The

BIGGEST
BOOK OF
HOCKEY
TRIVIA

Don Weekes

GREYSTONE BOOKS

D&M PUBLISHERS INC.

Vancouver/Toronto/Berkeley

Greystone Books
An imprint of D&M Publishers Inc.
2323 Quebec Street, Suite 201
Vancouver BC Canada V5T 4S7
www.greystonebooks.com

Library and Archives Canada Cataloguing in Publication
Weekes, Don
The biggest book of hockey trivia / Don Weekes
ISBN 978-1-55365-456-8
1. National Hockey League—Miscellanea 2. Hockey—Miscellanea
GV847.8.N3W4183 2009   796.962'64   C2009-903506-5

Editing by Anne Rose and Kerry Banks
Cover design by Peter Cocking and Heather Pringle
Cover photography (top) by Dave Reginek/Getty Images and
(bottom) Harry How/Getty Images
Printed and bound in Canada by Friesens
Printed on acid-free paper
Distributed in the U.S. by Publishers Group West

We gratefully acknowledge the financial support of the Canada Council
for the Arts, the British Columbia Arts Council, the Province of British
Columbia through the Book Publishing Tax Credit and the Government
of Canada through the Book Publishing Industry Development Program
(BPIDP) for our publishing activities.

Contents

Introduction

THIS BOOK CAME AS a great big surprise. In fact, it was never supposed to happen. The original plan—from a few years ago, when we decided to produce a definitive volume of the greatest trivia from our popular *Hockey Trivia* series—was to publish a one-off, then continue to publish more interactive trivia each season in our typical, smaller book size. But during the writing of that first "best of" book, 2005's *The Big Book of Hockey Trivia*, a lot of great hockey stories got yanked due to space considerations.

And that was also a little astonishing, given the 576-page girth of *Big Book*. In that door-stopper, we assembled enough trivia questions and games to rival the goal-scoring totals of Gordie Howe. Even *Sports Illustrated* was mildly impressed, noting that *Big Book* was "as big as *Moby Dick* and nearly as violent."

So here we are, four years later, with yet another thrashing hockey trivia monster—ready to tangle with even the most impassioned fan. And this time around, *The Biggest Book of Hockey Trivia* ramps it up with even more all-star facts, feats and firsts, including brand new trivia and completely updated material from past books. It's a one-two combination that will deke you out of your trivia mojo.

For example, who is the NHL's only 200-goal scorer without one 20-goal season? Trust us, it's no easy feat to accomplish. Or when did a position-player last tend goal during an NHL game? Here's a hint: it happened sometime between the invention of the Zamboni and the creation of separate team penalty boxes. Or which family has three brothers inducted into the Hockey Hall of Fame (and no, they're not anyone named Hull, Richard or Esposito)? The final score: *The Biggest Book of Hockey Trivia* picks up where the *Big Book* left us: with the best trivia collection of offbeat stories about your favourite snipers, heavy hitters and heroes between the pipes.

Just remember, hockey is full of surprises. So keep your head up and your stick on the ice.

Don Weekes
May 2009

1

Pumped

DURING THE PRE-GAME WARM-UP in the 1967 semifinals between Toronto and Chicago, Bobby Hull slapped a wicked shot over the end-boards and into the private booth of the Maple Leafs' owner, Harold Ballard. The misdirected blast struck Ballard's nose and broke it in three places. Hull was definitely pumped for the series, though the Hawks still lost in six. In this warm-up, we fire off a slew of questions to get you primed for upcoming trivia chapters.

Answers are on page 12

1.1 **What is the most number of points scored by a player in a season-opening game?**
A. Five points
B. Six points
C. Seven points
D. Eight points

1.2 **Who is the only player to score 200 career goals without having at least one 20-goal season?**
A. Defenseman Scott Stevens
B. Forward Eric Nesterenko
C. Defenseman Larry Robinson
D. Defenseman Nicklas Lidstrom

1.3 In how many consecutive seasons has Yanic Perreault led the NHL in faceoff-winning percentage?

A. Three straight times
B. Five straight times
C. Seven straight times
D. Nine straight times

1.4 In early hockey, what was the position name of the seventh man?

A. Rover
B. Point
C. Cover point
D. Rearguard

1.5 According to *Sports Illustrated,* what is the most unbeatable record in all of sports?

A. Wayne Gretzky's single-season 215 points
B. Bobby Orr's 46-goal season by a defenseman
C. Glenn Hall's 502 consecutive games streak
D. The Montreal Canadiens' five straight Stanley Cups

1.6 When did a forward or defenseman last tend goal during an NHL game?

A. 1960–61
B. 1970–71
C. 1980–81
D. 1990–91

1.7 Which NHL forward required an emergency tracheotomy to save his life, after he was struck in the throat by a puck in January 2000?

A. Adam Deadmarsh
B. Derek King

C. Trent McCleary

D. Benoit Hogue

1.8 **What is the most NHL teams from Toronto one player has suited up for?**

A. One team

B. Two teams

C. Three teams

D. Four teams

1.9 **In November 2003, what was the outdoor temperature at the Heritage Classic—the first outdoor NHL game played at Edmonton's Commonwealth Stadium?**

A. 21°F

B. 11°F

C. -1°F

D. -11°F

1.10 **What ended Al MacInnis's NHL career?**

A. An eye injury

B. Cartilage damage in his knees

C. Tendonitis

D. Stickmakers could no longer produce his preferred wood hockey sticks

1.11 **With what team and league did sniper Eric Stall lose his first tooth playing hockey?**

A. The Peterborough Petes in the OHL

B. The Lowell Lock Monsters in the AHL

C. The Carolina Hurricanes in the NHL

D. Stall has never broken any teeth

1.12 How many different teams did old-time centre Carl Voss play for during his eight-year NHL career?

A. Six different teams

B. Seven different teams

C. Eight different teams

D. Nine different teams

1.13 Who recorded the lowest goals-per-game ratio in a career of 1,000 games or more?

A. Craig Ludwig

B. Jay Wells

C. Brad Marsh

D. Ken Daneyko

1.14 Who has the lowest points-per-game ratio in a career of 1,000 games or more?

A. Luke Richardson

B. Brad Marsh

C. Ken Daneyko

D. Craig Ludwig

1.15 What is the longest time one individual has spent as a member of one NHL team?

A. 31 years

B. 41 years

C. 51 years

D. 61 years

1.16 Who was the only player to suit up for all five of the NHL's original charter teams?

A. Joe Malone

B. Dave Ritchie

C. Newsy Lalonde

D. Georges Vezina

1.17 **As of 2008–09, how many players in NHL history have recorded penalty shots in consecutive games?**

A. Only one—Eric Cole, with Carolina, in 2005–06

B. Two players

C. Three players

D. Four players

1.18 **As of 2008–09, what is the time of the fastest goal from the start of a season-opening game?**

A. Five seconds

B. 10 seconds

C. 15 seconds

D. 20 seconds

1.19 **How many fewer NHL regular-season career games did Mark Messier play than Gordie Howe?**

A. Only one game less than Howe

B. 11 games less than Howe

C. 51 games less than Howe

D. 101 games less than Howe

1.20 **How old was Gordie Howe when he retired from the NHL in 1980?**

A. 46 years old

B. 48 years old

C. 50 years old

D. 52 years old

1.21   Which is the only family to have three brothers inducted
       into the Hockey Hall of Fame?
       A. The Patrick family
       B. The Conacher family
       C. The Richard family
       D. The Cook family

1.22   Which superstar sniper scored the last NHL goal of the
       millennium?
       A. Eric Lindros
       B. Brett Hull
       C. Paul Kariya
       D. Jaromir Jagr

1.23   Who gave Pavel Bure his nickname—the Russian Rocket?
       A. A teammate
       B. A sports reporter
       C. A girlfriend
       D. A NASA scientist

1.24   In 2000–01, which Edmonton Oiler became the first NHLer
       in league history to twice score all three goals in a 3–0
       game?
       A. Ryan Smyth
       B. Doug Weight
       C. Bill Guerin
       D. Todd Marchant

1.25   Prior to March 19, 2006, when Toronto beat Pittsburgh 1–0
       on a penalty-shot goal, how many years had it been since
       an NHL game was won 1–0 on a penalty shot?
       A. One year
       B. 20 years

C. 70 years

D. No 1–0 game had ever been won on a penalty shot

1.26 **Among the hundreds of players to play in just one NHL game, how many have scored a goal in their lone appearance?**

A. None

B. Only one player, Brad Fast

C. Three players

D. 10 players

1.27 **Jordin Tootoo is the first NHL player with what racial background?**

A. Tootoo is First Nation (America)

B. Tootoo is Polynesian (Hawaii)

C. Tootoo is Aborigine (Australia)

D. Tootoo is Inuit (Canada)

1.28 **In 2006–07, which team's Zamboni drivers were accused of making bad ice for shootouts at the opponent's end of the rink?**

A. The Montreal Canadiens'

B. The Boston Bruins'

C. The Edmonton Oilers'

D. The Vancouver Canucks'

1.29 **Sam Battaglia, grandfather of journeyman winger Bates Battaglia, was famous for running what kind of business?**

A. Medicine

B. Crime

C. Entertainment

D. Agriculture

1.30 At the start of 2006–07, Los Angeles GM Dean Lombardi made a bet with Kings forward Alexander Frolov that, if Frolov "showed more determination with the puck," he (Lombardi) would read what Russian novel?

A. *Doctor Zhivago*
B. *The Brothers Karamazov*
C. *War and Peace*
D. *A Hero of Our Time*

1.31 In January 2006, how long were the pre-game retirement ceremonies honouring Steve Yzerman?

A. Less than 30 minutes long
B. Between 30 and 60 minutes long
C. Between 60 and 90 minutes long
D. More than 90 minutes long

1.32 Who was the only player to captain Steve Yzerman in NHL play?

A. Dale McCourt
B. Danny Gare
C. Reed Larson
D. Detroit had no full captain until Steve Yzerman

1.33 According to Jeremy Roenick, which injury was his most painful?

A. His fractured wrist
B. His shattered jaw
C. His fractured wrist, the second time
D. His broken nose, the eighth time

1.34 **Who scored the first goal in NHL history?**
  A. A pair of centres: Joe Malone and Newsy Lalonde
  B. Brothers Cy and Corb Denneny
  C. Hall of Famers Jack Adams and Art Ross
  D. A defenseman and a centre: Dave Ritchie and Joe Malone

1.35 **What player's streak was broken by the NHL lockout in 1994-95?**
  A. Mike Gartner's 15 consecutive 30-goal seasons
  B. Patrick Roy's nine consecutive 20-win seasons
  C. Wayne Gretzky's 14 consecutive All-Star appearances
  D. All of the above

1.36 **In April 2005, a group of Canadians took hockey to new heights by playing a game of shinny on what mountain?**
  A. Mount Aconcagua, Argentina
  B. Mount McKinley, Alaska
  C. Mount Everest, Nepal
  D. Mount Vinson-Massif, Antarctica

1.37 **What is the most goals scored in a single season by a major junior player who never made the NHL?**
  A. 70 goals
  B. 80 goals
  C. 90 goals
  D. 100 goals

1.38 **Which city has had the most NHL franchises?**
  A. Detroit
  B. Montreal
  C. New York
  D. Toronto

Answers

1.1 **B. Six points**

A whack of players in league history have scored five points in season openers, including Andy Bathgate, Phil Esposito and Gilbert Perreault. But the only player to notch six is forward Kevin Stevens, who scored twice and had four assists with Pittsburgh in a 7–4 win against Washington on October 5, 1990. Linemate John Cullen recorded five assists in the game.

1.2 **C. Defenseman Larry Robinson**

It is not easy to score 200 career goals without having at least one 20-goal season. As of 2008–09, only one player has ever managed the feat—Larry Robinson. The Big Bird compiled 208 career goals in his 20-year career, only getting close to the 20-goal plateau on two occasions (netting 19 goals for Montreal in 1976–77 and 1985–86). Comparatively, Scott Stevens totalled 196 career goals and had one 21-goal season; Eric Nesterenko played 21 seasons, scored 250 times and registered one 20-goal year (1957–58); and Nicklas Lidstrom passed the 200-goal mark in 2006–07, with a career-high 20 goals in 1999–2000.

1.3 **C. Seven straight times**

There is little statistical evidence that faceoffs win hockey games, which may explain why the art of winning draws is one of hockey's least appreciated one-on-one skills—one that gets little attention in player stat boxes and game reports. Further, since nearly every NHL team is almost average in faceoff wins, other aspects of play (such as giveaways and takeaways) tend to be more important and make up the difference after losing a faceoff. Still, this showdown to gain puck possession is played out about 60 times every game and, on occasion, leads to a crucial goal or prevents another team from scoring. Yet only a handful of forwards are very good at it; anyone with 53 per cent or better is usually a top 20 player on the draw. So it is remarkable that Yanic Perreault led the league with a figure higher than 61 per cent for seven seasons—almost as long as the statistic has been officially charted. How many players have accomplished anything close to that?

Yanic Perreault: Faceoff Gunslinger

SEASON	FO TOTAL	FO WINS	FO LOSSES	FO PERCENTAGE
1999–00	987	610	377	61.80
2000–01	1,055	661	394	62.65
2001–02	1,485	910	575	61.27
2002–03	1,156	727	429	62.88
2003–04	861	561	300	65.15
2005–06	899	559	340	62.18
2006–07	806	506	300	62.77

1.4 A. Rover

The rover, considered a fourth forward, was the key man on any club. Lined up between the three forwards and two defensemen, he was the best skater and all-round player, picking up a drop pass or rebound on the attack and returning to backcheck or bodycheck an opposing puck carrier. Yet the position was dropped in 1910, long before the NHL's first season in 1917–18, a decision that had less to do with "opening up the game" than basic economics: it was less expensive to ice six men.

1.5 C. Glenn Hall's 502 consecutive games streak

After analyzing the greatest records in professional sports, including Ty Cobb's .367 career batting average, the Boston Celtics' eight straight NBA championships and Jack Nicklaus's 20 major golf championships, *Sports Illustrated* in 1993 listed Hall's 502 consecutive complete games as the most unbreakable record in sports. From 1955 through 1962, in seven complete seasons with Detroit and Chicago, the maskless Hall never missed a start. And, while 502 is his regular-season total, the figure increases to 551 when Hall's 49 playoff games are included. As *SI* noted, Hall holds "the record of records … that won't ever be broken," especially with teams now carrying two goalies in an 82-game schedule and extended playoff format. However, Hall's ironman mark shouldn't be dismissed as just a product of his era. The quality of his play throughout his streak earned him NHL rookie of the year honours in 1956 and the Blackhawks a surprise Stanley Cup in 1961, as well as ensuring Hall a place on six All-Star teams before his astonishing record ended on November 7, 1962. He had strained his back at practice, possibly while fastening a toe strap. The next night, midway through the first period, the pain was so severe Hall removed himself from play.

1.6 A. 1960–61

Boston Bruins forward Jerry Toppazzini never shied away from any assignment. He had a warrior's instincts—and the scars to prove it after several career mishaps, including being cross-checked in the face so viciously by Ted Lindsay that doctors required photographs of him taken prior to the incident in order to reconstruct his face. Maybe that is why Bruins coach Milt Schmidt tapped the right-winger to tend goal, subbing for an injured Don Simmons, late in the third period of a 5–2 loss against Chicago on October 16, 1960. Topper not only filled the breach, he stepped into the crease without pads or a mask. Luckily, no shots were directed his way. Toppazzini is forever remembered, after a steady, albeit undistinguished 12-year career, as the last NHL position-player to play goal.

1.7 C. Trent McCleary

During a game between the Canadiens and Flyers at the Montreal Forum on January 29, 2000, Trent McCleary dove to block a Chris Therien slap shot and the puck hit him in the throat. The force of the blast fractured the Canadien winger's larynx and collapsed one lung, cutting off the flow of oxygen. Several emergency surgical procedures, including a tracheotomy on-ice just after the incident, cleared the airway, but it took several weeks and vocal cord operations before he regained the ability to speak. The incident left McCleary with a 15 per cent narrower air passage because of a partially paralyzed left vocal cord and scar tissue in his throat, prompting him to retire in September 2000.

1.8 C. Three teams

Our research found just one player, centre Corb Denneny, who skated with Toronto's three NHL teams—the Arenas, the St. Pats and the Maple Leafs—during his career. Denneny suited up for the Arenas in two NHL seasons (1917–18 and 1918–19) and then for four seasons with the St. Pats (1919–20 to 1922–23), winning Stanley Cups with each club. He later joined the Maple Leafs for their inaugural season, 1926–27. But Denneny's connection to Toronto doesn't end there. He also played for the Toronto Shamrocks and Toronto Blueshirts of the NHA, the predecessor to the NHL, and has worn more Toronto sweaters on more pro teams in Toronto than any other player.

1.9   C. -1°F

More than a game, more than a reunion, the Heritage Classic
had all the boyhood wonder and magic of a pick-up game on a
frozen pond under a crisp winter sky. There they were, larger
than life: Wayne Gretzky, Guy Lafleur and Mark Messier, Hall
of Fame thirty- and forty-somethings taking turns in the
time-honoured tradition of shovelling snow from the outdoor
rink built on the football field of Edmonton's Commonwealth
Stadium. A hockey first for the NHL, 57,167 fans had filled
the stands to watch two games—the old-timer Megastars
match and then the Montreal–Edmonton tilt—in sub-zero
temperatures, and from a distance that reduced the players
to ant-size proportions. Few came dressed to make a fashion
statement, but they all had an opinion about the temperature: freakin' *c-c-cold*. Montreal goalie José Théodore may have
had the best solution, though: his Canadiens pom-pom toque
was duct-taped to the top of his goalie mask. For the fun of
it, Edmonton's old-timers beat Montreal's greybeards 2–0;
and, for two points, the Canadiens won 4–3 over the Oilers.
Gretzky's daughter, Paulina, sang the national anthem.

1.10   A. An eye injury

A lot of shot-blockers and goalies drew a collective sigh of
relief in September 2005, when Al MacInnis retired his fear-
some slap shot. No longer would they face the Shot—that
100-mph howitzer responsible for many of the 1,274 points
MacInnis scored during his illustrious 22-year career. Indeed,
when he joined the NHL in the early 1980s, MacInnis had *only*
the Shot in his toolbox. "When he broke in with us, he was a
one-dimensional player," says Cliff Fletcher, former Calgary
GM. "He could shoot the puck and do it better than anybody.
But he wasn't a great defenseman. He had trouble turning, he wasn't strong and his skating had to be improved."

But MacInnis worked hard at making himself a complete player—honing his superior shooting skills while growing up, firing buckets of pucks against the family barn in Port Hood, Nova Scotia. "A lot of guys shoot hard," says Paul Coffey, "but nobody ever scattered on Al's teams when he was shooting. He *knew* where the puck was going." A seven-time All-Star who played in 12 All-Star games, MacInnis won the NHL's hardest-shot competition more times than any other player in its history. MacInnis ended his career after successive eye injuries, in 2001 and 2003, permanently damaged his peripheral vision.

1.11 **C. The Carolina Hurricanes in the NHL**
During a lifetime of playing with sticks and pucks, Stall defied the odds: he never lost a tooth in action. Then, in a game against St. Louis on January 15, 2006, the Hurricanes forward was initiated into hockey's rudimentary form of dentistry following a high stick from the Blues' Dennis Wideman that cut Stall's lip (requiring several stitches) and chipped half of one of his incisors. Still, "I've got a lot of chin scars, but I never lost a tooth," said Stall, who scored a hat trick in the 4–2 come-from-behind win.

1.12 **B. Seven different teams**
Carl Voss was one of hockey's most travelled players. He not only played for many teams in a short period of time, he played for a lot of teams when the league was relatively small. In fact, over eight seasons (between 1926–27 and 1937–38) Voss suited up for seven franchises in eight NHL cities—a period when the league only had 10 franchises. Even before he was named the NHL's first Calder Trophy winner as rookie of the year in 1933, Voss had worn the jerseys of a record three NHL clubs: the Toronto Maple Leafs, New York Rangers and Detroit

Red Wings. In the next five seasons, he would also play with the Ottawa Senators (whose franchise moved to St. Louis), St. Louis Eagles, New York Americans, Montreal Maroons and Chicago Blackhawks. But his travels during his playing career were an afternoon stroll compared to his life after retirement. In 1950, he became the first referee-in-chief of the NHL and other minor pro leagues, then travelled 60,000 miles per season to assess the work of officials in as many as 125 games each year. For this, Voss earned Hall of Fame status, and is one of the very few players to receive the honour as a builder.

1.13   C. Brad Marsh

Poster boy for scoring he's not, but Marsh read the defense very well and earned his keep playing stay-at-home hockey for more than 1,000 games. He scored one goal for every 47.2 games, or just 23 goals in 1,086 matches, from 1978–79 to 1992–93. In comparison, Luke Richardson and Ken Daneyko are red-hot snipers. As of 2008–09, Richardson ranks second, averaging one goal every 40 games; Daneyko ranks third with one goal every 35.6 games—while Marsh's protege has to be Mattias Norstrum, another blueline nobody, who retired after 903 games and just 18 goals.

Lowest Goals-Per-Game Average in NHL History*				
PLAYER	SEASONS	GOALS	GAMES	RATIO
Brad Marsh	1978–1993	23	1,086	47.2
Luke Richardson	1987–2009	35	1,417	40.5
Ken Daneyko	1983–2003	36	1,283	35.6
Craig Ludwig	1982–2000	38	1,256	33.1
Marc Bergevin	1984–2004	36	1,191	33.1

*Current to 2008–09

1.14   C. Ken Daneyko

Brad Marsh and Craig Ludwig had long careers as non-scorers in a goal-scoring sport, which says a lot about their commitment to the game. Each stuck to the blue line, netting only one point every five or more games—amongst the lowest ratios in NHL history. Ludwig scored a point every 5.7 games (222 points in 1,256 games) and Marsh scored a point every 5.4 games (on 198 points in 1,086 games). But Daneyko has everyone in his dust with a scorching 7.2 games per point, or 178 points in 1,283 games, while pulling up fast is Luke Richardson with 7.0 (201 points in 1,417 games), Marc Bergevin with 6.6 (181 points in 1,191 games) and Craig Berube with 6.1 (159 points in 1,054 games). Rob Ray, who quit before calling too much attention to his numbers, had only 91 points in 900 games, a ratio of one point for every 9.9 games. Unlike the others, however, he was a forward.

1.15   D. 61 years

The classic rink rat, Wally Crossman became a fixture at the Detroit Olympia when it opened in 1927. He worked as a soda jerk at a neighbourhood drugstore, sat in the balcony watching games for 25 cents and attended practices for free. Then in 1940, Red Wings GM Jack Adams hired Crossman as the club's dressing room attendant, a job he would hold for 61 years while watching 23 coaches come and go, enjoying a ring-side seat for seven Cup championships and getting his name inscribed on the Cup four times. Yet in all that time, Crossman was never paid. He taped sticks, cut oranges for the players to snack on between periods, did the laundry and opened and shut the door on the bench during games in return for just two free tickets to each game and tips from the players, before finally retiring after the 2000–01 season at age 90. "I've smelled enough sweat," he said. "I don't want to stay here until I'm 100. That's too long." Crossman died on January 29, 2003, at age 92.

1.16 B. Dave Ritchie

Ritchie was the only player to suit up for all five of the NHL's original charter teams. When the league began in 1917–18, his rights were owned by the Quebec Bulldogs. But since Quebec did not ice a team that year, he joined the Montreal Wanderers for four games before they withdrew from the league. The Ottawa Senators picked up Ritchie for the remaining 14 games of 1917–18. During the next several years, the defenseman then played with the Toronto Arenas, Quebec and the Montreal Canadiens, where he ended his career in 1925–26.

1.17 C. Three players

On November 9, 2005, Eric Cole became the first player to be awarded two penalty shots in one game, though he is not the first to record two penalty shots in back-to-back games. His second straight penalty-shot game, on November 11, was the third by an NHLer. Toronto's Mike Walton, in March 1968, and Esa Pirnes, in October 2003, are the other two. But Pirnes's two shots in two matches might be the exception in this rarest of accomplishments: Pirnes was playing in only his second and third career games. The Los Angeles forward missed both times, on October 10 against Pittsburgh's Marc-Andre Fleury and on October 12 against Chicago's Jocelyn Thibault.

1.18 B. 10 seconds

Kent Nilsson displayed his extraordinary gift for goal scoring in so many ways. In fact, Wayne Gretzky called Nilsson the most pure-skilled player he had ever seen. Nilsson's wizardry

with the puck also earned him the nickname "Magic Man,"
and after he ripped a goal past Quebec's Clint Malarchuk in
a record 10 seconds to open Minnesota's 1986–87 season, he
became the NHL's fastest season-opening goal scorer.

Fastest Goals in Season-Opening Games*

PLAYER	TEAMS/SCORE	DATE	TEAM/TIME
Kent Nilsson	Minnesota 4 vs Quebec 4	10/11/86	Minnesota 00:10
Ryan Walter	Washington 3 vs Buffalo 5	10/07/81	Washington 00:12
Denis Savard	Chicago 5 vs Pittsburgh 5	10/07/81	Chicago 00:13
Bill Mosienko	Chicago 1 vs Toronto 4	10/31/43	Chicago 00:13
Gus Bodnar	Toronto 5 vs New York Rangers 2	10/30/43	Toronto 00:15

*Current to 2008–09

1.19   B. 11 games less than Howe

The NHL lockout of 2004–05 prematurely ended the careers of
several veteran stars, including Ron Francis and Al MacInnis.
Even that warrior of a quarter-century of hockey Mark Messier
hung up his blades in 2005 after watching the league waste
the year—an unceremonious end to a glorious career that
spanned 1,756 games, a total just 11 shy of Gordie Howe's magic
number of 1,767. Only 11 games. But that's probably okay with
Messier, who could have broken Howe's famous record by playing in 2005–06. As Glen Sather remembers it: "He was never
the guy who wanted to get on the ice for an empty-net goal.
He always let somebody else do that. He was a great team guy."
And we would be remiss if we excluded the fact that 11 was the
same number Messier wore on his back during a distinguished
career that began in 1979–80 and ended in 2003–04.

1.20   D. 52 years old

Gordie Howe's durability is almost incomprehensible.
Between 1946 and 1989, his career spanned 32 pro seasons and

2,421 NHL and WHA games. During his last season, when he
was 52, he was almost *double* the age of most of his Hartford
teammates. Plus, he was one of only four Whalers to play
the entire 80-game schedule, and his 41 points bettered the
totals of 15 regulars on the bench. He also finished his career
with a lucky plus-9 and had one of the team's highest penalty
counts, 42 minutes, before scoring his last regular-season
goal on April 6, 1980. Ironically, that goal came against Rogie
Vachon of the Detroit Red Wings, the team with which Howe
played for 25 years and earned the nickname Mr. Hockey.
It was his 801st goal. (Assisting on the play: Ray Allison and
Detroit native Gordie Roberts, who was named after Howe
by hockey-loving parents when the Red Wing star was at his
peak in the 1950s.) Finally, Howe would score once more during the playoffs against Montreal, his greatest rival, before
retiring at age 52 on April 11. Today, there is little chance of
anyone ever challenging Howe as the oldest point-producing
NHLer. Greybeard Chris Chelios may have said it best when
asked if he felt old still playing at age 46: "Only every time I
think about Gordie Howe."

1.21   **B. The Conacher family**
It didn't happen until 1998, but the Hall of Fame finally had
its first family hat trick when Roy, younger brother of Charlie
and Lionel, was posthumously honoured in the veterans
category. Charlie, the Big Bomber, starred for Toronto in the
1930s on the Kid Line, with Joe Primeau and Busher Jackson,
and was inducted into the Hall in 1961. Lionel, the Big Train,
mastered hockey, football, wrestling and boxing and was
named Canada's athlete of the half-century in 1950; he was
a Hall inductee in 1994. Roy played 11 seasons with Boston,
Detroit and Chicago. In his rookie season he led the league in
goal scoring and followed up with six goals in the 1939 play-

offs, including the Stanley Cup winner for Boston. And even though he spent four years in the service during World War II, he still finished his career with 226 NHL goals—one more than brother Charlie.

1.22 B. Brett Hull

Brett Hull scored the last goal of the millennium in typical, dramatic fashion. In just one of two NHL games scheduled for December 31, 1999, he got the tying and winning goals in the third period of a 5–4 Dallas victory over the Mighty Ducks—his 600th and 601st career goals. And he scored them in his 900th game, a personal objective for Hull since the season began. "I wanted 600 in 900 games because they're round numbers and it's easier to do the math," he joked. The Stars' right-winger scored number 600 from the high slot on the power play, when he took a pass from Kirk Muller and fired a sizzler past goalie Guy Hebert. Hull added the winning goal two minutes later, his 601st and the game-winner and last goal of the millennium. It came at 8:49 of the third frame, approximately 9:30 PM Central Time in Dallas. "It's a neat thing, scoring the last goal of the millennium in the NHL," said Hull. So who scored the first goal of the new millenium? Seven NHL games were played on January 1, 2000, two of which were afternoon games: Tampa Bay in Florida and San Jose in Nashville. The Predators–Sharks game started at 2 PM Eastern Standard Time, one hour earlier than the Panthers–Lightning game that got underway at 3 PM at Florida's National Car Rental Center. Based on these starts, the first goal scored in Nashville would be the new millenium's first NHL goal. That distinction went to Sergie Krivokrasov, who scored at 0:22 of the first period in the 3–2 Predators win over San Jose.

1.23 **B. A sports reporter**

The nickname was applied to Bure after his electrifying NHL
debut with the Vancouver Canucks, in a game against the
Winnipeg Jets November 5, 1991. The 20-year-old Russian
wowed both the Vancouver crowd and the Jets with a series
of thrilling rushes, prompting *Vancouver Sun* sportswriter
Iain MacIntyre to note the next day: "If Winnipeg are the
Jets, then what do you call Pavel Bure? How about the Rocket?
It fits Bure perfectly. He is the fastest Soviet creation since
Sputnik." The name stuck, and soon the hockey world was
calling Bure the Russian Rocket. As Kerry Banks noted in his
1999 biography of the NHL star, *Pavel Bure: The Riddle of the
Russian Rocket:* "With its rolling alliteration and dual allusions
to Cold War weaponry and supersonic speed, the moniker
had an irresistible appeal."

1.24 **A. Ryan Smyth**

The odds of repeating such a feat are astronomical, as the NHL
record book shows. But when Ryan Smyth scored all three
goals in the Oilers' 3–0 win over St. Louis on November 14,
2000, he became the first player in league annals to notch
hat tricks in 3–0 games twice. Smyth scored two times in the
first period, then added an empty-netter in the third to duplicate his previous hat trick performance in a 3–0 victory over
Atlanta on March 13, 2000. Smyth's hat trick on November
14 was only the 11th time in the NHL's 83-year history that a
player scored all three goals in a 3–0 game.

1.25 **C. 70 years**

Yes, there was a series of blackouts, an electrical fire that
resulted in a 40-minute game delay, fans chanting "New A-
Re-Naaaa" and a video review of a nullified goal—all of which
had Toronto's Chad Kilger admitting "it was a bizarre game,

for sure." But the Mellon Center game's highlight was still Kilger's penalty-shot goal, which came after the forward was tripped by defenseman Rob Scuderi on a breakaway against Penguin goalie Marc-Andre Fleury. On the enusing penalty shot, the Toronto forward backed Fleury deep into the net and wristed a shot past his blocker and inside the left post. The only score of the game, Kilger's goal also avenged the Maple Leafs' 1–0 loss to the Rangers on a penalty shot by Bert Connelly on January 16, 1936—the only other occasion a 1–0 game was won on a penalty shot.

1.26   C. Three players

Although not household names, Rolly Huard, Dean Morton and Brad Fast still lived the dream of playing in the world's best league, if only for one game. But Huard, Morton and Fast are more than one-game wonders, they are the NHL's only goal-a-game one-game wonders. Huard played with Toronto on December 14, 1930, and scored in a 7–3 loss to Boston; Morton notched a goal for Detroit in a 10–7 loss to Calgary on October 5, 1989; and Fast made his debut in Carolina's final game of 2003–04, scoring the game-tying goal with 2:26 left in regulation time in a 6–6 finish against Florida. And though the whys and what ifs surrounding their departures may haunt Huard and Morton for years, Fast is still playing. After ping-ponging among European clubs for a few years, in May 2008 he signed a one-year deal with South Korea's Anyang Halla of the Asia Ice Hockey League.

1.27   D. Tootoo is Inuit (Canada)

NHLers have come from every nook and cranny across Canada, but Tootoo is the first player of Inuit descent drafted into the NHL. And it's a big surprise that the five-foot-eight winger made it, though not because he's almost a half-foot shorter than the average NHLer, but because Tootoo didn't play organized hockey until he was 14 years old. In his hometown of Rankin Inlet on the western shore of Hudson Bay, there weren't enough boys to ice more than one team at any age level. "I made history, I guess," said Tootoo after being selected 98th overall by the Nashville Predators in 2001.

1.28   **A. The Montreal Canadiens'**

In what might be the most brazen act of mischief by icemakers since Trent Evans buried a Canadian dollar coin under centre ice at the 2002 Olympics, Zamboni drivers at Montreal's Bell Centre provided a little hometown edge to the Canadiens on December 2, 2006, by clearing a narrower lane in the opposition's shooting zone for a shootout against the Toronto Maple Leafs. Pointing the finger was Toronto coach Paul Maurice, whose demand for an additional ice-scraping job to widen the path for his shooters was rejected by the referees. But upon video review, NHL official Mike Murphy said the swath of cleaned ice from the blue line to the crease of Cristobal Huet did look "narrower." It was the second time that Maurice had accused Montreal's Zamboni drivers of hindering his scorers during a shootout. In the first instance, on October 28, the Maple Leafs took the extra point. But on December 2, Toronto lost when Huet gave up one goal to Mats Sundin while Saku Koivu and Sheldon Souray connected for the Canadiens. The final score? Montreal and its Zamboni cheats: 4. Toronto: 3.

1.29   **B. Crime**

The real-life story of Sam "Teets" Battaglia is like a Mario Puzo novel, or, maybe, an episode of TV's crime drama *The Sopranos*. In fact, Puzo likely found inspiration for *The Godfather* and his popular trilogy of highly acclaimed movies in Mafia bosses such as Battaglia, the notorious don of the Chicago Outfit—the same crime empire that made Al Capone and Sam Giancana household names for their gambling, burglary and loansharking. As a goodfella, Sam Battaglia was arrested 25 times before he was finally jailed for extortion in 1967. He was released from prison and died of cancer in 1973, two years before Bates Battaglia was born. Interestingly, Bates found out about his grandfather's connections to the mob from friends, while playing street hockey.

1.30 **C. *War and Peace***
Russian literature and hockey are not often mentioned in the same sentence, but both subjects figured prominently in a wager made between Los Angeles's Alexander Frolov and Dean Lombardi. Before the start of 2006–07, Lombardi was trying to convince Frolov to play with more focus and resolve, when the Russian forward mentioned he had read Leo Tolstoy's *War and Peace*—not once, but twice. Given that the novel contains more than half a million words, this was no small boast. So Lombardi said he would read the gigantic book if Frolov showed more on-ice perseverance. The wager seemed to motivate Frolov, who subsequently led the Kings with a career-best 35 goals and 71 points. (No word yet on how Lombardi likes Tolstoy.)

1.31 **D. More than 90 minutes long**
Detroit owner Mike Ilitch may be Hockeytown's greatest fan, but when it comes to team celebrations he is the master of overkill. The guy who got no less than nine family members on the Stanley Cup in 1997—and set a record for more names engraved on the Cup than any other champion—raised the bar with the party he staged for Steve Yzerman on January 2, 2007, when the player's No.19 was hung at Joe Louis Arena.

Few people uttered anything but praise, however, until six weeks later at the league's GM meetings when the NHL introduced limits on the length of pre-game ceremonies. Yet if any player deserved such a celebration it was Yzerman—Detroit's distinguished leader and the NHL's longest-serving captain. The sold-out crowd was thrilled and stood for numerous ovations during the bash, which featured a mammoth seating arrangement at centre ice to accommodate the more than 40 guests, 27 of whom were introduced one by one before Yzerman took to the podium for his final farewell. By the time it was all over, the puck didn't drop until 8:34 PM Eastern Standard Time, more than 90 minutes after the scheduled 7 PM start time. Yzerman's fête was also a huge TV draw in Canada, with double the numbers of the game that followed: 916,000 viewers when Yzerman spoke and his jersey was raised compared to 400,000 for the 2–1 win against Anaheim.

1.32   B. Danny Gare
In the first three years of Steve Yzerman's 22-year NHL career with Detroit, Danny Gare was team captain. Gare got the "C" in his first full season with the Red Wings in 1982–83, the year before Yzerman joined the club as a rookie. When Gare was traded four years later, Yzerman assumed the captaincy, a post he held for 19 years, including his final season of 2005–06.

1.33   B. His shattered jaw
In the August 2004 edition of *Esquire* magazine, readers were treated to several amazing first-person accounts in an article called "What It Feels Like." The experiences ranged from what many would call insane (catching a great white shark), to the terrifying (surviving a tsunami) and the absurd (staying awake for 11 days). And Jeremy Roenick got some

ink with what it feels like "...to shatter your jaw," his most painful injury "by far," which he suffered in February 2004 while playing against the New York Rangers at MSG. Roenick detailed the gruesome facts better than any play-by-play announcer, too. Here's a sample: "I was on the ice, my face in a pool of blood. When I came to I felt like somebody was standing on the side of my face, stomping on it. When I went to bite down, my teeth didn't line up ... There were pieces of bone, of jaw, moving around, and I almost fainted ... There was actually a perfect broken-bone imprint of the puck in my jaw." Yet Roenick played again in six weeks—the bare minimum wait time.

1.34 **D. A defenseman and a centre: Dave Ritchie and Joe Malone**
The NHL's inaugural season, 1917–1918, began on December 19, 1917, with two games—the Toronto Blueshirts versus the Montreal Wanderers, and the Montreal Canadiens against the Ottawa Senators. It is widely believed that both contests were played in Montreal. But the Canadiens–Senators game actually took place at the Ottawa Arena on Laurier Avenue, where, attended by 6,000 rowdy fans, it began promptly at 8:30 PM, with the first goal scored by the Canadiens' Joe Malone at 6:30 of period one. In the other opening game, at the Montreal Arena, Montreal's Dave Ritchie netted the first goal between the Blueshirts and the Wanderers at 1:00 of the first period. Unfortunately, the Montreal game's start time remains unconfirmed. So, credit both the Wanderers' Dave Ritchie and Joe Malone of the Canadiens as the first goal scorers in NHL history.

1.35 **D. All of the above**
There are plenty of asterisks in the NHL record book due to 1994–95's lockout-shortened 48-game schedule. Not only did Gartner miss his first 30-goal season in 15 years (he scored just

12 goals in 1994–95), Roy, who won 17 games in 1994–95, ended his nine-year reign of 20-win seasons and Gretzky's record blitz of 14 straight All-Star games was halted. A few more broken streaks: Brett Hull's five consecutive 50-goal seasons (29 goals in 1994–95); Ray Bourque's five straight 80-point seasons (43 points in 1994–95); Ron Francis's streak of 13 20-goal seasons. For the first time in a quarter-century of NHL hockey, there were also no 100-point or 50-goal scorers, nor any 100-point teams.

1.36   C. Mount Everest, Nepal

On the morning of April 11, 2004, a group of Canadian climbers staged a game of shinny atop Mount Everest's Khumbu Glacier. Played in calm weather in front of a crowd of spectators at an elevation of 17,575 feet, it set a record as the highest game of hockey ever played—a tribute to the original 1972 Summit Series between Canada and the USSR. (In fact, prior to leaving for Everest, the Canadians were presented with original Team Canada jerseys by Ron Ellis, a member of Canada's 1972 Summit Series team and a former Toronto Maple Leaf star.) And though the Canadians were slated to play a team of Russian climbers, when the Russians didn't show, the Canadian climbers took on a squad composed of players from Australia, Nepal and the USA. Besides the rarefied elevation, the game also featured other oddities: the referee was a sherpa named Tsherling, a crevasse doubled as the penalty box and, at one point, the action was interrupted by three yaks that decided to cross the rink—or "glink," as the Canadians dubbed it. Canada won the record-breaking match 21–13.

1.37   D. 100 goals

The name Gary MacGregor is not well known, but MacGregor's career on-ice and in the record books is connected with many of hockey's elite. That's because in his final junior year, 1973–74,

MacGregor scored 100 goals in 66 games with Cornwall, a feat bested only by junior stars such as Mario Lemieux, Guy Lafleur and Pat LaFontaine. MacGregor was also one of Wayne Gretzky's first professional teammates with the WHA Indianapolis Racers before the team folded in 1978. So what led one of the CHL's highest-scoring players, a prospect who supposedly never lost a fight in junior hockey, to fall short of an NHL career? Apparently, in 1974, MacGregor was offered bigger money to play in the WHA, where he would get more ice time than with his NHL-drafted team, the Montreal Canadiens—where the competition for a roster spot at centre included Lafleur, Jacques Lemaire and Pete Mahovlich. So, rather than languish in the minors while waiting for an NHL break, MacGregor made the WHA his career choice and signed with the Chicago Cougars—and never played in the NHL. Still, he did net a 92–70–162 record in 251 WHA games between 1974 and 1979. Among junior players, the next-highest scorer without an NHL career is Jacques Locas Jr., who had 99 goals in 67 games with the Quebec Remparts in 1973–74.

1.38   B. Montreal
Some cities, including Toronto and Detroit, have had one franchise with three different names, others have played host to two different franchises, such as New York and Quebec. But Montreal was the only NHL city with three different NHL clubs: the Montreal Canadiens, Montreal Wanderers and Montreal Maroons. The Canadiens are the league's longest-existing franchise with the same name; the Wanderers played just two NHL games before they folded when their arena burned down in 1917–18; and the Maroons are remembered as Montreal's English team, winning two Stanley Cups between 1924–25 and 1937–38.

Game 1

Odd Man Out

IN EACH OF THE foursomes below, one name does not belong.
See if you can spot the odd man out.

Solutions are on page 558

1. Who didn't score 70 goals in a season?
   Teemu Selanne · Steve Yzerman · Jari Kurri · Bernie Nicholls

2. Who didn't post six straight 100-point seasons?
   Guy Lafleur · Brett Hull · Peter Stastny · Bobby Orr

3. Who wasn't a number one draft pick?
   Chris Pronger · Mats Sundin · Mike Modano · Joe Thornton

4. Who didn't score a Stanley Cup-winning goal?
   Mario Lemieux · Doug Gilmour · Kirk Muller · Wayne Gretzky

5. Who wasn't voted rookie of the year?
   Pavel Bure · Brian Leetch · Chris Drury · Patrick Roy

6. Who didn't compile 3,000 career penalty minutes?
   Dale Hunter · Chris Nilan · Dave Schultz · Marty McSorley

7. Who didn't win the Vezina Trophy?
   Grant Fuhr · Billy Smith · Tom Barrasso · Gerry Cheevers

8. Who didn't play 20 NHL seasons?
   Ron Francis · Marcel Dionne · Larry Robinson · Stan Mikita

9. Who didn't score five goals in a playoff game?
   Wayne Gretzky · Mario Lemieux · Darryl Sittler · Reggie Leach

10. Who didn't captain a Stanley Cup champion?
    Guy Carbonneau · Phil Esposito · Bob Gainey · Denis Potvin

2

19 Years and 213 Days

WHEN SIDNEY CROSBY WON the NHL scoring race in 2006–07, he became the youngest professional athlete in any North American sport to be crowned a scoring champion. Crosby, who was just 19 years and 213 days old, captured the Art Ross Trophy with 120 points. Wayne Gretzky was 20 years and 88 days old when he won the race in 1980–81. In this chapter, we champion scoring aces and rookie stars.

Answers are on page 42

2.1 In how many consecutive games did Evgeni Malkin score a goal at the start of his NHL career?
A. Four straight games
B. Five straight games
C. Six straight games
D. Seven straight games

2.2 Which is the only teammate trio to claim the top three spots in the NHL goal-scoring derby in two different seasons?
A. Montreal's Maurice Richard, Jean Béliveau and Bernie Geoffrion
B. Chicago's Bobby Hull, Stan Mikita and Kenny Wharram
C. Boston's Phil Esposito, Johnny Bucyk and Ken Hodge
D. Edmonton's Wayne Gretkzy, Jari Kurri and Glenn Anderson

2.3 Who is the oldest NHLer to record back-to-back 40-goal seasons?

  A. Teemu Selanne
  B. Wayne Gretzky
  C. Brett Hull
  D. Gordie Howe

2.4 Why was Bernie Geoffrion nicknamed Boom-Boom?

  A. Because of his rugged checks
  B. Because of his unpredictable temper
  C. Because of his boisterous trash talk
  D. Because of his thunderous slap shot

2.5 How many goalposts does Theoren Fleury claim to have hit during his disastrous 1999–2000 season, when he scored just 15 goals for the New York Rangers?

  A. 20 goalposts
  B. 30 goalposts
  C. 40 goalposts
  D. 50 goalposts

2.6 In 1944–45, during his historic 50-goal season in the six-team NHL, how many goalies did Maurice Richard score against?

  A. Five goalies
  B. Seven goalies
  C. Nine goalies
  D. 11 goalies

2.7 In 2006–07, who scored three goals in 100 seconds—the second-fastest even-strength hat trick in NHL history?

  A. Ray Whitney, with the Carolina Hurricanes
  B. Martin Havlat, with the Chicago Blackhawks

C. Sidney Crosby, with the Pittsburgh Penguins

D. Jonathan Cheechoo, with the San Jose Sharks

2.8 In 2006–07, for the first time since 1919, which two oppos-ing players produced natural hat tricks in the same game?

A. Ryan Smyth and Jonathan Cheechoo

B. Jonathan Cheechoo and Markus Naslund

C. Markus Naslund and Brad Richards

D. Brad Richards and Ryan Smyth

2.9 On October 31, 2001, the first time he returned to Texas to play his former team in Dallas, how many goals did Brett Hull score with Detroit against the Stars?

A. One goal

B. Two goals

C. Three goals

D. Brett Hull didn't score

2.10 Which player didn't score his first hat trick until he had more than 300 goals? (It happened in 2002–03.)

A. Adam Graves

B. Scott Mellanby

C. Trevor Linden

D. Phil Housley

2.11 What is the most game-winning goals scored by a player in one season?

A. 12 game-winners

B. 16 game-winners

C. 20 game-winners

D. 24 game-winners

2.12 How many seconds did it take Boston's Mike Knuble to
set the NHL record for two fastest goals from the start of a
game? (It happened in 2002–03.)

A. Seven seconds

B. 17 seconds

C. 27 seconds

D. 37 seconds

2.13 Who scored the fastest four goals in NHL history?

A. Peter Bondra

B. Mario Lemieux

C. Paul Kariya

D. Sergei Fedorov

2.14 In how many consecutive seasons did Gordie Howe finish in
the top 10 of the NHL scoring race?

A. 12 seasons

B. 15 seasons

C. 18 seasons

D. 21 seasons

2.15 Which player scored the most goals for an expansion team
in its first NHL season?

A. Blaine Stoughton, with Hartford, in 1979–80

B. Bob Kudelski, with Florida, in 1993–94

C. Brian Bradley, with Tampa Bay, in 1992–93

D. Wayne Gretzky, with Edmonton, in 1979–80

2.16 Who was the last NHLer to score at a goal-a-game pace
before Wayne Gretzky accomplished the same feat in
1981–82—with 92 goals in 80 games?

A. Maurice Richard

B. Gordie Howe

C. Mike Bossy

D. No one accomplished this feat before Wayne Gretzky

2.17 **Which teammates hold the record for the most power-play goals in one season?**

A. Mario Lemieux and Rob Brown, with the Pittsburgh Penguins

B. Tim Kerr and Brian Propp, with the Philadelphia Flyers

C. Joe Nieuwendyk and Joe Mullen, with the Calgary Flames

D. Todd Bertuzzi and Markus Naslund, with the Vancouver Canucks

2.18 **Who was the first NHLer to score 50 assists in 10 consecutive seasons?**

A. Gordie Howe

B. Adam Oates

C. Wayne Gretzky

D. Bernie Federko

2.19 **After Gordie Howe, which player has the most consecutive 20-or-more-goal seasons?**

A. Jaromir Jagr

B. Brendan Shanahan

C. Mats Sundin

D. Brett Hull

2.20 **If the NHL point-streak record is 51 games, what is the American Hockey League mark?**

A. 29 straight games

B. 39 straight games

C. 49 straight games

D. 59 straight games

2.21 Only a few NHLers have had a season in which they either scored or assisted on half of their teams' total goals. Who posted the highest single-season percentage of his club's total offense?

A. Steve Yzerman

B. Mario Lemieux

C. Marcel Dionne

D. Wayne Gretzky

2.22 In 1977–78, who set the Ontario Hockey Association (now the Ontario Hockey League) scoring record, with 192 points—a record he still holds?

A. The Ottawa 67s' Bobby Smith

B. The Oshawa Generals' Tony Tanti

C. The Cornwall Royals' Doug Gilmour

D. The Sault Ste. Marie Greyhounds' Wayne Gretzky

2.23 Wayne Gretzky took the fewest games to score 50 goals in a season. Which player was the fastest to reach 100 points from the start of a season?

A. Mario Lemieux

B. Pat LaFontaine

C. Steve Yzerman

D. Wayne Gretzky

2.24 In 2002–03, who scored a season-high seven points in one game?

A. Markus Naslund, with the Vancouver Canucks

B. Peter Forsberg, with the Colorado Avalanche

C. Jaromir Jagr, with the Washington Capitals

D. Dany Heatley, with the Atlanta Thrashers

2.25 In 2002–03, which Minnesota player passed Wild coach Jacques Lemaire on the NHL all-time scoring list?

A. Cliff Ronning

B. Andrew Brunette

C. Marian Gaborik

D. Jim Dowd

2.26 Who was the first NHLer to score 10 shorthanded goals in one season?

A. Marcel Dionne, with the Detroit Red Wings

B. Wayne Gretzky, with the Edmonton Oilers

C. Mario Lemieux, with the Pittsburgh Penguins

D. Dirk Graham, with the Chicago Blackhawks

2.27 No pair of teammates has ever dominated the NHL scoring chart like Phil Esposito and Bobby Orr with the Boston Bruins. For how many seasons did the duo rank one-two in the points parade?

A. Four seasons

B. Five seasons

C. Six seasons

D. Seven seasons

2.28 Which sniper has led the NHL in goal scoring for the most seasons?

A. Gordie Howe

B. Bobby Hull

C. Phil Esposito

D. Wayne Gretzky

2.29 What is the fastest time from the start of a game that a game-winning goal has been scored?

    A. At 0:07

    B. At 1:07

    C. At 2:07

    D. At 4:07

2.30 What is the highest goals-to-assists differential by a player in one season?

    A. A differential of 21

    B. A differential of 31

    C. A differential of 41

    D. A differential of 51

2.31 Besides Gordie Howe, who is the only other 42-year-old in NHL history to earn as many points as his age?

    A. Alex Delvecchio

    B. Igor Larionov

    C. Mark Messier

    D. Johnny Bucyk

2.32 Who is the youngest player in NHL history to lead or share the lead in goals in one season?

    A. Charlie Conacher, in 1930–31

    B. Bobby Hull, in 1959–60

    C. Wayne Gretzky, in 1981–82

    D. Rick Nash, in 2003–04

2.33 Amongst players who have scored 40 goals in a season, who holds the NHL record for scoring the highest percentage of them on the power play?

    A. Yvan Cournoyer, with the Montreal Canadiens

    B. Joe Nieuwendyk, with the Calgary Flames

C.   Luc Robitaille, with the Los Angeles Kings

D.   Dave Andreychuk, with the Buffalo Sabres

2.34   **What is the most number of points by an NHLer in his first game?**

A.   Four points

B.   Five points

C.   Six points

D.   Seven points

2.35   **What is the individual record for goals scored in the most consecutive regular-season games against the same opponent?**

A.   Six consecutive games

B.   Seven consecutive games

C.   Eight consecutive games

D.   Nine consecutive games

2.36   **Which sniper has finished runner-up in NHL scoring the most often?**

A.   Maurice Richard

B.   Ted Lindsay

C.   Bobby Hull

D.   Marcel Dionne

2.37   **Which NHLer holds the longest streak for scoring or assisting on consecutive goals scored by his team?**

A.   Jaromir Jagr, with the Pittsburgh Penguins

B.   Wayne Gretzky, with the Edmonton Oilers

C.   Mario Lemieux, with the Pittsburgh Penguins

D.   Steve Yzerman, with the Detroit Red Wings

Answers

2.1 **C. Six straight games**

Few rookies skate into the NHL record books after just six career games. For most, an NHL start is a kick-the-tires foray for their team followed by a one-way ticket back to the minors. And if they are successful at the NHL level, even fewer get mentioned in the same breath as Hall of Famers Joe Malone, Newsy Lalonde or Cy Denneny. Yet that's what Evgeni Malkin accomplished in 2006–07—or, more precisely, what he did between October 18 and November 1, 2006, when the 20-year-old Russian popped a goal in each of his first six games to become the first player since Malone, Lalonde and Denneny scored in their first six matches 89 years earlier during the NHL's inaugural season of 1917–18. Still, Malkin should own the record outright. No criticism intended, but Malone, Lalonde and Denneny weren't true rookies, considering they already had established playing careers when the league opened for business. In fact, Malone was 27 years old, Lalonde, 29, and Denneny, 25, in 1917–18. Note: Malone holds the all-time freshman record, after scoring goals in his first 14 games. Amongst modern players, Malkin's six topped Dmitri Kvartalnov's run of five for Boston in 1992–93.

2.2 **B. Chicago's Bobby Hull, Stan Mikita and Kenny Wharram**

Only three NHL teams have had three players sweep the top three spots in the goal-scoring parade. The first club to do it was the Montreal Canadiens in 1954–55, with Maurice Richard and Bernie Geoffrion tying for the league lead with 38 goals, and teammate Jean Béliveau one back at 37. But the

Chicago Blackhawks trio of Bobby Hull, Stan Mikita and Kenny Wharram did it twice during the 1960s. In 1963–64, Hull led all shooters with 43 goals, followed by Mikita and Wharram, who both netted 39. And in 1966–67, the Chicago trio did it again, with Hull potting 52 goals, Mikita, 35 and Wharram, 31.

2.3   **A. Teemu Selanne**
While the vast majority of 40-goal scorers (a whooping 86 per cent according to hockeybuzz.com) reach the milestone goal-count by age 29 or younger, Teemu Selanne, who already had four 40-goals-or-more seasons by that age, bucked the trend and notched consecutive campaigns of plus-40 goals at the ripe old ages of 35 and 36. Clearly, the lockout of 2004–05 agreed with the speedy Finn. He rested his broken knee and came through with two resurgence years in 2005–06 (40 goals) and 2006–07 (48). By comparison, Wayne Gretzky was 29 when he racked up his last 40-goal season, after which, in 1990–91, he broke 30 only twice more. As for Selanne, he's in good company when it comes to players with 40-goal seasons after age 35, an elite corps that includes Johnny Bucyk—the oldest 50-goal scorer—as well as Mario Lemieux, Phil Esposito, Mark Messier and Jaromir Jagr.

2.4   **D. Because of his thunderous slap shot**
When hockey writers of the 1950s first witnessed Geoffrion in practice slapping the puck with golf-swing shots, they called it a "slap" shot. Because of its inaccuracy and sheer velocity, the shot caused pucks to boom off the boards, a sound that echoed across the rink. After that, Geoffrion became "Boom-Boom" and the slap shot joined the wrist and backhand shots as one of the essential weapons in every scorer's arsenal.

2.5   B. 30 goalposts

After signing a career contract worth US$21 million over three
years, Theoren Fleury tanked in his first season in New York
and blamed his terrible 15-goal performance on bad luck: "I
bet you I hit 30 goalposts last year," he said. "If 15 of those had
gone in, I'd be at the average for my career." Ah, sure, Theo.

2.6   B. Seven goalies

Maurice Richard's historic 50-goal season in 1944–45 stands as
a benchmark for all snipers today. In the six-team NHL, seven
goalies participated in his record: Detroit's Harry Lumley gave
up 14 goals, followed by Mike Karakas of Chicago (8), Ken
McAuley of New York (8), Frank McCool of Toronto (8), Harvey
Bennett of Boston (6), Paul Bibeault of Boston (4) and Connie
Dion of Detroit (2). Bennett, the last surviving member of
the seven-goalie group, was in the Bruins' net for Richard's
celebrated goal on March 18, 1945. At the time, Bennett
complained to referee George Gravel that the puck had been
kicked in, a position he has always maintained despite the
enormity of Richard's accomplishment. Still, "he's too good an
athlete, he deserves everything he got," said Bennett to the
Hockey News. Ironically, the Rocket's big night was Bennett's
last as an NHL goalie. Subbing for an injured Frank Brimsek
(whom Richard once said was the most difficult to beat), the
19-year-old Bennett played just 25 games, winning 10 and losing 12, before being sent down to the minors, where he spent
a long career.

2.7   A. Ray Whitney, with the Carolina Hurricanes

Call it the Ray Whitney magic trick. In the second period of
a road game against the Boston Bruins on February 8, 2007,
the Hurricanes winger exploded for three goals in a span of
100 seconds. Whitney scored his first marker at 15:36, his sec-

ond at 16:45 and his third at 17:16, giving the 'Canes a 3–1 lead. But his third goal was greeted by a lone hat and a cascade of boos from disgruntled Bruins fans. "Things happen quick in this game," Bruins coach Dave Lewis said afterwards, "but normally, you don't want them to happen that quick." By the time second intermission rolled around, Whitney had also picked up an assist on Justin Williams's power-play goal. He then added another assist on Rod Brind'Amour's empty-netter in the third period to cap a five-point night in Carolina's 5–2 win. And, though Whitney's hat trick was well short of league record leader Bill Mosienko's 21-second hat trick, it comfortably beat the Whalers–Hurricanes franchise mark held by Ron Francis, who scored a hat trick in a span of 8:05 in 1985. Remarkably, it was only the second hat trick of Whitney's 15-year career.

2.8   A. Ryan Smyth and Jonathan Cheechoo

The NHL should have proclaimed October 12, 2006, official hat trick night. Why? Because between two games an unusually high number of natural hat tricks were tallied—three in all. First, the Devils' Brian Gionta scored three straight in a comeback win against Toronto; then, Ryan Smyth matched Jonathan Cheechoo's hat trick to help Edmonton erase a 4–1 deficit and earn a stunning 6–4 victory against San Jose. It was the first time in 87 years and only the second time ever that opposing players scored naturals in a single game. (Montreal's Didier Pitre and Ottawa's Jack Darragh each had natural hat tricks in the Canadiens' 10–6 win on January 16, 1919.) Smyth notched his three in an Oilers-record 2:01 on two deflections and a rebound, causing teammate Ethan Moreau to joke: "He scored three goals in 2:01, and the puck was on his stick for a total of four-tenths of a second. That's vintage Smitty." Smyth broke Wayne Gretzky's team mark of 2:18.

2.9   B. Two goals

Demonstrating a flair for the dramatic, Brett Hull set up one goal and scored twice in his first game against his former team, including the game-winner, which he wired past goalie Ed Belfour 52 seconds into overtime. For Hull, who signed with Detroit in the off-season after Dallas declined to offer him a contract, the result was sweet. Asked by reporters if he would be content to play second fiddle on the Red Wings' star-packed team, Hull replied: "I'll play the tuba. I don't care as long as we keep winning and having fun."

2.10   B. Scott Mellanby

Mellanby, the man who made the two-goal "rat trick" famous in Florida, scored his first-ever hat trick on March 6, 2003, when he knocked home career goals 324, 325, 326 and 327 against Phoenix in a 6–3 win. According to hockeydraftcentral.com, Mellanby was the first player in NHL history to reach the 300-goal mark without a hat trick. He was playing in his 1,209th game. In 2008–09, Mellanby looked to have some company in Petr Sykora, who posted a league-record 38 two-goal games without a hat trick. But then, on December 11, Sykora scored his first threesome, in Pittsburgh's 9–2 rout of the New York Islanders, for his 283rd, 284th and 285th career goals.

2.11   B. 16 game-winners

While the game-winning goal is a legitimate record, there is an element of luck associated with its accomplishment. That's because game-winners are sometimes decided not by the scorer, but by when the opposition pots its last goal in a loss. For example, in a 4–1 victory, the second goal scored by the winning team is considered the game-winner—since the losers didn't score more than once. If the opposition scores again, in a 4–2 result, the game-winner goes to the winning team's player who luckily netted the third goal. So, in some wins, game-winners are less a result of heroics then basic arithmetic. Still, only two players in league annals have been credited with 15 or more game-winning goals in one season. Phil Esposito scored 16 game-winners in back-to-back seasons, 1970–71 and 1971–72. Then, in 1983–84, Quebec's Michel Goulet earned an amazing 38 per cent of the Nordiques' 42 wins—with 16 game-winners.

2.12   **C. 27 seconds**
Knuble potted the fastest two goals from the start of a game in league history on February 14, 2003. Scoring at 0:10 and 0:27 against the Florida Panthers' Roberto Luongo, Knuble eclipsed a 28-year-old record of 33 seconds held by Chicago's John Marks. Setting an NHL standard was Knuble's way of celebrating his 400th career game, which he recorded a week earlier against Pittsburgh.

2.13   **A. Peter Bondra**
Bondra was in a gunner's groove on February 5, 1994. The Washington Capitals winger lit up Tampa Bay Lightning goalie Daren Puppa like a cheap cigar, snapping home four goals in a span of four minutes and 12 seconds in the first period. It was the fastest four-goal outburst in NHL history. To top things off, Bondra added a fifth marker in the Caps' 6–3 victory.

2.14   **D. 21 seasons**
Take a long look at that number. Incredible isn't it? For 21 straight seasons, Gordie Howe ranked among the NHL's top 10 scorers. And not only did Howe never have a bad year, he seemed impervious to injury: he didn't miss more than six games in any season during those 21 years. The string began

in 1949–50, Howe's fourth year in the league, and continued until 1969–70. Mr. Hockey led the loop in scoring six times and had one second-place finish and six thirds.

2.15 A. Blaine Stoughton, with Hartford, in 1979–80
Blaine Stoughton scored 56 goals in the Hartford Whalers' inaugural NHL season—the most by a player on a first-year NHL expansion team. His 50th goal came on March 28, 1980, outpacing Wayne Gretzky, who scored his first number 50 just five days later. That year Stoughton also tied Buffalo's Danny Gare and Los Angeles's Charlie Simmer for the 1979–80 goal-scoring lead—another first by an NHLer on a new team. Gretzky totalled 51 goals in 1979–80, Brian Bradley potted 42 in 1992–93 and Bob Kudelski hit the 40-goal mark in 1993–94.

2.16 A. Maurice Richard
Although a number of players recorded goal-a-game seasons during the NHL's formative years after 1917–18, it wasn't until 1944–45, when Richard scored 50 goals in 50 games, that the league had a modern-day benchmark for goal scoring. No scorer duplicated Richard's achievement of a goal-a-game pace until Gretzky, 37 years later, in 1981–82.

2.17 A. Mario Lemieux and Rob Brown, with the Pittsburgh Penguins
In 1988–89 the Penguins' power play usually meant one thing: a goal. It didn't matter who the opposition was or what combination of players were thrown together as a special team, Mario and the boys found a way to make their opponents pay for their transgressions. Pittsburgh established an NHL record with 119 goals on the man-advantage as Lemieux (31) and Brown (24) led the charge for a combined 55 power-play markers, the most ever by teammates in one season.

2.18 D. Bernie Federko

One of the few scoring stars on the blue-collar teams of the Harry Ornest-owned Blues, Federko got a lot of ice time, playing much of each season on two lines. He recorded this NHL first, scoring 50 assists or more, between 1978–79 to 1987–88.

2.19 B. Brendan Shanahan

Several big names—bigger than Brendan Shanahan's—have challenged Gordie Howe and his monster record of 22 consecutive seasons of 20 or more goals. Marcel Dionne and Brett Hull got to 17 straight seasons. Ron Francis totalled 20, but tripped up midway with an 11-goal year during the condensed 48-game schedule of 1994–95's player lockout. And Dave Andreychuk's career included 19 20-goal seasons interrupted by two defensive-oriented seasons in New Jersey. Only Shanahan has been a model of consistency, notching his 19th straight year of 20 or more goals in 2007–08. However, Howe's famous longevity mark is safe from Shanahan, who snapped his own streak by scoring just six times in 34 games in 2008–09.

2.20 B. 39 straight games

As of 2008–09, the longest point-scoring streak in AHL history belongs to Chicago Wolves right wing Darren Haydar, who set a new mark of 32 straight games with a goal and an assist in a 2–1 win over San Antonio on December 23, 2006. After eclipsing the 31-game record that Binghamton's Mike Richard set in 1987–88, Haydar, an Atlanta Thrashers free agent in 2006, extended his minor-league streak to 39, scoring 24 goals and 80 points between October 7, 2006, and January 6, 2007.

2.21 B. Mario Lemieux

Only four NHLers have ever had a season in which they figured in half their team's total goals. Joe Malone and Cy Denneny did it in the NHL's early days, when players often remained on the ice the entire game. Amongst modern-day players, only Mario Lemieux and Wayne Gretzky have duplicated the feat. Lemieux's 1988–89 performance is in a class by itself: he either scored or assisted on an amazing 57.3 per cent of the goals scored by the Pittsburgh Penguins that season—the highest percentage in NHL history. Yet despite his astonishing numbers, Lemieux didn't win the league MVP award in 1988–89. It went to Gretzky, who scored the same number of assists as Lemieux, but 31 fewer goals. Gretzky's MVP triumph over the high-scoring Lemieux was due to the fact that No. 99, in his first year with Los Angeles, took the Kings from being the fourth-worst team in the NHL to the fourth-best club—a 23-point jump in one season.

The NHL's Leading Scorers by Percentage of Team Scoring*

PLAYER	YEAR	G	A	POINTS	TEAM GOALS	PERCENTAGE
Mario Lemieux	1988–89	85	114	199	347	57.3
Joe Malone	1919–20	39	9	48	91	52.7
Mario Lemieux	1987–88	70	98	168	319	52.7
Wayne Gretzky	1984–85	73	135	208	401	51.9
Wayne Gretzky	1981–82	92	120	212	417	50.8
Cy Denneny	1924–25	27	15	42	83	50.6

*Current to 2008–09

2.22 A. The Ottawa 67s' Bobby Smith

In 1977–78, 20-year-old Bobby Smith of the Ottawa 67s waged a year-long battle with 17-year-old rookie Wayne Gretzky of the Sault Ste. Marie Greyhounds for the Ontario Hockey Association scoring title. When the smoke finally cleared, Smith, a three-year OHA veteran, had bested Gretzky by 10 points—192 to 182. He then went on to enjoy a distinguished 15-year NHL career with Minnesota and Montreal, but never outpointed the Great One again—though his total is still a league mark, as is Gretzky's 182 points by a rookie.

2.23   D. Wayne Gretzky
The ultimate team player, Wayne Gretzky routinely scored 100-point seasons. In 1983–84, he recorded the NHL's fastest 100 points in just 34 games. The following season he did it in 35 games. Mario Lemieux is the next fastest; he notched his quickest century mark in 36 games in 1988–89. Between them, Gretzky and Lemieux have combined to record the 12 fastest 100-point years.

2.24   C. Jaromir Jagr, with the Washington Capitals
Jagr matched his career high with seven points on three goals and four assists as the Capitals pounded the Florida Panthers 12–2 on January 10, 2003. Although Panthers owner Alan Cohen later complained that Washington had deliberately run up the score, Caps coach Bruce "Butch" Cassidy actually applied the brakes, with his team ahead 9–0 at the end of the second period. Jagr, who played just 14 minutes in the entire game, sat out most of the third period, losing any chance of breaking Darryl Sittler's single-game record of 10 points.

2.25   A. Cliff Ronning
On March 9, 2003, Ronning passed coach Jacques Lemaire with his 835th and 836th point to move into 98th spot on the all-time scoring list. In an exchange in front of the press,

Lemaire pointed out that Ronning needed 17 seasons to register 835 points, while he did it in 12 years. "Yeah, but you played with Guy Lafleur," Ronning argued. "Hey, you're playing with (Antti) Laaksonen and (Wes) Waltz," Lemaire replied.

2.26   A. Marcel Dionne, with the Detroit Red Wings
The shorthanded goal is one of those wonderful glitches in the game: it really isn't supposed to happen. In Dionne's fourth and final year with Detroit, 1974–75, he scored 47 goals—more than 50 per cent of them (25 goals) on special teams, including 10 shorthanded.

2.27   B. Five seasons
Esposito and Orr finished one-two in the NHL scoring race five times in six seasons (1969–70 to 1974–75). During that span, Esposito topped the chart four times and Orr twice. Boston's dynamic duo would have been six for six if not for the Flyers' Bobby Clarke, who edged Orr for second place in 1972–73 by three points, 104 to 101. Orr would have undoubtedly finished ahead of Clarke had he not missed 15 games due to injuries. In fact, Orr would have given Espo a run for first.

2.28   B. Bobby Hull
During his prime, Hull was not only the NHL's most powerful skater, he also possessed the hardest shot. (His high-velocity slapper was once timed at a terrifying 118.3 mph.) And those skills helped the Golden Jet top the NHL in goal scoring a record seven times in his career, though it's possible that Hull would have won more NHL goal-scoring races had he not jumped to the WHA in 1972–73. In 1974–75, he blasted in a WHA-record 77 goals with the Winnipeg Jets.

The NHL's Top Goal-Scoring Champs*

PLAYER	TEAM	TITLES
Bobby Hull	Chicago	7
Phil Esposito	Boston	6
Wayne Gretzky	Edmonton	5
Maurice Richard	Montreal	5
Charlie Conacher	Toronto	5
Gordie Howe	Detroit	5

*Current to 2008–09

2.29 A. At 0:07

Toronto's Charlie Conacher scored the fastest game-winner
in league history on February 6, 1932. According to local press
reports, "The near capacity crowd [in Toronto] had hardly
settled in their seats when Charlie Conacher opened the
scoring. Handed the puck by Busher Jackson from the opening faceoff, Conacher let loose a whistling drive from near
the blue line that found the top corner of the net. Wilf Cude
had little chance for the save." But Conacher's contribution
to his record is only half the story in the 6–0 win. Leaf goalie
Lorne Chabot stoned the Bruins through 60 minutes to help
preserve Conacher's early game-winner—one of old-time
hockey's least known pieces of trivia.

2.30 C. A differential of 41

In Brett Hull's case it is always better to receive than to give.
No NHLer has a higher goals-to-assist differential than Hull,
who recorded a league-busting 41 on 86 goals and 45 assists in
1990–91. The only other player to score at least 40 more goals
than assists in a season is Joe Malone, who notched 44 goals
and four assists in 1917–18. But Malone's numbers are suspect,
considering that proper tabulation for assists only began the
following season, 1918–19.

2.31 B. Igor Larionov

There is little chance of anyone ever challenging Gordie Howe as the oldest point-producing NHLer. His last season, 1979–80, was a 41-point campaign at the age of 52. But Larionov did equal another Howe mark, becoming just the second 42-year-old to record as many points as his age, when, in 2002–03, he scored 43 points. In the same season, and at the same age, 42, Mark Messier was another candidate, but registered only 40 points. Several other contenders have also come close, though not as 42-year-olds, including Johnny Bucyk (43 points in 1976–77 at age 41) and, more recently, Gary Roberts, who was almost 41 when he potted 42 points in 2006–07. As for Howe, in 1969–70, at age 42, he amassed a sizzling 71 points.

2.32 D. Rick Nash, in 2003–04

While everyone was watching Atlanta sniper Ilya Kovalchuk tear up the league, Rick Nash was finding his NHL legs in Columbus, developing a reputation as a young gun who would charge the net and pay the price for goals. Along with Jarome Iginla, the threesome tied for the goal-scoring title with 41 goals in 2003–04, though Nash was still a teenager (a good excuse for his wild minus-35), the first in league history to win or share the goal lead.

Youngest Goal-Scoring Leaders*

PLAYER	TEAM	SEASON	GOALS	AGE
Rick Nash	Columbus	2003–04	41	19 years, 293 days
Charlie Conacher	Toronto	1930–31	31	20 years, 92 days
Ilya Kovalchuk	Atlanta	2003–04	41	20 years, 354 days
Wayne Gretzky	Edmonton	1981–82	92	21 years, 68 days
Bobby Hull	Chicago	1959–60	39	21 years, 77 days
Charlie Conacher	Toronto	1931–32	34	21 years, 93 days
Wayne Gretzky	Edmonton	1982–83	71	22 years, 67 days

*From the Elias Sports Bureau; current to 2008–09

2.33 D. Dave Andreychuk, with the Buffalo Sabres

Dave Andreychuk may be the premier power-play specialist in NHL history: more than half of his career goals were scored when his team had the man-advantage, while many others came via deflections or rebounds that he banged in from the edge of the crease. At six foot four and 220 pounds, Andreychuk was a hard man to move once he parked himself near the goalie. And in 1991–92, with the Sabres, the big winger scored 28 of his 41 goals (68 per cent) on the power play. That's the highest percentage ever by a 40-goal scorer.

Highest Percentage of Goals on the Power Play*

PLAYER	TEAM	SEASON	G	PPG	PERCENTAGE
Dave Andreychuk	Buffalo	1991–92	41	28	.68
Joe Nieuwendyk	Calgary	1992–93	51	31	.61
Dave Andreychuk	Buffalo/Toronto	1992–93	54	32	.59
Luc Robitaille	Los Angeles	1991–92	44	26	.59
Tim Kerr	Philadelphia	1985–86	58	34	.59

*Since 1967–68; current to 2008–09, for players with 40-goal seasons or more

2.34 B. Five points

On February 14, 1977, Al Hill kept mumbling, "I can't believe it. I can't believe it." The rookie's state of disbelief was understandable. He had just scored a record five points for the Flyers in his NHL debut. Called up earlier that day from the AHL's Springfield Indians, Hill wasted no time getting on the scoreboard, blasting a 45-footer past St. Louis Blues goalie Yves Belanger only 36 seconds into the first period. Hill scored again on his second shot just 11 minutes later, then went on to add three assists in the Flyers' 6–4 win. Yet Hill was never able to duplicate his first-game magic. He scored just one point in eight more games that season and was sent back to Springfield, then bounced back and forth between the Flyers and the minors for eight seasons, while collecting an NHL career total of 95 points.

2.35 **C. Eight consecutive games**

Mike Knuble certainly enjoys playing against Buffalo. The right-winger scored goals against the Sabres in eight consecutive regular-season games to set an NHL record. The first four goals came when Knuble was with the Boston Bruins in 2003–04. The second four came in 2005–06, the year after the lockout, when he was a member of the Philadelphia Flyers. And in the first round of the 2006 playoffs, Knuble then scored his ninth straight goal against Buffalo in the first game of their 2006 playoff series, before being blanked in the next five games as Buffalo took the series. His regular-season streak against the Sabres was snapped when Buffalo crushed the Flyers 9–1 in their first meeting in 2006–07. Knuble shares the record with at least one other player: Alex Ovechkin, who scored seven straight times against Philadelphia in 2006–07, then tied Knuble's mark on November 2, 2008, with his eighth red light versus the Flyers. In his next game against Philly, on November 23, he went goal-less.

2.36 **A. Maurice Richard**

Interestingly, the player whose name is honoured on the new NHL goal-scoring award never won the Art Ross Trophy as the league's point-scoring champion. Not that Richard wasn't trying or anything. But, as the game's leading goal scorer, he was often outpointed by players who amassed greater point totals based on bigger numbers in the assist column than the goal column. For Richard, who usually recorded more goals than assists in a season, missing the Art Ross was his greatest disappointment. He finished second a record five times; twice, just one point behind the top scorer (including 1954–55, when Richard lost to teammate Bernie Geoffrion after being suspended for striking an official). Only old-timer Cy Denneny ties Richard for most runner-up finishes. But while Denneny also finished second five times, he did win a scoring championship (1923–24).

2.37   A. Jaromir Jagr, with the Pittsburgh Penguins

Jaromir Jagr began 1999–2000 proving what every team already knew: the so-called human highlight reel was almost impossible to shadow from the blue line in and rightly worth every penny of his league-leading us$10.4-million salary. In the best start to date of his lengthy career, Jagr scored 10 goals and 23 points in his first 11 games and, over a stretch of seven games between October 16 and November 4, had a hand in 15 straight Pittsburgh goals—setting a new league mark. Still, though Jagr counted seven goals and eight assists during this streak, the Penguins went winless, losing five and tying two. (The biggest beneficiary was Robert Lang, who scored five goals and two assists off the stick of the Czech superstar.) Note: in addition to his big slap shot and dazzling game of high-speed puck control, some of Jagr's success was a product of his extraordinary ice time and the lack of scoring depth on the injury-riddled Penguins. Coach Kevin Constantine had Jagr averaging 26:10 minutes per game. His 15 consecutive points accounted for more than a third of total player points earned during the Penguins' 0–5–2 run.

Game 2

What's in a Name?

TO MAKE IT IN THE NHL, they say you've got to have hockey in your blood. In fact, some NHLers can even boast having the league's initials in their family names. Discover the hockey players, teams and terms with N-H-L roots by using the clues in the right column to fill in the blanks on the left.

Solutions are on page 558

1. N A S H V I L L E — City of 1998 expansion club

2. G L E N N H A L L — The first butterfly-style goalie

3. N O H O L D S B A R R E D — Hockey term: anything allowed

4. B E R N I E N I C H O L L S — Kings 70-goal scorer

5. B E N C H C L E A R I N G B R A W L — Hockey term: team vs. team fight

6. R A N D Y H O L T — NHL record-holder for most penalty minutes in a game

7. K E V I N H A L L E R — Mighty Ducks defenseman in 1999-2000

8. P U N C H L I N E — Montreal's most famous old-time scoring trio

9. A N D Y V A N H E L L E M O N D — 1999 Hall of Fame referee

10. F I N A L W H I S T L E — Hockey term: end of game

3

Swan Song

WHEN CBC'S *Hockey Night in Canada* lost its venerable theme music in June 2008 over rights issues with songwriter Dolores Claman, the Canadian network took a surprisingly upbeat approach—at least in public. There was some finger-pointing within the corporation over losing what many consider Canada's second national anthem, but their solution to a new *Hockey Night* ditty was a theme-song contest. (Meanwhile, rival broadcaster CTV and its sports-channel partners TSN and RDS went on the power play with a reported seven-figure proposal to Claman, and scored, poaching the song that had been associated with *Hockey Night in Canada* since 1968.) During the summer of 2008, the CBC received more than 14,000 musical entries, which were reduced to five semifinalists, with themes then arranged by producer Bob Rock. After public voting, Colin Oberst's Canadian Gold was chosen as the new HNIC theme. Oberst's composition first aired on October 11, 2008. In this chapter we sing the praises of the media and all they've done to bring the game into our homes.

Answers are on page 68

3.1 Which NHL player launched his own entertainment company and hip-hop record label in 2005?
A. Jeremy Roenick
B. Anson Carter
C. Jarome Iginla
D. José Théodore

3.2 In 2000, CCM was asked to design a special type of skate for what kind of animal?

A. A dog

B. A bear

C. A chimpanzee

D. A kangaroo

3.3 In July 2003, which Dallas Star was surprised to discover his 1999 Stanley Cup ring being sold on eBay?

A. Guy Carbonneau

B. Brett Hull

C. Mike Modano

D. Ed Belfour

3.4 The late broadcaster Danny Gallivan coined the term "spin-o-rama" (or "spinnerama") to describe a deke first used by which NHLer?

A. Serve Savard, with the Montreal Canadiens

B. Denis Savard, with the Chicago Blackhawks

C. Andre Savard, with the Buffalo Sabres

D. None of the above; Danny Gallivan used "swirl-a-rama"

3.5 With which hobby was Bee Hive corn syrup once associated?

A. The collecting of NHL team pucks

B. The collecting of hockey cards

C. The collecting of game-worn jerseys

D. The collecting of autographed hockey sticks

3.6 During home games, which defunct NHL club was the first to play the rock anthem "Rock and Roll" (Part 2)—also known as "The Hey Song"?

A. The Kansas City Scouts

B. The Quebec Nordiques

C. The Winnipeg Jets

D. The Colorado Rockies

3.7 In a 1999 search for the top Zamboni driver of the year, how many votes did winner Jimmy "The Iceman" MacNeil receive?

A. Less than 1,000 votes

B. Between 1,000 and 100,000 votes

C. Between 100,000 and 250,000 votes

D. More than 250,000 votes

3.8 Which former Boston Bruins player is the mascot of the popular Boston-based punk rock group Dropkick Murphys?

A. Derek Sanderson

B. Cam Neely

C. Gerry Cheevers

D. Terry O'Reilly

3.9 On which television show did the Stanley Cup appear after the New York Rangers won the 1994 championship?

A. *Late Night with David Letterman*

B. *Coach's Corner,* with Don Cherry

C. *ABC's Wide World of Sports*

D. *The Tonight Show,* with Jay Leno

3.10 Where in Montreal was the once-famous Toe Blake's Tavern located?

A. On Mount Royal

B. On St. Catherine Street

C. At the Molson Brewery

D. Inside the old Montreal Forum

3.11 In which NHL arena did Jean-Claude Van Damme battle terrorists in the 1995 movie *Sudden Death*?

A. Pittsburgh's Civic Arena

B. Tampa Bay's ThunderDome

C. Los Angeles's Great Western Forum

D. New York's Madison Square Garden

3.12 Which musician recorded a controversial song about hockey violence in 2002, entitled "Hit Somebody!"?

A. Tom Waits

B. Warren Zevon

C. Neil Young

D. Weird Al Yankovic

3.13 In 2004, which NHLer made headlines when his likeness was inaccurately produced as an action figure?

A. Jarome Iginla

B. Donald Brashear

C. Kevin Weekes

D. Anson Carter

3.14 In what was considered a sportscasting first, both the play-by-play announcer and colour commentator called an NHL game from ice level between the benches. It happened in what season?

A. 2003–04

B. 2005–06

C. 2006–07

D. 2007–08

3.15 Which NHL team was the first to release a licensed version of the Monopoly board game?

A. The New York Rangers

B. The Minnesota Wild

C. The Colorado Avalanche

D. The Toronto Maple Leafs

3.16 In 2004, what unusual personal item of Bobby Hull's was auctioned off at his collectibles sale?

A. His false teeth

B. His jock strap

C. His farm's pitchfork

D. His hair-plug transplants

3.17 TV cameras have shot the game from every angle. But who first wore a camera on the ice during an NHL pre-season game?

A. It has never been done

B. Defenseman Larry Robinson

C. Goalie Kelly Hrudey

D. Referee Don Koharski

3.18 In 1996, a Canadian rock band called the Hanson Brothers launched a campaign to get which former hockey tough guy elected to the Hockey Hall of Fame?

A. Eddie Shack

B. Terry O'Reilly

C. John Ferguson

D. Tiger Williams

3.19 In 1955, on the night of the famous Richard Riot, what song did the organist play after a bomb exploded at the Montreal Forum?

A. The Platters' "Smoke Gets in Your Eyes"

B. Jackie Wilson's "Lonely Teardrops"

C. Percy Faith's "My Heart Cries for You"

D. Connie Francis's "Who's Sorry Now?"

3.20 Who was the first NHL player from outside North America to sign an endorsement contract with a Fortune 500 company?

A. Pavel Bure

B. Jaromir Jagr

C. Sergei Fedorov

D. Teemu Selanne

3.21 Who is considered hockey's first play-by-play announcer?

A. Norm Albert

B. Pete Parker

C. Foster Hewitt

D. None of the above

3.22 During the 1997 playoffs in Anaheim, which TV star accidentally exposed herself while singing the American national anthem?

A. Christina Applegate
B. Lucy Lawless
C. Roseanne Barr
D. Valerie Bertinelli

3.23 In 2006, eBay auctioned off an action figure of Buffalo goalie Clint Malarchuk—in what pose?

A. Lying on his back after a goal
B. Receiving an NHL award
C. Playing in an All-Star game
D. Suffering from a serious injury

3.24 How many pages did the New York Rangers team guide devote to Wayne Gretzky in his retirement year, 1998–99?

A. Four pages
B. Six pages
C. Eight pages
D. 10 pages

3.25 What did the Montreal press dub the 12 players who won five consecutive Stanley Cups in the 1950s?

A. Dickie's Dirty Dozen
B. The 12 Apostles
C. High Noon
D. Le Force Douze (The Force Twelve)

3.26 How often has a hockey player or team been voted *Sports Illustrated*'s Sportsman of the Year?

A. Only once

B. Two times

C. Four times

D. Six times

3.27 In 1996, Pavel Bure revived an old family business in Russia. What was it?

A. Vodka distilling

B. Watchmaking

C. Hockey-stick manufacturing

D. Sable farming

3.28 Who said: "I went to a fight and a hockey game broke out"?

A. Eddie Shack

B. Jay Leno

C. George Carlin

D. Rodney Dangerfield

3.29 Who was voted Canada's top newsmaker of 1997?

A. Mario Lemieux

B. Wayne Gretzky

C. Eric Lindros

D. Sheldon Kennedy

3.30 In 2006–07, which NHL team set a new North American record for most fans wearing wigs at a sporting event?

A. The San Jose Sharks

B. The Calgary Flames

C. The St. Louis Blues

D. The Philadelphia Flyers

3.31 Which team was the first to regularly play "The Hockey Song," by Stompin' Tom Connors, during its home games?

A. The Ottawa Senators

B. The Vancouver Canucks

C. The Edmonton Oilers

D. The Toronto Maple Leafs

3.32 According to a 2000 poll in the *Hockey News,* which season is considered number one in NHL history?

A. Maurice Richard's 50-goal season of 1944–45

B. Bobby Orr's 120-point season of 1969–70

C. Wayne Gretzky's 212-point season of 1981–82

D. Mario Lemieux's 199-point season of 1988–89

3.33 Which NHL tough guy played the role of New York Rangers enforcer Bob "Killer" Dill in the 2006 film about Maurice Richard, *The Rocket?*

A. Sean Avery

B. Andre Roy

C. Colton Orr

D. Brian McGrattan

3.34 Which hockey broadcaster first coined the phrase "dipsy-doodler"?

A. Danny Gallivan

B. Dan Kelly

C. Foster Hewitt

D. Dick Irvin

3.35 Gump Worsley opened a Montreal restaurant that featured "The Ranger Special" on the menu. What was this dish?
A. Pigs knuckles
B. New York cheesecake
C. Stuffed eggs
D. Chicken salad

3.36 In January 2007, which NHL team introduced "the Lay's Fan Zam," a custom Zamboni designed for entertaining rather than ice cleaning?
A. The Nashville Predators
B. The Florida Panthers
C. The Dallas Stars
D. The San Jose Sharks

Swan Song

Answers

3.1   **B. Anson Carter**
Anson Carter, one of the few black hockey players in the NHL, isn't shy about his love of hip-hop. During the 2005 NHL lockout, the dreadlocked Vancouver Canucks winger launched his own record label, Big Up Entertainment. "As of right now, we are building the ground level to be a multi-faceted entertainment company," Carter told AllHipHop.com. The first release from the independent label was the single "Passion and Pain," by Main & Merc of Richmond, Virginia. While the pair worked on their debut album, Carter then announced plans to turn Big Up into a full-blown media company, with sports, music and fashion divisions. The company's first film, *Bald*, a comedy similar to *American Pie*, is about a college student struggling to prevent his hair from falling out.

3.2   C. A chimpanzee

Andre Joly, manager of CCM's skate factory in St. Jean, Quebec, was more than a little sceptical when he received a phone call asking if the company could design a pair of hockey skates for a chimpanzee. "At first I thought it was a joke, and even after I received the chimp's foot tracing, I still thought it was a joke," admitted Joly. But the caller, film director Robert Vince, was serious. Vince needed the skates for Jack, the simian star of a new film he was making, *MVP: Most Valuable Primate.* "The skates we ended up designing basically combined a size-three junior skate with a size-eight toe cap," said Joly. Incredibly, it took Jack barely eight weeks to learn to skate, use a hockey stick and shoot a puck. But if hockey and chimpanzees still sound like an unlikely combo, Vince says that's because you don't know chimps. "They like anything that involves speed and aggression and feeling the wind blowing in their face."

3.3   C. Mike Modano

Looking for something special in hockey memorabilia? When Modano went shopping on eBay he found his own 1999 Cup ring. Funny, he thought it was at DeBoulle Jewellers in Dallas, where he had taken it to be duplicated and upgraded. But the jeweller thought it was to be sold and passed it on to a Florida man, who put the ring up for auction on eBay. Bidding on Modano's ring had hit US$20,000 before it was removed from the online site.

3.4   A. Serve Savard, with the Montreal Canadiens

While Denis Savard (and earlier, Bobby Orr) is more closely associated with the spin-o-rama, that shifty, on-the-fly 360-degree pivot to maintain puck possession against defensemen, it was Serge Savard whose original move to evade attacking forwards inspired the late CBC broadcaster Danny

Gallivan to announce, "... Savard avoids Clarke (Bobby) with a deft spinnerama move ..." Later, Denis Savard tried the technique, but only when he got to the NHL. "It started off with me just turning my back to the defenseman to keep the puck away," Savard told the *Hockey News*. "Then I thought about it, and said, 'Hey, this could be a pretty good move.' So I practised it and perfected it."

3.5 **B. The collecting of hockey cards**

For thousands of Canadian youngsters from 1934 to 1967, the best hockey cards came from the St. Lawrence Starch Co. Ltd., makers of Bee Hive corn syrup. Compared to today's high-gloss cards, a Bee Hive black-and-white might resemble those grainy snapshots from grandmother's family photo album in the attic. But they were magic to the kids who collected them. With mailed-in proof of purchase (a collar off a two-pound can earned a single photo, a five-pound can was worth two), fans received a colour photo of their favourite star mounted on a 4¼- by 6¾-inch card. Bee Hives were produced in three series: 1934 to 1943, 1944 to 1964 and 1964 to 1967. And the photo promotion proved a bonanza for Bee Hive, which quadrupled production to become Canada's largest-selling corn syrup in the 1930s, with more than 2,500 photos mailed daily from its St. Lawrence business office in Port Credit, Ontario. Today, an entire set of Bee Hive's 601 cards, if it exists, is worth CDN$75,000.

3.6 **D. The Colorado Rockies**

The Rockies didn't accomplish much during their brief six-year NHL-stint in Colorado, but they did leave behind one little-known first that went on to become an institution at American sporting events: their theme song, Gary Glitter's glam-rock classic "Rock and Roll" (Part 2). Played when the home team scored or won, the "Hey Song" was then dropped from many arena playlists after Glitter's conviction for sexual abuse of a child in 2005. In 2006, the NFL asked teams to stop playing the tune, though several pro clubs had already pulled the sports anthem after the singer was convicted and imprisoned on child pornography charges in 1997.

3.7   **C. Between 100,000 and 250,000 votes**
When California-based Zamboni announced its search for the top driver of 2000, with the winner to clean the ice at the NHL All-Star game in Toronto, a number of candidates, including celebrities such as Garth Brooks and Bill Murray, received nominations. In time, the contest turned into a two-man race between Jimmy "The Iceman" MacNeil of the Brantford Civic Centre in Ontario, and legendary Detroit Red Wings iceman Al Sobotka. The Zamboni website received more than a million hits during the campaign; MacNeil's 177,566 votes eclipsed Sobotka's by an easy 80,000.

3.8   **D. Terry O'Reilly**
Formed in 1996, Dropkick Murphys are a seven-man band that play loud Irish-infused punk rock. The members are also die-hard Boston Bruins fans. But of all the players who have worn the black-and-gold, tough guy Terry O'Reilly is the band's favourite, and they often wear his No. 23 jersey at their concerts. "Watching O'Reilly as a kid, he was just the type of player who made you feel you could get out there and do it, too," said bass player Ken Casey in an interview with NHL. com. "That was just his way, and I think people can identify with it. And that's how we approach our music. We want people to come to a show and feel like they could step up on the stage and do it, too." O'Reilly's jersey has become a Casey trademark, a look adopted by many of the band's fans. And

when the group toured Australia in 2005, they constantly ran into Aussies sporting Bruins garb, specifically O'Reilly sweaters. "They said they just wanted us to feel at home," said Casey.

3.9 **A. *Late Night with David Letterman***

Following the Rangers' Cup victory in 1994, the trophy made a surprise guest appearance on *David Letterman*. During the show's monologue, Letterman casually leaned back, looked over at his desk and said to band leader Paul Shaefer: "Hey Paul, what's that behind my desk?" Of course, everyone knew something was up. Letterman walked over, pulled out the Stanley Cup to wild applause, then brought out Mark Messier, Brian Leetch and Mike Richter. After a brief interview with the trio, Letterman then placed the Cup onstage, where it remained for the entire show, in front of 20 million viewers.

3.10 **B. On St. Catherine Street**

Little more than a two-minute cab ride from the Montreal Forum, between a cigar shop and Leader's Bowling Lanes, was the non-descript entrance of Toe Blake's Tavern at 1618 St. Catherine Street West. In the days before "Women Welcome" establishments, Toe Blake's was a sanctuary for the boys, where they could chin wag until the wee hours over pints of ale and a few stogies. Topics ranged from which Canadien dynasty had the better talent or who was better, Gordie or Maurice, to some old Maroons story that became taller with each telling. Blake's tavern was the mecca for hockey philosophers and armchair coaches, a preserve steeped in hockey knowledge—second only to the Canadien coach's office at the Forum. Today, the entire block has been replaced by a mall complex.

3.11 A. Pittsburgh's Civic Arena

Many of the scenes in the film *Sudden Death,* in which Jean-Claude Van Damme plays a fire chief fighting a deadly duel with terrorists during Game 7 of the Stanley Cup finals, were shot during an actual game between the Penguins and the Blackhawks at Pittsburgh's Civic Arena. The Igloo was chosen as the backdrop for the action thriller because Penguins owner Howard Baldwin was one of the film's producers. In fact, the movie was based on an idea proposed by Baldwin's wife, Karen.

3.12 B. Warren Zevon

Warren Zevon, a die-hard hockey fan, and Mitch Albom, a Detroit sportswriter, collaborated on "Hit Somebody!" The tongue-in-cheek tune relates the story of Buddy, from the fictional Canadian border town of Big Beaver, who dreams of scoring goals but is really only good at beating up other players. When Buddy tries to argue he's more than your average goon, his coach replies: "The fast guys get paid, they shoot, they score. Protect them Buddy, that's what you're here for. Protection is what you're here for. Protection—it's the stars that score. Protection—kick somebody's ass." Although it earned critical acclaim, "Hit Somebody!" was not well received by the NHL, which banned the tune from the playlist at NHL arenas.

3.13 A. Jarome Iginla

When the three-inch Jarome Iginla figure rolled off the production line in 2004, officials with McFarlane Toys, the licensed manufacturers of NHL figures, had to be a little red-faced. In the two-pack set containing a miniature likeness of Iginla and Saku Koivu, the Iginla figure had the lighter skin pigmentation of the two players. Because of a mistake made in the skin-wash process, the fair-skinned Koivu had a deep suntan and Iginla was as pale as his real-life Nordic counter-part. But this was good for sports memorabilia collectors, who see a spike in demand for collectibles with even the tiniest imperfections.

3.14   C. 2006–07

The claim that announcers get a better sense and feel for the game by being close to the players, coaches and officials at ice level was first tested when the Canadian all-sports net-work TSN placed Chris Cuthbert and Glenn Healy between the teams' benches to call the New York Rangers–Buffalo Sabres match on December 1, 2006. With TV numbers hurt-ing (and tanking in the U.S.), broadcasters had begun looking for "unique experiences" in order to sell hockey to dwindling television audiences. Did the experiment work? Cuthbert admitted that "it's pretty special, not perfect," referring to some sightline problems from the low position. Still, the *Globe and Mail* called it a historic success and not just a gimmick, suggesting that having two announcers rink-side did bring viewers closer to the action. TSN also televised games using a one-up, one-down system—a play-by-play man in the booth and an analyst at ice level. And in a November 15 game, colour commentator Pierre McGuire conducted another first by inter-viewing the Senators' Mike Fisher, who was standing on the ice during a stoppage in play. FSN Detroit was the first U.S. tele-vision outlet with play-by-play at ice level. Ken Daniels called the Red Wings–Ottawa Senators game on December 12, 2006. Mickey Redmond stayed in the press box for his game analysis.

3.15   B. The Minnesota Wild

Talk about capping your expenses. Following the 1999 release of the league's version of Monopoly, in 2006 Hasbro licensed the first NHL team-themed edition of its popular board game to the Minnesota Wild. In the Wild Collector's US$45-edition, franchises cost only $160 and arenas just $900; the prime real estate spaces of Boardwalk and Park Place have been replaced by Jacques Lemaire and his goalie and nephew, Manny Fernandez; the usual game pieces have been substituted with pewter tokens of the Wild logo, hockey skates and, naturally, a Zamboni, and instead of houses and hotels, there are now warming huts and arenas. Unfortunately, however, Monopoly's famous jail remains a jail—instead of what any puckhead would rightfully argue should be a penalty box.

3.16   A. His false teeth

One of the more bizarre items on the block at Bobby Hull's collectibles auction in 2004 was his partial upper plate. The famous choppers of Hull's trademark smile were apparently lost during a trip to Switzerland in the 1950s and later mailed back to him. When the booty from the auction was finally counted, the Golden Jet's false teeth had fetched US$575.96.

3.17   C. Goalie Kelly Hrudey

In a 1991 Rangers–Kings exhibition game at Caesar's Palace in Las Vegas, Hrudey's helmet was wired with a microcamera, permitting viewers to experience hockey from the player's perspective for the first time.

3.18   D. Tiger Williams

Rock music's Hanson Brothers (who are not related to the Hanson brothers of *Slapshot* fame) kick-started their crusade to get Williams into the Hockey Hall of Fame at the October 1996 launch of their CD *Sudden Death*. The album features 15 songs about girls, beer and hockey, including "Stick Boy," "Third Man In," "Rink Rat" and a tune called "He Looked a Lot Like Tiger Williams," in which the NHL's all-time penalty leader is likened to a doctor, a traffic cop and God. Included with each CD was a ballot, which the Hansons asked people to sign and return, boosting Williams for the Hall ahead of "some of those fancy-schmancy, no-hitting prima-donna whining millionaire goal sucks." In response to the campaign, Williams said he doubted he would ever make it into the Hall, but if he did he knew the ideal spot. "I should be in the refs' section, because I made their lives interesting. The only time they got their mugs on TV was when they were in the middle of a fight wiping my blood off their faces."

3.19   **C. Percy Faith's "My Heart Cries for You"**

On the eve of the 1955 playoffs, during a Detroit–Montreal match, someone set off a tear-gas bomb in the Forum to protest the suspension of Maurice Richard, who had deliberately hit a linesman during a brawl earlier that week. The suspension included the season's final three games and the playoffs, with Richard's scoring lead, the Canadiens' first-place finish and the Stanley Cup at stake. And for Montreal's French-Canadian fans, losing Richard—their idol and the Canadien's best player—was a slap in the face. The game was cancelled and the Montreal streets erupted in riots. Only a radio appeal by Richard quieted the city. All was lost: the Rocket's scoring title, the Habs' first-place finish and the Stanley Cup. To this day, Jean Béliveau believes that with Richard's help the Canadiens would have won the Stanley Cup in 1955. As for what musical selection the organist played as putrid smoke filled the Forum and fans began their exodus, that would be "My Heart Cries for You."

3.20   **C. Sergei Fedorov**

In October 1995, the smooth-skating Red Wing superstar inked a three-year endorsement deal with Nike Inc., the

American shoe and sportswear colossus, to promote its fledgling roller- and ice-hockey divisions. Fedorov and fellow endorsers Brian Leetch and Scott Stevens gave the company its first shot of prime-time hockey exposure when they hit the ice wearing new Nike skates, with the famous "Swoosh" logo, at the 1996 NHL All-Star game in Boston.

3.21 **A. Norm Albert**

On February 8, 1923, *Toronto Star* reporter Norm Albert—not Foster Hewitt—called the first play-by-play of a hockey game. Hewitt himself noted the fact in his *Star* column the next day, pointing out that Albert's presentation was "the inaugural broadcasting by radio for a hockey game play-by-play." Hewitt's voice wasn't heard on hockey's other pioneer broadcast, though. A westerner, Pete Parker, called a game between the Regina Capitals and the Edmonton Eskimos of the WCHL on Saskatchewan radio on March 14, 1923, eight days before Foster Hewitt's historic "first" broadcast from the Mutual Street Arena in Toronto.

3.22 **B. Lucy Lawless**

The Anaheim Mighty Ducks booked the statuesque Lawless, best known for starring in the TV series *Xena: Warrior Princess*, to sing the "Star Spangled Banner" for a playoff game against Detroit at the Arrowhead Pond on May 6, 1997. However, the five-foot-eleven New Zealand actress, wearing a skimpy, low-cut dress, drew plenty of attention for reasons other than her singing voice, when she exuberantly spread her arms to belt out that final note and suffered a wardrobe malfunction. "I was wearing a *Playboy*-type outfit, and when I lifted my arms for the big finish, out popped my breasts," she said in an interview. "Obviously, I was mortified." The Red Wings plucked the Ducks 5–3.

3.23   **D. Suffering from a serious injury**
Sports memorabilia hit a new low in 2006, when eBay
auctioned off a customized McFarlane figurine of Clint
Malarchuk's near-fatal skate slash of March 22, 1989. The
small, hand-painted ornament depicted the Buffalo goalie
crouched over a pool of blood on the ice, clutching his
throat. Bidding was cut off early, at $40, due to the outcry
over bad taste.

3.24   **D. 10 pages**
Every season, NHL clubs publish team guides—complete with
regular-season and playoff records, franchise histories and
current-player profiles. Each team member usually gets two
pages devoted to his career, though exceptions are made for
players such as Mark Messier, who receive four pages because
of their star power and contributions to hockey. Wayne
Gretzky and Mario Lemieux received even more play, however. In 1996–97, Lemieux's retirement season, the Pittsburgh
Penguins devoted eight pages to the Magnificent One and his
career. And in the 1998–99 New York Rangers guide, Gretzky
was given a 10-page spread, highlighted with a year-by-year
compendium of facts and statistics as well as a short biography, "The Legend of '99."

3.25   **B. The 12 Apostles**
The "12 Apostles" inherited the glory and soul of the
Canadiens and turned winning the Stanley Cup into a spring
rite for an NHL-record five consecutive seasons. The only
Canadiens to play on all five championships: Maurice Richard,
Jean Béliveau, Jacques Plante, Dickie Moore, Claude Provost,
Doug Harvey, Jean-Guy Talbot, Donnie Marshall, Bernie
Geoffrion, Tom Johnson, Bob Turner and Henri Richard.

3.26 **C. Four times**

Compared to the three other big North American team
sports, hockey is underrepresented amongst winners of *Sports
Illustrated*'s Sportsman of the Year prize. Since the magazine
was founded in 1954, *SI* has honoured only hockey's Bobby
Orr (1970), the gold-medal U.S. Olympic team (1980), Wayne
Gretzky (1982) and Bob Bourne (1987)—the latter named one
of eight "Athletes Who Care" by *SI*, for his work with humani-
tarian causes. Of course, the first three honourees are obvious
choices. Orr revolutionized his blue line position and became
the first defenseman to win the NHL scoring title in 1970; the
American "Miracle" Olympic team stunned the world to take
gold before a hometown crowd at Lake Placid in 1980, and
Gretzky became the face of hockey with his jaw-dropping
212-point season in 1981–82, outdistancing his closest rival
by 65 points. Bourne, though, was a less obvious choice for
a sports award that is usually presented to athletes for their
athletic prowess. He was singled out for his significant and
valuable efforts with a school for handicapped children after
his infant son Jeff was diagnosed was spina bifida; Bourne
and his wife have devoted countless hours to the disease.

3.27 **B. Watchmaking**

In 1996, Pavel Bure revived the family watchmaking business founded by his great, great, great grandfather in Czarist
Russia. The business venture made headlines, but for all the
wrong reasons. ESPN reported that Bure's business partner,
Anzor Kikalichvili, was a member of the Russian mafia and
involved with money laundering, extortion and drug dealing.
Bure denied the report.

3.28 D. Rodney Dangerfield

A favourite on the comedy circuit, Mr. Respectability first cracked hockey's best one-liner on *The Tonight Show Starring Johnny Carson* in 1983.

3.29 D. Sheldon Kennedy

Newspaper editors and broadcast news directors voted Sheldon Kennedy Canada's top newsmaker of 1997, citing his courage in going public about the years of sexual abuse he endured from junior coach Graham James. In a year of hockey-related sexual-abuse scandals, Kennedy gave the sport back its dignity, the editors remarked. As a result, Kennedy's bravery inspired other men to come forward with their own stories of abuse. Kennedy played with Detroit, Calgary and Boston before retiring in 1997 to run a treatment facility in British Columbia for sexually abused youngsters.

3.30 D. The Philadelphia Flyers

The Flyers had a dismal season in 2006–07, but they did create a buzz of excitement on October 30, 2006, when fans were given bright-orange wigs by the team for a game against the Chicago Blackhawks at the Wachovia Center. The hairy handouts were part of an effort to break the *Guinness Book of World Records* stat for "most fans wearing wigs—single venue." The Flyers had unofficially broken the old record—of 6,213 fans—at a Detroit–Pistons game on March 19, 2004, by gathering 9,315 signatures from the 18,876 fans attending the 2006 game.

3.31 A. The Ottawa Senators

"The Hockey Song," written and made famous by Stompin' Tom Connors, is often sung at hockey arenas both large and small. The song is split into three verses, each describing a period of play in a typical game, and is well-known for its catchy chorus: "Oh, the good old hockey game, is the best game you can name. And the best game you can name, is the good old hockey game!" The song first appeared on Connors's 1973 album, *Stompin Tom and the Hockey Song*, but the tune did not attain major popularity until 1992, when the Ottawa Senators began playing it at their games. Fans quickly took a liking to the song and it spread throughout the NHL.

3.32   **B. Bobby Orr's 120-point season of 1969–70**
In *Century of Hockey*, the *Hockey News* polled 20 hockey experts and chose Orr's 1969–70 season as the best in league history—ahead of Wayne Gretzky's record 212-point season in 1981–82. During 1969–70 Orr scored 33 goals and 120 points to become the first defenseman in history to win the Art Ross Trophy as scoring champion. He also won every important individual award available, including the Hart Trophy as league MVP, James Norris Trophy as best defenseman and, in the playoffs, the Stanley Cup and Conn Smythe Trophy as postseason MVP. In a Canadian Press report, Orr said: "People say to me: 'How'd you put up numbers like that?' I was blessed with an ability to play the game and to skate. But I was always allowed to play my style, whereas what is happening in the game today is we're not letting players create. It starts long before the pros. It starts with kids. They (coaches) want to teach the trap. If you have a young defenseman who can skate, they want him to throw the puck up along the glass. They don't want him to skate past centre ice. That's really hurting us. It's not fun for the kids. We're not letting them create."

3.33   **A. Sean Avery**
Several NHL players had small roles in the 2006 biopic about Maurice Richard, *The Rocket*, including Mike Ricci as Elmer Lach, Vincent Lecavalier as Jean Béliveau and Ian Laperriere

as Boom Boom Geoffrion. But the most memorable cameo belonged to Sean Avery, who played New York Rangers bruiser Bob "Killer" Dill. In the film, Dill is called up from the minors by the Rangers for the sole purpose of goading Richard into a fight, only to be pummelled twice by the Montreal star. Yet, though the movie was faithful to the facts in most respects, this incident is a dramatization. Dill tangled twice with Richard during a game on December 17, 1944—once on the ice and then again in the penalty box—and was flattened by Richard in both exchanges, but he was not brought up to the NHL by the Rangers solely for this purpose. In fact, Montreal traded Dill to the Rangers midway through the previous season, and he played nine games against the Canadiens without tangling with Richard before their famous December 1944 bout.

3.34   C. Foster Hewitt

"Dipsy-doodler" is not in any dictionary, but it has long been in hockey's lexicon thanks to Foster Hewitt and, later, Danny Gallivan. In the 1940s, Hewitt called Maple Leafs superstar Max Bentley a "dipsy-doodler" to describe the forward's slight build and adroit skating and stickhandling skills. Gallivan, a wordsmith in his own right, made "dipsy-doodler" a hockey standard in the 1960s.

3.35   D. Chicken salad

The Gumper had a great sense of humour, particularly about his teammates. With Ranger backchecking often non-existent, his years in the New York nets were packed with 50-shot games. But Worsley took the puck barrage in stride and tossed the last laugh: chicken salad, "The Ranger Special."

3.36 C. The Dallas Stars

The Stars' 2007 addition to the NHL's endless parade of marketing gimmicks made its debut at American Airlines Center during the second intermission of a game against the Pittsburgh Penguins on January 27. The Lay's Fan Zam, however, does not clean ice (its on-board water tank, normally used to flood the rink's surface, was removed to create a seating area for up to 10 people)—instead, its sole purpose is to entertain. To this end, the pimped-up Zamboni is fitted with a 110-cubic-inch Harley Davidson engine, 24-inch chrome rims and a chrome steering wheel, plus a sound system with seven 1,200-watt amplifiers, strobes and neon lights, hydraulics, a smoke machine and three Xbox 360 systems with individual 19-inch monitors. It is also equipped with hockey-stick-shaped exhaust pipes and a front grille that features an operating 52-inch plasma television. At each home game, fans register to take a ride in the flashy vehicle, and, presumably, acquire a craving for potato chips.

Game 3

Hockey Crossword 1

Solutions are on page 558

ACROSS

1. Ranger _____ Mironov
4. Short for Daniel
6. Man-advantage or _____ play
9. Steve Yzerman's team and home ice
10. Buffalo second-string goalie Mika _____
12. Devils sniper Patrik _____
13. D-man ____ Iafrate
14. Carolina-Columbus wing Robert _____
16. Goalie makes a stop
19. Edmonton D-man Eric _____
20. Florida team
22. Toronto's 1960s Cup-winner Ron _____
23. Goalie Arturs _____
26. Montreal D-man Craig _____
27. Opposite of loss
29. Commercial
30. Threesome

31. 1994 Ranger Cup-winner Jay _____
32. He _____ the gloves

DOWN

1. Vancouver D-man from 1998–99 to 2002–03, Murray _____
2. 2003–04 rookie points leader, Michael _____
3. Thin
4. Montreal winger Pierre _____
5. Ranger centre Petr _____
6. Islander great, captain Denis _____
7. 1980s Red Wing winger Paul _____ (no relation to Tiger Woods)
8. Long-time Ranger-Bruin sniper Jean _____
11. Boston's Bobby _____
13. 2003–04 LA centre Sean _____
14. Calgary's first choice in 2001, Chuck _____

84

15. Panther Lyle _____
16. D-man sniper Mathieu _____
17. Team from Ottawa
18. Washington team
21. Capital of Canada
24. Style of _____ of hockey
25. Dallas team
28. Playing surface

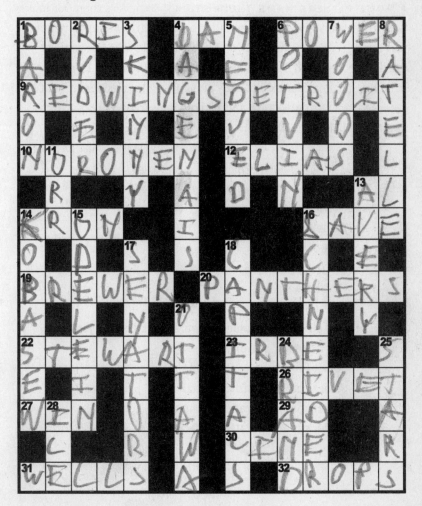

4

Men with Pucks

SOME PLAYERS NAME THEIR STICKS, some kiss them for luck and others give them pep talks, but Petr Klima's superstition was unique. The eccentric Czech forward would only use a stick until he scored with it. Then he'd deliberately break the lumber, believing that each stick had only one goal in it. Considering that he recorded 408 regular-season and playoff goals in his career, Klima must have been an equipment manager's worst nightmare.

Answers are on page 94

4.1 **What is the name of the new millenium's revolutionary skate with heated blade?**
   A. BladeRunner
   B. Ice Rockets
   C. Thermablade
   D. HotShots

4.2 **Atlanta star Ilya Kovalchuk wears No. 17 on his jersey in honour of which player?**
   A. Soviet forward Alexander Maltsev
   B. Soviet goalie Vladislav Tretiak
   C. Soviet sniper Alexander Yakushev
   D. Soviet superstar Valeri Kharlamov

4.3 In what decade did the NHL introduce the goal crease?

A. The 1920s

B. The 1930s

C. The 1940s

D. The 1950s

4.4 After winning an automobile for copping the MVP award at the 1989 NHL All-Star game, Wayne Gretzky announced he was giving his prize to someone else. Who?

A. His father, Walter

B. His wife, Janet

C. His agent, Michael Barnett

D. His former teammate, Dave Semenko

4.5 In 1999, a company unveiled a new hockey stick with what feature?

A. A crooked shaft

B. A twisted blade

C. A rubber handle

D. A pre-taped blade

4.6 Which three-time Stanley Cup-winning Montreal Canadien was the last Boston player to wear No. 4 before the number was given to Bobby Orr?

A. Al Langlois

B. Reggie Fleming

C. Andre Pronovost

D. Marcel Bonin

4.7 When did the average weight of NHL players first reach 200 pounds?

A. 1989–90

B. 1993–94

C. 1997–98

D. 2001–02

4.8 What colour were WHA pucks?

A. The WHA used only black pucks

B. Grey

C. Violet

D. Several different colours, including red and orange

4.9 What was the last unused sweater number in NHL history (a rookie took it in 2006–07)?

A. No. 64

B. No. 74

C. No. 84

D. No. 94

4.10 What incident persuaded Toronto Maple Leaf Brian Conacher to wear a helmet for the first time at the 1968 All-Star game?

A. A heartbreaking letter from a fan

B. A trial rule to test helmet use among elite NHLers

C. A player bet that Conacher lost

D. Another NHL player's on-ice death

4.11 In 2006–07, which goalie with connections to the old Winnipeg Jets wore a mask featuring players from that team?

A. Curtis Joseph, with the Phoenix Coyotes

B. Nikolai Khabibulin, with the Chicago Blackhawks

C. Robert Esche, with the Philadelphia Flyers

D. Mikael Tellqvist, with the Phoenix Coyotes

4.12 Who was the first American player to have his jersey number retired by an NHL team?

A. Pat LaFontaine, with the Buffalo Sabres

B. Neal Broten, with the Dallas Stars

C. Rod Langway, with the Washington Capitals

D. Mike Richter, with the New York Rangers

4.13 On March 3, 1968, which arena hosted the only double-header in NHL history?

A. Boston Garden

B. The Montreal Forum

C. Chicago Stadium

D. Madison Square Garden

4.14 Why does Sidney Crosby wear No. 87?

A. No. 87 represents his date of birth

B. No. 87 is the number his father wore

C. No. 87 is the only number that no other NHL player has worn

D. No. 87 matches the number of goals he scored in peewee hockey

4.15 If you spin a puck and slide it on the ice at the same time, what happens?

A. It stops spinning first

B. It stops sliding first

C. It stops spinning and sliding at exactly the same time

D. None of the above

4.16 Which Canadian arena celebrates the opening of each NHL season with the playing of bagpipes?

A. Air Canada Centre, in Toronto

B. General Motors Place, in Vancouver

C. Scotiabank Place, in Ottawa

D. Rexall Place, in Edmonton

4.17 What is the maximum allowable width of a goalie sweater?

A. 22 inches

B. 26 inches

C. 30 inches

D. 34 inches

4.18 When built, how far was the Bruins' Fleet Center from Boston Garden, the team's original home rink?

A. Nine inches

B. Nine feet

C. Nine city blocks

D. Nine miles

4.19 In what decade was the first modern-day goalie pad invented?

A. The 1910s

B. The 1920s

C. The 1930s

D. The 1940s

4.20 Which uniform number(s) has been retired by the league?

A. No. 1

B. No. 9

C. No. 99

D. All of the above

4.21 Who wore two different masks and sets of equipment in 2006–07: one to go with his team's regular uniforms and one to match his team's vintage third jerseys?

A. Ryan Miller, with the Buffalo Sabres

B. Dwayne Roloson, with the Edmonton Oilers

C. Roberto Luongo, with the Vancouver Canucks

D. Marc-Andre Fleury, with the Pittsburgh Penguins

4.22 What did the word "Moo-lay" on the shaft of Ryan Smyth's stick refer to when he played with the Edmonton Oilers?

A. The shaft of his custom stick

B. His hairstyle

C. His pre-game routine

D. His penchant for milk

4.23 In what year was the centre red line introduced?

A. 1943–44

B. 1945–46

C. 1947–48

D. 1949–50

4.24 What sports figure's image was former Ottawa goalie Ray Emery asked to remove from his mask in February 2006?

A. Tennis babe Maria Sharapova's

B. Baseball slugger Barry Bonds's

C. Basketball bad boy Dennis Rodman's

D. Boxer and ear-biter Mike Tyson's

4.25 What is the most number of NHL arenas a player has competed in during his career?

A. Less than 25 arenas

B. Between 25 and 35 arenas

C. Between 35 and 45 arenas

D. More than 45 arenas

4.26   The Buffalo Sabres put player numbers on the front of their
       uniforms in 2006–07. But which team did so before them?
       A.   The Colorado Avalanche
       B.   The Boston Bruins
       C.   The old Winnipeg Jets
       D.   The New York Rangers

4.27   Who owns the puck with which Maurice Richard scored
       his 325th NHL goal—in November 1952—to break Nels
       Stewart's all-time record?
       A.   His brother, Henri
       B.   Queen Elizabeth II
       C.   The Hockey Hall of Fame
       D.   The Canadian Museum of Civilization

4.28   Why did Mike Ricci switch to sweater No. 40 while playing
       with the San Jose Sharks in 2005–06?
       A.   To honour a deceased NFL player
       B.   It was the lowest number available on the roster
       C.   As a favour to a family member
       D.   His usual sweater numbers, 9 and 18, were taken

4.29   According to the Hockey Hall of Fame, the world's oldest
       hockey stick was carved in what year?
       A.   1752
       B.   1802
       C.   1852
       D.   1902

4.30   At a 2006 auction of Jacques Plante memorabilia, who
       made the highest bid for Plante's 1960's-era goalie mask?
       A.   Jacques Plante's family
       B.   Goalie José Théodore

C. A Canadian museum

D. The Hockey Hall of Fame

4.31 In the last 50 years of NHL hockey, two Toronto Maple Leaf players with the same sweater number have recorded the club's best finishes in individual scoring. What is that jersey number?

A. No. 10

B. No. 14

C. No. 22

D. No. 27

4.32 How did ex-NHL coach Jacques Demers come to own the last hockey stick used by Wayne Gretzky in a Stanley Cup finals game?

A. He purchased it at an auction

B. He found it in an empty locker

C. He traded it for his Stanley Cup ring

D. He asked Gretzky for it

4.33 In which decade did an NHL goaltender first wear a mask in a regular-season game?

A. The 1920s

B. The 1930s

C. The 1940s

D. The 1950s

4.34 In 2001–02, which goalie wore a mask adorned with the image of Eddie—the menacing mascot of the heavy metal band Iron Maiden?

A. Roman Turek, with the Calgary Flames

B. Martin Biron, with the Buffalo Sabres

C. Mike Dunham, with the Nashville Predators

D. Nikolai Khabibulin, with the Tampa Bay Lightning

4.35 Which Original Six arena was the first to have a four-sided clock, the first to use Herculite glass and the first to install separate penalty boxes?

A. Maple Leaf Gardens
B. The Detroit Olympia
C. The Montreal Forum
D. Madison Square Garden

4.36 In 1997–98, what word did Dallas Star defenseman Darryl Sydor stitch on his jersey?

A. Mom
B. Defense
C. Courage
D. Peace

4.37 In what year did the NHL first require all teams to dress a backup goalie during game play?

A. 1950
B. 1955
C. 1960
D. 1965

Men with Pucks

Answers

4.1   **C. Thermablade**

No less an authority than Wayne Gretzky has endorsed Thermablade technology, which he says is "an advantage that can't be ignored." It's hard to knock the Great One on anything hockey-related, and the physics of the heated skate blade do back up his claims. Because skating is made possible by a microscopic layer of water on the ice that acts as a lubricant between ice and skate blade, a heated blade creates a thicker layer of water, which then improves lubrication (only the topmost layer of ice is heated by the blade). As inventor Dr. Alain Haché states: "The heated blade system offers the double advantage of allowing the skate to glide on warmer, more slippery ice without making it softer." A battery and electronics, integrated into the heel of the blade, are connected to a resistor that heats the thermablade to 41°F, with a full charge lasting 75 minutes of ice time and recharging of the batteries taking about two hours. According to the skate's founders, the benefits include faster acceleration, tighter turns and increased control.

4.2 D. Soviet superstar Valeri Kharlamov

Even though Ilya Kovalchuk was born two years after Kharlamov's death in 1981, the Atlanta sniper wears No. 17 in memory of the late Soviet hockey star—considered among the best forwards on the Soviet team that played Team Canada in the historic Summit Series of 1972. In fact, Kharlamov was so highly regarded by the Canadian players that, in Game 6, Bobby Clarke paid him the ultimate compliment: a two-hand slash that broke the Soviet's ankle. (Kharlamov missed Game 7 and played injured in Game 8; the Soviets lost both games and the series.) Although Kharlamov never set any scoring records, his inventive play and virtuosity with the puck in bypassing defensemen were pure wizardry. Racing down the ice, his body would be a blur as he wove and deked to fake out the opposition—a style of play that would be studied and adopted by the next generation of superstars, including Wayne Gretzky and Igor Larionov. In another tribute to Kharlamov, each year the Soviet newpaper *Sovetsky Sport* awards Russia's top NHLer the Kharlamov Trophy. And, nominated by his fellow Russian

NHLers, the winner in 2003–04 was Kovalchuk, with 58 out of 63 votes. It was an honour truly befitting Atlanta's No. 17.

4.3   B. The 1930s

After decades of playing hockey without a formalized territory for goaltenders, in 1932–33 the NHL created an imaginary 10-foot no-screening zone in front of the goal. Then in 1934–35, painted right on the ice, an actual crease appeared—eight feet wide and five feet deep—to define the goalie's turf, and skaters were forbidden to interfere with netminders in this 40-square-foot area. And though throughout the years the crease has changed size, in 1998 it was altered again, to eight feet wide by four feet six (with a rounded top)—almost the same dimensions as first conceived in 1934–35.

4.4   D. His former teammate, Dave Semenko

The 1989 NHL All-Star game was held in Edmonton, where Wayne Gretzky, who had been traded to Los Angeles before the start of the season, celebrated his return to Northlands Coliseum by notching a goal and two assists and copping MVP honours. Afterwards, Gretzky surprised everyone, including the recently retired Semenko, by announcing he was giving the Dodge truck he had won as the game's MVP to his former Oiler teammate and on-ice protector.

4.5   A. A crooked shaft

In February 1999, International Marketing Management of Oak Park, Illinois, introduced the UB Offset. The stick has a "hands forward" design—a shaft that snakes back half an inch just above the heel of the blade—and supposedly improves passing, shooting and stickhandling by enabling players to hold the puck further back in their stance. Approved for use in the NHL and IHL (1945–2001), the UB Offset was first used by defenseman Steve Gosselin, with the Chicago Wolves.

4.6 A. Al Langlois

Nicknamed "Junior," Langlois won Cups with Montreal in 1958, 1959 and 1960 before being traded to New York, Detroit and Boston—where, in 1965–66, he played his last NHL season wearing the Bruins' No. 4. The following year, No. 4 was handed to Orr, who made it his own forever.

4.7 C. 1997–98

Once near extinction on NHL ice, the small-framed player has made a strong comeback in recent years. Thanks to the crackdown on obstruction and interference in 2005–06, speed is back, and so are the smurfs. Still, the league has never been bigger. In 1981–82, the average NHLer stood six feet tall and weighed 188.1 pounds. In 1997–98, the average player weight broke 200 pounds with a mean of 200.2 pounds. And by 2002–03, the average height had reached six foot one and the average weight had risen to 204.1 pounds.

4.8 D. Several different colours, including red and orange

The pucks used in the NHL are always black, but in its first year of operations, 1972–73, the WHA experimented with red-, orange-, yellow-green- and blue-coloured pucks. However, such experiments were a failure. The dyes affected the chemical nature of the pucks, making them more susceptible to cuts and chips and causing them to bounce crazily—no matter how cold officials got them before the game.

4.9   C. No. 84

Even though he ranked 11th in points among rookies, Montreal's Guillaume Latendresse still drew considerable attention in 2006–07. And when Hall of Fame goalie Patrick Roy got on Latendresse's case, saying the teenager was only playing with the Canadiens because he was French, Latendresse fired back: "I thought I was the one who was 19 years old." To prove his readiness, after replacing Chris Higgins on the Habs' top line, the rookie then scored four goals in a five-game span. But his first claim to fame came in his debut on October 6, 2006, when he wore No. 84 on the back of his Habs jersey—the first player to wear the number. Eighty-four was the last unused number in the NHL. At least one NHLer has donned every other number from one to the now-retired 99.

4.10   D. Another NHL player's on-ice death

Very few players wore helmets at All-Star games before Brian Conacher donned headgear for the first time at this annual celebration. Conacher's decision was prompted by the death of Minnesota's Bill Masterton, who had died just a day earlier, on January 15, 1968, from an on-ice injury. In a game against Oakland, Masterton lost his balance after being checked by two Seals, hit his head on the ice and was then carried off on a stretcher. He never recovered. The tragedy cast a pall over the All-Star match, which became less about showcasing hockey's finest and more about the divisive debate over mandatory helmet use. Montreal's J.C. Tremblay also wore a helmet for the 1968 All-Star game, but Tremblay had worn one all year. And though some sources suggest that Conacher was the first helmeted All-Star, Gordie Howe probably wore a helmet at the 1950 All-Star game after sustaining severe head injuries in

March 1950. In 1934, defenseman Eddie Shore also wore a helmet at a game involving All-Stars, but that was a benefit game to honour Ace Bailey.

4.11 D. Mikael Tellqvist, with the Phoenix Coyotes

Paying tribute to former players on goalie masks is a relatively new phenomenon, with Jocelyn Thibault's artful "Jacques Plante" mask from Thibeault's 1995–96 season with Montreal one of its earliest examples. Designed by artist Michel Lefebvre, the illustration depicts the "pretzel" style fibreglass model worn by the legendary Plante, hockey's first masked goalie. Similarly, Mikael Tellqvist had illustrations of past greats painted on both his Toronto and Phoenix masks. Tellqvist's Maple Leafs face protector was emblazoned with Johnny Bower and fellow Swede Borje Salming, while his Phoenix mask, in recognition of the Coyotes' roots in Winnipeg, sports Jets legends Tomas Steen on the left side and Bobby Hull on the right. Meanwhile, hockey's latest trend in mask art favours more recently retired players. In February 2007, Montreal rookie Jaroslav Halak's mask featured Patrick Roy—wearing a Canadiens jersey and raising the Stanley Cup.

4.12 C. Rod Langway, with the Washington Capitals

Among the more than 100 NHLers with retired numbers, only six Americans have been so distinguished. Rod Langway— two-time Norris Trophy winner (1983 and 1984) as the league's best defenseman—was honoured on November 26, 1997, with his No. 5 raised to the rafters by Washington during the Capitals' last game at U.S. Air Arena. (The opponent that night: the Montreal Canadiens, the only other team for which Langway played.) Despite Langway being the most unlikely player to save a franchise, his trade from Montreal to the Caps in 1983 signalled a new beginning for Washington, which had suffered eight long years as the NHL's doormat. The son of a U.S. Armed Forces father, Langway was born at an American army hospital within the Maag Compound in Taipei, Taiwan. And though the long-time captain only scored 51 goals in 994 career games, he was a fearless leader, best known for his shot-blocking skills. Other Americans with retired numbers include Neal Broten, whose No. 7 was retired a few months after Langway's by the Dallas Stars, on February 7, 1998; Mike Richter, honoured on February 4, 2004; Pat LaFontaine (March 3, 2006); Brett Hull (December 5, 2006) and Brian Leetch (January 24, 2008).

4.13   D. Madison Square Garden

After the roof of the Philadelphia Spectrum blew off in a howling snowstorm in 1968, the Flyers were forced to play several "home" games at out-of-town arenas while repairs were made to the Spectrum. The team played at the Colisée in Quebec City and at Toronto's Maple Leaf Gardens, where on March 3 it became the only NHL arena to host a double-header as Philadelphia battled the Oakland Seals to a 1–1 tie in an afternoon game. Afterwards, in the regularly scheduled nightcap, the hometown Rangers downed Chicago 4–0.

4.14   A. No. 87 represents his date of birth

Several NHL stars have selected unconventional uniform numbers. Mario Lemieux chose No. 66 because it was the reverse of Wayne Gretzky's 99. Jaromir Jagr picked No. 68 because it represented the year of the Prague Spring, 1968's short-lived surge of social reform in his home country of Czechoslovakia. In Sidney Crosby's case, the motivation is numerical symbolism. The Penguins phenom wears No. 87 because it represents the year, month and day of his birth: August 7, 1987.

4.15   C. It stops spinning and sliding at exactly the same time

This can be proven easily in a home experiment. No matter how fast a puck spins or slides, when both motions are applied the puck comes to a complete stop—with its spin and forward motion ceasing at the same time. While logic would suggest that rotation should not influence linear movement, as Dr. Alain Haché writes in *The Physics of Hockey*, the two motions do *not* act independently of each other. "The time it takes for the puck to stop spinning *and* sliding is always exactly the same," says Haché. Try it. He's right.

4.16   A. Air Canada Centre, in Toronto

The playing of bagpipes has been a Toronto tradition since the Maple Leaf Gardens' first hockey game—on November 21, 1931, when 13,542 spectators watched the 48th Highlanders march onto the ice playing "Happy Days Are Here Again" to christen the Maple Leafs' new home. The bagpipe custom continued when the club moved to its new barn in 1999, with bagpipe players leading the parade from the Gardens to the Air Canada Centre. And today, before each season's home opener, "The Maple Leaf Forever" is still played as it was for almost seven decades in the Gardens' hallowed halls—a reminder of the Leafs' rich hockey heritage and a welcome to fans.

4.17   C. 30 inches

With scoring at an all-time low and goalies using their super-sized equipment to full advantage in the 1990s, a number of new rules came into effect in 1998–99. As a result, today's netminders must not wear jerseys measuring more than 29 1/2 inches across the chest or 30 inches at the hem. (There is no limit on length measurement, but a jersey is illegal "if it covers any area between the legs.) The new rules have also done away with "tying down" of sweaters at the wrists, which creates tension, or a "webbing effect," in the armpit area.

4.18 A. Nine inches

Constructed almost wall-against-wall, the Bruins' state-of-the-art Fleet Center was built less than the length of a stick blade away from Boston Garden, the beloved facility where sports legends such as Red Auerbach, Bobby Orr and Larry Bird dazzled audiences for 67 years. The Garden was torn down in 1998, three years after the Fleet Center opened in September 1995.

4.19 B. The 1920s

Emil "Pop" Kenesky is generally credited with inventing, in 1924, the first quasi-modern goalie leg-pads. Kenesky was working as a harness-maker in Hamilton, Ontario, when Jake Forbes, an NHL goalie for the Hamilton Tigers, asked him to repair the cricket pads he had been using. The result was an unusual combination of horse hide, felt and rubberized canvas, with kapok for stuffing in the front and deer hair on the sides. Kenesky's big, thick, leather pads ended a long losing streak for Forbes, and the Hamilton craftsman became the pad-maker of choice for goaltending's elite. His handiwork (and later that of his son, Jack) protected the legs of every top netminder during the six-team era and on, including Tony Esposito's and Ken Dryden's. Remarkably, Kenesky's pad design has undergone very few changes over the years. In fact, it has stayed essentially the same for five decades—with the exception of an added scoop at the pad's base for shock absorption and padding that fits around either side of the skate. Yet during the 1990s, hockey's first family of goalie pads finally closed up shop, unable to compete as old-world tradesmen in a high-tech age of lighter and more water-resistant materials.

4.20 C. No. 99

After the Great One's retirement in 1999, the NHL announced
that no player in the league would ever again wear No. 99—
not that any player in his right mind would consider it. But the
famous double-nines didn't always command a Wayne Gretzky-
like respect. In fact, almost a half-century before Gretzky, in
1934–35, three different Montreal Canadiens donned No. 99
without any obvious impact. And in modern-day hockey, a few
more 99s sprouted up around the league, perhaps in the hope
of capturing the Gretzky—pre-retirement—magic. Toronto's
Wilf Paiement, who entered the NHL the same season as
Gretzky (1979–80), wore No. 99 for three years with the Maple
Leafs. And soon after, Winnipeg boasted Rick Dudley in a Jets
No. 99 uniform, though "I went to Edmonton for a game and
the fans gave me such a hard time," Dudley said. "So I thought,
'Maybe they are right. Maybe I should not wear this number.'
I took it off."

4.21 C. Roberto Luongo, with the Vancouver Canucks

Roberto Luongo made a major fashion statement in 2006–07
as the first NHL goalie to don two different sets of equipment,
depending on which jersey his team was wearing that game.
When the Canucks were clad in their regular killer-whale jerseys, Luongo suited up with a mask featuring the Vancouver
skyline, a bear tearing through a goalie mask and the Lions
Gate Bridge. And on those nights when the club donned its
throwback blue-green-and-white jerseys, Luongo wore colour-
coordinated pads and a cream-coloured vintage mask designed
to resemble the face protectors of the early 1970s, when the
Canucks entered the league. The otherwise unadorned mask
sported a graphic of that bearded lumberjack-on-skates Johnny
Canuck, the cartoon character the team was named after, on
its side.

4.22   B. His hairstyle

Smyth is the only player in NHL history to score all the goals in one game on two occasions, scoring hat tricks in 3–0 wins on March 13, 2000, and November 14, 2000. Smyth's custom-made shafts from Hespeler feature a maple leaf, his late grandmother's initials and the word "Moo-lay," which his teammates jokingly used to pronounce "mullet"—after his coif of choice.

4.23   A. 1943–44

The Rangers' Frank Boucher and men such as Art Ross of Boston and Hap Day of Toronto revolutionized the game when they introduced the centre red line to hockey in 1943–44. The line sped up the action, enabling players to pass the puck from their own zone to centre ice. It also reduced offside infractions and the grinding style of play that were so common under the old rules and instead prompted players to carry the puck over the blue line. While at one time strong forechecking teams could trap opponents in their zone for long periods, the new rules also gave defenders greater mobility to counterattack through speed and passing. The offensive potential proved potent in 1943–44, when four teams surpassed the 200-goal mark, an NHL first.

4.24   D. Boxer and ear-biter Mike Tyson's

Ray Emery's mask of Mike Tyson lasted all of one game, a 5–0 loss to Boston on January 30, 2006. And if the Bruins' pounding wasn't enough to prompt Emery to reconsider his design choice, Senators GM John Muckler provided the knock-out blow when he reminded Emery, an avid boxing fan, that Tyson was a convicted rapist and abuser of women. "Growing up, he [Emery] always had boxers on his helmet, and I appreciate that Tyson was an idol to him as a boxer," said Muckler.

"But after discussions about Tyson's past… [Emery] said he'll no longer wear it [the boxer] on his face mask." The Tyson illustration was quickly painted over with a safer pick: an image of Canadian boxing legend George Chuvalo.

4.25 **D. More than 45 arenas**
There are no official league records of such trivia, but in this age of new franchises and buildings, a few veterans have broken the plus-50 mark in rinks played in. In 1999–2000 at least four players, three of them Sharks, hit the 50-rink milestone. San Jose's Gary Suter and Ron Sutter bagged number 50 at Phillips Arena in Atlanta on February 11, 2000; Vincent Damphousse followed with his 50th NHL arena shortly after. On February 13, 2000, Larry Murphy then stepped onto the ice at Denver's Pepsi Center to play hockey on his 50th NHL rink. Murphy has also skated in a few neutral-site games in extinct venues in Atlanta and Cleveland. But what are the 20-year veteran's favourite and least-favourite haunts? Old Maple Leaf Gardens in Toronto is a fond memory, and not because of the booing he received as a Maple Leaf but because it was where he saw his first game as a child. Calgary's Stampede Corral, however, was a bust. The rink was small, the boards a foot higher than normal and the player benches were two parallel rows—forcing players in the back row to climb by players in the front to get to the ice.

4.26 **B. The Boston Bruins**
The Buffalo Sabres introduced a new jersey logo (dubbed the "Buffaslug") in 2006–07, then added player numbers to the front of their uniforms—a wrinkle copied later in the season by the Dallas Stars. But the Sabres are not the first NHL team to do this. In 1936–37, the Boston Bruins put uniform numbers on both the backs and fronts of their jerseys, an

uninspiring concept that the club stuck with for 12 years before introducing its familiar spoked-B crest.

4.27   **B. Queen Elizabeth II**
Who would have guessed? The puck that Maurice Richard scored his 325th goal with to break Nels Stewart's all-time NHL record on November 8, 1952, is owned by Queen Elizabeth II. The inscribed, gold-plated puck was presented to the Queen in 1955 by the Montreal Canadiens, evidently because she had expressed an interest in Richard's career after watching him play—in person—at the Montreal Forum during the 1951–52 season.

4.28   **A. To honour a deceased NFL player**
During his 15-year NHL career, Mike Ricci wore only No. 9 or 18, but after hearing about Pat Tillman, he switched to No. 40. Tillman, a four-year defensive safety with the NFL Arizona Cardinals, turned down a lucrative US$3.6-million contract in 2002 to enlist with the U.S. Army Rangers in the wake of the terrorist attacks in New York on September 11, 2001. "My great grandfather was at Pearl Harbour and a lot of my family has gone and fought in wars, and I really haven't done a damn thing as far as laying myself on the line like that," Tillman told NBC News after 9/11. But after joining Operation Mountain Storm to fight Al-Queda in Afghanistan in April 2004, Tillman's battalion came under enemy fire in a roadside ambush. Tillman was killed in action, and his heroic sacrifice to save his unit from Afghan insurgents quickly became the stuff of media legend. Then Tillman's family found out the true horror of his death. Contrary to official army accounts, he was shot in the head by a U.S. soldier from just 35 metres away, just moments after signalling he was a "friendly."

Before a U.S. congressional panel three years later, his brother accused the Pentagon of fabricating "deliberate and calculated lies" to boost American morale during wartime. Tillman was the first NFLer killed in combat since Buffalo tackle Bob Kalsu died in the Vietnam War in July 1970. "When I heard the [original] story, it really touched me," said Ricci. "This is a way to pay tribute to what's he's done." Tillman wore No. 40 with the Cardinals.

4.29 C. 1852

After the Hockey Hall of Fame verified in 2002 that Gord Sharpe—of Peterborough, Ontario—owned the world's oldest existing hockey stick, Mark O'Connell—of Beaverton, Ontario—decided to have his attic treasure evaluated, too. And though there is no firm date on the exact age of the O'Connell relic, it has been dated to 1871, likely making it the oldest manufactured stick in the world. As well, compared to Sharpe's handcrafted piece of hickory, O'Connell's is a one-piece stick, 42 inches in length, with a steam-bent blade. And in faded black script on the side of the blade: the maker's name, Ditson, which means it was likely made before 1871, the year American sporting goods owner Henry A. Ditson linked up with baseball star George Wright. Interestingly, the earliest stick-producers stamped their company name on the blade—rather than the shaft, as is the practice with current manufacturers. As for Sharpe's stick, it was carved in the early 1850s by a distant relative, Alexander Rutherford Sr., at his farm outside Lindsay, Ontario. Sharpe auctioned it on eBay for approximately CDN$2 million in 2007. O'Connell, who found his stick in the attic of his cottage in Orillia, Ontario, plans to sell his, too.

4.30   **C. A Canadian museum**

One of the crown jewels in the 2006 auction of more than 50 Jacques Plante hockey items, including trophies and Stanley Cup rings, was Plante's 1960s pretzel-style mask, the third one used by Plante in NHL play. The fibreglass, caramel-coloured face protector, first worn in 1963 after the netminder was traded to the New York Rangers, was purchased by the Canadian Museum of Civilization in Ottawa for almost US$19,000. The Montreal auction house Classic Collectables conducted the auction on behalf of Plante's Swiss widow, Caroline Raymonde Plante. The money raised went to a foundation to train Swiss goalies.

4.31   **D. No. 27**

As of 2008–09, no Toronto player has won the Art Ross Trophy as regular-season scoring leader since Gord Drillon captured the award in 1938. The best any Leaf has done in scoring in the last half-century (since Max Bentley's third place in 1950–51) is two third-place finishes, both by No. 27s: Frank Mahovlich, with 84 points in 1960–61, and Darryl Sittler, with 117 points in 1977–78.

4.32   **D. He asked Gretzky for it**

It was a gutsy move by anyone's standards, but the request for Gretzky's silver Easton hockey stick also came from an opponent who only moments before had snatched victory away from the L.A. Kings at the 1993 Stanley Cup finals. And, the appeal came from the same man who had outed Marty McSorley in Game 2 for using an illegal stick, a penalty that turned the series in Montreal's favour. But Jacques Demers, who had known Gretzky since their WHA days, asked anyway. Montreal was jubilantly celebrating its 24th Stanley Cup and the two men were shaking hands in the customary lineup after the game, when the Great One graciously obliged. It turned out to be Gretzky's last stick from a Stanley Cup finals match.

4.33   **B. The 1930s**

Today it is considered a netminder's single most important piece of equipment, but the goalie mask was once regarded as a symbol of cowardice—an impractical device that restricted vision. Then in 1959, Montreal's Jacques Plante slipped on a homemade fibreglass mask in a game against New York and changed the face of goaltending forever. Still, the distinction of being the first goalie to wear a mask belongs to the Montreal Maroons' Clint Benedict, who first wore a face protector in 1930 after a rising 25-foot blast from Howie Morenz smashed Bendict's nose and cheekbone. "I saw it at the last split second and lunged," Benedict said. "Wham, I was out like a light and woke up in the hospital." A reporter recalled that the puck had "crushed in the side of Benny's face like an eggshell," an injury that forced Benedict to use a crude leather mask—modified either from a football face mask (in use at the time) or a boxer's sparring mask. But the contraption didn't work. "The nosepiece protruded too far and obscured my vision on low shots," said Benedict. So after a 2–1 loss to Chicago, he threw out the mask and tried a wire-cage-type protector, "but the wires distracted me. That's when I gave up." Benedict continued to play, maskless, but later that season another Morenz shot struck him in the throat, ending his career. "You know, if we had been able to perfect the mask I could have been a 20-year man," he concluded, though he held no grudges against Morenz. Benedict played 17 seasons and was inducted into the Hockey Hall of Fame in 1965.

4.34 **A. Roman Turek, with the Calgary Flames**

The Czech goalie has been a serious fan of Iron Maiden since he was a teenager, and considers his backstage meeting with the heavy metal band at a concert in Germany the thrill of a lifetime. At the time, Turek was playing with Nurenberg of the German Elite League, when, as he admitted in an interview with the *Calgary Sun*: "After the concert, one guy took me to their locker room and they gave me CDs, a T-shirt and a hat. I already played with the group's mascot, Eddie, painted on my mask, but they signed it and I just said, 'Oh, my God! That's my dream come true.' " "Eddie" is also Turek's nickname and the name of his son.

4.35 **A. Maple Leaf Gardens**

When the Gardens closed its doors to NHL hockey on February 13, 1999, it signalled the end of an era: the last of the Original Six buildings. Each of the six rinks—Madison Square Garden, Detroit Olympia, Montreal Forum, Boston Garden, Chicago Stadium and the Gardens—were as unique in character and history as the teams that called them home. But MLG might be a little more special: it was the first hockey building with a four-sided clock (1932), Herculite glass (1947), escalators (1955) and separate penalty boxes (1963). Separating penalized players began after an on-ice fight between the Leafs' Bob Pulford and the Canadiens' Terry Harper carried over into the Gardens' "shared" box. And while this was neither the first nor the last sin-bin fight, it did deliver an early knockout punch to end the problem.

4.36   A. Mom

Since NHL rules don't permit personal patches on the outside of jerseys, Sydor stitched one word—Mom—on the *inside* of his sweater, a tribute to his mother, Anne Sydor, who died on October 19, 1997. Before Anne, 55, suffered a heart attack in Edmonton, the last night of her life was spent watching her son on CBC's *Hockey Night in Canada*, as Dallas defeated Toronto 5–4.

4.37   D. 1965

Although many teams already had two goalies—a regular starter and a spare for practice—it was not until the 1965 play-offs that the NHL ruled that all clubs must have a netminder on the bench, dressed to play. Before the rule change, home teams would provide a spare if either club sustained an injury to their starter. The spares, usually amateur and practice goalies or club trainers, sat in the stands and only dressed when needed, delaying games for long stretches. That tradition, and the split-second careers of transient replacements such as Detroit trainer Lefty Wilson, ended with the two-goalie system.

Game 4

The Best Rookie Class Ever?

FOR THE FIRST TIME in league history, rookies from two NHL Entry Drafts became available at the same time in one regular season. Blame the 2004–05 lockout for the embarrassment of riches in freshman talent and the plethora of records and firsts these newbies established in 2005-06. With such depth, it may be the best rookie class ever. But it comes with an asterisk, considering that the lockout doubled the influx of first-year players. Match the 11 rookies with their records below. Pay attention, some set more than one mark.

Solutions are on page 558

Sidney Crosby	Dion Phaneuf	Henrik Lundqvist
Ryan Miller	Marek Svatos	Jussi Jokinen
Ray Emery	Alexander Ovechkin	Josh Harding
Kari Lehtonen	Antero Niittymaki	

1. He set an NHL rookie record for most shots on goal in one season.

2. He is the first goalie to play his first NHL game and record his first win in a shootout.

3. **SC** He is the youngest player in NHL history to score 90 and 100 points.

4. **DP** He is only the third rookie defenseman to reach the 20-goal plateau in one season.

5. **AO** He is the second rookie in NHL history to record 50 goals and 100 points in one season.

6. **HL** He set the New York Rangers record for most wins by a rookie goalie.

7. **AO** He is the first rookie to lead an NHL regular season in shots on goal.

8. **MS** He tied the NHL rookie record with nine game-winning goals in one season.

9. **SC** He is second in most points by a rookie who entered the league in the same year he was drafted.

10. **JJ** He led all players in shootout goals during 2005–06.

11. **KL** He recorded the best save percentage in shootouts during 2005–06.

12. **AO** He is only the fourth rookie in NHL history to reach the 50-goal mark in one season.

13. **AE** He tied the league record for most goaltending victories in a calendar month.

14. **SC,AO** They are the first two rookies in NHL history to score 100 points in a single season.

15. RM, RE, KL, HL, AM These five rookie goalies equalled the league record for most freshmen, with 20 wins in one season.

5

The Rookies

MARIO LEMIEUX MAY BE FAMOUS for his 1984 debut, with its first-game, first-shift, first-shot goal, but Washington's Alexander Ovechkin is the only number one draft pick in league history to score a *pair* of goals in his NHL debut. Ovechkin refused to let his team lose—twice answering with goals, first on a slap shot, then on a wrist shot, and each time bulging the twine less than 90 seconds after his opponents took the lead. "I feel my dreams come true," Ovechkin said at the time. "I play in the NHL. First game. First win." The 20-year-old Russian's dominance in Washington's 3–2 win against Columbus was a big sign of things to come.

Answers are on page 121

5.1 **Who scored a goal against the most teams in his rookie season?**
  A. Alexei Yashin, in 1993–94
  B. Alexei Kovalev, in 1992–93
  C. Alexandre Daigle, in 1993–94
  D. Alexander Ovechkin, in 2005–06

5.2 **Who is the first rookie defenseman to score at least 75 points in one season?**
  A. Ray Bourque, in 1979–80
  B. Larry Murphy, in 1980–81
  C. Gary Suter, in 1985–86
  D. Brian Leetch, in 1988–89

5.3 Which goalie had the most shutouts in his rookie season?

A. Martin Brodeur

B. Tony Esposito

C. Mike Richter

D. Terry Sawchuk

5.4 A select few rookies have scored a point their first NHL shift. But who did it in the fastest time from the start of a game?

A. Dave Christian, with the Winnipeg Jets

B. Mario Lemieux, with the Pittsburgh Penguins

C. Bobby Carpenter, with the Washington Capitals

D. Evgeni Malkin, with the Pittsburgh Penguins

5.5 Since the 1967–68 expansion, what is the fastest time a rookie has scored his first NHL goal in his first game (from the opening faceoff)?

A. Before the 10-second mark

B. Between the 10- and 20-second marks

C. Between the 30-second and one-minute marks

D. After the one-minute mark

5.6 Who set a rookie point-scoring streak in 2006–07?

A. Paul Stastny, with the Colorado Avalanche

B. Anze Kopitar, with the Los Angeles Kings

C. Jordan Staal, with the Pittsburgh Penguins

D. Evgeni Malkin, with the Pittsburgh Penguins

5.7 In 2006–07, after breaking Teemu Selanne's rookie record by scoring a point in each of 18 straight games, Paul Stastny set a new rookie scoring streak of how long?

A. An 18-game stretch

B. A 20-game stretch

C. A 22-game stretch

D. A 24-game stretch

5.8 What is the NHL record for the longest point-scoring streak to start an NHL career?

A. Eight straight games

B. 10 straight games

C. 12 straight games

D. 14 straight games

5.9 Which NHL rookie recorded the most penalty minutes in his 1990s debut?

A. Gino Odjick, with the Vancouver Canucks, in 1990–91

B. Mike Peluso, with the Chicago Blackhawks, in 1990–91

C. Brad May, with the Buffalo Sabres, in 1991–92

D. Link Gaetz, with the San Jose Sharks, in 1991–92

5.10 The NHL All-Rookie Team has been selected since 1982–83. Who is the only player to be voted NHL rookie of the year and not be elected to the team?

A. Tom Barrasso, with the Buffalo Sabres, in 1983–84

B. Pavel Bure, with the Vancouver Canucks, in 1991–92

C. Chris Drury, with the Colorado Avalanche, in 1998–99

D. Andrew Raycroft, with the Boston Bruins, in 2003–04

5.11 Who was the first NHL rookie to lead the league in plus-minus?

A. Bill Hajt, with the Buffalo Sabres, in 1974–75

B. Ray Bourque, with the Boston Bruins, in 1979–80

C. Andrej Meszaros, with the Ottawa Senators, in 2005–06

D. No rookie has ever led in plus-minus

5.12 Wayne Gretzky scored his 500th career goal into an empty Vancouver net. Which rookie netminder was pulled for the extra attacker, resulting in that famous goal?

A. Richard Brodeur

B. John Garrett

C. Troy Gamble

D. Kirk McLean

5.13 What was so special about rookie rearguard Brent Seabrook's first NHL goal—scored in 2005-06?

A. He was celebrating his birthday

B. He scored in overtime

C. He was moved up to play forward

D. He scored on the shootout

5.14 Who holds the all-time record in Canada's three junior leagues for most goals scored in one season by a rookie?

A. Pat LaFontaine, with the QMJHL, in 1982-83

B. Tony Tanti, with the OHL, in 1980-81

C. Don Murdoch, with the WHL, in 1974-75

D. Wayne Gretzky, with the OHL, in 1977-78

5.15 Before Sidney Crosby and Evgeni Malkin did it with Pittsburgh in 2006-07, which NHL team tandem last won both the league and rookie scoring races in the same season?

A. It had never happened before

B. Bryan Trottier and Mike Bossy, with the New York Islanders

C. Bernie Geoffrion and Bobby Rousseau, with Montreal

D. Bobby Hull and Billy Hay, with Chicago

5.16 **How many goals did Steve Yzerman score as a rookie?**

A. More than Guy Lafleur in his rookie season

B. More than Steve Larmer in his rookie season

C. More than Luc Robitaille in his rookie season

D. More than Dale Hawerchuk in his rookie season

5.17 **As of 2008–09, how many rookies have scored 100-or-more-point seasons in their NHL debut? Name them, too.**

A. Five rookies

B. Seven rookies

C. Nine rookies

D. 11 rookies

5.18 **Which rookie led his team in scoring during 1994–95's 48-game season?**

A. Paul Kariya, with the Anaheim Mighty Ducks

B. David Oliver, with the Edmonton Oilers

C. Peter Forsberg, with the Quebec Nordiques

D. Radek Bonk, with the Ottawa Senators

5.19 **Even though hockey greats Guy Lafleur and Marcel Dionne were selected ahead of this pick in his draft year, he was still the first NHL rookie to break the 40-goal barrier. Who was he?**

A. Bob Nystrom

B. Bill Barber

C. Rick Martin

D. Steve Shutt

5.20 **Which tough guy owns the NHL record for most fighting majors by a rookie?**

A. Paul Laus, in 1996–97

B. Joe Kocur, in 1985–86

C. Reed Low, in 2000–01

D. Stu Grimson, in 1990–91

5.21 **Prior to Alexander Ovechkin, how many players have been named NHL player of the month and rookie of the month in the same month?**

A. None

B. Only one player

C. Two players

D. Four players

5.22 **In 1947, who beat Gordie Howe to win the Calder Trophy as the NHL's top rookie?**

A. Howie Meeker, with the Toronto Maple Leafs

B. Jim Conacher, with the Detroit Red Wings

C. Fern Flaman, with the Boston Bruins

D. Leo Gravelle, with the Montreal Canadiens

5.23 **In 2006–07, which rookie broke Jack Hamilton's 64-year record as the youngest player to score a hat trick?**

A. Jordan Staal, with the Pittsburgh Penguins

B. Jiri Hudler, with the Detroit Red Wings

C. Evgeni Malkin, with the Pittsburgh Penguins

D. Dustin Penner, with the Anaheim Mighty Ducks

5.24 **Amongst rookies with 45 goals in their first season, who owns the highest proportion of his team's goals?**

A. Mike Bossy, with the New York Islanders, in 1977–78

B. Joe Nieuwendyk, with the Calgary Flames, in 1987–88

C. Teemu Selanne, with the Winnipeg Jets, in 1992–93

D. Alexander Ovechkin, with the Washington Capitals, in 2005–06

5.25 In 2000–01, which rookie goalie led the NHL in both goals-against average and save percentage?

A. Marty Turco, with Dallas

B. Evgeni Nabokov, with San Jose

C. David Aebischer, with Colorado

D. Roman Cechmanek, with Philadelphia

5.26 In 2006–07, which rookie record(s) did Jordan Staal smash with Pittsburgh?

A. The youngest player to score on a penalty shot

B. The youngest player with two shorthanded goals in a game

C. Most shorthanded goals by a rookie

D. All of the above

5.27 How many rookies have recorded a hat trick in their first NHL game?

A. It has never happened

B. Only once: Alex Smart did it in 1942–43

C. Two times

D. Three times

5.28 Which rookie owns the NHL record for most goals in one Stanley Cup finals series?

A. Howie Morenz, with the 1924 Montreal Canadiens

B. Johnny Gagnon, with the 1931 Montreal Canadiens

C. Roy Conacher, with the 1939 Boston Bruins

D. Mike Rupp, with the 2003 New Jersey Devils

5.29 As of 2008, who is the most recent rookie to score a Stanley Cup-winning goal?

A. Travis Moen, with 2007's Anaheim Mighty Ducks

B. Mike Rupp, with 2003's New Jersey Devils

C. Dick Duff, with 1962's Toronto Maple Leafs

D. There hasn't been one since Roy Conacher in 1939

Answers

5.1   **D. Alexander Ovechkin, in 2005–06**
Playing in a 30-team NHL might be an unfair advantage for any
rookie trying to top Teemu Selanne's record of goal scoring
against 21 teams in a season. But with the league's unbalanced
schedule in 2005–06, teams played against 24 clubs—only one
more than the number Selanne faced as a freshman in 1992–
93's 24-team league. And that one extra opponent could make
all the difference. Alexander Ovechkin beat Selanne's 21 count
and recorded goals against 22 of Washington's 24 opponents in
2005–06—the most teams any rookie has ever scored upon. In
fact, Ovechkin totalled 52 of the Capitals' 230 goals for an NHL-
best 22.6 per cent—scoring against every team the Capitals
challenged (except San Jose and Los Angeles).

5.2   **B. Larry Murphy, in 1980–81**
Few first-year defensemen have been afforded the ice time
Murphy received in his rookie start, with coach Bob Berry
believing Murphy could easily make the transition from
junior hockey to the NHL. In fact, Murphy's rookie-record
76 points was fourth in team scoring, behind only the Triple
Crown Line of Marcel Dionne, Dave Taylor and Charlie
Simmer, each of whom finished in the NHL's top 10.

5.3   **B. Tony Esposito**
Esposito earned the moniker "Tony O" in his first full NHL
season, 1969–70, by zeroing Chicago's opponents a record
15 times in 63 games for a sizzling 2.17 GAA. That's a shutout
almost every fourth start during his rookie year. Along with

his new alias, Esposito also won the Calder and Vezina trophies and was named to the First All-Star Team. Other rookies with double-digit shutout records: Hainsworth (14) in 1926–27, Tiny Thompson (12) in 1928–29 and Sawchuk (11) in 1950–51. Martin Brodeur, the next career shutout king, notched just three zeroes in his rookie campaign. Surprisingly, the Rangers' Mike Richter went without a shutout until his third NHL season.

5.4   C. Bobby Carpenter, with the Washington Capitals

Few NHL prospects experience an NHL start faster than Bobby Carpenter's. Still in high school, he was labelled the Can't-Miss Kid in a *Sports Illustrated* cover story in February 1981. Four months later, the 17-year-old from St. John's Preparatory School in Danvers, Massachusetts, became Washington's first pick (third overall in 1981) and the first player to go straight from a U.S. high school into the NHL. Four months later, he was on league scoresheets in his first NHL match, with a goal and an assist against Buffalo's Don Edwards for a 5–3 Capitals loss on October 7, 1981. As quickly as he made it into the world's best league, he was in the record books, too, setting up Ryan Walter on a breakaway against Edwards that netted the Capitals' first goal of 1981–82, only 12 seconds after the opening faceoff. Rookie Dave Christian of the Winnipeg Jets bested Carpenter with his first point (a goal) just seven seconds after he stepped on the ice for the first time. But Christian's goal came at 1:07 of the first period, well after the 12-second mark (from an opening faceoff) of Carpenter's point.

5.5   B. Between the 10- and 20-second marks

It was a great start for a rookie in his season home opener. Just 18 seconds after the puck was dropped on October 10, 1974, Danny Gare, a 20-year-old winger up from the Calgary Centennials, scored his first NHL goal on his first shift against the NHL's top scoring line: the Bruins' Phil Esposito, Wayne Cashman and Ken Hodge. What a night! Gare and the Sabres pounded the Bruins 9–5. Prior to expansion, the fastest time is 15 seconds—by Gus Bodnar (1943–44). More recently, Alexander Mogilny did it in 20 seconds (1989–90).

5.6 A. Paul Stastny, with the Colorado Avalanche

Anyone watching Paul Stastny in 2006–07 could see why the strapping 21-year-old centre was making the rookie-of-the-year race tight for rivals Evgeni Malkin and Jordan Stall. Stastny "plays well beyond his years," Colorado captain Joe Sakic remarked during the freshman's 18-game point-scoring streak, the longest on NHL record by a rookie. But Stastny's natural feel for the action may have something to do with his gene pool—after all, he is the son of superstar Peter Stastny, the league's most prolific scorer after Wayne Gretzky in the 1980s. "He's got a hockey sense that you can't teach," Avalanche coach Joel Quenneville commented during Stastny's stellar year. Stastny, who wears his father's No. 26, earned the rookie record after assisting on a Milan Hejduk goal on March 11. (The previous mark of 17 games was set by Teemu Selanne in 1992–93.) As well, during his record stretch (which began February 3), Stastny scored eight goals and 18 assists with a plus-10—beating his father's franchise record of one point or more in 16 straight games. The streak also included 15 consecutive road games with a point, January 13 to March 17—a rookie record that busted the league's 13-game mark posted by his uncle, Marion Stastny, in 1981–82. Oh yeah, the bloodlines are there.

5.7 B. A 20-game stretch

After smashing Teemu Selanne's NHL mark of 17 to set the new rookie run at 18 games of one point or more, Paul Stastny bumped the count to 20 matches—giving pause to any future freshman with plans of erasing the Stastny name from the NHL record book. During his February 3 to March 17 streak, the red-hot Stastny—with 11 goals, 18 assists and a plus-12 rating—shot into contention for the coveted Calder Trophy and led Colorado in its playoff bid to within one point of contention. The scoring drive made the 21-year-old the third-youngest player in league annals to notch a 20-game point streak (at 21 years and 80 days old), compared to league leaders Mario Lemieux (20 years and 161 days old on the last day of his 28-game streak in 1985–86) and Wayne Gretzky (21 years and 36 days old on the last day of his 24-game streak in 1981–82).

5.8   **D. 14 straight games**
There's no official NHL record for point-scoring streaks by rookies—and that's unfortunate, because more fans should know of Dmitri Kvartalnov, or, more specifically, of what he pulled off as a freshman with Boston in 1992–93. Kvartalnov enjoyed a long career in Europe, including appearances with the Soviet national team at the 1989 and 1991 World Championships. Yet, by NHL standards, he was a flash-in-the-pan, his rise to prominence as swift as his sudden departure as a 112-game player who scored 42 goals and 91 points in just two seasons with the Bruins. Still, Kvartalnov's stellar start included a remarkable 14-game point-scoring streak that jump-started his NHL career and earned the 26-year-old rookie 12 goals and 22 points between October 8 and November 12, 1992. As well, he scored an unprecedented five of those goals in his first five games, a feat topped only by Evgeni Malkin's six in 2006–07.

5.9   **D. Link Gaetz, with the San Jose Sharks, in 1991–92**
No rookie in the 1990s accumulated more box time than San Jose's Link Gaetz in 1991–92. In just 48 games with the Sharks,

Gaetz amassed 326 penalty minutes—just six minutes more than rookie Mike Peluso's 320 in 1990–91. But unlike the one-dimensional Peluso, who carved out an NHL career as a full-time enforcer, Gaetz didn't—despite his superior hockey skills. Nicknamed "Missing Link," Gaetz was a devastating blend of size, skill and meanness, though off-ice troubles with alcohol affected his availability and play. Still, Gaetz became a legitimate heavyweight who would hit anyone—anywhere, anytime. In a widely publicized quote by Sharks scout Chuck Grillo, he was affectionately called "one of the meanest kids living." Unfortunately Gaetz never developed the proper mental approach. After his rookie year, 1991–92, he never played in the NHL again.

NHL Rookies with Most Penalty Minutes in the 1990s

PLAYER	TEAM	SEASON	GP	PIM
Link Gaetz	San Jose	1991–92	48	326
Mike Peluso	Chicago	1990–91	53	320
Brad May	Buffalo	1991–92	69	309
Gino Odjick	Vancouver	1990–91	45	296
Krzysztof Oliwa	New Jersey	1997–98	73	295

5.10 **B. Pavel Bure, with the Vancouver Canucks, in 1991–92**

This is a weird one. How does a Calder Trophy winner not make the NHL All-Rookie Team? Apparently, only if his name is Pavel Bure. Since both the rookie of the year and players of the All-Rookie Team are chosen by members of the Professional Hockey Writers Association, you would expect some consistency in the balloting. But in 1992, the media reps were having trouble deciding between Bure's record of 34–26–60 in 65 games or Tony Amonte's 35–34–60 in 79 games. So, in schizophrenic fashion, they picked Bure as the NHL's top rookie but selected Amonte, and not the Russian Rocket, as the All-Rookie Team's right-winger. To top off the snub with a little humiliation, Bure then watched his Calder runner-up, Nicklas Lidstrom, make the cut as a member of the All-Rookie Team that same year.

5.11   **D. No rookie has ever led in plus-minus**
Since 1968, when plus-minus was first tabulated by the NHL, no freshman has won the statistic that measures a player's performance based on goals scored versus goals-against while he is on the ice. But a few players have come very close, including Andrej Meszaros in 2005–06 and Blake Wheeler in 2008–09. Meszaros benefited greatly from playing on first-place Ottawa, but it was his heavy shot and positional play that earned the rookie defenseman from Slovakia an impressive plus-34, just one back of league leaders Wade Redden and Michal Rozsival, each with plus-35. And in Wheeler's case, the Boston rookie used his size, speed and puck control to garner a robust plus-36, just one point behind teammate and league leader David Krejci's plus-37. In the process, Wheeler played 81 games and scored 21 goals on the Bruins' third line and penalty kill in 2008–09. "I've never seen a guy that big move that fast," veteran defenseman Aaron Ward observed in the *Boston Herald.*

5.12   **C. Troy Gamble**
The Great One scored number 500 into an empty net on November 22, 1986. Looking on helplessly from the bench was Troy Gamble, who, after allowing four goals (two by Gretzky himself), was pulled for the extra attacker. In the final minute, Gretzky squeezed the shot home, bulging the net for the 500th time. Edmonton beat the Canucks 5–2. It was Gamble's first NHL game.

5.13 **B. He scored in overtime**

It may not be a league first, but Brent Seabrook still made quite an impression with his first NHL goal. The rookie defenseman earned a 6–5 win for Chicago after the Blackhawks had blown a three-goal lead in the third period on November 2, 2005. Seabrook fired a wrist shot past the Blues' Patrick Lalime just 35 seconds into overtime. "It's awesome," Seabrook said. "I'm thrilled right now. I'm going to keep that puck."

5.14 **A. Pat LaFontaine, with the QMJHL, in 1982–83**

American-born Pat LaFontaine cut a wide swath through the porous ranks of the Quebec Major Junior Hockey League in 1982–83, his rookie year. A native of St. Louis, Missouri, who learned hockey in Detroit before playing junior in Montreal, LaFontaine scored 104 goals in 70 games with the Verdun Junior Canadiens and amassed more goals than any other freshman in Canadian junior hockey history. Next best: Don Murdoch, with 82 goals for Medicine Hat in 1974–75; Tony Tanti, with 81 goals for Oshawa in 1980–81; and Ladislav Nagy, with 71 goals for Halifax of the QMJHL in 1998–99. Wayne Gretzky and Mike Bossy each potted 70 goals in their respective rookie seasons.

5.15 **D. Bobby Hull and Billy Hay, with Chicago**

With top-five picks in five successive drafts between 2002 and 2006, Pittsburgh finally had its breakout year in 2006–07. The Penguins' kiddie corps rocked the league with a slew of firsts, mosts and youngest records, including scoring titles by Sidney Crosby and rookie Evgeni Malkin. Crosby, the youngest scoring champion in NHL history, led all scorers with 120 points; Malkin topped all freshman, compiling 85 points. The last team to capture both scoring titles: the Chicago Blackhawks in 1959–60, when Bobby Hull won the Art Ross Trophy with 81 points and Billy Hay was best among first-year players with 55 points. Only seven other teams in league history have boasted rosters with duo scoring champs in one year. The Montreal Maroons remain the lone team to sport a rookie who led all players in scoring. Nels Stewart, who joined the NHL at age 22, won the scoring title with 42 points in 36 games during 1925–26.

5.16 **A. More than Guy Lafleur in his rookie season**
Yzerman made a big impression in his rookie season, scoring 39 goals for Detroit in 1983–84. The only rookie from our all-star group of Lafleur, Hawerchuk and Robitaille to score fewer goals in his first season is Lafleur, who counted a respectable 29 goals in 1971–72. Robitaille (45), Hawerchuk (45) and Larmer (43) all outscored Yzerman in their inaugural NHL campaigns.

5.17 **B. Seven rookies**
Considering the magnitude of the achievement, 100-or-more rookie points, it's remarkable that even seven players reached such scoring heights as freshmen, though the list could be one name longer with a new leader at the top: Wayne Gretzky. But the Great One's WHA year prior to joining the NHL disqualified him from any rookie statistics, or at least that's the NHL's verdict (despite insisting that Gretzky's WHA records don't officially count towards his pro point totals). Still, Gretzky amassed a 51–86–137 record in his first NHL season, 1979–80, enough to potentially hand the Great One several rookie marks—including most points by a freshman.

The NHL's All-Time Top Point-Scoring Rookies*

PLAYER	TEAM	SEASON	GP	G	A	POINTS
Teemu Selanne	Winnipeg	1992–93	84	76	56	132
Peter Stastny	Quebec	1980–81	77	39	70	109
Alex Ovechkin	Washington	2005–06	81	52	54	106
Dale Hawerchuk	Winnipeg	1981–82	80	45	58	103
Joe Juneau	Boston	1992–93	84	32	70	102
Sidney Crosby	Pittsburgh	2005–06	81	39	63	102
Mario Lemieux	Pittsburgh	1984–85	73	43	57	100

*Current to 2008–09

5.18 A. Paul Kariya, with the Anaheim Mighty Ducks

During 1994–95's abbreviated season, Kariya was the only
rookie to lead his team in scoring, with a 18–21–39 record—
10 points more than the tally of teammate Shaun Van Allen.
Kariya was selected fourth overall in the 1993 NHL Entry
Draft, following two seasons split between Canada's national
Junior and Olympic teams and the University of Maine Black
Bears, where he became the first freshman to win the Hobey
Baker Award as top U.S. college player (1992–93). That year,
Kariya helped the Black Bears win the NCAA national cham-
pionship, scoring three assists in the third period of the final
game to lead Maine from a 4–2 deficit to a 5–4 victory over
Lake Superior State. Kariya was also a member of Canada's
gold-medal-winning team at the 1992–93 World Junior
Championships.

5.19 C. Rick Martin

The left-winger on the Buffalo Sabres' famed French
Connection Line, Rick Martin had the heavy shot and soft
hands of a natural goal scorer. While first-pick Lafleur scored
29 goals and second-pick Dionne, 28, Martin (fifth-pick
overall) blew an NHL-rookie-record 44 goals past opposition

netminders in 1971–72. And Martin was just heating up. In both his third and fourth NHL campaigns he lit the lamp 52 times. But Martin's career came to a premature end when he was forced to retire because of knee miseries in 1982. Had he played a few more years in good health, he would surely be a member of the Hall of Fame.

5.20 B. Joe Kocur, in 1985–86

Kocur hit the league hard in 1985–86. The Detroit Red Wings recruit dropped his gloves and slugged it out 36 times in just 59 games, which set not just a new rookie record but an NHL mark as well. Until broken bones in his hands forced him to cut back on the hostilities, Kocur was the NHL's most feared knockout artist. He was finally dethroned by veteran pugilist Paul Laus in 1996–97, when Laus racked up 39 fighting majors in 77 games.

5.21 C. Two players

Since the inception of the Rookie of the Month Award in 1983–84, only three NHLers have won the double distinction of top player and rookie honours in the same month. Alexander Ovechkin, who notched both awards in January 2006 after scoring a league-leading 21 points in 14 games (11–10–21), joined Washington Capitals goalie Jim Carey (March 1995) and Winnipeg Jets winger Teemu Selanne (January 1993). Ovechkin, who had seven multiple-point games, recorded his first hat trick on January 13 in a 3–2 overtime win against Anaheim, including what became known as "the Goal"—while rolling on his back at full speed—against Phoenix in a 6–1 win on January 16. Yet Ovechkin's numbers speak more to the anemic play of the Capitals. He netted 28 per cent of the Capitals' goals and earned points on 53 per cent of its goals, 21 of 40. Washington won five and lost 10 games that month.

5.22 A. Howie Meeker, with the Toronto Maple Leafs

Howe's first-season totals (7–15–22 in 58 games) did not excite Calder voters, who instead awarded Meeker top rookie honours after he posted an impressive 27–18–45 in 55 games with Toronto. Meeker's best freshman start came on January 8, 1947, when he shell-shocked Chicago's Paul Bibeault with the 12th, 13th, 14th, 15th and 16th NHL markers—one of three five-goal games by a rookie (Mickey Roach's and Don Murdoch's are the others) in league history. Meeker would play another seven NHL seasons without equalling his rookie year point output.

5.23 A. Jordan Staal, with the Pittsburgh Penguins

His teammates nicknamed him Gronk, after a comic book character. Apparently, Jordan Staal's huge size—six foot four—makes him scary, which is how many already felt about his rookie campaign in 2006–07, when he set an unprecedented number of "youngest" records in penalty shots and shorthanded goals. Then, on February 10 against Toronto, Staal notched the game's first two goals and the overtime winner in the Penguins' 6–5 victory over the Maple Leafs to become the youngest player ever to score a hat trick. He was just 18 years and 153 days old when he scored four times against the Rangers on December 4, 1943, more than a month younger than Jack Hamilton (who was 18 years and 185 days old).

5.24 C. Teemu Selanne, with the Winnipeg Jets, in 1992–93

In his first NHL season, in 1992–93, Selanne was responsible for 23.6 per cent of the Jets' total offensive output—76 of Winnipeg's 322 goals. By comparison, Alexander Ovechkin's rookie campaign with Washington in 2005–06 netted him 52 goals and a close second to Selanne, for a 22.6 per cent share of the Capitals' 230 goals. Only four other freshmen qualify with 45 goals or more, but none are above the 20th percentile. And while Pavel Bure holds the mark among all modern-day players, with 29.5 per cent of Florida's goals during 2000–01, Selanne probably has the highest ratio ever achieved by a rookie.

5.25 **A. Marty Turco, with Dallas**
Goalie Ed Belfour's erratic behaviour off-ice and his clashes with Dallas coach Ken Hitchcock led to increased ice time for backup Marty Turco in 2000–01, and the freshman responded by posting sterling numbers. In 26 games, Turco led all goalies with a 1.90 GAA and a .925 save percentage, a double-first for a rookie netminder.

5.26 **D. All of the above**
When 2006–07 began, Pittsburgh had no big expectations of Jordan Staal. The club figured on playing him for a maximum of nine games before returning him to the OHL Peterborough Petes—enough time for the Penguins to test drive their 2006 first-rounder while preventing the first year of his three-year entry-level contract from kicking in. However, Staal played so well that he jumped to the Penguins' second line just four months after draft day. The 18-year-old played anything but like a teenager, and, within a month, proved just how much the NHL was now a young man's game. No, Pittsburgh never figured on Staal for 2006–07. Nor did many netminders. And his success came in part from being able to get a shot off while holding the puck far from his body. Staal figures he has a wingspan that can sweep the puck from one side of his body to the other by as much as 10 feet. "I think it kind of fools goalies when I have it stretched out and I just let it go. They're not expecting a shot," the six-four Staal has said.

Jordan Staal's Rookie Records of 2006–07

DATE	OPPONENT	ACHIEVEMENT	AGE
Oct. 21	Columbus	Two Shorthanded Goals	18 years, 41 days
		• Youngest player with two SH goals in a single game, including penalty shot goal (*surpassed Radek Dvorak: 20 years, 278 days*)	
		• Only player to score more than one SH goal before his 19th birthday	
		• Youngest player to score two goals in a single game in 63 years (*previously Bep Guidolin: 18 years, 12 days*)	
		• Youngest player to score on a penalty shot (*surpassed Nathan Horton: 18 years, 224 days*)	
Nov. 25	NYR	Overtime Penalty Shot	18 years, 76 days
		• First rookie with OT penalty shot since league adopted rule in 1984–84	
		• Tied several rookies with most penalty shots (2) in one season (*only David Vyborny has two PS goals, 2000–01*)	
Mar. 6	Ottawa	Seventh Shorthanded Goal	18 years, 177 days
		• Set rookie record with his 7th SH goal (*surpassed Gerry Minor and John Madden: six SH goals*)	

5.27 D. Three times

No matter what Fabian Brunnstrom does in his NHL career, he will forever be remembered for his debut on October 15, 2008. Brunnstrom is one of only a trio of NHLers to score three goals in their first game, matching the feats of Alex Smart (with the Montreal Canadiens) in a 5–1 win against Chicago on January 14, 1943, and Real Cloutier (with the Quebec Nordiques), who pumped three goals in his—and Quebec's—first NHL game on October 10, 1979. Unfortunately, the Nords lost their home opener to Atlanta 5–3. But Cloutier, a former WHA scoring champion, tied the 36-year-old mark for most goals in a first game established by Smart. Brunnstrom, the much ballyhooed unrestricted free agent, helped the Stars to a 6–4 win over Nashville. "I don't think you can knock the smile off his face right now," said Dallas goalie Marty Turco. Interestingly, Brunnstrom was a healthy scratch in the first two games of the season. "We just want to make sure he's ready," said coach Dave Tippett.

5.28   C. Roy Conacher, with the 1939 Boston Bruins
Younger sibling of the famous Hall of Fame Conachers, Lionel and Charlie, brother Roy began his NHL career in grand fashion, scoring a league-high 26 goals in his freshman year, 1938–39—only the second time a rookie has led the NHL in goals. Then in the playoffs, Conacher played even better, notching six goals, including five in the finals—still an NHL rookie record. To cap off this Cinderella story, the Bruins then won the Stanley Cup on Conacher's Cup-winner, on April 16, 1939. According to the local papers, "Conacher's winning goal was the prettiest thing of the night. [Eddie] Shore started it at his defense by passing to Cowley, who skidded the puck across the ice when checked at the Toronto defense. Conacher, flying like the wind, took it in stride and hung the rubber behind [Turk] Broda with 18 minutes of the second period gone." And though few rookies ever get as much ice time as he did during those playoffs, after his stellar debut Conacher was handed a regular shift on Boston's second line, with Bill Cowley and Mel Hill.

5.29   B. Mike Rupp, with 2003's New Jersey Devils
Rookie Mike Rupp may not have known just how exclusive an NHL club he entered when he scored New Jersey's Stanley Cup-winning goal in 2003. Since its inception in 1918, the NHL has seen only five freshmen score Cup-winners, and none since Roy Conacher managed it in 1939—until Rupp. Still, Toronto's Corb Denneny gets a bye into the club, since he

scored the NHL's first Cup-winning goal in 1918, in the league's first season, when all players could be classified as rookies. As for the great Howie Morenz, he began his Hall of Fame career notching the winner of Montreal's first NHL Stanley Cup, in 1924. Then, in 1926, Nels Stewart capped a string of rookie feats—including becoming the only rookie to win a regular-season scoring title—by potting the Montreal Maroons' winner of 1926. Thirteen years later, Roy Conacher won the Cup for Boston in 1939. But Rupp had the least playoff experience of all five rookies. The third-line centre played in only 26 regular-season matches and just four in the Devils' drive for the Cup in 2003. Yet he figured in all three goals of New Jersey's 3–0 victory in the hardest game to win: a do-or-die seventh and deciding match, in which he scored what stood as the Cup-winner, then set up Jeff Friesen for New Jersey's second and third assurance goals to win the championship. Even more impressive, it was Rupp's first playoff goal ever—and only the second time in NHL history that a player's first postseason marker was a Cup-winner; Pete Kelly did it in 1936.

Rookie Stanley Cup-winning Goal Scorers*

PLAYERS	TEAMS	YEAR	RS GP	RS G	PS GP	PS G
Corb Denneny	Toronto	1918	21	20	6	3
Howie Morenz	Montreal	1924	24	13	6	7
Nels Stewart	Maroons	1926	36	34	8	6
Roy Conancher	Boston	1939	47	26	12	6
Mike Rupp	NJD	2003	26	5	4	1

*Current to 2008
RS GP=regular-season games played; RS G=regular-season goals
PS GP=postseason games played; PS G=postseason goals

Game 5

The Third Jersey

MORE THAN JUST SUPPLYING additional income, the third jersey gave a completely new look to the league's more traditionally dressed clubs. Some teams hit the mark with their alternate logos and sweater designs, but others struck out, including the Dallas Stars, who, after making about us$400,000, mothballed their incredibly unpopular third jersey in April 2006. In this game, match the teams in the left column with their third-jersey designs.

Solutions are on page 560

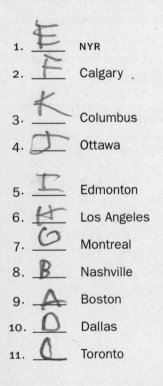

1. __E__ NYR

2. __F__ Calgary

3. __K__ Columbus

4. __J__ Ottawa

5. __I__ Edmonton

6. __H__ Los Angeles

7. __G__ Montreal

8. __B__ Nashville

9. __A__ Boston

10. __D__ Dallas

11. __C__ Toronto

A. Brown bear

B. Sabre-tooth tiger protruding out of a triangle

C. Replica of a 1938 jersey

D. Bull's head with a star constellation

E. The *Statue of Liberty*'s head

F. Horse head snorting fire

G. Replica of a 1945 jersey

H. Coat of arms

I. Drop of oil in a gear-like design

J. A Roman's head, looking out

K. A star, wrapped in the Ohio State flag

6

True or False?

AFTER HIS RECORD-BREAKING STREAK of five straight shutouts in January 2004, Phoenix goalie Brian Boucher collected
only four wins during the rest of the season in 27 games played. *True
or False?* It's true. Boucher fell apart after his much-publicized run
of shutouts, going 4–17–6 over the next 27 starts to average almost
four goals-against per game—not the performance Coyote GM Mike
Barnett expected after trading Sean Burke in early February to make
Boucher Phoenix's number one man. In this chapter we change the
pace and challenge you to a series of right-or-wrong questions.

Answers are on page 142

6.1   Alexander Ovechkin is the first player since Terry Sawchuk
to be named to the NHL's First All-Star Team in his first
three seasons. *True or False?*

6.2   In 2006–07, Daniel Alfredsson, with Ottawa, became the
first NHL player in 86 years to score game-winning goals in
four straight games. *True or False?*

6.3   Gordie Howe is the oldest player to appear in a game for
the Detroit Red Wings. *True or False?*

6.4   Maurice Richard did not win the Hart Trophy as MVP in the
season that he became the first NHLer to score 50 goals in
50 games. *True or False?*

6.5 One of Jarome Iginla's birth names is Elvis. *True or False?*

6.6 No team has ever led the NHL in both goals scored and goals allowed in the same season. *True or False?*

6.7 The last man to win the Lady Byng Trophy as the NHL's most gentlemanly player with zero penalty minutes was a defenseman. *True or False?*

6.8 The Philadelphia Flyers' famous 35-game unbeaten streak is the longest amongst the four major-league sports. *True or False?*

6.9 No player has ever won the Calder Trophy as the NHL's outstanding rookie and then spent the next season in the minors. *True or False?*

6.10 A player with just one NHL game behind him had a hockey championship trophy named after him. *True or False?*

6.11 No member of the 2005–06 Phoenix Coyotes was with the Winnipeg Jets in 1995–96, the last season before the Canadian team relocated to Arizona. *True or False?*

6.12 Before Sidney Crosby, Jordan Staal and Kristopher Letang scored for Pittsburgh in a 2006–07 game against the New York Rangers, no team had ever iced three teenaged goal scorers in the same match. *True or False?*

6.13 The lowest sweater number that has not been retired by an NHL team is 13. *True or False?*

6.14 Jaromir Jagr is the only NHLer to be traded immediately after recording a 50-goal season. *True or False?*

6.15 Hockey visors do not affect a player's vision. *True or False?*

6.16 The first player to sign a pro contract with the Toronto Maple Leafs in 1927 was an American. *True or False?*

6.17 The Calder Trophy for rookie of the year is the only NHL trophy a player can win just once in his career. *True or False?*

6.18 No player has ever scored goals in his first regular-season games more than two seasons in a row. *True or False?*

6.19 Luc Robitaille is the highest-scoring left-winger in NHL history. *True or False?*

6.20 To improve their pugilistic skills, players can attend hockey fight school. *True or False?*

6.21 When the net is intentionally or accidentally dislodged from its moorings, a referee whistles the play dead. *True or False?*

6.22 Although Boston, Toronto, Chicago, Detroit, New York and Montreal are known as "Original Six" teams, they are not the founding clubs of the NHL. *True or False?*

6.23 In June 2004, the *Tampa Tribune* ran an editorial stating that the Lightning had lost Game 7 of the Stanley Cup finals. *True or False?*

6.24 No non-goalie has ever worn No. 1 on his sweater. *True or False?*

6.25 In 2007, Sidney Crosby became the youngest player voted to the starting lineup of an NHL All-Star game since fan balloting began in 1986. *True or False?*

6.26 Despite a 6–2–2 record and 1.29 goals-against average with the Phoenix Coyotes in January 2004, a month when he notched four of his NHL-record five consecutive shutouts, Brian Boucher was not named the league's defensive player of the month. *True or False?*

6.27 While playing together in Florida, Pavel and Valeri Bure only helped each other score one goal as Panthers. It came when Valeri assisted on Pavel's 400th career goal. *True or False?*

6.28 No NHLer since 1967–68 has won the goal-scoring race with less than 10 power-play goals. *True or False?*

6.29 The odds of becoming an NHL star are approximately 15,000 to one. *True or False?*

6.30 In 2006–07, 18-year-old rookie Jordan Staal scored more goals than his older brother, Eric Stall, did. *True or False?*

6.31 In 2006–07, Chris Chelios became the first player in NHL history to still be playing in the league when he became eligible to collect his NHL pension. *True or False?*

6.32 The first woman goalie to win a pro hockey game was an American. *True or False?*

6.33 The Lester B. Pearson Award pays tribute to the NHL's most outstanding player, as judged by the players themselves. No player has ever won it with two different teams. *True or False?*

6.34 No player has ever led his team in goals, assists, points and penalty minutes in the same season. *True or False?*

6.35 In 2006–07, Jacques Lemaire's Minnesota Wild was a league-leader in shootout wins. *True or False?*

6.36 A 2006 medical report on bodychecking in hockey leagues for 11-year-old boys found *no* evidence that bodychecking increases the rate of serious injuries. *True or False?*

6.37 No 40-year-old player has ever posted a 100-point season. *True or False?*

6.38 Between the two dynasty teams of the 1980s, the New York Islanders outscored the Edmonton Oilers in four Stanley Cup championships. *True or False?*

6.39 During the 1920s and early 1930s, before Detroit became the Red Wings, the team was known as the Cougars and then the Falcons. No player has ever played for Detroit under all three team names. *True or False?*

6.40 An old-time player once scored a hat trick in overtime. *True or False?*

6.41 No NHL player has ever scored 70 goals in a season and not been elected to either the First or Second All-Star Team. *True or False?*

6.42 Sidney Crosby is the shortest player ever selected number one overall in the NHL Entry Draft. *True or False?*

6.43 The game-winning goal that defeated the Toronto Maple Leafs in their last game at Maple Leaf Gardens was scored by former Leaf captain Doug Gilmour. *True or False?*

6.44 Gordie Howe's dog is named Rocket. *True or False?*

6.45 In 2005–06, despite the NHL's clampdown on obstruction, comebacks by teams were *down* in the first season under the new rules. *True or False?*

6.46 Wayne Gretky scored his first 50th goal on the same night that Guy Lafleur scored his last 50th. *True or False?*

True or False?

Answers

6.1 **True**

There hasn't been an NHL start like this since the great Terry Sawchuk backstopped consecutive First All-Star Teams in his first three seasons in the early 1950s. It only took 55 years of All-Star voting, but Alexander Ovechkin repeated Sawchuk's feat when he was named First All-Star in 2005–06, 2006–07 and 2007–08. Equally impressive, in each of those seasons Ovechkin led the NHL in shots. Ovechkin's next target? As of this writing, it's matching Bill Durnan's four All-Star team appearances in his first four seasons. Durnan did it in the 1940s.

6.2   **True**

Daniel Alfredsson became only the second player in NHL history to score the game-winning goal in four consecutive games, when the Senators captain potted the decisive marker in a 5–2 victory over the Washington Capitals on January 16, 2007. (Alfredsson also scored in his next game, versus the Vancouver Canucks, but Roberto Luongo stopped 34 shots in the 2–1 Canucks win.) According to the Elias Sports Bureau, the only NHLer with more consecutive game-winners is Montreal Canadiens forward Newsy Lalonde, who netted five straight in February 1921.

6.3   **False**

When Chris Chelios played in 2005–06's season opener in Detroit against the St. Louis Blues, on October 5, he was 43 years, 253 days old. Gordie Howe was 43 years and four days old in his last Red Wings game, in 1971. Chelios extended his mark with the Red Wings in 2008–09, playing in 28 games at age 47.

6.4   **True**

You have to wonder what more Maurice Richard could possibly have done to impress the Hart Trophy voters. In 1944–45, the 23-year-old winger set a new NHL record by scoring 50 goals in 50 games. Yet the MVP went to Richard's Montreal linemate Elmer Lach, who won the scoring title and set a new league record for assists, with 54. In retrospect, it's difficult to understand the voters' logic. Goal scoring is normally regarded as the more prestigious of the two categories, and Richard's mark was clearly a more impressive achievement. Interestingly, Lach's assist mark was erased just five years on by Ted Lindsay, while Richard's total of 50 goals was not eclipsed until 21 years later, when Bobby Hull notched 54 in 1965–66. The Rocket's milestone of 50 goals in 50 games lasted 36 seasons, until 1980–81, when Mike Bossy demolished it.

6.5   True

Iginla's full name on his birth certificate is Arthur-Leigh Elvis Adekunle Jarome Jij Junior Iginla. Luckily, Jarome became his first name of choice, as few hockey players could get away with Adekunle, Jij, or even Elvis, which Iginla inherited from his father, a Nigerian-born, Canadian-trained lawyer who adopted the King of Rock's first name to better integrate into North American society. "He thought it was like Mike or Mark. He didn't realize who Elvis was," Jarome once said. Iginla was born in Edmonton to Susan Schuchard and Elvis Iginla on Canada Day, 1977.

6.6   False

Two teams have led the NHL in goals scored and goals allowed in the same season. In both cases, it was a Chicago club. With Dick Irvin and Babe Dye providing most of the fire-power, the 1926–27 Blackhawks posted a league-high 115 goals in 44 games. But the Hawks also gave up 116 goals, the most in the league, and finished third in the American Division with a 19–22–3 record. In 1947–48, led by Doug Bentley and Roy Conacher, Chicago fired a league-best 195 goals while allow-ing a loop-high 225-against. The leaky defense hurt. Chicago finished in last place.

6.7   True

Although Bill Quackenbush never spent more than 17 min-utes in the penalty box in any of his 13 NHL seasons, he was no cream puff. In fact, the burly rearguard was known for his bruising but clean bodychecks. But in 1949, with Detroit,

Quackenbush became the first D-man to win the Lady Byng Trophy as the NHL's most gentlemanly player, and the last player to win the award with 0 PIM.

The NHL's Penalty-Free Lady Byng Winners*							
PLAYER	YEAR	TEAM	GP	G	A	P	PIM
Syl Apps	1941–42	Tor	38	18	23	41	0
Bill Mosienko	1944–45	Chi	50	28	26	54	0
Bill Quackenbush	1948–49	Det	60	6	17	23	0

*Current to 2008–09

6.8 True

It's a record that won't likely be challenged, given that today's teams play with five-minute overtimes and shootouts to settle tie games. But Philadelphia's 35-game unbeaten streak is still a record-book phenomenon. The Flyers played 85 days and 19 different teams without losing a single game between October 14, 1979, and January 7, 1980. Not one team in the league, except Washington, which they never played, could knock the Flyers off their streak of 25 wins and 10 ties—until on December 22 they beat Boston 5–2 and destroyed Montreal's record unbeaten streak of 28 games (22 wins and six ties), set in 1977–78. Among the contenders in other major-league sports, the Flyers also eclipsed the NFL's Canton Bulldogs mark of 25 wins between 1921 and 1923, Major League Baseball's New York Giants streak of 26 in a row in 1916 and the NBA's Los Angeles Lakers run of 33 straight wins in 1971 and 1972.

6.9 False

In the 1950s, NHL players had little clout when it came to negotiating with management. Witness the example of Gump Worsley. After winning the Calder Trophy as the NHL's top rookie in 1952–53, the New York Rangers netminder figured he was well within his rights to ask for a $500 raise on his $7,500 salary the following fall. His opinion was not shared by Rangers general manager Frank Boucher, however, who demoted Worsley to the Vancouver Canucks of the Western Hockey League and replaced him with American Hockey League veteran goalie Johnny Bower. However, as they did the year before, the club finished out of the playoffs, while the Gumper had a far better time of it out west. The WHL Canucks finished in first place and their netminder was declared both outstanding goaltender and league MVP. The following fall, Bower played the bulk of the season on the Pacific Coast while Worsley reclaimed his starring role in Manhattan.

6.10   True

Goalie Joe Turner played his only NHL game for Detroit on February 5, 1942. Soon after, he joined the U.S. Marine Corps and was killed in action in 1944. Then in 1945, governors of the newly formed International Hockey League, seeking to name their championship trophy, chose to honour Turner. The Turner Cup was presented annually to the champions of the IHL before the minor pro league was disbanded in 2001. In 2007, the United Hockey League officially became the International Hockey League and, in tribute to the original IHL, restored the Turner Cup as a championship trophy.

6.11   False

When the wrecker's ball demolished the ancient Winnipeg Arena in March 2006, the only Coyote still tied to Phoenix's former club was 29-year-old centre Shane Doan, who joined the Jets in their final NHL season, 1995–96, after being drafted seventh overall by the club in 1995. "Those are huge moments that I'll always remember," Doan recalls of his rookie campaign in the old barn. Doan became team captain in 2003–04 and, as of 2008–09, is still a Jet/Coyote.

6.12 **False**

Pittsburgh made the most of its lengthy stay in the NHL basement between 2001–02 and 2005–06, deciding the future of the franchise with five successive top-five draft picks: Ryan Whitney, fifth overall in 2002; Marc-Andre Fleury, first in 2003; Evgeni Malkin, second in 2004; Sidney Crosby, first in 2005, and Jordan Staal, second in 2006. The hockey world was soon hailing the Penguins' youth corps as the second coming of the Edmonton Oilers' 1980s nucleus of Gretzky-Messier-Anderson-Coffey. Now, all Sid and the kids had to do was live up to the hype. And they got a good start on October 12, 2006, when 19-year-old Crosby scored and 18-year-olds Staal and Kristopher Letang each notched their first NHL goals to pull out a 6–5 win against the New York Rangers. It marked just the ninth time an NHL team has iced a trio of teenage goal scorers in one game, and the first time since teens Dave Andreychuk, Paul Cyr and Phil Housley scored for Buffalo in a 6–4 win against Edmonton on October 17, 1982. Crosby's game-winner, with just 3.3 seconds remaining in regulation time, produced the NHL rarity.

6.13 **True**

With so few players wearing unlucky No. 13, none of the NHL's 30 franchises will retire the number anytime soon. However, one possible candidate who could change the league's lowest unretired number from No. 13 to No. 20 (the next lowest number not retired) is Toronto's former captain Mats Sundin. But it's an unlikely scenario considering Toronto's weird policy of differentiating between retired and honoured numbers. And as great as Frank Mahovlich, Johnny Bower and Tim Horton

were to the Maple Leafs, their numbers have only been honoured, not retired. Of course, the highest number not retired
by a team is No. 98.

6.14   False

Two NHLers besides Jaromir Jagr have been traded after 50-goal
seasons. Only a couple of months after he notched 55 goals
for the Los Angeles Kings in 1987–88, Jimmy Carson was sent
to the Edmonton Oilers as part of the blockbuster deal that
brought Wayne Gretzky to the Kings. Carson scored 49 goals
for the Oilers in 1988–89, but soon after that his career took
a dive. He never again scored as many as 35 goals in a season
and was out of the NHL by age 28. Pavel Bure was dealt to the
Florida Panthers by the Vancouver Canucks midway through
1998–99, after scoring 50 the previous year. Bure forced the
trade by refusing to report to the Canucks.

6.15   True

In 2004, researchers at Université de Montreal's School of
Optometry subjected a number of NHL player visors to a battery of tests with state-of-the-art equipment, to determine
if there are any significant differences between the ability
to see with or without a visor. The researchers recruited 18
amateur hockey players—10 men and eight women—to complete a series of tests three times: once wearing an Itech visor,
once wearing an Oakley visor and once without a visor. The
conclusions were clear: visors in no way affect visual percep-
tion, colour contrast or peripheral vision. But don't expect
the results to change many minds. It was Eric Lindros who
compared wearing a visor to "driving in a rainstorm without
windshield wipers."

6.16   True

The first player Conn Smythe signed after he purchased the St. Patricks and patriotically renamed them the Toronto Maple Leafs was Carl Voss, an American from Chelsea, Massachusetts. Voss held an impressive sports legacy as a Canadian football champion with Queen's University in 1923 and 1924 and Memorial Cup finalist with the Kingston Frontenacs in 1926. He played just 14 games in Toronto, but won rookie of the year honours in 1933 with Detroit and scored the Stanley Cup-winning goal for Chicago in 1938. In 1950 Voss was named the first referee-in-chief of the NHL.

6.17   True

By definition, the Calder is a one-time trophy for a player, awarded to the NHL's top rookie. The winner is chosen by the Professional Hockey Writers' Association, but the honour confers no guarantee of a stellar career. Still, despite such Calder-winner flops as Willi Plett, Steve Vickers and Brit Selby, the association's track record at predicting future stars has been surprisingly accurate, including such notable Calder-winners as Dany Heatley, Peter Forsberg and Martin Brodeur.

6.18   False

There may be a few snipers who have equalled Florida winger Kristian Huselius's feat of netting a goal in first games in three consecutive seasons, but, according to our research, we would be surprised to find another NHLer who has scored those three goals on the first shots of each season. In 2001–02, the Swedish rookie potted his first career goal on his first shot on net in Florida's first game, a 5–2 loss to Philadelphia on October 4; then, in 2002–03, he netted his first of the season, again on his first shot in his first game, a 4–1 loss to Chicago

on October 17; and, in 2003–04, Carolina became the third
team to discover that Huselius makes his first shot count,
when he potted his first goal on his first blast in the Panthers'
season-opener, a 3–1 win against the Hurricanes on October 9.
Even more scary, Huselius repeated the feat for a fourth time
in 2008–09, when he scored a goal on his first shot as a Blue
Jacket in Columbus's season-opener against Dallas.

6.19   True

Luc Robitaille surpassed Bobby Hull's NHL record of 610 career
goals by a left-winger on January 18, 2002, when he tipped
a point shot past Washington Capitals goalie Olaf Kolzig to
open the scoring in a 3–1 Detroit win. Ironically, Robitaille's
linemate during the historic game was Brett Hull, Bobby's
son. Weirder still, Brett scored Detroit's second goal later
in the opening period to tie his father's career mark of 98
game-winning goals. Since then, Brendan Shanahan (656 as
of 2008–09) and Dave Andreychuk (640) have both eclipsed
Hull's left-wing career total.

6.20   True

In the summer of 1999, Dustin McArthur, an Eastern Hockey
league player, opened up the first hockey fight school, in
Sarnia, Ontario. McArthur's logic was simple. "By no means is
it to create fighters," he said in a *National Post* story. "The idea
is to teach hockey players how to best defend themselves." In
the school's inaugural season, 30 students learned the fun-
damentals of boxing and hockey fighting, including how to
punch, how to hold, how to tie up an opponent and how to
duck. Then in 2007, NHL brothers Aaron and Derek Boogaard
staged their first fight camp—for young hockey players—at
a Regina training centre. The clinic registered students aged
12 to 18. "We're showing them the little things that would

help them out, rather than learning the hard way and getting hurt," said Derek Boogaard at the time.

6.21 **False**

In his first game with the New York Islanders, on March 1, 2007, Ryan Smyth played heads-up hockey after the St. Louis net was accidentally dislodged by linemate Jason Blake during a second-period Islanders attack. Parked at the Blues' crease, with play continuing, Smyth used his skate to inch the post back atop its moorings only a few seconds before Marc-Andre Bergeron's bad-angle shot deflected off a St. Louis player and into the net past Curtis Sanford. The referee had watched the play from behind the cage, ready to whistle no goal had the net not been in legal position. (When a net is deliberately dislodged to prevent a goal, the player is penalized under NHL rule 51(c).)

6.22 **True**

There is nothing "original" about the Original Six except for the Toronto Maple Leafs and Montreal Canadiens, two of the five founding-member clubs of the NHL in 1917–18. After that first season, the league soon ballooned into a 10-team circuit with franchises in markets such as Pittsburgh, St. Louis and Ottawa, and both Montreal and New York had two NHL teams, each competing in the same market. When the Brooklyn Americans folded in 1941, the league downsized to six teams and went on a 25-year hiatus from expansion—the era fondly remembered as the golden age of hockey with the Original Six teams. It lasted from 1942–43 to 1966–67.

6.23 **True**

"Stop the presses" should have been the rallying cry after the Tampa Bay Lightning won the Stanley Cup in 2004. The *Tribune* had prepared two editorials—one for a win and one for a loss. But despite the correct text being placed in the paper's computers, the editorial that appeared in 275,000 copies of the *Tribune* opened with: "The Tampa Bay Lightning didn't win the National Hockey League's Stanley Cup last night. But the team had a championship season nevertheless." The correct editorial, which never made ink, credited the Lightning for generating pride and excitement in the community.

6.24 False

The circumstances under which Montreal defenseman Herb Gardiner broke hockey's longstanding tradition and wore No. 1 during 1926–27 and 1927–28 can be traced back to November 28, 1925, and the final game of Canadiens great Georges Vezina. After appearing in 325 consecutive regular-season games, Vezina was forced to retire because of tuberculosis. Sadly, the Hall of Fame netminder died months later. Out of respect, no Canadiens goalie donned No. 1 for four years, until George Hainsworth wore it in 1929–30. However, during that four-year period, the No. 1 sweater was handed to a couple of defensemen, including Gardiner, and, when he was traded, D-man Marty Burke. Babe Seibert, another rearguard, also wore No. 1—for Montreal in the late 1930s.

6.25 True

Sidney Crosby appears destined to demolish any number of league records, including a few All-Star marks. In 2007, at 19 years and five months of age, Crosby became the youngest player voted to the NHL All-Star lineup by fan ballot, eclipsing Jaromir Jagr, who was 19 years and 11 months old when he set the record in 1992. Sid the Kid topped all players with 825,783 votes and registered the second-highest vote count since balloting to select All-Star starters began in 1986. Jagr amassed a record 1,020,736 in 2000, but his mark didn't last long, cut down by another Crosby total: 1,713,021 votes in 2009's balloting, which was undoubtedly fuelled by the increase in Internet accessibility in the nine years since Jagr's All-Star selection. It's also worth noting that at 1986's All-Star match, rookie Wendel Clark was just 19 years and four months old (two months younger than Crosby), but Clark wasn't voted in as a starter that year.

6.26 True

Boucher must have been scratching his noodle after the NHL named Ottawa defenseman Wade Redden defensive player of the month for January 2004. Redden led all Senators in ice time as the team earned a season-best 10–4–2–0 record, but Boucher set two modern-day NHL records with five straight shutouts and a streak of 332 minutes and one second without allowing a goal. All but one of his zeroes came in January 2004.

6.27 False

Because of Pavel's trade to the New York Rangers and a knee injury that cost Valeri 37 games, the Bure brothers only played together for 26 games with Florida in 2001–02. The Panthers went 5–14–5–2, but the two combined for 18 goals and 20 assists. Pavel's 400th career goal was assisted on by brother Valeri.

6.28 False

Conventional wisdom suggests that a player has to capitalize on the power play to put up big goal numbers. But there are a few exceptions. Since the NHL began compiling power-play stats in 1967–68, four players—Bobby Hull, Steve Shutt,

Wayne Gretzky and Keith Tkachuk—have led the league in goals while counting fewer than 10 on the power play. Hull did it first, tallying only eight of his league-high 44 goals on the man-advantage in 1967–68.

6.29 **True**

In a study titled *The Straight Facts About Making It in Pro Hockey*, researcher and author Jim Parcels tracks 30,000 children who played hockey in Ontario, all of whom were born in 1975. By the age of 15, three-quarters of the study group had given up the sport. At 16 years old, only 232 were drafted by the OHL and only 105 ever played in an OHL game. And at the NHL draft, two years later, only 48 were selected—and of those, only 26 played an NHL game. Only two players—Todd Bertuzzi and Jason Allison—amongst Parcels's original group of 30,000 became NHL stars. As his study shows, there are a few ways to climb the hockey hierarchy and play at the NHL level, but the overwhelming odds don't change much in another draft year, with another junior league or with a scholarship to an American college.

6.30 **False**

Anyone who thought Jordan Staal would challenge his brother in goal totals in 2006–07, raise your hand. No one? Jordan's first season with Pittsburgh surprised most fans, including the Penguins, who got 29 goals from the 18-year old—just one less than the 30 that Carolina earned with his brother, Eric. The numbers had people talking family dynasty—and sibling rivalry. Was Eric just suffering from a Stanley Cup hangover, or did Jordan instantly mature into a bonafide NHLer? "I told him, I'm coming for him," said Jordan. "But I didn't expect it to be this close."

6.31 **False**

Chris Chelios is the second player to double dip at age 45, collecting an NHL pension while still receiving his US$1.15-million salary from Detroit. In the process, Chelios joined Toronto backup netminder Johnny Bower, who, at age 45, started drawing pension cheques during his last season, 1969–70. The legendary Gordie Howe was also eligible for his NHL retirement fund at age 45, but was playing alongside his sons in the WHA at the time. Still, when Howe returned to the NHL at age 51 in 1979–80, he too drew a league pension and salary. Chelios's first game as an NHL pensioner came in a 2–1 loss to St. Louis the day after his birthday, on January 26, 2007. He recorded 20 shifts in 17:11 of ice time, had one shot on net and blocked two more—not the accomplishments of a typical pensioner. Chelios was in his 23rd season.

6.32 **True**

Fourteen months after Canadian national women's team goalie Manon Rheaume appeared in a 1992 NHL exhibition game with the Tampa Bay Lightning, American Erin Whitten began playing with the East Coast Hockey League's Toledo Storm. On October 30, 1993, in a 6–5 win over the Daytona Bombers, Whitten became the first female goalie to record a victory in a professional game. Her start in hockey came in high school while playing on the boys' team in her hometown of Glens Falls, New York. Whitten then moved up to women's university hockey in New Hampshire and then to the United States national women's team, where she played in four Women's World Championships.

6.33 **False**

The Pearson has long been overshadowed by the more prestigious Hart Trophy, which is awarded to the NHL's regular-season MVP as chosen by the Professional Hockey Writer's Association. But the Pearson is the one trophy that the players have a say in, in terms of who receives it. And on several occasions, both hockey writers and players have voted alike and agreed on the same league MVP, including in 1990 and 1992, when Mark Messier won the Hart and Pearson each season. But Messier's success came with different teams: Edmonton, followed by New York, an NHL exclusive.

6.34   False

This feat is not so remarkable. It was recently accomplished by Darcy Tucker with Tampa Bay in 1998–99 and Theo Fleury with Calgary in 1997–98. In 1999–2000, Boston's Joe Thornton led in all three offensive categories with a 23–37–60 record while compiling a club-high 82 minutes in the box.

6.35   True

As the architect of some of the game's most stifling defense-oriented teams, Jacques Lemaire surprised more than a few hockey aficionados when his Minnesota Wild finished 2006–07 with a league-high 10–7 shootout record—equalling four other teams with 10 wins in its surprising 104-point season. And it wasn't because Lemaire changed strategies to suit the new NHL. Instead, it was more of the same Lemaire, only now he was playing the trap at lightning speed with better players, while still stressing positional play, especially in the neutral zone. The Mad Trapper had everyone in the right spots on the ice. But what about teaching the uncoachable art of the shootout? Minnesota's 10–7 record can be credited to four players, including Mikko Koivu, with a league-high eight goals, and Petteri Nummelin, who notched six in seven shots. General manager Doug Risebrough's spending spree in the summer of

2006 didn't hurt, either. Risebrough turned one of the league's lowest payrolls into a salary-cap-busting us$42.1 million.

6.36   False

After Hockey Canada changed its age classifications for minor hockey, allowing 11-year-old boys to play with 12-year-olds in peewee divisions (where bodychecking was permitted), researchers found that the rate of injuries among the 11-year-olds doubled and that serious injuries, such as concussions and bone fractures, tripled. Data from emergency rooms in the Edmonton region was examined during a four-year period: two years before and two years after the NHL's policy change. Overall, 86 of every 1,000 11-year-old players visited hospital emergency rooms after the rule change, compared to 41 per 1,000 players when no checking was permitted in the same age group. Across Canada, at least 9,000 hockey players under age 16 are treated in hospitals for injuries, with 85 per cent of those injuries due to bodychecking. The research was published in the July 2006 edition of the *Canadian Medical Association Journal*.

6.37   False

They don't make them like they used to. Or do they? Several recent players have had success into their 40s, including Chris Chelios and Igor Larionov. But only Mark Messier managed to sneak into the top tier of greybeards amongst a select few Original Six veterans when, in 2000–01, he bested Dave Keon's 62 points. Even so, the best offensive season ever registered by a 40-year-old player belongs to Gordie Howe, who racked up 103 points on 44 goals and 59 assists in 1968–69, before turning 41 the day the season ended. The ageless Howe also ranks third and fourth on the list of highest output by an elder statesman.

Best Offensive Seasons by 40-Year-Olds

PLAYER	TEAM	SEASON	AGE	G	A	P
Gordie Howe	Detroit	1968–69	40	44	59	103
Johnny Bucyk	Boston	1975–76	40	36	47	83
Gordie Howe	Detroit	1967–68	40	39	43	82
Gordie Howe	Detroit	1969–70	42	31	40	71
Alex Delvecchio	Detroit	1972–73	40	18	53	71
Mark Messier	New York Rangers	2000–01	40	24	43	67
Dave Keon	Hartford	1979–80	40	10	52	62

*Current to 2008–09

6.38 True

Because of the sheer volume of team and individual records established by the Gretzky-led Oilers during their dynasty years of the 1980s, we tend to overlook the scoring prowess of the Islanders in their glory days. Between 1980 and 1983, the Isles, led by Mike Bossy, Bryan Trottier and Denis Potvin, scored an amazing 87 goals in just 19 final-round games to capture four Stanley Cups. By comparison, Edmonton's powerhouse needed more games (22) and scored fewer goals (85) to win its four championships.

6.39 False

Only four NHLers can say they played for all three Detroit teams in the NHL: Ebbie Goodfellow, Reg Noble, Larry Aurie and Herb Lewis. Before the winged wheel became synonymous with Detroit, the Red Wings had two names: the Cougars (1926–27 to 1929–30) and then the Falcons (1930–31 and 1931–32). Yet Detroit struggled under both names until grain millionaire James Norris purchased the franchise in 1932 and renamed the team the Red Wings. Norris chose a logo similar to the emblem of the Montreal Amateur Athletic Association, a sporting club of which he was a member. Also, the MAAA

Winged Wheelers had won the first Stanley Cup in 1893, and this became Norris's inspiration for his own NHL franchise. He kept long-time coach and general manager Jack Adams, who had already begun assembling a nucleus of players of championship stature. Adams then picked up Noble, Goodfellow, Aurie and Lewis in the late 1920s—who each wore the sweaters of all three Detroit teams. Noble was sold to the Montreal Maroons for $7,500 after just five games as a Red Wing in 1932, but Goodfellow won three Stanley Cups and captained the team in the late 1930s and early 1940s before becoming a player-coach. Adams paired wingers Aurie and Lewis in 1928, and for the next 11 seasons they played on Detroit's first line, each becoming team scoring leader at least once. Aurie and Lewis were centred first by Cooney Weiland and later by Marty Barry. With Weiland, Aurie and Lewis's line averaged just 150 pounds, but their playmaking often outshone Toronto's famous Kid Line. In 1935, Adams then stuck Barry betwen the two little wingers to give the unit more beef, and Detroit won consecutive Stanley Cups in 1935–36 and 1936–37.

6.40   True

Ken Doraty set a record that can never be broken when he scored an overtime hat trick in a game between the Toronto Maple Leafs and Ottawa Senators on January 16, 1934. In those days there were no sudden-death endings. Instead, the NHL tried to decide tie games with an extra 10-minute period. Doraty netted three totals in the overtime stanza and the Leafs won 7–4.

6.41   False

Centre Bernie Nicholls of Los Angeles was not voted to either the First or Second NHL All-Star Team in 1989, despite racking up 150 points on 70 goals and 80 assists to place fourth in league scoring. Mario Lemieux and Wayne Gretzky, who ranked one-two in the points parade, claimed the two All-Star centre positions.

6.42 False

As is the custom with reporting "upper- and lower-body" injuries, NHL teams typically play fast and loose with a player's height and weight, particularly when stats are smaller than the NHL average of six foot one and 201 pounds. Which explains why, though Sidney Crosby doesn't need any extra edge in stature among the league's elite, sources list his height as both five foot ten and five foot eleven. Despite the discrepancy, however, there was no issue of size at the 2005 NHL Entry Draft, where Crosby was selected first overall by Pittsburgh. Historically, several other number one picks were five foot eleven, but Crosby is the shortest first-overall draftee since Dale McCourt was chosen first by Detroit in 1977. McCourt is five foot ten.

6.43 True

While wearing the "A" for Chicago, Gilmour, once the heart and soul of the Maple Leafs, scored the Blackhawks' game-winner against Toronto at the Maple Leaf Gardens finale, February 13, 1999. Gilmour scored the Hawks' third goal in the 6–2 victory.

6.44 True

In a November 2006 *Hockey News* feature about his life after hockey, Gordie Howe revealed that he named his little dog, Rocket, after Howe's fiercest on-ice rival, Maurice Richard. (No word on whether Howe was able to teach the "cute little bugger" to fetch or heel, something the great Richard never tolerated from his NHL masters.)

6.45 False

Clutch-and-grab hockey has rarely paid heed to one of sports'
most exciting plays, the comeback. Before the crackdown on
fouls such as hooking and holding, the NHL never averaged
better than one comeback every 12.2 games, and in the least-
active year on record, 2001–02, it was once every 15.9 games.
But after the rule changed, teams trailing after two periods
won one every 8.4 games, or 147 in 1,230 contests, during
2005–06. Dallas had the best numbers with 12 comebacks,
followed by Los Angeles's 10.

6.46 True

The torch was truly passed from one era's superstar to the
next on April 2, 1980, when Lafleur and Gretzky each scored
their 50th goal of the season. It was the sixth and final time
Lafleur would score 50 and the first of nine for the Great One.

Game 6

The Last Original Six Survivor

WHO WAS THE LAST Original Six player (pre-1967) to play in the NHL? Unscramble the old-timers' names below by placing each letter in the correct order in the boxes (each name starts with the boldest letter), then unscramble the letters in the circled and diamond-shaped boxes. The circled boxes spell our secret Original Six survivor, and the diamond-shaped boxes, the team he played with his entire 17-year career. The letters in the darkened circles are his initials; the letter in the darkened triangle is the initial of his team's name. *Solutions are on page 561*

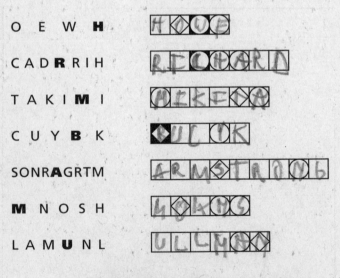

O E W **H**

CAD **R** RIH

T A K I **M** I

C U Y **B** K

SONR **A** GRTM

M N O S H

L A M **U** N L

of

162

7

Welcome Back, and a Few Goodbyes

THE IRONY OF BRETT HULL'S just-came-back-to-say-goodbye season of 2005–06 is that, after years of publicly admonishing the NHL for its defense-oriented play, diluted talent and poor marketing, when the league finally revamped its product with rules to increase scoring and speed of play, the Golden Brett was too old to play the NHL's new, exciting game. "Isn't that always the way it goes? The guy who pushes for the changes, who makes the world better, doesn't get to enjoy what he's worked for," said Dallas Stars centre Mike Modano. After 18 NHL seasons, Hull, age 41, played just five games for Phoenix post-lockout. As for Hull's legacy, only Wayne Gretzky and Gordie Howe have scored more than Hull's 741 career goals. In this chapter, we revisit the historic, born-again season of 2005–06.

Answers are on page 172

7.1 What is the greatest number of NHL games played in one night? (It happened in 2005–06.)

A. 12 games

B. 13 games

C. 14 games

D. 15 games

7.2 In 2005–06, the NHL's first season with a zero-tolerance policy on obstruction, teams enjoyed how many power plays compared to the previous season, 2003–04, when there were a league-wide 10,427 power-play opportunities?

A. There were fewer—between 8,000 and 10,000 power plays

B. There were the same—between 10,000 and 11,000 power plays

C. There were more—between 11,000 and 13,000 power plays

D. There were more than 13,000 power plays

7.3 In a January 2006 game against the Phoenix Coyotes, which NHL rookie did Wayne Gretzky call "a phenomenal player"—while describing one of his goals as "pretty sweet"?

A. Alexander Ovechkin, with the Washington Capitals

B. Dion Phaneuf, with the Calgary Flames

C. Sidney Crosby, with the Pittsburgh Penguins

D. Marek Svatos, with the Colorado Avalanche

7.4 In 2005–06, which NHLer claimed to have a Japanese samurai amongst his ancestors?

A. Sniper Paul Kariya

B. Tough guy Tie Domi

C. Goalie Jamie Storr

D. Big mouth Jeremy Roenick

7.5 In 2005–06, which NHL club celebrated a victory by sending its entire team onto the ice when the first star was announced after the game?

A. The Vancouver Canucks

B. The New York Rangers

C. The Buffalo Sabres

D. The Atlanta Thrashers

7.6 In 2005–06, which NHL goalie won a wager with his team's captain by eating a live cockroach?

A. Marty Turco, with the Dallas Stars
B. Vesa Toskala, with the San Jose Sharks
C. Ray Emery, with the Ottawa Senators
D. Cristobal Huet, with the Montreal Canadiens

7.7 What was the so-called "Shanahan Summit"?

A. A meeting between hockey aficionados to discuss making the game more exciting
B. A team of barnstorming All-Stars during the 2004–05 lockout
C. A nickname for the 2005 World Junior Championships
D. Brendan Shanahan's personal top 10 list of NHL snipers

7.8 In 2005–06, how many more faceoffs did Rod Brind'Amour take than any other player?

A. Less than 100 faceoffs
B. Between 100 and 200 faceoffs
C. Between 200 and 300 faceoffs
D. More than 300 faceoffs

7.9 What was the difference between Joe Thornton and Jonathan Cheechoo's salaries when they became San Jose linemates in 2005–06?

A. Less than US$1 million
B. Between US$1 and US$3 million
C. Between US$3 and US$5 million
D. More than US$5 million

7.10 Which NHL team served up the "Pizza Line" in 2005–06?

A. The San Jose Sharks

B. The Ottawa Senators

C. The Philadelphia Flyers

D. The Colorado Avalanche

7.11 During the lockout of 2004–05, who produced the "Bring It Back" TV commercials featuring abandoned 19,000-seat arenas and melting ice?

A. Molson

B. General Motors

C. Nike Canada

D. The NHL Players Association

7.12 In 2005–06, which NHL team set a regular-season record for most wins when trailing after 40 minutes?

A. The Dallas Stars

B. The New York Rangers

C. The Detroit Red Wings

D. The Toronto Maple Leafs

7. 13 Who scored the most shootout goals in 2005–06?

A. Sergei Zubov, with the Dallas Stars

B. Miroslav Satan, with the New York Islanders

C. Jussi Jokinen, with the Dallas Stars

D. Viktor Kozlov, with the New Jersey Devils

7.14 Under the new NHL rules adopted in 2005–06 governing shootouts, who is credited with the game-winning goal in a shootout win?

A. No one is credited

B. The first player to score in the shootout

C. The last player to score in the shootout

D. All players from the winning team who scored

7.15 **In 2005–06, how many consecutive games did Buffalo's Martin Biron win after switching his goalie stick brand?**

A. Four games in a row

B. Seven games in a row

C. 10 games in a row

D. 13 games in a row

7.16 **What 2005–06 story was hockey analyst Glenn Healy talking about when he said, "I got to buy some of those drugs that Boston's been smoking"?**

A. The 2006 Winter Olympics in Torino, Italy

B. The Joe Thornton trade

C. The firing of Bruin general manager Mike O'Connell

D. The NHL's new substance abuse program

7.17 **What is the most points recorded by an NHL team on a road trip?**

A. 13 points

B. 15 points

C. 17 points

D. 19 points

7.18 **What NHL first did rookie goalie James Howard of Detroit accomplish in his first two career games of 2005–06?**

A. He received two fighting majors

B. He faced two penalty shots

C. He earned assists in both games

D. He was involved in two shootouts

7.19 In 2005–06, in terms of ice time, which player—earning a minimum of US$450,000—delivered the best bang for the buck for his team?

A. Jamie Heward, with the Washington Capitals
B. Jarred Smithson, with the Nashville Predators
C. Cristobal Huet, with the Montreal Canadiens
D. Mark Hartigan, with the Columbus Blue Jackets

7.20 What is the NHL record for most victories by a netminder in one month?

A. Eight wins
B. 10 wins
C. 12 wins
D. 14 wins

7.21 Complete the following quote by veteran NHL defenseman Mathieu Dandenault, who, after playing his first game as a Montreal Canadien in 2005–06, said: "I don't really feel a part of Montreal yet," because . . . .

A. "I haven't moved into my condo."
B. "I haven't scored my first point here."
C. "I haven't won a Stanley Cup here."
D. "I haven't been booed yet."

7.22 What was Jaromir Jagr referring to in 2005–06 when he said, "I'll bet all my money they're legal"?

A. His pre-game meds
B. His elbow pads
C. His hockey sticks
D. His goaltender's leg pads

7.23 Who did Olli Jokinen credit for rescuing his NHL career, after the one-time Florida sniper signed a multi-year contract with the Panthers in 2005–06?

A. European scout Niklas Blomgren

B. General Manager Mike Keenan

C. Coach Jacques Martin

D. Veteran Joe Nieuwendyk

7.24 On March 3, 2006, the night Pat LaFontaine's number was retired in Buffalo, which Toronto Maple Leaf was playing in his 1,000th NHL game against the Sabres?

A. Tie Domi

B. Eric Lindros

C. Mats Sundin

D. Ed Belfour

7.25 After tying Terry Sawchuk's NHL-win record of 447 in November 2005, how many more games did Ed Belfour need to break the old-timer goalie's mark?

A. Two games

B. Four games

C. Six games

D. Eight games

7.26 How many victories did Ottawa goalie Ray Emery record to set the NHL mark for most consecutive wins from the start of a career?

A. Five consecutive wins

B. Seven consecutive wins

C. Nine consecutive wins

D. 11 consecutive wins

7.27 In 2005–06, what was the most shootout wins recorded by a goalie?

A. Seven shootout wins

B. Eight shootout wins

C. Nine shootout wins

D. 10 shootout wins

7.28 In 2005–06, how many rounds was the longest shootout?

A. Five rounds

B. 10 rounds

C. 15 rounds

D. 20 rounds

7.29 In 2005–06, which player scored the controversial shootout goal that brought about a video-review rule change?

A. Brad Richards

B. Jeremy Roenick

C. Alexander Ovechkin

D. Jussi Jokinen

7.30 Who is the first NHL rookie to lead the league in shots on goal since 1967–68?

A. Guy Lafleur, in 1971–72

B. Mike Bossy, in 1977–78

C. Wayne Gretzky, in 1979–80

D. Alexander Ovechkin, in 2005–06

7.31 In 2005-06, which NHL goalie donned a mask that was emblazoned with the image of a gangster holding a gun and smoking a cigar?

A. Antero Niittymaki, with the Philadelphia Flyers

B. Mathieu Garon, with the Los Angeles Kings

C. Manny Legace, with the Detroit Red Wings

D. Nikolai Khabibulin, with the Chicago Blackhawks

7.32 In 2005-06, who became the first NHL player to be awarded two penalty shots in one game?

A. Erik Cole, with the Carolina Hurricanes

B. Milan Hejduk, with the Colorado Avalanche

C. Ryan Smyth, with the Edmonton Oilers

D. Mike Modano, with the Dallas Stars

7.33 Which NHL team was Sidney Crosby's favourite when he was growing up?

A. The Montreal Canadiens

B. The New York Rangers

C. The Pittsburgh Penguins

D. The Toronto Maple Leafs

7.34 Which team recorded the NHL's first win by shootout?

A. The Toronto Maple Leafs

B. The Ottawa Senators

C. The Pittsburgh Penguins

D. The Calgary Flames

7.35 Several successful NHL teams iced rosters with multiple Europeans in 2005-06. What was the most players from one European country on an NHL team that season?

A. Five Europeans from one country

B. Six Europeans from one country

C. Seven Europeans from one country

D. Eight Europeans from one country

7.36 **Which NHL team record did the Detroit Red Wings break in 2005–06?**

A. Most wins in one season

B. Most road wins in one season

C. Fewest losses in one season

D. Most road losses in one season

7.37 **The average number of goals scored per game in the NHL rose from 5.1 to 6.1 in 2005–06. How many years has it been since the league had a season with a larger increase?**

A. 20 years

B. 35 years

C. 50 years

D. 75 years

Welcome Back, and a Few Goodbyes

Answers

7.1 **D. 15 games**

The NHL's strategy after emerging from the lockout that wiped out 2004–05 was a season-opening night unlike any other in the league's 87-year history. Several story lines dominated the headlines, including the Lightning finally raising its Stanley Cup banner in Tampa Bay; Wayne Gretzky's coaching debut; the first game of 18-year-old phenom Sidney Crosby; many new rules to crack down on fouls, and the first ever shootout. Also, to bring the fans back, ticket prices were slashed overall by 7.5 per cent, two-thirds of NHL clubs cut ticket costs and all 30 teams were in action on the same night for the first time since 1928–29, when the league had 10 teams. The 15-game total eclipsed the previous mark of

14, which had been done nine times. A record 275,447 fans showed up for the comeback celebration on October 5, 2005.

7.2 D. There were more than 13,000 power plays

When Stephen Walkom was appointed as the NHL's new director of officiating in August 2005, his directive was ice clear: stop all the hooking, holding and cross-checking by bringing in a consistent standard of rule enforcement for the entire season. That didn't mean no contact, either, it meant no fouling in the bump-and-grind play. And, if goals and power-play starts are any indication, Walkom realized his mandate: the crackdown on obstruction created more offensive opportunities in the following season, 2005–06. To prove it, here are a few numbers to bang around. Goal scoring was up 18 per cent, or one goal per game, from a five-year low of 5.1 goals per game in 2003–04 to 6.1 in 2005–06—the largest percentage increase since 1929–30. As well, there were 10,427 power plays in 2003–04 and 14,390 in 2005–06, a whopping leap of 28 per cent thanks to Walkom and the NHL's zero-tolerance edict. This led to 2,545 power-play goals—826 more than in 2003–04, when 1,717 were scored on the man-advantage.

7.3 A. Alexander Ovechkin, with the Washington Capitals

Wayne Gretzky knows something about greatness, so when he praises a player his comments reverberate throughout the hockey world. "You know, he's a phenomenal player and he's been a tremendous influence in the game," said Gretzky after his Phoenix Coyotes were whipped 6–1 by the Capitals in January 2006. The Great One was talking about Ovechkin's two-goal, three-point contribution in the win and, more specifically, the effort he made on the goal "that was pretty sweet." After being sent sprawling by a hit from Coyotes defenseman Paul Mara, the 20-year-old Russian slid past goalie Brian Boucher towards the corner boards, rolled from his back to his chest and tapped the puck with his stick blade in a blindsided effort to score from a near-impossible angle. The puck whipped past a startled Boucher, who had given up on the play. "I saw the net, then I saw the puck, but not at the same moment. I shot the puck without really knowing where the net or I was," said Ovechkin of what many have called the greatest goal of 2005–06.

7.4 C. Goalie Jamie Storr

Few NHLers are of Asian heritage, with Paul Kariya being the most famous. Less well-known is Philadelphia's Jamie Storr, who doesn't look part-Asian (like Kariya)—until he dons his mask, which is decorated with his mother's initials and Japan's Rising Sun on the back, fiery dragons on the side and, leaving no mistake as to his identity, his name written in Japanese on the front. But the mask and its oriental motif are just part of Storr's warrior arsenal. He claims to also have the blood of Japan's most famous soldiers in his veins. "I have been told that my mother's grandfather was a samurai, so I have the blood of a samurai," says Storr. Storr's mother and father met in Brampton, Ontario, in 1967. His mother, Keiko, was born December 7, 1941—the day Japan bombed Pearl Harbour.

7.5 C. The Buffalo Sabres

It's the kind of team spirit that coaches kill for. After stressing production in even-strength situations, Buffalo coach Lindy Ruff saw his Sabres annihilate the Los Angeles Kings 10–1 on January 14, 2006, with six even-strength goals, three more on the power play and another on a shorthanded breakaway. "Pretty well everyone chipped in," said Ruff. "It was a great team effort from top to bottom. The forward lines did a lot of work down low, controlled play, cycled the puck and got rewarded for it." Rookie forward Jason Pominville and Jochen Hecht scored three goals apiece, and Pominville with a natural hat trick. "It's awesome," said Pominville. "It doesn't happen too often. So it's fun to see the team work hard and have it finally pay off." Twelve Sabres earned 27 individual points, while Chris Drury got the third star and Pominville the second. When Hecht was named the game's first star, the entire team then skated onto the ice. "It was a good night for everybody on our team," said Hecht. "Everybody played hard and everybody deserved the first star."

7.6 C. Ray Emery, with the Ottawa Senators

His teammates already knew Ray Emery was a different kind of character, but just how different became clear when the Senators goalkeeper accepted a $500 bet from captain Daniel Alfredsson to gobble a cockroach that had scuttled across the floor of the team's dressing room during an October 2005 game against the Carolina Hurricanes. "I'd crush on *Fear Factor*," said Emery, who used the $500 to obtain an elaborate new tattoo on his right arm that reads "Anger Is a Gift." The choice of tattoo probably didn't sit well with Ottawa's coaching staff, as they'd ordered Emery to take an anger management course.

7.7 A. A meeting between hockey aficionados to discuss making the game more exciting

NHL fans knew the league had finally got it right after witnessing the first night of hockey in 2005–06. In Nashville's opener, Steve Sullivan took the puck in San Jose's corner, faked out Sharks winger Marco Sturm and turned defenseman Tom Preissing into a pretzel before sliding a pass to winger Scott Walker at the far post for a tap-in. Sullivan later said that, a few years earlier, he would have been sticked between the legs and pinned against the glass after his second move—exactly the kind of clutch-and-grab hockey Brendan Shanahan was trying to eliminate when he organized a two-day conference of players, coaches, GMs, on-ice officials and media in December 2004. Shanahan's credibility as a veteran scorer, tough guy and Cup-winner made him the perfect player to pull together such a diverse group to share ideas on how to open up the game and make hockey fun again, as with Sullivan's "dipsy-dos" on the tap-in goal by Walker. Shanahan wasn't solely responsible for the crackdown on interference or the other rule changes that tweaked the game in 2005–06, but his summit established the NHL competition committee that was the first step in injecting more entertainment into the game.

7.8 D. More than 300 faceoffs

There's not much that Rod Brind'Amour didn't do for Carolina in 2005–06—or, for that matter, any team the two-way centre played for in his lengthy NHL career. That's because the versatile Brind'Amour never took a game off. Even at age 35, he led all forwards in ice time, with an average of 24:29 per game in 2005–06. And those numbers were usually earned against the other team's top line, including on penalty kills and faceoffs, which Brind'Amour managed 2,145 times—winning 1,267 of them, almost 350 more faceoffs than any NHLer, for a winning percentage of 59.11 in 2005–06. He was also the Hurricanes' triggerman on 44 per cent of their draws, besting rival Joe Thornton, who had 37 per cent of San Jose's faceoffs. (The NHL has been keeping statistics on faceoffs since 1997–98.)

7.9 D. More than US$5 million

No matter how good a tandem looks on paper, teaming your best shooter with your top playmaker isn't always successful. In fact, finding the right chemistry between players usually happens by accident, because a great scoring duo—with each player feeding off the other—demands a skill set that can't be practised or taught. Which is why San Jose's blockbuster trade for Joe Thornton in November 2005 and his subsequent pairing with Jonathan Cheechoo proved more a stroke of luck than genius. In theory, superstar centre Thornton would be double-teamed, providing more space for Cheechoo to score, while Thornton, a left-shooting centre, would complement Cheechoo's right shot. But in reality, the pair clicked from the start. While Thornton drew the fire, he could still make seam passes into quiet areas that Cheechoo skated into to get an open shot and finish the play—making the duo the league's most lethal twosome and turning Cheechoo into a bona fide sniper. The pair captured NHL trophies as point and goal leaders, with Thornton amassing a league-high 125 points and Cheechoo besting all scorers with 56 goals (Thornton assisted on 38 of them). But salary-wise, the two couldn't be much further apart. When they became linemates, Thornton was earning us$6.66 million and Cheechoo, us$760,000—a us$5.9-million difference. Late in 2005–06, Cheechoo signed a five-year us$15-million contract extension. Good thinking.

7.10 **B. The Ottawa Senators**

When the Senators line of Daniel Alfredsson, Jason Spezza and Dany Heatley began running roughshod over the opposition early in the 2005–06 season, the *Ottawa Citizen* ran a contest to find a name for the high-powered trio. Unfortunately, the winning entry, the Cash Line, generated little enthusiasm. Instead, many people referred to the trio as the Pizza Line. That's because, for several years, the pizza chain Pizza Pizza had been running a promotion that awarded a free slice of pie to every fan with a ticket stub for an Ottawa home victory in which the team scored five or more goals. And initially, the low-scoring Senators were no threat to Pizza Pizza's ovens.

However, in 2005–06, the Sens reached the magic number five in their first three games. So, fearing a loss of dough, in the literal sense, Pizza Pizza changed its slice standard to six goals. But with Alfredsson, Spezza and Heatley lighting the lamp, the team hit the six-goal mark six times in its first 19 home games, filling fans' stomachs and giving Pizza Pizza a steady dose of acid indigestion.

7.11   C. Nike Canada

During the NHL lockout, the Canadian airwaves were saturated with commercials lamenting the lack of hockey, such as Molson Canadian's 30-second montage of weepy fans singing the 1980s Culture Club hit "Do You Really Want to Hurt Me?" in the beer-maker's "Hockey, Please Come Back" campaign. But Nike made a more forceful appeal to Canadians and their collective passion for hockey with its simple "Bring It Back" spot, which featured the stark image of a vacant arena interior— silent except for the crackle of melting ice.

7.12   A. The Dallas Stars

Mike Modano nailed it when he said, "We just keep finding ways to dig ourselves out of holes." In fact, the 2005–06 Dallas Stars were regular-season backhoes when entering the third period behind: first tying the NHL record with their ninth come-from-behind victory in a 2–1 win against Vancouver on March 11, then, with a 4–3 win against San Jose on March 18, 2006, breaking the benchmark held by both the 2001–02 Toronto Maple Leafs and 2002–03 Boston Bruins. "I think all nine of them have been different, whether it's getting bombed early and me getting pulled or a tight game like [Saturday's]," goalie Marty Turco told the *Dallas Morning News* after the March 11 win. The Stars' record-setting 10th win when trailing after 40 minutes was won in a shootout and without the help of Jussi Jokinen, who surprisingly missed his attempt after converting his first nine shootout chances. In fact, four of the record 10 comeback wins were by shootout, which only debuted in 2005–06. Dallas also maintained a perfect record with an NHL-best 10–0 in shootouts. (The record for most wins by a team trailing after 40 minutes is unofficial and probably only dates back to the 1990s.)

7.13   C. Jussi Jokinen, with the Dallas Stars

Without question, the most anticipated rule change in 2005–06 was the introduction of the shootout. The controversial one-on-one tiebreaker had fans standing in their seats and traditionalists condemning it as anti-team and, even, unhockeylike. Sure. Meanwhile, little-known Jussi Jokinen turned goalies inside out and converted a perfect nine of nine shootouts, until late season, when on March 18 he missed the net on his 10th attempt against San Jose's Vesa Toskala. Jokinen was merely mortal after that, finishing the year with a league-high 10 shootout goals on 13 tries for a stellar 76.9 shoot-percentage, the highest of any player with six or more attempts. The Oilers' Alex Hemsky led all shooters with 14 tries, but scored only five times, for a 35.7 per cent scoring ratio. Surprisingly, the worst shooter was Colorado sniper Joe Sakic, who was held scoreless on seven attempts.

7.14   A. No one is credited

Shootout goals and goals-against are not credited in individual statistics. According to Rule 89b, Note 6, the player who scores the game-winner in a shootout does not receive credit for the goal in his personal stats, and the losing goalkeeper is not charged with the extra goal-against. Further, regardless of the number of goals scored during the shootout, the final score is always a one-goal difference between opponents, based on the score at the end of overtime. The visiting team shoots first. In 2005–06, there were 330 goals on 981 attempts, with goalies stopping two of every three shots. Edmonton played a league-high 16 games, going 7–9; Dallas netted the most shootout wins, with a 12–1 record.

7.15 D. 13 games in a row

Martin Biron is no hockey pitchman—until it comes to talking about his Montreal-brand goalie paddle. And why shouldn't he be effusive about the Finnish hockey equipment manufacturer? After the Sabres goalie switched to Montreal's composite shaft—with wooden paddle and blade—in early November 2005, he went on a 13-game tear between November 15 and December 17. Not that Biron wasn't happy with his Koho-ccm sticks; he just got a little bored waiting for a start as backup to number one man Ryan Miller. That boredom got Biron talking to Buffalo defenseman Teppo Numminen—the owner, product tester and player representative for Montreal Sports in the North American market. Brion got his new sticks almost at the same time as Miller went down with a broken right thumb, a lucky break for Biron. The Sabres gelled and Biron earned the longest streak by an NHL goalie since Detroit's Chris Osgood won the same number in 1995–96. During that stretch, Buffalo won nine road games, almost equalling its own NHL record of 10, set in 1983–84.

7.16 B. The Joe Thornton trade

The deal stunned everyone. First, because it was Joe Thornton, the face of the Boston franchise. Then, because Boston's star captain had just signed a three-year contract worth us$20 million. And finally, because of what the Bruins received in return. Frankly, it looked like a bag of pucks. But Wayne Primeau, Marco Strum and Brad Stuart injected life into the underachieving Bruins as the season progressed. Still, in 532 career games, Thornton had 454 points, just 108 fewer than the combined totals of Primeau, Strum and Stuart, who played in 918 more games than the hulking forward centre. The deal had Glenn Healy wondering what herb the Bruins' executives were ingesting to make them believe that dealing Thornton was a good idea. It wasn't, and, late in the season, Boston general manager Mike O'Connell was fired.

7.17   **C. 17 points**

The Philadelphia Flyers were road warriors during a gruelling three-week, 11-game marathon in 2005–06, notching an impressive 8–2–0–1 record to claim honours for the most productive road trip in NHL history. No team in league annals has come home with 17 points. But NHL schedulers take note: the Flyers' tank was running on empty. Philadelphia lost two of its last three away games and its return to the Wachovia Center was a disaster, with the club dropping its first three home games and losing in overtime to Colorado, in a shootout to Carolina and in regulation time to Boston. Philadelphia's 11-game swing matched the longest trip in modern NHL history. Eighteen years earlier, the Calgary Flames played 11 consecutive games away from the Saddledome when, in February 1988, the Winter Olympics came to town. But they didn't fare as well, going 5–5–1 for 11 points.

7.18   **B. He faced two penalty shots**

A few goalies in NHL history have faced back-to-back penalty shots in consecutive games, and, in one case, two in one game. But in an NHL first of its kind for a rookie, James Howard faced penalty shots in his first two career starts. In his NHL debut, against Los Angeles on November 28, 2005, Howard gave up a goal to Joe Corvo on a penalty shot in a

5–2 win. Then, in his next game, on December 1, the Red Wing freshman went one-on-one with Calgary's Shean Donovan, who failed to convert on his attempt with 1:11 remaining. Donovan never got his shot off, but the Flames won 3–2.

7.19   **A. Jamie Heward, with the Washington Capitals**
Among minimum-salary players in 2005–2006, Jamie Heward more than proved his value for Washington. After stops in four NHL cities and three Swiss clubs, the us$450,000-defenseman led the Capitals with 21:51 minutes per game, ranked 22nd in the NHL with 29.0 shifts per game, recorded 140 shots on goal and blocked more than 100. He also recorded seven goals on 28 points—a career high. But Cristobal Huet was a strong challenger. The Montreal goalie, who earned just above minimum compensation (us$456,000), led the league with a .929 save percentage in 36 games and took the Canadiens to a playoff spot after a seventh-place finish in the Eastern Conference.

7.20   **C. 12 wins**
Ray Emery was once known only as Domink Hasek's backup. However, that lowly status changed in late 2005–06, whe he exploded onto the scene with a torrid March campaign. Emery was named defensive player of the month and rookie of the month after leading all goaltenders with a 12–2–2 record, including two shutouts, a 2.09 goals-against average and a .925 save percentage. His 12 wins also tied a league record for most victories in a calendar month, set first by Bernie Parent, with Philadelphia, in March 1974.

7.21   **D. "I haven't been booed yet."**
He said it with a grin, but Mathieu Dandenault knows how harsh the media spotlight can be on a French player with the Canadiens and how fast Montreal's loyal fans can jump on an

underachiever. That kind of attention turned his defensive predecessor, the much-maligned Patrice Bresebois, into a human bull's-eye and finally forced him into hockey anonymity in blissful Denver. As one Montreal scribe stated: "If you haven't been booed, you're not a Canadien." Patrick Roy was also driven out of town by boos one famously fateful night in Montreal in 1995, and Hall of Famer Bernie Geoffrion got the Forum boobirds chirping for having the nerve to win the scoring title from Maurice Richard in 1955. Tough crowd, those Frenchies.

7.22 C. His hockey sticks

After making headlines in 2004 for an online gambling habit that drained him of a reputed us$500,000, Jaromir Jagr should probably think twice about further references to betting—or to using illegal sticks. His bravado may have cost the Rangers two points and a win in their game against Atlanta on March 8, 2006. Referee Don Koharski, who nailed Jagr twice for using an illegal stick, penalized him during overtime and then disqualified him in the shootout in the 3–2 loss to the Thrashers. Asked if the illegal-stick call felled the Rangers, New York coach Tom Renney said, "Jag's a pretty good scorer. He had a better than 50–50 chance of scoring, so yeah, maybe." But it was not Jagr's first offense for playing with a banned blade. After the Capitals called for a measurement in a game against Washington on November 26, 2005, the five-time scoring champion was nabbed with a prohibited stick at the start of overtime. After that game, Caps goalie Ollie Kolzig said, "We played with him for three years so we all knew." After the Olympic break in 2006, the NHL instituted a rule requiring that all players involved in shootouts must have their sticks measured. As well, sticks must not have more than a half-inch curve.

7.23   B. General Manager Mike Keenan

Iron Mike was notorious for his motivational strategies. And
though his hard-line approach failed to inspire several notable
underachievers, many of his whipping boys matured under
his demanding tutelage. Still, Keenan's whine mellowed with
age. With the Panthers, his seventh team, he used a new, softer
approach to rejuvenate the career of Olli Jokinen, for example,
a fading prospect who was on his third club in four years.
Keenan gave Jokinen more ice time and named him captain.
The Finn responded stat-wise and, at the 2006 trading deadline, showed that his loyalty went beyond big money. "Before
Mike came here I was playing fourth line," Jokinen said in a
National Post story. "...he really pushed me hard and gave me
all kinds of chances to play, and I proved what kind of player I
am." Jokinen's new contract was a four-year us$21-million deal,
though soon after, the Panthers axed Keenan. In 2008, Jokinen
was moved to Phoenix, and later that season was traded again,
rejoining Keenan, this time as a member of the Calgary Flames.

7.24   A. Tie Domi

Few thought Tie Domi would ever achieve the 1,000-game
milestone. The odds of long-term NHL success usually run
against any player with a fists-first philosophy. But Domi
proved to be more than tough. He matched his pugilistic
skills with a tireless work ethic and hard-driving ambition
that kept him in a Maple Leaf uniform longer than any other
teammate except Mats Sundin. It's a notable achievement,
considering Domi only scored his 100th goal in October 2005,
almost 15 years after his first. Still, the fourth-line winger with
3,515 career penalty minutes couldn't inspire Toronto. They
were outclassed 6–2 in Domi's 1,000th game against Buffalo, a
team celebrating its own past beneath the freshly hung banner of Pat LaFontaine's No. 16.

7.25   C. Six games

The game had 15 goals, 14 power plays and four lead changes, but when it was finally over, Ed Belfour had secured his place in history. The 40-year-old goalie's 448th career-win came in a 9–6 victory against the New York Islanders on December 19, 2005—a feat that took Belfour six tries in a three-week span to accomplish after tying the great Terry Sawchuk with win number 447 on November 28. "It took forever," said Belfour. "The guys just played unbelievable. It took nine goals, but I'm really thankful and honoured."

7.26   C. Nine consecutive wins

It took Ray Emery four years, but the Ottawa rookie didn't complain, considering his real estate in the record books. After going 1–0–0 as backup to Patrick Lalime in 2002–03 and 2–0–0 for his second and third career wins in 2003–04, Emery went on a 6–0 tear in early 2005–06 for nine straight wins, erasing Bob Froese's record run with Philadelphia of eight straight wins from a career start. Emery capped the record with his first NHL shutout, a 4–0 whitewash versus Montreal on November 29, 2005.

7.27   B. Eight shootout wins

During the first shootout season, three goalies shared the lead with eight wins: Dallas's Marty Turco, Martin Brodeur of New Jersey and the Islanders' Rick DiPietro. Brodeur and DiPietro, who played in a league-high 11 games, each had three losses; Turco registered only one. DiPietro faced the most shots (41) and Brodeur had the best save percentage (.763) of the three. Washington's Olaf Kolzig, with four wins and five losses, had 44 shots-against in one-on-one play, the most amongst all netminders. But the season's big surprise was star netminder Miikka Kiprusoff of Calgary, who netted only one win in eight shootout games and allowed 12 goals on 23 shots. It was the worst save percentage (.478) among goalies with at least one shootout victory in 2005–06.

7.28   **C. 15 rounds**

During its first season featuring the shootout format to determine the outcome of tied games, the NHL recorded 145 matches involving shootouts, though none longer than the marathon 15-round duel between the New York Rangers and Washington Capitals on November 26. Based on the new rules, if the score remains tied after each team has taken three shots, the shootout proceeds to a sudden-death format with each team shooting once in successive rounds. A winner is declared only when one team scores in the round. In the New York–Washington game, rookie netminder Henrik Lundqvist went head-to-head against counterpart Olie Kolzig as the Rangers' Michael Nylander, Ville Nieminen and Jason Strudwick all scored to keep the shootout going, with Nylander matching the Capitals' Andrew Cassels goal in the second round, Nieminen equalling Brian Willsie's sixth-round score and Strudwick countering Bryan Muir's 14th-round goal. Then, in the 15th round, after the Caps' Matt Bradley wrist shot failed, defenseman Marek Malik fooled Kolzig on a trick shot with his stick between his skates. "I was watching everything before me," said Malik, the third-to-last shooter available on the Ranger bench. "Olie was unbelievable. He stopped everything, from shots, moves. I just thought to myself, 'Maybe I'll surprise him.' I tried the move and it worked." It was Malik's first goal of the regular season. "You have to have guts to do that move," said Jaromir Jagr. "In front of 20,000 people watching you, it's not that easy to do." The trick goal ended the NHL's longest shootout in the 15th round to give New York a 3–2 win over Washington. "It was actually kind of fun," said loser Kolzig to the Associated Press. "On this stage, Madison Square Garden, Saturday night ... I didn't expect Malik to pull off a move like that.

7.29   B. Jeremy Roenick

Hockey would be something less than it is without Jeremy Roenick. The skating mouthpiece with the flashy hockey skills brings opinion, drama and passion to the game every night. Not surprisingly, he is also no stranger to controversy. So Roenick's move to Los Angeles in 2005–06 seemed inspired, except for the fact that it produced one of his lowest scoring seasons. Among the highlights: his controversial shootout goal against Nashville on November 5, 2005. Replays showed Roenick scored on a rebound by playing the puck twice in a fall that sent Predator goalie Tomas Vokoun into the net with the puck. The NHL later made the first in-season rule change to allow video reviews of shootouts.

7.30   D. Alexander Ovechkin, in 2005–06

Only the combination of a once-in-a-generation player on a scoring-challenged team in rebuilding mode, playing under nearly obstruction-free rules, could produce such an NHL first. Along with numerous other NHL and franchise rookie records, Washington's Alexander Ovechkin broke the league rookie mark for most shots in a season. In a 4–3 loss to Carolina on April 5, 2006, he recorded five shots to total 388, one more than Teemu Selanne's freshman mark of 387 in 1992–93. Then, with seven games remaining in the Capitals' schedule, Ovechkin notched another 37 for a league-best 425 shots in 2005–06. Ovechkin is the only rookie to top all players in one season since shot counts were first tabulated in 1967–68, with his highest total coming against Tampa Bay on March 23, 2006, when he tallied 13 shots. It's not an official record, but it is considered the most by any player since Brian Leetch's 13 in a game against Washington on January 4, 1989. (Ray Bourque is said to have netted an unofficial record of 19 against Quebec, on March 21, 1991.)

7.31 A. Antero Niittymaki, with the Philadelphia Flyers

When Antero Nittymaki played in Finland, his nickname was Antsu, but during his short NHL stint in February 2004, Flyers coach Ken Hitchcock started calling Nittymaki "Frank," after the infamous Prohibition-era mobster Frank Nitti. Once Nittymaki understood what the nickname meant, he had his mask repainted with a gangster theme. The design depicts Frank Nitti smoking a cigar and holding a gun, with smoking bullets below. Said Hitchcock: "I guess I was the first to call him that. I never thought in my wildest dreams he would go and put it on his bloody mask."

7.32 A. Erik Cole, with the Carolina Hurricanes

Erik Cole became the first player with two penalty shots in one NHL game, scoring on the first as the Hurricanes chalked up a franchise-record eighth straight victory, a 5–3 win over the Buffalo Sabres on November 9, 2005. The Carolina winger was awarded the first shot while his club was shorthanded in the third period, after being hauled down from behind by Jochen Hecht. The goal gave the Hurricanes a 4–1 lead. Later in the third, Cole was hooked by Dmitri Kalinin and granted another penalty shot, which was foiled by Martin Biron. "I made the move I wanted, but not the shot I wanted," said Cole. In his next game, two nights later, Cole earned yet another penalty shot. But he couldn't beat Florida's Roberto Luongo.

7.33   A. The Montreal Canadiens

As a youngster, Sidney Crosby's favourite players were Wayne
Gretzky, Steve Yzerman and Mario Lemieux—but the team
he dreamed of playing for was the Montreal Canadiens. That
fantasy didn't materialize. Crosby's first NHL game against
Montreal, on November 10, 2005, however, did have a fairy
tale ending. The 18-year-old sensation scored the first goal
of the contest and later notched the game-winner, with the
Penguins posting a 3–2 shootout victory on home ice. After
teammates Mark Recchi and Mario Lemieux were denied
by Canadien goalie José Théodore, Crosby skated in, faked
Théodore to his knees and roofed a backhand into the top of
the net—sending the netminder's water bottle skyward and
the Mellon Arena crowd into a frenzy. "It's so amazing, it's
hard to believe," Crosby said later. "I was just fortunate to get
that shot. I got lucky with that shot."

7.34   B. The Ottawa Senators

The first shootout win in NHL history went to Ottawa on the
first night of NHL play in 2005–06. With Toronto 2–2 and 1:02
remaining in regulation time, Daniel Alfredsson scored to
tie the game. Then, after a scoreless five-minute overtime,
the Ottawa captain connected again on the Senators' first
attempt under the new shootout format to settle tied games.
The Leafs' Jason Allison and Eric Lindros failed in their efforts
against Dominik Hasek, but Dany Heatley scored on Ottawa's
third chance, clinching the win with two points for the
Senators. Toronto coach Pat Quinn, no fan of the shootout,
was diplomatic about the outcome, saying, "I'm not one of the
ones that like the game being settled this way." The Leafs' Ed
Belfour is the first netminder in NHL history to suffer a shootout loss. Heatley and Alfredsson's sticks were subsequently
sent to the Hockey Hall of Fame.

7.35 C. Seven Europeans from one country

Not since Scotty Bowman successfully united the Russian Five of Igor Larionov, Vladimir Konstantinov, Slava Fetisov, Slava Kozlov and Sergei Fedorov on the Detroit Red Wings have NHL teams been so Euro-centric as in 2005–06. European players have a home on every NHL roster, but the New York Rangers, Detroit Red Wings and Dallas Stars took Bowman's original plan to heart and injected their lineup with as many as seven regulars from one European country. Although some called them the Czech Rangers, Swedish Red Wings and Finnish Stars, "It's not a master plan" said Detroit general manager Ken Holland in a *USA Today* interview. "We never said we want to get seven Swedes, but when we got four or five and they played well, you start to think, 'If you grow up playing a similar style of hockey, you might have pretty good on-ice chemistry.'"

Teams with Most Europeans from One Country in 2005–06

TEAM	COUNTRY	NUMBER OF PLAYERS
Detroit	Sweden	7—Nicklas Lidstrom, Henrik Zetterberg, Tomas Holmstrom, Mikael Samuelsson, Niklas Kronwall, Andreas Lilja and Johan Franzen
NYR	Czech Republic	7—Jaromir Jagr, Martin Straka, Martin Rucinsky, Petr Sykora, Petr Prucha, Marek Malik and Michal Rozsival
Dallas	Finland	6—Jere Lehtinen, Jussi Jokinen, Niko Kapanen, Antti Miettinen, Niklas Hagman and Janne Niinimaa

7.36 B. Most road wins in one season

One of the teams expected to be hit hardest by the NHL's new economic structure in 2005–06 was Detroit. But the free-spending Red Wings showed surprising resiliency under the league's US$39-million salary cap. Defenseman Mathieu Schneider may have had the best answer when he said,

"I think the reality is, guys really want to play here." As a result, the Red Wings kept many core players, including Pavel Datsyuk, Brendan Shanahan, Henrik Zetterberg, Nicklas Lidstrom and Manny Legace, who netted an NHL-record 10 wins in October to hand Detroit an early lead in the Western Conference. Another key to success was coach Mike Babcock, who kept his club poised against third-period comebacks with his "Keep your foot on the gas, just keep playing" philosophy to avoid falling into a defensive shell. As a result, Detroit scored more goals in the third period (107) than any other frame, finished second behind Ottawa in total shots (2,796) and outshot opponents a league-high 62 times in 82 games. The Wings also became the all-time-best road warriors, tying New Jersey's 28-win mark in 1998–99 on April 3 with a 2–1 shootout win against Calgary and then setting a new high of 31 victories on the road to cap 2005–06.

7.37   D. 75 years

The rule changes introduced by the NHL to boost offense after the lockout wiped out the 2004–05 season proved a smashing success. Teams scored a total of 7,443 goals in 2005–06, an average of 6.1 per game and an 18 per cent increase over the average of 5.1 goals scored in 2003–04. The rise marked the largest percentage-increase in goal scoring since 1929–30, when the goals-per-game average jumped from 2.9 to 5.9 thanks to a new rule that permitted forward passing inside all three zones. The boost in overall goal scoring was reflected in substantial point-total increases by numerous players, including Carolina's Eric Staal, who posted the biggest jump of 69 points. All told, five players recorded 50 goals, the most since eight players reached the mark in 1995–96.

Game 7

Lockout Lingo

THE DEFINITIVE QUOTE of 2004–05's NHL labour dispute may be in the *2006 NHL Guide and Record Book.* Opposite the year 2004–05, atop the list of previous Stanley Cup winners and team rosters dating back to 1892, is the line "No Cup Winner." In this game, match the individuals below with their familiar quotes about hockey's longest lockout.   *Solutions are on page 561*

PART 1

Flyers goalie Robert Esche

LA Kings forward Sean Avery

Former NHL great Marcel Dionne

Mike Lupica, the *New York Daily News*

Ottawa enforcer Rob Ray

Wayne Gretzky

TV host Jay Leno

1. __RE__ "I think there are a lot of great owners out there, but there's a madman leading them down the wrong path."

2. __OL__ "Fans are disappointed, but the action is expected to save over 3,000 teeth."

3. __WG__ "I felt, OK, maybe Mario and I don't have the answers... I just feel disappointed and, quite frankly, I'm a little embarrassed."

4. __RR__ "I'd cross the line in a second. Why wouldn't I?"

5. __MD__ "Why should you pay a kid, coming out of junior, who hasn't done anything, a million bucks?"

6. *HC* "I still say the (New York) Rangers haven't looked this good in the month of March since '94."

7. *SH* "We burned a year for nothing. We didn't win anything. We didn't prove anything. We didn't get anything. We wasted an entire season."

PART 2

Flyers GM Bobby Clarke

Gary Bettman

Greg Cote, the *Miami Herald*

Bob Goodenow

Devils GM Lou Lamoriello

Jim Armstrong, the *Denver Post*

All-time minor-league goal leader Kevin Kerr

1. *BG* "Players are not greedy."

2. *JA* "Sure, a lot of people have been hurt by the NHL lockout, but the ones I really feel for are Canadian. I mean, how much curling can a man take?"

3. *KK* "I'll come and play for thirty grand and a jersey and meal money, just to say I had a chance to play in the NHL... Maybe they'll realize what it means for some of us guys to play in the NHL."

4. *BC* "Someone has to grab Goodenow by the throat and tell him, 'Look after the Canadian cities.'"

5. *GC* "The NHL and its players are still meeting, with discussions now centring on a two-game regular season followed by a one-period sudden-death playoff."

6. *CL* "All we have to do to solve [the problem] is to do what the cardinals are doing to get a new Pope. They are not leaving the room until there is white smoke."

7. *GB* "If we don't have a new CBA, so that our players can start the season with us in October, we will not open on time."

8

The Rearguards

DURING THE SIX-TEAM ERA, a defenseman's primary role was to take care of his own end. Traditional rearguards, such as Allan Stanley, Leo Boivin and Butch Bouchard, for example, plied their trade with heavy hits and solid backchecking, and in the process produced some of the most competitive low-scoring games in the history of hockey. But there was another, smaller, group of intrepid blueliners, whose on-ice skills surpassed the standard defensive and positional play of their contemporaries. These players could control the tempo and flow of a game—by leading a headlong rush through traffic or delivering pinpoint passing right on the tape. And if Bobby Orr changed hockey by reinventing how his position was played, he did it in the tradition of these maverick D-men, an elite cadre that includes Doug Harvey, Pierre Pilote and Tim Horton. In this chapter, we champion the offensive strengths of some of the NHL's best defensemen—and a few others worth remembering.

Answers are on page 202

8.1 Who was the first defenseman in NHL history to score 20 goals in a season?
A. Doug Mohns
B. Frank "Flash" Hollett
C. Pat Egan
D. Red Kelly

8.2   Why did Bobby Orr wear sweater No. 4?

    A.   Boston rookies were given the lowest number available

    B.   Orr was No. 4 with the OHA Oshawa Generals

    C.   Four is Orr's lucky number

    D.   Orr was handed the number after a veteran defenseman didn't make the team

8.3   In 2006–07, which NHL defenseman became the new iron-man among blueliners?

    A.   Cory Sarich, with the Tampa Bay Lightning

    B.   Mathieu Dandenault, with the Montreal Canadiens

    C.   Karlis Skrastins, with the Colorado Avalanche

    D.   Chris Chelios, with the Detroit Red Wings

8.4   Which defenseman scored the most goals in one season during the 1990s?

    A.   Sandis Ozolinsh

    B.   Al MacInnis

    C.   Gary Suter

    D.   Kevin Hatcher

8.5   Defensemen in old-time hockey once lined up behind one another on faceoffs, rather than side by side. What brought about the change?

    A.   A few multi-sport athletes from Canadian football

    B.   Hockey's seventh position, the rover, was eliminated

    C.   The advent of the faceoff circle

    D.   There were too many injuries

8.6 If Wayne Gretzky's 51-game consecutive-point-scoring streak is the NHL record for all skaters, what is the longest point-scoring streak for a defenseman? Name the record holder, too.

A. Eight games

B. 18 games

C. 28 games

D. 38 games

8.7 Only Bobby Orr and Paul Coffey have cracked the 40-goal plateau. Which other defenseman failed to reach 40 goals in a season by just one goal?

A. Kevin Hatcher

B. Ray Bourque

C. Doug Wilson

D. Denis Potvin

8.8 What is the record for most goals by a defenseman in one season?

A. 46 goals

B. 48 goals

C. 50 goals

D. 52 goals

8.9 Which rearguard held the NHL scoring record for most points in a season before Bobby Orr broke it in 1968–69?

A. Pierre Pilote, with the Chicago Blackhawks

B. Babe Pratt, with the Toronto Maple Leafs

C. Doug Mohns, with the Chicago Blackhawks

D. Red Kelly, with the Detroit Red Wings

8.10 During his 15-year NHL career, how many goals did stay-at-home defenseman Brad Marsh score?

    A. Three goals

    B. 23 goals

    C. 43 goals

    D. 123 goals

8.11 As of 2007–08, who was the last defenseman to win the Hart Trophy as league MVP?

    A. Bobby Orr, with the Boston Bruins

    B. Denis Potvin, with the New York Islanders

    C. Ray Bourque, with the Boston Bruins

    D. Chris Pronger, with the St. Louis Blues

8.12 In 2002–03, which Montreal defenseman did Canadiens fans nickname "Breeze-By"?

    A. Karl Dykhuis

    B. Patrice Brisebois

    C. Stephane Quintal

    D. Patrick Traverse

8.13 As of 2008–09, which same-team duo most recently finished one-two atop the NHL scoring list for defensemen in the same season?

    A. Scott Niedermayer and Chris Pronger, with Anaheim, in 2006–07

    B. Nicklas Lidstrom and Chris Chelios, with Detroit, in 2001–02

    C. Gary Suter and Al MacInnis, with Calgary, in 1987–88

    D. Bobby Orr and Carol Vadnais, with Boston, in 1974–75

8.14 After playing his last game in 1947, which old-time defenseman was immediately inducted into the Hockey Hall of Fame and had his number retired by his team?

A. Eddie Shore, with the Boston Bruins
B. Dit Clapper, with the Boston Bruins
C. Lester Patrick, with the New York Rangers
D. Howie Morenz, with the Montreal Canadiens

8.15 Besides Bobby Orr, how many other defensemen in NHL history were regular-season offensive leaders, either in goals, assists or points?

A. None, Bobby Orr is the only one
B. Two defensemen
C. Four defensemen
D. Six defensemen

8.16 In modern-era hockey, what is the greatest number of defensemen to rank among the NHL's top 10 scorers in one season?

A. There has never been more than one defenseman in the top 10
B. Two defensemen
C. Three defensemen
D. Four defensemen

8.17 As of 2008–09, who was the last defenseman to finish in the top 10 of NHL scoring leaders?

A. Paul Coffey
B. Al MacInnis
C. Brian Leetch
D. Nicklas Lidstrom

8.18 Which two defensemen in 1998–99 passed Tim Horton's record of 1,446 regular-season games—the most of any NHL rearguard?

A. Paul Coffey and Larry Murphy

B. Larry Murphy and Ray Bourque

C. Ray Bourque and Scott Stevens

D. Scott Stevens and Craig Ludwig

8.19 Which team manager suspended his two top defensemen for roughness during the 1923 playoffs?

A. Leo Dandurand, with the Montreal Canadiens

B. Art Ross, with the Hamilton Tigers

C. Pete Green, with the Ottawa Senators

D. Charles Querrie, with the Toronto St. Patricks

8.20 Who holds the NHL record for most regular-season appearances by a defenseman—without winning the Stanley Cup?

A. Al MacInnis

B. Larry Murphy

C. Doug Mohns

D. Harry Howell

8.21 What is the NHL record for most power-play goals by a defenseman in a season?

A. 15 power-play goals

B. 17 power-play goals

C. 19 power-play goals

D. 21 power-play goals

8.22 Who is the first defenseman to record 500 career points?

A. Pierre Pilote

B. Bill Gadsby

C. Doug Harvey

D. Red Kelly

8.23 How many Devils teammates did Ken Daneyko play with during his 20-year career in New Jersey?

A. 120 teammates

B. 170 teammates

C. 220 teammates

D. 270 teammates

8.24 As of 2007–08, when was the last time a defenseman won the Lady Byng Trophy as the league's most gentlemanly player?

A. 1983–84

B. 1973–74

C. 1963–64

D. 1953–54

8.25 Who was the first blueliner to score 1,000 career points?

A. Ray Bourque

B. Bobby Orr

C. Denis Potvin

D. Brad Park

8.26 Paul Coffey played on which team when he scored his 300th NHL goal?

A. The Edmonton Oilers

B. The Pittsburgh Penguins

C. The Los Angeles Kings

D. The Detroit Red Wings

8.27 **In what season did Bobby Orr become the first defenseman in NHL annals to win the scoring race?**

A. 1968–69

B. 1969–70

C. 1970–71

D. 1971–72

8.28 **Which defenseman recorded the best plus-minus number in one season during the 1990s?**

A. Marty McSorley

B. Chris Pronger

C. Vladimir Konstantinov

D. Scott Stevens

8.29 **Before the introduction of three- and four-round playoff hockey in 1967, who held the NHL playoff record for most points by a defenseman in postseason play of two rounds (semifinals and finals)?**

A. Tim Horton, with the Toronto Maple Leafs

B. Red Kelly, with the Detroit Red Wings

C. Leo Boivin, with the Boston Bruins

D. Jacques Laperriere, with the Montreal Canadiens

8.30 **Who was the only defenseman to become a leading playoff scorer during the six-team era (1942–43 to 1966–67)?**

A. Bobby Orr

B. Tim Horton

C. Pierre Pilote

D. Allan Stanley

8.31 Which defenseman owns the NHL record for most consecutive games without a goal?

    A. Doug Harvey

    B. Ken Daneyko

    C. Craig Ludwig

    D. Rich Pilon

8.32 Which defenseman reached 1,000 career points in the
fewest games?

    A. Denis Potvin

    B. Paul Coffey

    C. Ray Bourque

    D. Bobby Orr

The Rearguards

Answers

8.1   **B. Frank "Flash" Hollett**

They called him "Flash" because, under the tutelage of
Boston's Eddie Shore and Dit Clapper, Hollett became one of
early hockey's great rushing defensemen. His adeptness at
stickhandling and setting up scoring plays on the rush proved
invaluable to the Bruins during their Stanley Cup campaigns
of 1939 and 1941. Yet despite Hollett recording two 19-goal
seasons for Boston, manager Art Ross unwisely traded him to
Detroit, where Flash again performed All-Star manoeuvres on
the blue line, finally notching the first 20-goal season (1944–45)
by a defenseman. Hollett's record stood until Bobby Orr's 21
goals in 1968–69.

8.2 **D. Orr was handed the number after a veteran defenseman didn't make the team**

When Bobby Orr arrived at the Bruins' training camp in 1966 he was handed a few numbers, including No. 30 and No. 27, both of which he wore for eight pre-season exhibition games before coach Harry Sinden settled on a low number—one traditionally reserved for the blue line corps. The story goes that after Junior Langlois was injured and failed to make the team, Orr got Langlois's No. 4. Interestingly, Orr was first offered Bruin great Dit Clapper's old No. 5, but he turned it down and took No. 4 because it was closer to No. 2, his uniform number in Oshawa. Boston's No. 2 wasn't available, as it had been retired in honour of Eddie Shore. "When I started, the numbers were all assigned and we didn't care about the number, we just wanted the sweater," said Orr.

8.3 **C. Karlis Skrastins, with the Colorado Avalanche**

When this endurance record was smashed, many hockey fans had the same reaction: a blank stare followed by the inevitable, Karlis who? Fair enough. Among the game's ironmen, only a handful of names resonate with fans. Doug Jarvis and Tim Horton, sure. But Karlis Skrastins? Skrastins must be hockey's least known ironman—or he was until February 8, 2007, when he broke Horton's 486-game durability mark for defensemen in his 487th consecutive match, a 6–3 loss to the Atlanta Thrashers. "He's as under-the-radar as any guy I've ever been around," Colorado coach Joel Quenneville confirmed in a Canadian Press story. "He's one guy that really doesn't want attention, doesn't want accolades." Skrastins's near-anonymous streak began on February 21, 2000, and ended on February 24, 2007, a remarkable seven-year stretch that saw him play through several injuries before a bad knee forced him out on

February 25. The 32-year-old rearguard had played 495 straight games. "If I can be sure I can play the game I usually play when I'm healthy, I'm going to play, because pain is part of our game," Skrastins once said about playing injured. (Ironically, he was nicknamed Scratch by his teammates, a play on his last name.) Horton's streak lasted from February 11, 1961, to February 4, 1968. Jarvis holds the overall record of 964 consecutive games, tallied during 13 seasons, 1975–76 to 1987–88.

8.4 D. Kevin Hatcher

No defenseman during the 1990s put up Bobby Orr- or Paul Coffey-like regular-season goal totals, but one D-man came close: Kevin Hatcher. The rearguard exploded in 1992–93 with the Washington Capitals, recording an unexpected 34 goals— second only to team leader Peter Bondra, with 37. Hatcher's 34-goal tally is six better than any other blueliner's during the 1990s.

Top Goal-Scoring Defensemen During the 1990s

PLAYER	TEAM	SEASON	GP	GOALS
Kevin Hatcher	Washington	1992–93	83	34
Paul Coffey	Pittsburgh	1989–90	80	29
Al MacInnis	Calgary	1989–90	79	28
Al MacInnis	Calgary	1990–91	78	28
Al MacInnis	Calgary	1993–94	75	28
Sandis Ozolinsh	San Jose	1993–94	81	26
Jeff Brown	St. Louis	1992–93	71	25
Al Iafrate	Washington	1992–93	81	25

8.5 A. A few multi-sport athletes from Canadian football

The hockey faceoff has seen several modifications and rule changes, most of them to do with players infringing on the draw. For example, rearguards have little impact in the faceoff area, but their original positions on faceoffs did change after a few multi-sport players from Canadian football's Toronto Argonauts played in the Ontario Hockey Association's 1906 championship game. Instead of lining up in the usual tandem stance on faceoffs (with players behind one another), these blueliners positioned themselves side by side, like defensive linemen in football. Shortly thereafter, all defensemen were aligned an equal distance from the faceoff.

8.6 **C. 28 games**

As difficult as it is to imagine anyone even coming close to Wayne Gretzky's 51-game scoring streak, the same could be said about fellow Edmonton Oiler Paul Coffey's mark of 28 games by a defenseman. Two years after Gretzky managed his 1983–84 all-time record, Coffey scored 55 points in a 28-game stretch with the offense-oriented Oilers. Bourque, also no offensive slouch, ranks a distant second with a 19-game streak and 27 points. Not surprisingly, four of the top five positions in this category date to the 1980s. And the rankings haven't changed much since 1991–92, when Brian Leetch recorded a 16-game stint and knocked Bobby Orr out of the top five. Orr had two streaks of 15 games during the 1970s, equalled later during the 1990s by Steve Duchesne and Chris Chelios. Chelios is the last blueliner to take a serious run at the top five, with 15 consecutive games in 1995–96.

The NHL's Longest Point Streaks by Defensemen*

PLAYER	TEAM	SEASON	G–A–P	GAMES
Paul Coffey	Edmonton	1985–86	16–39–55	28
Ray Bourque	Boston	1987–88	6–21–27	19
Ray Bourque	Boston	1984–85	4–24–28	17
Brian Leetch	NYR	1991–92	5–24–29	17
Gary Suter	Calgary	1987–88	8–17–25	16

*Current to 2008–09

8.7   C. Doug Wilson

Few rearguards have ever amassed the stratospheric numbers produced by defensemen Bobby Orr and Paul Coffey, who together have authored six of the eight-best goal-producing seasons by rearguards. Only Chicago's Doug Wilson orbits in Orr-Coffey space—thanks to his Norris Trophy-winning season of 1981–82, when he scored 85 points and 39 goals, just one shy of the illusive 40-goal mark. With his speed, mobility and monster slap shot, Wilson engineered 14 goals on the power play for the Blackhawks, a team with the third-highest regular-season goal count in franchise history—332. At the other end, Chicago gave up an all-time club-high 363 goals, while the 24-year-old defenseman earned a plus-one. Although five Hawks notched 30 goals or more that year, the only one to outscore Wilson was Al Secord, with 44 markers. Wilson was only the second defenseman in NHL history to score 30 goals in a year.

8.8   B. 48 goals

After Bobby Orr scored 46 goals in 1974–75, few figured another defenseman could top such a mind-boggling number. But 11 years later, in 1985–86, Paul Coffey smashed Orr's mark, tallying 48 goals. An extraordinarily gifted skater, with the rushing and puckhandling skills of Orr, Coffey was perfectly suited to Edmonton's firewagon style of play. More than just a fast skater, though, Coffey had a talent for making plays at lightning speed. And while some criticized his defensive-end work, he finished the season with a plus-61 rating. Yes, Coffey did surprise Orr's fans by outscoring the great Bruin, but they could take some comfort in knowing that Coffey finished 1985–86 with 138 points, one point less than Orr's NHL record of 139 points in 1970–71.

The NHL's Top Goal-Scoring Defensemen*

PLAYER	TEAM	SEASON	SCHEDULE	GOALS
Paul Coffey	Edmonton	1985–86	80	48
Bobby Orr	Boston	1974–75	80	46
Paul Coffey	Edmonton	1983–84	80	40
Doug Wilson	Chicago	1981–82	80	39
Bobby Orr	Boston	1970–71	78	37
Bobby Orr	Boston	1971–72	78	37
Paul Coffey	Edmonton	1984–85	80	37
Kevin Hatcher	Washington	1992–93	84	34

*Current to 2008–09

8.9 **A. Pierre Pilote, with the Chicago Blackhawks**

Before Orr scored 64 points in 1968–69 to establish the new NHL season point total for defensemen, Chicago captain Pierre Pilote held the record with 59 points in 1964–65. Pilote, a three-time Norris Trophy winner and eight-time All-Star, broke Babe Pratt's 21-year-old mark of 57 points set in 1943–44. Mohns, a sometimes-blueliner, wasn't playing rearguard in 1967–68, the season he scored 60 points on a line with Stan Mikita and Kenny Wharram. Kelly's highest season total as a defenseman was 54 points, in 1950–51.

8.10 **B. 23 goals**

Brad Marsh was the archetypal journeyman—with little natural talent, he had to work harder than most players to stay in the world's best league. In 15 seasons with six teams, he scored only 23 goals in 1,086 games, and every one of them was a testament to his work ethic. Still, Marsh's dogged efforts brought him to the 1993 All-Star game, where, ironically, he scored a goal.

8.11   D. Chris Pronger, with the St. Louis Blues

Few defensemen have ever dominated an NHL team so completely in one season that they received MVP honours. Voters
for the Hart Trophy are typically more impressed by forwards
with big goal numbers, which have a big impact on a team's
success, than by the defensive positions of goaltender and
defenseman. In fact, in NHL history, fewer than 10 rearguards
have had their names etched on the Hart—and only two of
those players managed it in the last 65 years. Since Babe Pratt
won the Hart in 1944 and Bobby Orr captured it in 1970, 1971
and 1972, only Chris Pronger has put together a Hart-worthy
year (in 1999–2000). And as important as Ray Bourque and
Denis Potvin were to their respective teams, neither managed the silverware. What *did* Pronger do, though? He led
the NHL in plus-minus (plus-52), led his team in assists (48),
finished second among NHL defensemen in points (62) and
finished third on his team in points and penalty minutes (92).
Numbers aside, Pronger is also a world-class athlete. As one
scouting report said: "He blends his physical play with good
offensive instincts and skills. His defensive reads are excellent… he patrols the point smartly… and he has a nasty
streak with his stick." Further, Hart voters were likely swayed
by what happened to the Blues in 1999–2000. The team unexpectedly won the Presidents' Trophy by finishing first overall
with an all-time franchise-high of 114 points, and in the process scored the third-highest goal count (248) while allowing
the fewest goals (165). It is the first and only time St. Louis led
all teams in points in one season.

8.12   B. Patrice Brisebois

Brisebois, the last remaining link to the Canadiens' 1993
Stanley Cup, is not the first player branded by Montreal's
merciless fans and its media with a catchy but unflattering

nickname. The oft-criticized Brisebois earned the "Breeze-By" moniker for his spotty defensive play, not unlike another much-criticized member of the Habs, goalie Andre "Red-Light" Racicot. As Racicot later said, "They booed Stephane Richer out of town and look what they did to Patrick (Roy). It's (Montreal) a stupid place to play but life goes on." Perhaps not surprisingly, then, for a short time during Montreal's ill-fated 2002–03 season, Brisebois was diagnosed with an irregular heartbeat due to work-related stress. In 2005, he then signed as a free agent with Colorado, where he played two seasons in virtual anonymity, only to return to hellfire in Montreal for further scrutiny of his blue line duties. Go figure.

8.13   C. Gary Suter and Al MacInnis, with Calgary, in 1987–88
Since 1967–68, only two pairs of rearguards from the same team have led all defensemen in scoring. The New York Islanders iced the Potvin brothers in 1975–76, with Denis collecting 98 points and Jean earning 72—certainly a league first for siblings. And despite the pairings of such high-profile blue line stars as Lidstrom-Chelios, Niedermayer-Pronger and Orr-Vadnais, the most recent defensive duo with a one-two league finish is Gary Suter (91 points) and Al MacInnis (83) with the first-place Calgary Flames in 1987–88.

8.14   B. Dit Clapper, with the Boston Bruins
The night Dit Clapper played his last game, February 12, 1947, must have been a little like Wayne Gretzky's last match. Clapper had a brilliance and genius for the game that few players possessed during his era. He made multiple All-Star appearances, won three Stanley Cups and in his best season scored 41 goals—in the 44-game schedule of 1929–30, when he played right wing. He was also the first 20-year man in NHL history. And though Clapper never transcended the sport

like the Great One, he was so highly regarded that the league inducted him into the Hall and the Bruins retired his No. 5 immediately after his February 12 game. A few elite players are a lock for such honours after retirement, but no one has ever been accorded the privilege without delay like Clapper.

8.15   B. Two defensemen

Although Bobby Orr is the first and only rearguard to win an NHL scoring title, two old-time blueliners led or tied the league in assist totals (something that Orr also did multiple times). Counting helpers in hockey's early days was sometimes suspect, but the NHL *Guide and Record Book* lists two defensemen as assist leaders. In 1917–18, Harry Cameron, with Toronto, tied forwards Cy Denneny and Reg Noble with a league-high 10 assists in the 22-game schedule. Then in 1921–22, Cameron bested the circuit by notching 17 assists. Two years later, in 1923–24, Georges Boucher, with Ottawa, then led the league with 10 assists in 24 games. And both Cameron and Boucher also won several Stanley Cups between them and are Hockey Hall of Fame members. (For the record, old-timer Eddie Gerard tied Newsy Lalonde with a league-best 10 assists in 1918–19, but Gerard played defense and left wing at the time.)

8.16   B. Two defensemen

In the game's early days, defensemen such as George Boucher, King Clancy and Harry Cameron represented their blue line peers in the NHL's top 10. But in modern-day hockey, only a few rearguards have had such success—and only once have two defensemen managed it in the same season. In 1973–74, Bobby Orr came second (to Phil Esposito) with 122 points, and Brad Park, with the Rangers, finished tied for 10 with 82 points.

8.17 A. Paul Coffey

It has been said (with some levity) that Paul Coffey only *really* started playing defense under Scotty Bowman in Detroit. But the fact is, Bowman built an offensive system for his 1995 Stanley Cup finalists around the skating skills of Coffey. If Coffey, at left defense, ever got caught out of position after a scoring sortie into the opponent's zone, the left-winger stayed back to cover for him. It's a classic example of Bowman utilizing his best players' talents to optimum advantage. As a result, Coffey rarely got caught, registering a team-leading 58 points and a plus-18 rating in lockout-shortened 1994–95, a tribute as much to Bowman's system as his own all-round abilities. As well, Coffey remains the last defenseman to crack the top 10, finishing tied for sixth place with a 14–44–58 record. The last blueliner with top-10 status in a full season is Brian Leetch, who achieved it in 1991–92. Both Coffey and Bobby Orr can claim the most top-10 finishes among D-men—with six each.

8.18 B. Larry Murphy and Ray Bourque

Not one but two defensemen passed Tim Horton and took the lead among rearguards for most career games played in 1998–99. Murphy topped Horton on February 5, 1999, in his 1,447th league game; Bourque did it two months later on April 5, 1999. And since then, two other rearguards have eclipsed Horton: Scott Stevens, with 1,635 games, and Chris Chelios, who leads all blueliners with 1,644 in 2008–09. As well, Luke Richardson may next break Horton's mark. He had 1,417 career games in 2008–09.

8.19 A. Leo Dandurand, with the Montreal Canadiens

So vicious were the attacks by Montreal defensemen Sprague Cleghorn and Billy Couture in the first game of the 1923

Montreal–Ottawa playoffs that Dandurand didn't even wait for the league to take action; he fined and suspended his own players. In one incident, after a pretty Ottawa goal by Cy Denneny, Couture clubbed the Senator player as he was returning to take his position for the faceoff; later, Cleghorn cross-checked Lionel Hitchman in the face, knocking him out cold. Despite Montreal's rough tactics, however, Ottawa won the game 2–0, though in the return match, the Canadiens pulled off a 2–1 victory despite the absence of their suspended rearguards, Couture and Cleghorn. Still, in the two-game, total-goals series, it wasn't enough to get by the Senators, who claimed the round by a 3–to–2 goal margin, leaving Dandurand, a true sportsman, to reflect on his self-imposed suspensions.

8.20   D. Harry Howell
When Harry Howell retired from NHL play in 1972–73, he led all Cup-less players, with 1,411 games in 21 seasons. Since then, Phil Housley, Mike Gartner and Scott Mellanby have each played more regular-season matches without a championship, but Howell remains hockey's most frustrated rearguard. Bluelining for New York, California and Los Angeles between 1952 and 1973, Howell never played on a first-place team nor made the Stanley Cup finals.

8.21   C. 19 power-play goals
For all of his weaknesses on the blue line, including easily being beat one-on-one and taking bad penalties, Sheldon Souray turned around his image as a lumbering rearguard in the speedy NHL with a career year in 2006–07. Leading Montreal to a league-high 22.8 per cent success rate of 86 power-play goals in 378 opportunities, Souray's laser beam slap shots set a new NHL mark among defensemen—19 goals

on the man-advantage, with his record-setting 19th coming against the Rangers' Henrik Lundqvist in a 3–1 loss on April 5. The previous league mark of 18 power-play goals was held by the Islanders' Denis Potvin in 1975–76 and matched by Adrian Aucoin of Vancouver in 1998–99. In 1985–86, forward Tim Kerr set the all-time record at 34 goals.

8.22 B. Bill Gadsby

A superb two-way defenseman, Gadsby narrowly beat Doug Harvey in the race to be the first rearguard to record 500 points. Gadsby scored the league's first 500th on November 4, 1962, just months ahead of Harvey's 500th. Red Kelly, who amassed 452 points while patrolling the blue line for Detroit, would have been the first to reach the mark, but he was converted into a centre after his trade to Toronto in 1959–60. When Gadsby retired in 1965–66, he ranked 20th among NHL scorers.

8.23 C. 220 teammates

Daneyko is the most unlikely fit among the top one-team players in NHL history. A defenseman who didn't score a goal in six of his 20 seasons with New Jersey, Daneyko ranks fourth all-time amongst one-team NHLers, with 1,283 career games, behind only such prolific scorers as Detroit's Alex Delvecchio (1,549 games), Chicago's Stan Mikita (1,394) and Steve Yzerman (1,514). During his one-team career, Daneyko played with 220 Devils teammates and outlasted 10 New Jersey head coaches, and is the only Devil to play in all of the franchise's 173 playoff games before May 13, 2003, when he was a healthy scratch for Game 2 of the New Jersey–Ottawa Conference finals. Coach Pat Burns suggested the veteran made costly mistakes during a 3–2 loss in Game 1, to which Daneyko replied: "Do I buy it? No."

8.24 D. 1953–54

Defenseman Nicklas Lidstrom might have been the best bet
to break with a half-century tradition of Lady Byng winners
from the forward ranks. But the Detroit rearguard finished
runner-up for four years—1999, 2000, 2001 and 2003—to keep
Red Kelly's 1954 Lady Byng the last by a rearguard. Kelly was
named most gentlemanly player three times: in 1950–51
(24 penalty minutes), 1952–53 (eight minutes) and 1953–54
(18 minutes).

8.25 C. Denis Potvin

As of 2008–09, only six defensemen in NHL history have
scored more than 1,000 points. Potvin reached the milestone
first, on April 4, 1987, after a Mikko Makela shot ricocheted
off Potvin's arm and sailed past Sabre goalie Jacques Cloutier
into the Buffalo net. Potvin recorded 290 goals and 710 assists
to reach point number 1,000. So who are the other five rearguard gunners? Ray Bourque (1,579 points), Paul Coffey (1,531),
Al MacInnis (1,274), Phil Housley (1,232) and Larry Murphy
(1,216). Potvin concluded his career with 1,052 points.

8.26 B. The Pittsburgh Penguins

Coffey played on nine NHL teams, but his most productive
seasons as a goal scorer came in Edmonton and Pittsburgh.
During those years he racked up career goals faster than
many forwards, scoring his 300th while playing for the
Penguins on January 5, 1991. It was his 777th game and
11th NHL season.

8.27 B. 1969–70

Because the position is primarily defensive in nature, blueliners are rarely expected to be prolific goal scorers. But
Bobby Orr altered that mindset with his historic first-place

finish in 1969–70's scoring race. After collecting 41, 31 and 64 points between 1966–67 and 1968–69, Orr sent the hockey world reeling by firing 33 goals and 87 assists for 120 points, to become the first rearguard to win the Art Ross Trophy as the league's scoring champion. Orr's 33 goals also established another milestone: the NHL's first 30-goal season by a blueliner. He was just 22 years old.

8.28   C. Vladimir Konstantinov

The best plus-minus during the 1990s belongs to Detroit's Vladimir Konstantinov, the veteran Soviet rearguard who recorded a decade-high plus-60 in 1995–96. The Red Wings didn't win the Stanley Cup that season, but they finished the year with a league-record 62 wins and placed four players—Konstantinov, Sergei Fedorov, Viacheslav Fetisov and Vyacheslav Kozlov—amongst the top five plus-minus leaders, the only time in the 1990s that one team has so dominated the plus-minus column. After winning the Cup in 1997, Konstantinov suffered career-ending injuries in an automobile accident.

8.29   A. Tim Horton, with the Toronto Maple Leafs

Despite what Punch Imlach or any other NHL coach demanded of Horton, he always played the game his way. Although he listened to advice, picking from it what he could use, Horton remained true to his own hockey sense, developing skills that went far beyond the one-dimensional defensive game he was taught. As a result, his independence challenged some, but it also made him one of the league's most explosive, rushing rearguards. Then, during the 1962 Stanley Cup finals, Horton established the defenseman's record in playoff scoring, amassing 16 points (three goals, 13 assists) in 12 games. His biggest point? It came against Chicago on Dick Duff's Cup-winning goal, a result of one of the classic end-to-end rushes that made Horton a dominant player of the great Leaf teams of the 1960s.

8.30 C. Pierre Pilote

Pilote should be classed with the Orrs, Robinsons and MacInnises in the playoff record books, given that he was the only Original Six defenseman to earn top points in a post-season scoring race. He would win the Norris Trophy as top rearguard on three successive occasions and play in eight All-Star games, but perhaps Pilote's greatest achievement came mid-career in Chicago's breakthrough playoff year of 1961. The Hawks' D-man led the rush and worked the corners, besting Chicago's marquee gunners, Bobby Hull and Stan Mikita, to tie Gordie Howe as playoff scoring leader and record 15 points. It was Chicago's last Cup to date; Pilote was named captain of the Blackhawks the following season.

8.31 B. Ken Daneyko

Although the NHL keeps no such official record, Rich Pilon should still thank Ken Daneyko for erasing his name from this mark in hockey's hall of shame. In April 2002, Pilon's futility mark of 245 games without a goal was broken by Daneyko, who went on to establish his own NHL dry-spell streak of 256 straight goal-less games between February 9, 1999, and October 25, 2002, when he potted one against Martin Biron in a 2–1 New Jersey win at Buffalo. Daneyko took it all in stride: "I'm like an NHL linesman. I score about every five years." Obviously, the Devils rearguard kept the puck, one of only 36 to enter an opponent's net off his stick during his 1,283-game career. Daneyko also scored five times in playoff action, including a goal that came during his regular-season goal-less run in the 2000 Stanley Cup finals.

8.32 B. Paul Coffey

Paul Coffey notched his 1,000th nhl point in his 770th regular-season game, reaching the milestone in 163 games less than his closest pursuer, Ray Bourque. but Bobby Orr likely would have been the fastest rearguard to reach the millennium mark if he had stayed healthy for another season. Orr retired in 1978–79 after scoring 915 points in only 657 games.

The NHL's 1,000-Point Defensemen*

PLAYER	TEAM	DATE	GAME NUMBER
Paul Coffey	Pittsburgh	12/22/90	770
Ray Bourque	Boston	02/29/92	933
Denis Potvin	NYI	04/04/87	987
Al MacInnis	St. Louis	04/07/98	1,056
Phil Housley	Washington	11/08/97	1,081
Brian Leetch	Boston	10/18/05	1,151
Larry Murphy	Toronto	03/27/97	1,228

*Current to 2008–09

Game 8

Hockey Crossword 2

Solutions are on page 562

ACROSS

1. Full name of 13-year D-man, mostly with Hartford, initials A.B., 1988–2001
5. _____ Roenick
7. Detroit's Sergei _____
8. _____ Messier
10. LA winger Nelson _____
11. Major department store in Canada
13. D-man Lyle _____
15. NJ's D-man Scott _____
19. Forward Vincent _____
22. Long-time Hawk, 1994 Cup-winner with NYR, winger Steve _____
24. Initials of American state where Devils play
26. Retired Hartford Washington D-man, initials S.K., Scot _____
28. 1980s–1990s centre, mostly with Oilers, Mark _____
30. Four-game tryout with Pens in 1998–99, initials P.S., Pavel _____
32. _____ open net
33. Father
35. Last name with the letter "U" three times, Buffalo Chicago centre Christian _____
36. Goalie makes a stop or _____
37. Pittsburgh-NYR centre Petr _____

DOWN

1. Ottawa captain Daniel _____
2. Veteran winger, mostly with Buffalo, Donald _____
3. Veteran D-man with St.Louis-Vancouver, initials M.B., Murray _____
4. Montreal D-man Craig _____
5. Jaromir _____
6. Old-time 1940s All-Star tough guy Pat _____
8. Chicago-Edmonton winger, initials E.M., Ethan _____
9. Old first name, rhymes with "hip"
12. 500-goal scorer, one-time Leaf Dave _____
14. 35-game Flyer in 1990s, Yanick _____

16. 2001–02 Toronto winger Garry _____
17. Ottawa-Vancouver D-man _____ Salo
18. NYR D-man Brian _____
20. Cartilage between joints in knee, starts with "M"
21. 2002–03 Pittsburgh centre Martin _____
23. _____ MacInnis

25. _____ Béliveau
27. 2001–02 Florida D-man Brad _____
28. Veteran Florida D-man, tough guy Paul _____
29. Pavel _____
31. _____ Belfour
34. Old-timer scoring champ Babe _____

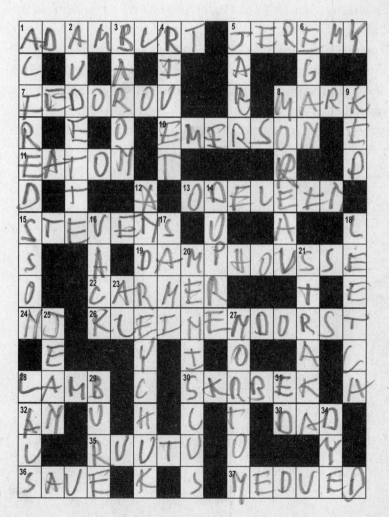

9

Only the Firsts

WHICH SCORING TRIO first recorded 300 points in an NHL season? Several lines come to mind, including Los Angeles's Triple Crown Line, which earned Marcel Dionne, Charlie Simmer and Dave Taylor bragging rights as the first unit to feature three 100-point scorers. The trio managed it in 1980–81. But a full decade earlier, the Nitro Line of Phil Esposito, Ken Hodge and Wayne Cashman became the most explosive offensive force in NHL history when they tallied 336 points, powered by Esposito's record-setting 152 points. The feat was even more amazing considering Hodge and Cashman rarely played on the Bruins' power play.

Answers are on page 229

9.1   In which NHL city did the first professional hockey game take place?
    A. Montreal
    B. Toronto
    C. Pittsburgh
    D. Ottawa

9.2   Who was the NHL's first scoring champion?
    A. Reg Noble, with the Toronto Arenas
    B. Joe Malone, with the Montreal Canadiens
    C. Cy Denneny, with the Ottawa Senators
    D. Frank Nighbor, with the Ottawa Senators

9.3 Who is the only NHL player to lead the league in power-play goals and shorthanded goals—in the same season—twice in his career?

A. Pavel Bure
B. Wayne Gretzky
C. Mario Lemieux
D. Jaromir Jagr

9.4 Who was the first NHL goalie awarded an assist?

A. Johnny Mowers, with the Detroit Red Wings
B. Tiny Thompson, with the Boston Bruins
C. Turk Broda, with the Toronto Maple Leafs
D. Bert Gardiner, with the Boston Bruins

9.5 In what season did an NHLer first play more games than the regular-season schedule allowed for?

A. During the NHL's 30-game schedule of 1924–25
B. During the NHL's 48-game schedule of 1934–35
C. During the NHL's 50-game schedule of 1944–45
D. During the NHL's 70-game schedule of 1954–55

9.6 Who is the first Russian-born player to log 1,000 NHL games?

A. Pavel Bure
B. Alexander Mogilny
C. Sergei Fedorov
D. Alex Kovalev

9.7 Since regular-season overtime was instituted in 1983–84, in which season did a player score the first overtime penalty-shot goal in NHL history?

A. 1990–91

B. 1996–97

C. 2000–01

D. It has never happened

9.8 Who was the first NHL goalie to have his number retired?

A. Ed Giacomin, with the New York Rangers

B. Bernie Parent, with the Philadelphia Flyers

C. Terry Sawchuk, with the Detroit Red Wings

D. Turk Broda, with the Toronto Maple Leafs

9.9 What NHL first occurred in the game between the Chicago Blackhawks and the Toronto Maple Leafs on December 2, 1950?

A. There was not a single penalty called

B. The game was delayed by a bomb threat

C. Three goalies were picked as the three stars

D. The two opposing coaches engaged in a fist fight

9.10 Which player is usually credited with pioneering hockey's first slap shot—long before Bernie Geoffrion popularized *his* slapper?

A. Alex Shibicky, with the New York Rangers

B. Charlie Conacher, with the Toronto Maple Leafs

C. Sweeney Schriner, with the New York Americans

D. No one, Geoffrion was the first

9.11 Who scored the first goal at both Toronto's Maple Leaf Gardens and Chicago Stadium?

A. Charlie Conacher

B. Joe Primeau

C. Dick Irvin

D. Harold "Mush" March

9.12 In 2003, who became the first hockey player to have a classical musical composition written about one of his goals?

A. Bill Barilko

B. Bobby Orr

C. Wayne Gretzky

D. Peter Forsberg

9.13 What hockey first did Robbie Ftorek and teammate Claude Larose accomplish with the Cincinnati Stingers in the WHA?

A. They each recorded two penalty shots in one game

B. They each assisted on Wayne Gretzky's first pro goal

C. They each wore the same jersey number for the Stingers

D. They each share credit for scoring the first goal in Stinger history

9.14 Who was the first player from a post-1967 expansion team to lead the NHL in playoff scoring?

A. Bill Goldsworthy, with the 1968 Minnesota North Stars

B. Red Berenson, with the 1971 St. Louis Blues

C. Rick MacLeish, with the 1974 Philadelphia Flyers

D. Bryan Trottier, with the 1980 New York Islanders

9.15 Who was the first player to speak out publicly against the NHL Players Association during the lockout of 2004–05?

A. John Madden, with the New Jersey Devils

B. Chris Chelios, with the Detroit Red Wings

C. Mike Commodore, with the Calgary Flames

D. Brett Hull, with the Detroit Red Wings

9.16 Who was the first high-profile player to walk away from the entire NHL 2004–05 season because of the lockout?

A. Markus Naslund

B. Peter Forsberg

C. Jaromir Jagr

D. Vincent Lecavalier

9.17 Who was the first NHL head coach to hire an assistant coach?

A. Fred Shero, with the Philadelphia Flyers

B. Scotty Bowman, with the Montreal Canadiens

C. Lynn Patrick, with the St. Louis Blues

D. Al Arbour, with the New York Islanders

9.18 In 1999–2000, who was the first NHLer to score a goal during the new four-on-four overtime format?

A. Brett Hull, with the Dallas Stars

B. Brian Savage, with the Montreal Canadiens

C. Valeri Bure, with the Calgary Flames

D. Mike Ricci, with the San Jose Sharks

9.19 Who is the first player to lead the NHL in penalty minutes in his first two seasons?

A. Chris Nilan

B. Bob Probert

C. John Ferguson

D. Keith Magnuson

9.20 Who was the first goalie in NHL history to record a shutout?

A. Georges Vezina, with the Montreal Canadiens

B. Chuck Gardiner, with the Chicago Blackhawks

C. Lorne Chabot, with the New York Rangers

D. George Hainsworth, with the Montreal Canadiens

9.21 **Who was the first U.S. president to attend an NHL game while in office?**

A. John F. Kennedy

B. Ronald Reagan

C. George Bush

D. Bill Clinton

9.22 **Who was the first European-trained player to captain an NHL team?**

A. Stan Mikita, with the Chicago Blackhawks

B. Lars-Erik Sjoberg, with the Winnipeg Jets

C. Peter Stastny, with the Quebec Nordiques

D. Mats Sundin, with the Toronto Maple Leafs

9.23 **Who is the first player to score a goal in the NHL *before* scoring his first goal in junior hockey?**

A. Kris Draper

B. Michel Goulet

C. Neal Broten

D. Jimmy Carson

9.24 **Which NHL team was the first to use a European-trained goalie?**

A. The Quebec Nordiques

B. The New York Islanders

C. The Philadelphia Flyers

D. The Toronto Maple Leafs

9.25 In what decade did an NHL team first travel to a game by airplane?

A. The 1920s

B. The 1930s

C. The 1940s

D. The 1950s

9.26 Who was the first NHLer to test positive for banned steroids?

A. Bryan Berard

B. Zdeno Chara

C. Matthew Barnaby

D. José Théodore

9.27 Which was the first NHL team to win the Stanley Cup with an American-born coach?

A. The Montreal Canadiens

B. The New York Rangers

C. The Chicago Blackhawks

D. The Pittsburgh Penguins

9.28 Who was the first player of Asian ancestry to play in the NHL?

A. Jim Paek

B. Steve Tsujiura

C. Larry Kwong

D. Paul Kariya

9.29 Which Boston player was scratched from his team's lineup in January 1958, prompting the Bruins to call up minor leaguer Willie O'Ree—the first black man to play in the NHL?

A. Right-winger Leo Labine

B. Centre Bronco Horvath

C. Centre Don McKenney

D. Left-winger Johnny Bucyk

9.30 Who was the first player to publicly admit to participating in the NHL's substance abuse program?

A. Brett Thomas

B. Ken Daneyko

C. Randy Ellis

D. Réne Lacroix

9.31 What professional hockey first did Antero Niittymaki accomplish while playing with the AHL Philadelphia Phantoms in April 2004?

A. He was the first European goalie with a 30-win season

B. He was the first pro goalie credited with an overtime goal

C. He was the first AHL goalie fined for illegal pads

D. He was the first pro goalie with a shootout win

9.32 In 1998–99, what hockey first did Vince Riendeau achieve?

A. Riendeau was the first North American to play in a Russian hockey league

B. Riendeau was the first NHLer from North America to play in a Russian hockey league

C. Riendeau was the first North American to play in a Swedish hockey league

D. Riendeau was the first NHLer from North America to play in a Swedish hockey league

9.33 Who was the first goalie to score a goal and record a shutout in the same game?

A. Chris Osgood

B. Ron Hextall

C. José Théodore

D. Martin Brodeur

9.34 In a game on March 26, 1931, Bruins coach Art Ross tried what newspapers of the day called "an amazing manoeuvre" with goalie Tiny Thompson. It was an NHL first. What was Ross's "manoeuvre"?

A. He forced Thompson to serve his own penalty

B. He invented goalie skates for Thompson

C. He pulled Thompson to add an extra forward

D. He taught Thompson to shoot the puck into the neutral zone

9.35 Which enforcer publicly admitted, "I'm the first person to go through stage four in the substance abuse program and get back to hockey"?

A. Louie DeBrusk

B. Dave Semenko

C. Bob Probert

D. Brantt Myhres

9.36 In November 1926, Hal Winkler became the first goalie in NHL history to record a shutout in his first game. In what other famous shutout first did he participate?

A. He played in the NHL's first 0–0 scoreless game

B. He played in the NHL's first playoff shutout

C. He recorded a shutout in his last NHL game

D. He played opposite the first goalie to record a shutout in his first playoff game

9.37 In what year did a Zamboni first appear on NHL ice?

A. 1949

B. 1955

C. 1961

D. 1967

Answers

9.1 **C. Pittsburgh**

It may be one of hockey's most unbelievable believe-it-or-not facts. More than a decade before the NHL was founded in 1917–18, and years before any other pro league started up, a small and short-lived league called the International Hockey League operated a five-team circuit that paid salaries to its players. In its inaugural game on December 9, 1904, a Portage Lakes team from Houghton, Michigan, beat hometown Pittsburgh 6–3 with the first pro goal ever scored by Barney Holden of Portage Lakes. At the time, the Stanley Cup was awarded to the best amateur team and players, most of whom wanted to earn money playing the game they loved. Some played for one of the five original IHL teams: Pittsburgh; Sault Ste. Marie, Ontario; and Michigan's Sault Ste. Marie, Portage Lakes and Calumet. The league's top recruits included Hall of Famers Fred "Cyclone" Taylor and Joe Hall.

9.2 **B. Joe Malone, with the Montreal Canadiens**

In the league's inaugural season, 1917–18, Malone was supposed to play for the Quebec Bulldogs. But 10 days before the official formation of the new circuit, the Bulldogs folded and its players were divided up among the other four clubs. With Malone, the Montreal Canadiens obtained Quebec's top marksman, and he set a torrid scoring pace—averaging more than two goals per game during the 22-game regular season. For the star centre it was like shooting fish in a barrel. On the strength of multiple three-, four- and five-goal games, he potted 44 goals in 20 matches and established a still-standing league record to become the NHL's first scoring leader. To equal Malone's 2.20 goals-per-game ratio today, an NHLer would have to net 180 goals in an 82-game schedule.

9.3   C. Mario Lemieux
There are power-play specialists and there are penalty-killing specialists, and then there are a few rare individuals, including Mario Lemieux, who excel as both. The Magnificent One led the NHL with 31 power-play and 13 shorthanded goals in 1988–89, then duplicated the feat in 1995–96, when the Penguins superstar topped the league with 31 power-play goals and eight shorthanded tallies.

9.4   B. Tiny Thompson, with the Boston Bruins
In old-time hockey, few goalies ever received assists, either because the nature of the game created little opportunity or simply because they were not credited. But there are a few recorded instances of point-scoring goalies, including Bert Gardiner (in 1943–44) and Johnny Mowers (in 1941–42). Even earlier, though, Tiny Thompson passed out to Babe Siebert on two of the defenseman's goals in a 4–1 victory against Toronto on January 14, 1936. It remains the earliest official recognition of a goalie assist, though netminders had assisted on goals before Thompson.

9.5   A. During the NHL's 30-game schedule of 1924–25
Well before modern-day players Jimmy Carson and Bob Kudelski set a regular-season standard of 86 games, defenseman Lionel Hitchman played 31 games in a 30-game schedule by splitting 1924–25: 12 games with the Ottawa Senators and 19 games with the Boson Bruins. It was the first time an NHLer played more games than in the regular-season schedule.

Hitchman then went on to enjoy his greatest years with the Bruins, where he was paired on the blue line with Eddie Shore, a puck rusher who fit perfectly with the stay-at-home defenseman.

9.6 C. Sergei Fedorov

The highs and lows that came with being a Soviet defector never deterred Sergei Fedorov from his ultimate goals. Along with roommate and friend Alexander Mogilny, he represented the new generation of Russian superstar—bound for international fame and glory while still playing under the strict Soviet hockey model established by coach Viktor Tikhonov. It came as little surprise then, just a year after Mogilny defected in 1989, that Fedorov followed suit and signed with the Detroit Red Wings (his draft team from the previous summer). But hockey proved to be the easy part. Adapting to a new language and culture meant some "horrible tough times" for both men, who found solace in one another's on-ice success. The statistics reflect an ongoing competitive streak: as Fedorov played in game number 1,000 as a Columbus Blue Jacket on November 30, 2005, for example, Mogilny had logged a close-second 975 games. Fedorov's assist that night against Minnesota gave him a career 431–592–1,023—compared to Mogilny's two-point evening—and 471–565–1,036 record. The pair had abandoned their Soviet homeland many years earlier, but the two friends were still close—separated only by 13 points.

9.7 C. 2000–01

The first penalty shot in overtime occurred between the New York Rangers and the Nashville Predators on December 23, 2000, at Madison Square Garden. With a 2–2 score, Nashville's

David Legwand was awarded a penalty shot after being up-ended at 3:17 in overtime. Then, on the one-one-one, he deked Kirk McLean and popped the goal for a 3–2 win—the first overtime goal on a penalty shot in NHL history. "I knew a lot of the guys had their toes crossed in their skates. Some of the guys were looking, and others said they couldn't. I sort of peeked," said Nashville coach Barry Trotz.

9.8 **B. Bernie Parent, with the Philadelphia Flyers**
It is surprising, considering all the great goalies who have played the game, that no puck stopper had his number retired until October 11, 1979, the date Bernie Parent's No. 1 was taken out of circulation. Parent secured a place in Philadelphia hockey history by leading the Flyers to Stanley Cups in 1974 and 1975. His brilliance between the pipes in those two post-seasons earned him back-to-back Conn Smythe Trophies as MVP of the playoffs and prompted the appearance of a famous placard at the Spectrum: "Only God Saves More Than Parent."

9.9 **C. Three goalies were picked as the three stars**
Being a goalie in the days before the advent of the mask was a hazardous job, a fact never more evident than during the game between Chicago and Toronto at Maple Leaf Gardens on December 2, 1950. In the second period, a shot struck Toronto goalie Al Rollins above the left eye and he had to be carried off the ice on a stretcher. He was replaced by backup Turk Broda, who had been watching the game from the stands. A few minutes later, Chicago goalie Harry Lumley was struck in the face by a deflected puck and left the ice to undergo repairs. Then, during the third period, Lumley went to the Chicago bench to receive medical aid and, during the delay, the crowd began to boo—until it was announced that Lumley

was playing with a broken nose. The game ended in a scoreless draw, and its three stars then announced: Lumley, Broda and Rollins, three goalies—an NHL first.

9.10 A. Alex Shibicky, with the New York Rangers

The first slap shot has many claimants, dating back to the 1920s' Babe Dye and Didier Pitre (the latter was called Cannonball because of his heavy shot). However, players such as Bernie Geoffrion are usually credited with being the first to utilize it during the early 1950s. But almost two decades before the Boomer unleashed his shot, it has been established that Alex Shibicky was winding up and blasting his own slappers. "It was a snap shot from the hip," according to his son, Alex Jr. Shibicky caught on with the Rangers in 1935–36 and was almost immediately teamed with linemates Neil and Mac Colville, with the trio learning every detail of the game from veterans Bill and Bun Cook—including an innovative technique for shooting the puck that Shibicky first tried in practice, then pioneered in a game in 1937. But Shibicky's claim is also not without its challengers, including Bun Cook, who may also have used the slap shot in game play. Shibicky, however, is adamant that "Bun never used the slapper in a game. I did, but it was his idea." Still, no matter who was first, Shibicky's unit soon clicked, and it was dubbed the Bread Line by sportswriters who considered the trio the "bread and butter" of the Rangers. In 1940, with the Bread Line and the Cook brothers firing on all cylinders, New York then won the Stanley Cup, its last championship before Mark Messier led the Blueshirts to 1994's Cup. When Shibicky died in July 2005, the NHL made plans to send the Stanley Cup to the Vancouver area to commemorate his accomplishments.

9.11 D. Harold "Mush" March

The five-foot-five, 155-pound March, who was nicknamed after a cartoon character, scored the inaugural goals at two Original Six stadiums. The Chicago Blackhawk winger's first brush with history came on November 21, 1929, when he scored the first goal at Chicago Stadium against Alex Connell in a 6–5 loss to the Ottawa Senators. Two years later, on November 12, 1931, March scored the first goal at Maple Leaf Gardens against netminder Lorne Chabot in a 2–1 Blackhawks triumph over Toronto. But the biggest goal of March's career came on April 10, 1934, when he netted the overtime winner that gave Chicago its first Stanley Cup. March, who died at age 93 in January 2002, received a final tribute on the opening day of the 2001–02 season, when he dropped the puck for the ceremonial opening faceoff at Chicago's new United Center.

9.12 B. Bobby Orr

"The Goal," a musical tribute to Orr's famous 1970 Stanley Cup-winning goal, was performed for the first time on July 18, 2003, at the 2003 Festival of the Sound—Parry Sound, Ontario's annual classical music festival. Orr, who was born in Parry Sound, was in the audience to hear the piece, which was composed by Eric Robertson for brass quintet and narrator. The tribute was part of the grand opening of the new Charles W. Stockey Centre for the Performing Arts and the Bobby Orr Hall of Fame.

9.13 C. They each wore the same jersey number for the Stingers

Both Ftorek and Larose had good reason for wanting sweater No. 8 in Cincinnati. Larose had enjoyed a successful NHL career with No. 8, while Ftorek had worn the number his entire pro career as a tribute to ex-Bruin Fleming Mackell. And in an unprecedented move, Cincinnati received special permission from the league so that both players could wear the Stingers' No. 8 during 1977–78.

9.14   A. Bill Goldsworthy, with the 1968 Minnesota North Stars
Surprisingly, a player from an expansion team led the NHL play-off scoring race in 1968. Even odder, the player came from the Minnesota North Stars, a team that failed to make the finals. Bill Goldsworthy collected 15 points in 14 games to pace all playoff scorers. The top scorer on the Cup-champion Montreal Canadiens that year was Yvan Cournoyer, with 14 points.

9.15   A. John Madden, with the New Jersey Devils
Even though the NHLPA was quick to admonish players who openly admitted to considering a salary cap, a fair number still stepped forward, the first being John Madden on the first day of the lockout. "The only problem I'm having with things is believing whose numbers are right and whose numbers are wrong. Those are the big issues. And if it needs to have a cap, give it a cap, you know?" Madden told the *Newark Star-Ledger*. The next day, Madden skated around the issue, reworking his comments to say that he would support his union in the event that it accepted a cap.

9.16   B. Peter Forsberg
Less than a week after NHL commissioner Gary Bettman indefinitely postponed the 2004–05 season, starting September 15, 2004, 155 NHLers began playing in Europe. The most notable among that group? Peter Forsberg, who signed on September 18 to play with his old club, MoDo, in the Swedish Elite League. The Colorado Avalanche centre committed to the entire season, irregardless of any settlement in the labour dispute. "It has always been my dream to come back and play for my home team and win a championship,"

said Forsberg, who certainly wasn't in Sweden to match his NHL income, considering his reported $22,000-a-month salary. Still, Forsberg received a hero's welcome in his native country, where he played just 33 games and earned a 13–26–39 record before breaking his wrist on January 20, 2005. MoDo failed to win its championship, a feat the club last managed in 1979.

9.17 **C. Lynn Patrick, with the St. Louis Blues**

In the first season of NHL expansion, in 1967–68, St. Louis GM and head coach Lynn Patrick hired 34-year-old Scotty Bowman as his assistant. Bowman's job was to handle the defense corps while Patrick oversaw the forwards. After the slumping Blues won only four of their first 16 games, Patrick then also handed over the offense reins to Bowman, telling him, "You're ready to coach the team." He was right. Under Bowman's command, St. Louis reached the Stanley Cup finals. Four years later, the concept of the full-time assistant coach became a reality in the NHL when Philadelphia's Fred Shero hired Mike Nykoluk (and later Barry Ashbee) to help run the Flyers in 1972. Today, assistant coaches are as common—and as essential—behind the bench as trainers.

9.18 **D. Mike Ricci, with the San Jose Sharks**

The first player to register an overtime goal in the NHL's inaugural season of four-on-four was Mike Ricci, who scored the historic marker in a four-on-three power play against Edmonton on October 7, 1999. The format's fast-paced play increased scoring chances, but, again, hot goaltending prevailed: 13 of the first 15 overtime games in 1999–2000 finished in a tie, with goalies stopping 90 of 92 overtime shots. The first scorer in true four-on-four play (with neither team being penalized) was Valeri Bure, in a 3–2 overtime win October 13, 1999.

9.19 D. Keith Magnuson

Keith Magnuson didn't win many fights during his career, but he would fearlessly trade punches with anyone. After breaking into the NHL with Chicago in 1969–70, the hard-nosed defenseman racked up 100 or more penalty minutes in each of his first six seasons—and led the loop in his rookie and sophomore seasons with 213 and 291 PIM, respectively, a feat no other NHLer duplicated until Daniel Carcillo managed it in 2007–08 and 2008–09. A fan favourite and team leader, Magnuson adopted coach Billy Reay's defensive mantra of "None Against," striving at all costs to keep the puck out of his own net. Selected in 2001 as a member of the Blackhawks' 75th-anniversary All-Star team, Magnuson died in a car accident on December 15, 2003. Carcillo amassed 324 and 254 minues in his first two seasons, split between Phoenix and Philadelphia.

9.20 A. Georges Vezina, with the Montreal Canadiens

On February 18, 1918, Georges Vezina became the first net-minder to record a shutout, when the Montreal Canadiens defeated the Toronto Arenas in a 9–0 bombing. It was the 29th game of the NHL's first season as a league. Vezina joined the Canadiens of the National Hockey Association in 1910–11 and didn't miss a game for 15 years, playing a remarkable 367 consecutive regular-season and playoffs games. After his death from tuberculosis in 1926, the Montreal Canadiens donated the Vezina Trophy to honour his memory. Vezina was one of the original 12 individuals elected to the Hockey Hall of Fame.

9.21 D. Bill Clinton

The first sitting U.S. president to attent an NHL game was Bill Clinton, who watched the Washington Capitals defeat

the Buffalo Sabres 3–2 on May 25, 1998, at Washington's MCI
Centre. "It (hockey) is much more exciting in person, even,
than on television—no offense to ESPN," Clinton said
during the second-period intermission. "I love this. It's fasci-
nating." The American president sat in the luxury suite
of Capitals owner Abe Poulin. Unfortunately, Clinton left the
arena before Todd Krygier's overtime goal gave Washington
a 3–2 victory.

9.22   B. Lars-Erik Sjoberg, with the Winnipeg Jets
Before the Winipeg Jets crashed, burned and rose again in
the desert as the Phoenix Coyotes, they, more than any other
team, developed the first European-North American link in
hockey. Sjoberg, already a 30-year-old veteran Swedish defenseman, was amongst the first Europeans lured by Winnipeg.
Sjoberg played six seasons with the Jets: his first five in the
WHA and his last, 1979–80, as an NHLer when the two leagues
merged. Sjoberg's experience on European ice prepared him
well for North American play. After he became the Jets' captain in 1975, he led the team to three Avco World Trophies in
four years. And when Winnipeg became an NHL franchise in
1979, Sjoberg, still wearing the "C," became the league's first
European-trained captain.

9.23   A. Kris Draper
A combination of unusual circumstances allowed Kris Draper
to score a goal in the NHL before he had played a single game
in junior hockey. Draper joined the Canadian National hockey
team on a full-time basis at age 17 in 1988–89. The following
season he was selected 62nd overall in the 1989 NHL Entry
Draft by the Winnipeg Jets and, on October 4, 1990, made
his NHL debut with a goal against the Toronto Maple Leafs.
After playing two more NHL games, Draper was then sent

down to the Ottawa 67s of the Ontario Hockey League, where he scored 19 goals in 39 games. Later that season, Draper then played seven games for Moncton in the AHL, where he scored twice.

9.24   B. The New York Islanders

The first European-trained goalie to don the pads in the NHL was Sweden's Goran Hogosta, who made his debut on November 1, 1977, for the New York Islanders against the Atlanta Flames. Hogosta replaced an injured Billy Smith and played nine minutes, getting credit for a shared shutout in the Isles' 9–0 win. After this relief stint, however, Hogosta did not make another NHL appearance until 1979–80, his last big-league season, when he played 21 games for the Quebec Nordiques.

9.25   A. The 1920s

Although air travel did not become a common mode of transportation for NHL teams until the 1960s, the New York Rangers made history in December 1929, when then-club-president Colonel John Hammond hired the Curtis-Wright Corporation to transport the team to Toronto via airplane. Hammon was clearly not a superstitious man: the plane left on Friday the 13th. But flying didn't help the Blueshirts. They lost 7–6.

9.26   A. Bryan Berard

This is not the kind of first any athlete wants on his record. But Bryan Berard will forever be remembered as the first NHLer busted for steroid use, after he tested positive for the banned substance 19-norandrosterone in November 2005. Ironically, Berard did not face disciplinary measures from the NHL for the result because the test was not part of the league's program.

Rather, as a U.S. Olympic team candidate, Berard was caught by the U.S. Anti-Doping Agency and barred from international hockey for two years. Of the 250 athletes tested who were eligible for Olympic teams, Berard was the only one to test positive. (Later, during pre-Olympic drug testing in January 2006, José Théodore tested positive for a hair-restoration drug known as Propecia, a prescription product that is banned as a masking agent.) "No question, I'm embarrassed about it," said Berard, who insists the steroid was in a supplement he took to get ready for the 2005–06 NHL season.

9.27 A. The Montreal Canadiens

Strange, but true. The Montreal Canadiens, perhaps the team most closely identified with Canadian hockcy, was the first NHL club to win the Stanley Cup with an American coach. The year was 1924 and the coach was Leo Dandurand, a native of Bourbonnais, Illinois, who moved to Canada in 1905 and later served as a referee in the National Hockey Association, the predecessor to the NHL. One of the top sports entre-preneurs of his day, Dandurand was also the director of the Montreal Royals baseball team and founder of the Montreal Alouettes football team. After purchasing the Canadiens with two partners in 1921 for US$11,000, he coached the club from 1921 to 1926, then again in 1934–35, before selling the team.

9.28 C. Larry Kwong

The son of a Chinese grocer in Vernon, British Columbia, Larry Kwong grew up dreaming of one day skating in the NHL. He finally got his shot after a long slog through the minors ended with a call-up by the injury-riddled New York Rangers on March 13, 1948. But the right-winger's stay with the big club was painfully brief. Kwong played just one shift in the game against the Canadiens at the Montreal Forum before being returned to the New York Rovers of the Eastern Hockey League. Kwong later played for the Valleyfield Braves of the Quebec Senior League, where he thrived under coach Toe Blake, winning the league's MVP award in 1950–51 and leading the club to the senior title. But after his one New York minute, he never got another crack at the big time.

9.29 A. Right-winger Leo Labine

Willie O'Ree is often called the Jackie Robinson of hockey for being the first black player in the NHL. But for all his on-ice talent, O'Ree never had an impact on the sport like Robinson, who broke the colour barrier and cleared a path for thousands of black ballplayers to follow. O'Ree was simply the first. Yes, it was a courageous act, but, despite O'Ree's efforts to prove that he belonged in the NHL, no other black athlete played in the league until 1974, when Mike Marson was drafted by Washington. O'Ree's big break came on January 18, 1958, when the Bruins' hard-hitting winger Leo Labine was laid low by the flu and O'Ree played left wing on a line with Don McKenney and Jerry Toppazzini. Within two games, O'Ree was back with the Quebec Aces, arguably hockey's best team outside the NHL. O'Ree's historic rise to hockey supremacy is compelling because he could see with only one eye—a disability he hid well enough to sustain a 21-year pro career. Even so, O'Ree faced no challenge greater than the prejudice against the colour of his skin. In February 1998, he was named director of youth development for NHL Diversity.

9.30 B. Ken Daneyko

Devils mainstay Ken Daneyko voluntarily turned himself over to the NHL's substance abuse program in November 1997, becoming the first "known" NHLer to take part in the no-fault rehab plan run jointly by the league and the NHL Players

Association. "I'm an alcoholic, I cannot drink," he said in 1998. "It took me a long time to admit that to myself, much less anyone else. I'd been getting by, faking it, but hockey was the only good thing I was doing." According to Daneyko, he never drank heavily before a game or played drunk. "The only control in my life was hockey." (The other three multiple-choice players in our question are fictitious.)

9.31 **B. He was the first pro goalie credited with an overtime goal**
They've scored game-winners and power-play goals and recorded shutouts while scoring a goal, but until Antero Niittymaki, no netminder had ever potted an overtime goal—or a shorthanded one. Niittymaki managed both at once on April 11, 2004, in a game between the Hershey Bears and Philadephia Phantoms of the AHL. With the teams deadlocked 2–2 midway through overtime, Hershey coach Paul Fixter pulled goaltender Phillippe Sauve during a power play in a last-game gamble to qualify for the Calder Cup playoffs. But the five-on-three man-advantage failed during the ensuing attack when Shane Willis's wild pass back to the point left the Phantom zone, rebounded off the boards at centre ice and slid into Hershey's vacated net. Niittymaki was the last Phantom to touch the puck and was credited with the OT goal.

9.32 **B. Riendeau was the first NHLer from North America to play in a Russian hockey league**
Riendeau, who played 184 games in eight NHL seasons with Montreal, St. Louis, Detroit and Boston, made hockey history in February 1999 when he became the first former NHLer (from outside Russia) to join the Russian Hockey League. Riendeau backstopped for Lada Togliatti, a club based in

the industrial city of Togliatti, 700 kilometres southeast of Moscow. Although Riendeau could have played elsewhere in Europe, he told the *National Post* that he chose Russia because "I'm not your typical type of guy. This is a chance to deal with a new culture, a new language. To me, this is life, trying new things." And Riendeau's first on-ice experience in Russia was positive: after back-to-back victories in the nets, his teammates all came up to him. "I've no idea what they were saying, but they seemed happy," said Riendeau. (In 1990 Todd Hartje became the first North American to play in Russia, but Hartje never made it to the NHL.)

9.33 **C. José Théodore**
Five other netminders potted goals in the NHL before José Théodore managed it, but Théodore is the first backstopper to score while picking up a shutout. "I couldn't believe it," Théodore said. "Guys like Hextall and Brodeur can think about scoring, but I can only dream about it. I don't really have a good shot." Théodore insists he wasn't trying to score when he flipped the puck at the empty net late in the game against the New York Islanders on January 2, 2001. But it kept rolling towards the Islanders' net and sealed Montreal's 3–0 victory. "I just wanted to clear the puck down the middle. If you aim for the boards, there's always a chance of a penalty… When I saw the puck sliding towards the goal—and I did have time to watch it—it was an extraordinary feeling," Théodore said.

9.34 **C. He pulled Thompson to add an extra forward**
Ross was the first coach to yank his goalie for an extra attacker. In the 1931 Montreal–Boston semifinals, with one loss already and behind 1–0 in Game 2, Ross gambled in the

dying moments and pulled Tiny Thompson to add a forward. The scheme didn't work; Boston still lost to Montreal 1–0. But what the day's sports pages called an "amazing manoeuvre" caught on and soon became standard game strategy.

9.35   D. Brantt Myhres

Hockey tough guy Brantt Myhres's worst enemies have always been his own demons. After a 154-game, 687-penalty-minute career in the NHL, he hit the league's limit of four go-arounds in its substance abuse program: 28 days the first time; then two months, six months and, finally, a full year of rehab that forced Myhres to miss all of 2003–04. It's safe to say Myhres was a very good active alcoholic, conning the system until stage four—his last shot at playing and staying sober. The bottle has long been considered an occupational hazard with heavyweights (because of the stress of fighting for a living), but don't expect Myhres—the recovering alcoholic—to be an on-ice pacifist. Shortly after his last rehab stint, he received an eight-game suspension for an ugly bench-clearing brawl between Lowell and Norfolk in an AHL game on December 11, 2004. Myhres's last fight came in an exhibition game in 2005 when he was auditioning for Calgary's enforcer job. He tangled with Edmonton's Georges Laraque, who TKOed Myhres's NHL career with a smashing left hand that crushed bones around Myhres's left eye socket. Myhres played another 34 games for the Flames' AHL Omaha farm team, but he said no to every opponent who engaged him. In 2007, he was an agent-in-training for Rich Winter's firm.

9.36   D. He played opposite the first goalie to record a shutout in his first playoff game

On April 2, 1927, four months after Winkler became the first goalie to notch a shutout in his first career game, he became part of another first when Lorne Chabot of the Rangers earned a shutout against Winkler in a New York–Boston 0–0 tie during the Stanley Cup semifinals. Like Winkler's history-making regular-season shutout debut, Chabot became the first rookie goalie to earn a zero in his first playoff game, with Winkler in goal for both historic shutout firsts. Ironically, during that season Winkler was sent to the Bruins, with Chabot replacing him in the New York nets. This means that both Winkler and Chabot played for the same team, the New York Rangers, when they each recorded their landmark rookie shutouts.

9.37 B. 1955

The Zamboni was invented in 1945 by Frank Zamboni, a rink attendant at Paramount Studios in Hollywood, California. The idea of a motorized ice-cleaner caught the attention of figure skater Sonja Henie, and with her support, Zamboni was able to build a prototype. (Before the Zamboni, NHL rinks were cleaned and flooded between periods by workers using shovels and barrels of water.) The Zamboni made its NHL debut on March 10, 1955, in a 0–0 tie between the Canadiens and the Maple Leafs at the Montreal Forum. It was a bumpy baptism. During the game, Habs fans grew so angry with the Leafs' stifling, defensive play that they littered the ice with garbage, including pigs feet.

Game 9 ─────────

The First Five-Team 20-Goal Man

WHO WAS THE FIRST NHLER to record 20-goal seasons with five different teams? Most of the players listed below have scored 20 goals with at least two different clubs; some have done it with three; others, such as Doug Gilmour, with four teams, and a select few, such as Eddie Shack and Mike Gartner, are five-team 20-goal men. Their names, such as Adam Oates, appear in the puzzle horizontally, vertically, diagonally or backwards. After you've circled all 45 words, read the remaining letters in descending order to spell our unknown shooter. As a bonus we've circled a few words, including FIVE and TEAMS and the first name of our mystery 20-goal man, DEAN PRENTICE

Solutions are on page 562

Amonte	Carson	Dionne	Gartner	Guerin
Larionov	Mullen	Nolan	Robitaille	Stastny
Turgeon	Andreychuk	Arnott	Clark	Esposito
Gilmour	Hull	MacInnis	Muller	Oates
Roenick	Shanahan	Yashin	Bathgate	Coffey
Five	Goulet	Kovalev	Messier	Murphy
Palffy	Selanne	Sundin	Zhamnov	Bure
Dean	Francis	Gretzky	Kurri	Mogilny
Nicholls	Recchi	Shack	Teams	Nieuwendyk

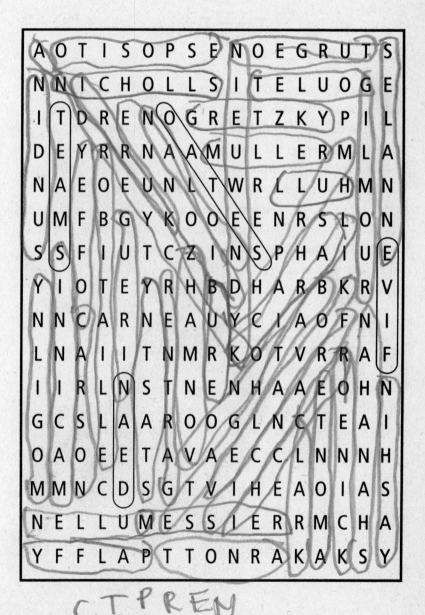

```
A O T I S O P S E N O E G R U T S
N N I C H O L L S I T E L U O G E
I T D R E N O G R E T Z K Y P I L
D E Y R R N A A M U L L E R M L A
N A E O E U N L T W R L L U H M N
U M F B G Y K O O E E N R S L O N
S S F I U T C Z I N S P H A I U E
Y I O T E Y R H B D H A R B K R V
N N C A R N E A U Y C I A O F N I
L N A I I T N M R K O T V R R A F
I I R L N S T N E N H A A E O H N
G C S L A A R O O G L N C T E A I
O A O E E T A V A E C C L N N N H
M M N C D S G T V I H E A O I A S
N E L L U M E S S I E R R M C H A
Y F F L A P T T O N R A K A K S Y
```

CTPREN

10

Team Tricks

CHICAGO'S BILL MOSIENKO bagged the NHL's quickest hat trick, in 21 seconds, on March 23, 1952. But what is the team record for three goals? Almost two decades after Mosienko's feat, the Boston Bruins set the team version, scoring a trio of goals just one second faster than Mosienko managed it. The Bruins' three-goal outburst came in 20 seconds, as Johnny Bucyk (at 4:50), Ed Westfall (at 5:02) and Ted Green (at 5:10) scored in rapid succession during the third period of an 8–3 win over Vancouver on February 25, 1971. More recently, Washington missed the Bruins' mark by one second, with a team hat trick in 21 seconds, to tie Mosienko and the Blackhawks' record. In this chapter, we focus on team spirit.

Answers are on page 257

10.1 **Which two teams have played the most regular-season games against one another?**
A. The Montreal Canadiens and the Boston Bruins
B. The Chicago Blackhawks and the Detroit Red Wings
C. The New York Rangers and the Boston Bruins
D. The Toronto Maple Leafs and the Montreal Canadiens

10.2 **Which team was first to invite the fathers of players on a road trip?**
A. The Nashville Predators
B. The Los Angeles Kings

C. The Edmonton Oilers

D. The Pittsburgh Penguins

10.3 **From what historical event does Columbus's NHL team take its namesake, the Blue Jackets?**

A. The U.S. Civil War

B. The first atomic bomb

C. The Indian Wars

D. The Kent State Riot of 1970

10.4 **Which club's record streak of 487 consecutive home sell-outs came to an end in 2006–07?**

A. The Edmonton Oilers'

B. The Colorado Avalanche's

C. The Toronto Maple Leafs'

D. The Detroit Red Wings'

10.5 **Which Central Hockey League team made history in 2005 by icing pro hockey's first brother-sister duo?**

A. The Austin Ice Bats

B. The Wichita Thunder

C. The Tulsa Oilers

D. The Odessa Jackalopes

10.6 **Of all defunct NHL teams, which one recorded the greatest number of losses?**

A. The California/Oakland Seals

B. The New York/Brooklyn Americans

C. The old Ottawa Senators

D. The Montreal Maroons

10.7 In 2003–04, which NHL general manager told fans to stay away if they were going to boo his players?

    A. Bobby Clarke, with the Philadelphia Flyers

    B. Glen Sather, with the New York Rangers

    C. Larry Pleau, with the St. Louis Blues

    D. Bob Gainey, with the Montreal Canadiens

10.8 What is the most number of regular-season games played by a franchise before its first playoff match?

    A. Less than 300 games

    B. Between 300 and 500 games

    C. Between 500 and 700 games

    D. More than 700 games

10.9 How many points could an NHL team record if they lost all 82 games in a season, in overtime?

    A. 22 points

    B. 41 points

    C. 62 points

    D. 82 points

10.10 What is the record for the longest undefeated streak in overtime games by a team?

    A. 16 overtime games

    B. 26 overtime games

    C. 36 overtime games

    D. 46 overtime games

10.11 What is the most points recorded by an NHL team on a road trip?

    A. 13 points

    B. 15 points

C. 17 points

D. 19 points

10.12 What is the record for longest winning streak on the road in one season?

A. 10 road games

B. 12 road games

C. 14 road games

D. 16 road games

10.13 What is the team mark for most consecutive games (from the start of a season) that a player has recorded two-goal nights?

A. Three straight games

B. Five straight games

C. Seven straight games

D. Nine straight games

10.14 In 2003–04, how many home games did Pittsburgh lose, establishing a new NHL record for ineptitude?

A. 13 games

B. 14 games

C. 15 games

D. 16 games

10.15 The Pittsburgh Penguins snapped an NHL-record, 14-game home losing streak on a tying goal by defenseman Marc Bergevin in 2003–04. How long had it been since Bergevin last scored a goal?

A. 42 games earlier

B. 62 games earlier

C. 82 games earlier

D. 102 games earlier

10.16 Even though Pittsburgh lost more games in a row in 2003–04 than any other team in NHL history (home and away), the streak is not a league record. Why?

A. One of the losses was in overtime

B. One of the losses was a postponed game

C. One of the losses was a neutral-site game

D. There is no official NHL record for most consecutive losses

10.17 What is the NHL team record for most consecutive games without going into overtime?

A. 29 straight games

B. 49 straight games

C. 69 straight games

D. 89 straight games

10.18 Which NHL team is associated with the "334 Club"?

A. The New Jersey Devils

B. The New York Islanders

C. The New York Rangers

D. All of the above

10.19 What is the greatest number of games a team has finished above .500 during the regular season and still not made the playoffs?

A. Four games

B. Eight games

C. 12 games

D. 16 games

10.20 Which is the first pro hockey team to win 50 or more games in five successive seasons?

A. The Houston Aeros of the AHL

B. The Quad City Mallards of the UHL

C. The Tulsa Oilers of the CHL

D. The Hersey Bears of the AHL

10.21 **Which NHL team started a 2005–06 game with a 1–0 lead?**

A. The Carolina Hurricanes

B. The Toronto Maple Leafs

C. The Edmonton Oilers

D. The Nashville Predators

10.22 **What famous event in Montreal Canadiens history took place on March 11?**

A. The legendary Howie Morenz was honoured with a rare funeral service at the Montreal Forum

B. The Canadiens played their last game at the Montreal Forum

C. The death and sweater retirement of Hall of Famer Bernie Geoffrion

D. All of the above

10.23 **Which team has gone the longest without an NHL scoring champion?**

A. The Chicago Blackhawks

B. The New York Rangers

C. The Toronto Maple Leafs

D. The Ottawa Senators

10.24 **Which modern-era NHL team has been blanked the most times in a season since the record was set in 1928–29?**

A. The Washington Capitals, in 1974–75

B. The Ottawa Senators, in 1992–93

C. The San Jose Sharks, in 1992–93

D. The Columbus Blue Jackets, in 2006–07

10.25 What is the greatest number of hat tricks by all teams in one season?

A. 109 hat tricks
B. 139 hat tricks
C. 169 hat tricks
D. 199 hat tricks

10.26 Which regular-season champion finished a record 27 points ahead of the second-place team?

A. The 1943–44 Montreal Canadiens
B. The 1977–78 Montreal Canadiens
C. The 1983–84 Edmonton Oilers
D. The 1995–96 Detroit Red Wings

10.27 Which team led the NHL in goals scored for the most consecutive seasons?

A. The Maurice Richard-Jean Béliveau-era Montreal Canadiens
B. The Bobby Hull-Stan Mikita-era Chicago Blackhawks
C. The Bobby Orr-Phil Esposito-era Boston Bruins
D. The Wayne Gretzky-Mark Messier-era Edmonton Oilers

10.28 Which 1990s team posted the largest single-season improvement in points in NHL history?

A. The 1992–93 Quebec Nordiques
B. The 1993–94 San Jose Sharks
C. The 1996–97 Dallas Stars
D. The 1998–99 Toronto Maple Leafs

10.29 Which team has scored the most power-play goals in one season?

A. The 1977–78 Montreal Canadiens
B. The 1983–84 Edmonton Oilers

C. The 1988–89 Pittsburgh Penguins

D. The 1992–93 Detroit Red Wings

10.30 What is the least amount of goals scored by a post-1967 expansion team in its inaugural NHL season?

A. 123 goals

B. 153 goals

C. 183 goals

D. 213 goals

10.31 Which expansion team set an NHL attendance record in its first season?

A. The San Jose Sharks, in 1991–92

B. The Tampa Bay Lightning, in 1992–93

C. The Mighty Ducks of Anaheim, in 1993–94

D. The Atlanta Thrashers, in 1999–2000

10.32 How many wins did the Buffalo Sabres register in 2006–07 to tie the NHL record for most victories from the start of a season?

A. Six straight wins

B. Eight straight wins

C. 10 straight wins

D. 12 straight wins

10.33 Which NHL team had its 66-year-old record of best road start in a season destroyed by the Buffalo Sabres in 2006–07?

A. The Toronto Maple Leafs

B. The Boston Bruins

C. The Detroit Red Wings

D. The New York Americans

10.34 Which team recorded the NHL's most efficient power play since expansion in 1967–68?

A. The Philadelphia Flyers, in 1973–74

B. The Montreal Canadiens, in 1977–78

C. The New York Islanders, in 1981–82

D. The Calgary Flames, in 1987–88

10.35 At the start of 2006–07, how many games did the Anaheim Ducks lose in their NHL 16-game unbeaten streak?

A. None

B. One game

C. Two games

D. Four games

10.36 In 1999–2000, how many of the Florida Panthers' team records did Pavel Bure break?

A. Three records

B. Five records

C. Seven records

D. 21 records

10.37 Which Original Six team was saddled with "Muldoon's Curse"?

A. The Toronto Maple Leafs

B. The Boston Bruins

C. The Chicago Blackhawks

D. The Montreal Canadiens

10.38 Where does the world's longest-surviving hockey club come from?

A. Nova Scotia (The Halifax Hockey Club)

B. Montreal (McGill University)

C. Boston (Harvard University)

D. Oxford, England (The Oxford Ice Hockey Club)

Answers

10.1   B. The Chicago Blackhawks and the Detroit Red Wings
Considering that Montreal and Toronto were both members
of the NHL when the league was created in 1917, one might
logically assume they would have played more games against
one another than any other pair of teams. But that's not the
case. As of 2008–09, Chicago and Detroit have met 703 times—
10 more times than Montreal and Toronto's Maple Leafs (and
its predecessors, the Arenas and St. Patricks). Given the fact
that the Hawks and the Red Wings did not join the league
until 1926, how could they overtake Montreal and Toronto in
recent years? Try: unbalanced schedules and increased interdi-
vision play.

10.2   A. The Nashville Predators
The first team to invite the fathers of players on a road trip
was probably the Nashville Predators. The club asked its
players' dads to accompany their sons during the franchise's
inaugural season of 1998–99, and have held an annual "Dads'
Trip" ever since, including a father-son outing in 2006–07
when 23 fathers made a two-game road trip to Philadelphia
and St. Louis. Since then, Minnesota, Pittsburgh and the
Islanders have all rewarded NHL fathers for sacrifices made
in supporting their sons' dreams. (Players' moms have often
played larger roles, but it would be "kind of weird" bringing
them along, according to the Wild's Mark Parrish.)

10.3 **A. The U.S. Civil War**

The Blue Jackets name honours Ohio's contribution to American history, specifically its involvement in the Civil War, given that Ohio sent more of its citizens into battle for the Union Army than any other state in the union. The city of Columbus manufactured the blue uniforms worn by Union soldiers, and the uniform colour of the Blue Jackets, Capital Blue, is similar to that worn by the Union Army. The 13 stars in the team logo represent each of the original 13 U.S. colonies. Even the Blue Jackets' mascot, Stinger, sports a blue Civil War cap.

10.4 **B. The Colorado Avalanche's**

Some people doubted that Denver could support an NHL franchise when the Quebec Nordiques relocated to the mile-high city in 1995–96. The NHL's Colorado Rockies were a disaster on-ice and didn't draw well in their six-season run before the franchise moved to New Jersey in 1982, and the World Hockey Association Denver Spurs lasted less than a season prior to their departure to Ottawa. But Denver fans responded to the Avalanche, which won the Stanley Cup its first year in town, and the team was soon selling out on a nightly basis. Their home sellout streak began on November 9, 1995, and lasted until October 16, 2007, when the Avalanche hosted Chicago. The official attendance of 17,681 in that Blackhawks game was 326 seats short of capacity in the Pepsi Center, ending the longest recorded sellout streak in NHL history at 487 games.

10.5 **C. The Tulsa Oilers**

On January 28, 2005, Angela Ruggiero became the first female non-goaltender to play in a U.S. men's professional hockey game, when she laced them up for the Tulsa Oilers in a Central Hockey League tilt against the Rio Grande

Valley Killer Bees. Making the occasion doubly memorable, Ruggiero's brother, Bill, was the Oilers' goaltender. Together, the Ruggieros became the first brother-and-sister pairing in a North American professional game. "It was all that I could ask for," said the 25-year-old rearguard after Tulsa's 7–2 victory over the Killer Bees. Ruggiero, who won gold, silver and bronze as a member of the 1990, 2002 and 2006 U.S. Women's Olympic Teams, played 13 shifts that totalled 13:05, recorded an assist on the game's final goal, finished plus-two and did not shy away from physical contact. Seconds after being checked in her third shift of the game, she answered with a hit of her own by knocking a Killer Bees player into the boards. "I'm used to getting hit," said Ruggiero. "There was definitely a lot of contact, but it was all clean. That's hockey. It's a rough game."

10.6   B. The New York/Brooklyn Americans
The Seals quit the NHL just in time. Between 1967–68 and 1975–76, California collected 401 losses, one less than the Americans' 402.

10.7   D. Bob Gainey, with the Montreal Canadiens
Few sports fans have ever been publicly skewered the way Gainey admonished Montreal fans after they booed their favourite target, Patrice Brisebois, in a November 2003 game at the Bell Centre. Gainey coolly fired back at the boo-birds: "A bunch of gutless bastards, to be honest. They're jealous people, yellow people," he said. "Our message to them is to stay away. We don't need you." That kind of criticism of the public would not be tolerated from just anyone. But Gainey, one of hockey's most respected players and team builders, got everyone on side, including his players.

10.8 D. More than 700 games

The best spin to put on the early history of the Washington Capitals might be that they had a long-term struggle for respectability. But in reality, they were *the* club to pillage for points. The Caps' growing pains were considerable: lacklustre talent; dismal performances that set all-time league lows in fewest wins and most losses; a parade of management changes that included the hiring of 26-year-old Gary Green, the youngest coach in NHL history, and an eight-year playoff jinx that dragged on for a record 720 games before the Capitals' first playoff series in 1983. What broke the cycle of mediocrity and ended Washington's postseason curse? A crucial six-player trade with the Montreal Canadiens. The franchise subsequently delivered its first .500 season in 1982–83, followed by its first playoff spot, which ended in a divisional semifinal loss to the Stanley Cup-champion New York Islanders.

10.9 D. 82 points

Considering today's rules that guarantee a point in an overtime loss, a club could conceivably lose every game of the season in overtime and still earn 82 points, which was once considered .500 hockey and enough to secure a playoff spot.

10.10 C. 36 overtime games

This remarkable record was set by the Boston Bruins between 1934 and 1938, when the NHL played 10-minute overtimes in games that were deadlocked after 60 minutes. The Bruins posted nine wins and 27 ties during the streak—which began December 30, 1934, in a scoreless draw against the New York Rangers. Four years later, almost to the day, the same Rangers finally brought Boston's overtime run to an end with a 2–1 defeat on December 31, 1938. After the loss, the Bruins went undefeated for their next 12 overtime contests.

10.11 C. 17 points

The Philadelphia Flyers were road warriors during a gruelling, three-week, 11-game marathon in 2005–06, notching an impressive 8–2–0–1 record to claim honours for the most productive road trip in NHL history. No other team in league annals has ever come home with 17 points. But NHL schedulers take note: The Flyers' tank was running on empty. Philadelphia lost two of its last three away games and its return to the Wachovia Center was a disaster, with the club dropping its first three home games and losing in overtime to Colorado, in a shootout to Carolina and in regulation time to Boston. Still, Philadephia's 11-game swing did match the longest trip in modern NHL history. Eighteen years earlier, the Calgary Flames played 11 consecutive games away from the Saddledome when, in February 1988, the Winter Olympics came to town. But they didn't fare as well as Philly, going 5–5–1 for 11 points.

10.12 B. 12 road games

The advent of regular-season overtime and the shootout has changed the title holders of many NHL records. This may not be an across-the-board phenomenon, but check out the leaders for the longest winning streak on the road in one season. Before overtime in 1983–84, the best road run was eight games (held by five teams, all equalling the mark between 1971–72 and 1981–82). But in the first season of overtime, 1983–84, the Buffalo Sabres set a new record of 10 successive wins on the road between December 10, 1983, and January 23, 1984. Surprisingly, none of those victories were overtime decisions, but all the other leaders—St. Louis, with 10 straight road wins in 1999–2000, New Jersey, with 10 in 2000–01, Buffalo, with 10 in 2006–07, and San Jose, with 10 in 2007–08—sustained their streaks with at least one overtime or shootout win. One argument is that the teams still had to win those road games, but it was with an advantage not available to previous record holders. Currently, the Detroit Red Wings lead this category with 12 successive victories away between March 1 and April 15, 2006. The Red Wings did it with two shootout victories.

10.13 C. Seven straight games

It's always big trivia news when a long-standing NHL record is broken, even one as obscure as the Calgary Flames' seven-game streak in this category. Daymond Langkow made history and put the Flames in the NHL record book by scoring twice in a 4–3 victory against the Los Angeles Kings on October 18, 2007. It marked the seventh consecutive match to start the season that a Calgary player had potted two goals, breaking a little-known record held by the Ottawa Senators, who accomplished the feat twice—in 1917–18 and again in 1920–21. Further, Langkow made the team record a little personal: his first goal was his 200th career marker, his second his 500th career point. The veteran centre was also the biggest contributor to Calgary's record, notching three of seven two-goal games during the historic run. The other double red-lights came courtesy of Kristian Huselius, with two, and Matthew Lombardi and Jerome Iginla, with one each. Calgary won three and lost four during the stretch.

10.14 B. 14 games

If teams hung banners from the rafters for their NHL records, as they do for their championships, Pittsburgh's Igloo would be festooned with some doozies. Next to the banner celebrating the league's longest winning streak of 17 games in 1992–93, fans could be reminded of the Penguins' embarrassing 14-game home losing streak of 2003–04—the longest in NHL history. The moribund Penguins took losing to new depths that season by bettering the four previous record-holding teams (with 11 straight defeats) by three losses. (To add salt to Pittsburgh's wound, the four clubs—Boston, Washington, Ottawa and Atlanta—all suffered their slide as first-year expansion clubs.) The December 31 to February 22 skid was also on course to set another league mark for futility at home—the longest home winless streak. But the Penguins won on March 6 and halted their fall at 16 games, one short of the record 17 winless games held by Ottawa and Atlanta.

10.15 D. 102 games earlier

You know your team is in deep trouble when it needs a goal from Marc Bergevin. The veteran blueliner notched just his 36th goal in 1,181 career games to snap Pittsburgh's 14-game home losing streak on March 2, 2004. Bergevin's weak wrist shot from the point fluttered past the Islanders' Garth Snow at 1:46 of the third period for the 3–3 tie with New York. "I saw the replay—it was a laser beam," joked Bergevin of his first goal in precisely 102 games. Bergevin hadn't scored since November 23, 2002.

10.16 A. One of the losses was in overtime

No one has talked to the Washington Capitals or the San Jose Sharks about Pittsburgh's 18-game losing streak in 2003–04, but they are probably not happy with the St. Louis Blues. In a losing stretch that could have changed the NHL record book and displaced Washington and San Jose from the top spot for most consecutive losses (with 17), one of the Penguins' 18 defeats was in overtime, a 3–2 loss to St. Louis on February 14. Had the Blues beat the hapless Penguins in regulation time, hockey's losingest team would be Pittsburgh. Instead, their official record is 0–17–0–1, and the Capitals and Sharks remain the beacons of incompetence.

10.17 B. 49 straight games

The San Jose Sharks detest overtimes, but they hate shootouts even more. In 2005–06, they finished 30th among the NHL's 30 teams with an awful 1–7 shootout record. But in OT, the Sharks had a very respectable 9–4. Then again, overtime often leads to the dreaded shootout. So San Jose played a once-bitten-twice-shy game in regulation in 2006–07, going 49 matches without an extra period from October 6 to January 30, the longest streak since the five-minute overtime rule was introduced in 1983–84.

10.18 A. The New Jersey Devils

On January 22, 1987, a good old-fashioned New Jersey blizzard dropped 15 inches of snow and created the "334 Club": the 334 fans who braved road conditions to watch the Devils' 7–5 win against the Calgary Flames at the Meadowlands. Only 13 Devils made it for the start of the game, which was delayed by one hour and 46 minutes.

10.19 D. 16 games

Finishing 16 games above .500 would easily assure a playoff berth today, but in 1969–70, the defending-champion Montreal Canadiens went 38–22–16 and still failed to make the postseason. The reason was the NHL's unbalanced divisional playoffs format. Montreal's division, the East, featured strong, established teams, while the West was composed of third-year expansion clubs. Although the teams played an interlocking schedule, only four teams from each division (rather than the top eight overall) made the playoffs. Montreal's 92 points— which would have led the West and was only seven points back of the East division-champion Blackhawks and Bruins—left it tied with the New York Rangers for the fourth and final playoff spot. New York qualified for the postseason because it had scored more goals than Montreal.

10.20 B. The Quad City Mallards of the UHL

It's a record unmatched by any other team in professional hockey history. In March 2001, the United Hockey League's Quad City Mallards, based in Moline, Illinois, completed their "Drive of Five" with five consecutive seasons of 50 or more regular-season wins—and that's in a 74-game schedule. With three Colonial Cups also in that span, the Mallards are something of a success at rewriting the record books, both on and off the ice. In 2002 and again in 2004, the Iowa-Illinois border team collected 50th wins for an unprecedented sixth and seventh time in eight years. The Mallards also set UHL records for total season and average attendances and, in just their eighth season, almost hit the three-million mark in all-time attendance. As a result, all Quad City season ticket-holders were rewarded with free tickets to home playoff games as well as a "Legends Bobblehead Series," a limited-edition five-bobblehead set. Moreover, the Mallards are amongst the first in pro hockey to broadcast all of their games live over the Internet. As well, in February 2004, Cam Severson became the first former Mallard to score a point in the NHL while playing with the Anaheim Mighty Ducks.

10.21 D. The Nashville Predators

How do you win a game after scoring the exact same number of goals as your opponent? Just ask the Predators. On January 23, 2006, the team was spotted a one-goal lead over its opponents, the Detroit Red Wings, before the start of a game, and the 1–0 advantage proved the difference in the Predators' subsequent 3–2 win, in which each team scored only twice. The match was a make-up for a November game that was stopped during the first period when Detroit's Jiri Fischer suffered a seizure and collapsed on his team's bench. Fischer was revived by cardio-pulmonary resuscitation and a defibulator, and the game was postponed, allowing the Predators to keep their 1–0 lead for a later date. "Obviously it made a difference because they beat us by the one goal," Detroit centre Jason Williams said after the win. Nashville is the first team to start a game with a 1–0 lead, Detroit the first to trail on the scoreboard before the opening faceoff.

10.22 D. All of the above

Few dates hold as much significance in the storied history of the Club de Hockey Canadien as March 11. On that date, Montreal fans pay tribute to several events—most recently, the death of Bernie "Boom-Boom" Geoffrion on March 11, 2006. Just hours after Geoffrion's death from stomach cancer in an Atlanta hospice, the Canadiens retired his famous No. 5 in an emotional 40-minute banner-raising ceremony at centre ice at the Bell Centre. In attendance was the Geoffrion family, including his wife Marlene—daughter of the great 1930s NHL star Howie Morenz. In the last moments of his life, the Boomer had insisted that all of his family be there for his sweater retirement, as his banner would be raised next to Morenz's retired No. 7. "The first time dad took my mom on a date, he took her to a boxing match at the Forum," said son Danny Geoffrion. "He told her that, one day, his sweater would hang up there next to her father's. Today, he kept that promise." Long criticized for not retiring several jersey numbers of past greats, the Canadiens finally scheduled the Geoffrion celebration for March 11—to coincide with the 10th anniversary of the last Habs game at the Forum, where

Geoffrion starred for 14 years. It was also 69 years to the day after 12,500 fans attended funeral services at the Forum for his father-in-law, Howie Morenz. As well, the Canadiens were playing the New York Rangers, a team Geoffrion played for and coached after his playing career ended with Montreal in 1964. And in the 1–0 Montreal win, Craig Rivet, fittingly, scored on a slap shot—the shot Geoffrion popularized and the inspiration for his famous nickname.

10.23 C. The Toronto Maple Leafs

As hockey-savvy as Maple Leaf fans are, few would know the name Gord Drillon. That's because most Leaf fans weren't even born when Drillon led the league with 52 points and won the scoring title in 1937–38. New York hasn't seen a Ranger win the crown in almost as long. Bryan Hextall Sr. netted a league-high 56 points in 1941–42.

10.24 D. The Columbus Blue Jackets, in 2006–07

One of hockey's most embarrassing and, apparently, safest team records belongs to the Chicago Blackhawks. For going on 80 years now, the Hawks have led the NHL in most games blanked in a season after humiliating themselves with 20 zeroes in the 44-game schedule of 1928–29. (In that era, before the introduction of the red line and without forward passing in the offensive zone, shutouts were commonplace. The Pittsburgh Pirates suffered a similar fate that same season with 18 zeroes.) But the Blackhawks' one-off record should not be taken lightly, as Columbus found out in 2006–07 by being held off the scoresheet 16 times to set a modern-day record, surpassing the 14 shutout defeats of Pittsburgh in 1969–70 and Minnesota in 2000–01. Note: The 1928–29 Hawks own a few other train-wreck records that the Blue Jackets should also stay clear of, including most consecutive games shutout (8), fewest goals in a season (33) and lowest goals-per-game average (0.75). Chicago finished 1928–29 with a 7–29–8 record; Columbus had a 33–42–7 mark in 2006–07.

10.25 B. 139 hat tricks

Remember when hockey was about scoring goals? Even though 1981–82 ranks fourth-highest in scoring (6,741 goals), it leads all seasons in hat tricks. Wayne Gretzky netted an all-time-high 10 three-or-more-goal games that year. The 1980–81 season featured the second-most hat tricks: 133.

10.26 D. The 1995–96 Detroit Red Wings

Scotty Bowman's Red Wings played superb hockey in 1995–96, racking up a record of 62–13–7. No other team has ever won more games or finished so far ahead of the competition. Detroit's 131-point tally was 27 points better than the second-place Colorado Avalanche managed. However, Colorado got the last laugh, upsetting Detroit in the Western Conference finals and going on to win the Stanley Cup. Yet as good as the Red Wings were in 1995–96, in relative terms, the two teams that rank second and third on the all-time chart were even more dominant. In 1929–30, Boston finished 26 points ahead of the next-closest team in a 44-game schedule, and in 1943–44, Montreal had a 25-point cushion over the runner-up in a 50-game schedule.

10.27 A. The Maurice Richard-Jean Béliveau-era Montreal Canadiens

The 1950s may not have been a high-scoring decade, but you would have had trouble convincing the rest of the NHL that the Canadiens lacked firepower. Beginning in 1953–54, the Habs embarked on an amazing record streak of 10 straight seasons as the NHL's top-scoring team. In comparison to Montreal's dominance, the Wayne Gretzky-Mark Messier-era Edmonton Oilers, hockey's highest-scoring club, strung together only six successive regular seasons as the league's best scorers. By the time Montreal's run ended in 1963–64, the Flying Frenchmen had added five Stanley Cups to their trophy case.

10.28 B. The 1993–94 San Jose Sharks

Under rookie coach Kevin Constantine, San Jose made the playoffs for the first time in 1993–94, improving its 1992–93 record by 58 points while jumping from 24 to 82 points. The dramatic turnaround eclipsed the 52-point leap by the 1992–93 Quebec Nordiques as the largest single-season improvement in NHL history. The Sharks' surge was sparked by the crafty play of veteran forwards Igor Larionov and Sergei Makarov, the maturation of young defenseman Sandis Ozolinsh and the acrobatic netminding of Arturs Irbe. San Jose continued its inspired play in the postseason, upsetting top-seeded Detroit, before falling to Toronto in seven games.

10.29 C. The 1988–89 Pittsburgh Penguins

Powered by Mario Lemieux's 31 power-play goals, the Penguins amassed a league-record 119 man-advantage goals during 1988–89. Remarkably, none of the NHL's highest-scoring teams (such as the 1980s Edmonton Oilers and 1970s Montreal Canadiens) rank among the premier power-play clubs in the NHL record book. After the Pens, the 1992–93 Detroit Red Wings scored 113 times on the advantage and the 1987–88 New York Rangers 111 times.

10.30 B. 153 goals

The 1967–68 Oakland Seals hold the NHL record for futility in goal scoring by an expansion club. The punchless Seals scored a record-low 153 times and averaged just 2.07 goals per match during the 74-game schedule, to finish in the NHL cellar with a 15–42–17 record. But even that goal mark was in jeopardy during the 2000–01 season, when Jacques Lemaire's Minnnesota Wild, playing in eight more games than Oakland, scored just 168 goals in 82 contests. Though if averages mean anything, Minnesota fared worse due to its longer schedule, with 2.05 goals per game. The Wild's goal count was also close to the low of 170 goals set by the New York Islanders in 1972–73 and tied by the Atlanta Thrashers in 1999–2000. The most goals scored by an NHL expansion team is 303, registered by the former WHA Hartford Whalers in 1979–80. Among expansion clubs starting from scratch, the Tampa Bay Lightning registered the most in its debut: 245 goals in 1992–93.

10.31 D. The Atlanta Thrashers, in 1999–2000

Fans were easier to come by than wins for the Thrashers in 1999–2000. Atlanta set an expansion-team record by averaging 17,205 fans per game in its first season, including 14 sellouts. But audience loyalty brought few victories, as the Thrashers challenged league standards for futility in the win column with a 14–61–7 record. The mark was the fourth-worst record for an expansion club since 1970, with the fourth-highest loss total ever and second-most defeats at home (29). "It's been a hard year," lamented goalie Damian Rhodes.

10.32 C. 10 straight wins

It's a good thing that Buffalo didn't have to play Toronto before it recorded its 10th consecutive win from the start of 2006–07. Otherwise, the Maple Leafs might have halted the Sabres' streak earlier, considering the Leafs' cherished 1993–94 record of 10 straight victories was on the line. Still, at the first opportunity—in Buffalo's 13th game—the Leafs took revenge, handing the Sabres their first defeat in regulation, a 4–1 setback on November 4, 2006. The result: Buffalo only tied Toronto's record 10-win streak after the Sabres' 11th game ended in a 5–4 shootout loss to Atlanta. "I'm a little ticked off," said Sabres goalie Ryan Miller. "It would have been fun to be on our own; a little piece of history."

10.33 A. The Toronto Maple Leafs

While Buffalo had to settle for sharing with Toronto the NHL's longest winning streak from start of season (see previous answer, 10.33), in 2006–07 the Sabres took some solace in establishing a new league mark for the best road start. The team demolished the Maple Leafs' long-standing run of seven road wins (to start 1940–41) with a record-setting road-win streak of 10 victories between October 4 and November 13, 2006. Since 1940, only the 1985–86 Philadelphia Flyers and 2005–06 Detroit Red Wings have managed to tie Toronto's mark.

10.34 B. The Montreal Canadiens, in 1977–78

It rarely paid to take a penalty against the Scotty Bowman-led Montreal Canadiens. In 1977–78, Bowman's special teams scored 31.9 per cent of the time they iced an extra attacker. The raw numbers are even more impressive. Montreal amassed 73 power-play goals on 229 advantages, with Guy Lafleur (15) and Steve Shutt (16) accounting for 31 goals. According to the Elias Sports Bureau, Montreal recorded the league's best power-play percentage since expansion in 1967. Bowman's Canadiens lost just 10 games that season. Today, the best teams rarely score above a 25 per cent efficiency rate.

10.35 D. Four games

When is a loss not really a loss? Only in an NHL game, where the league can suspend reality by ignoring the final score and award one point to the losing team. Of course, this doesn't happen in regulation, but it does in an overtime or shoot-out situation. By this standard, with at least a point in each of its first 16 games, Anaheim could argue that it owns the longest unbeaten streak to start a season. Why? They topped the league's previous best 15-game start (Edmonton's 12–0–3 record in 1984–85) with an 8–0–4–4 record between October 6 and November 9, 2007. And during that time they collected a league-high 28 points, one more than the Oilers' 27 points in 1984–85. But in those first 16 contests Anaheim suffered three shootout losses, which the NHL didn't have in 1984–85—and one overtime defeat in their 13th game, a certain streak-breaker during the Oilers' run. As a result, and rightly so, the NHL record book has Edmonton with the longest undefeated streak to start a season.

10.36 D. 21 records

Floridians haven't seen a hometown athlete like Pavel Bure since Dan Marino at his peak. In short order, Bure erased 21 team records in almost every category for goals, including goals in a period (3), in a game (4), in a season (58), game-winners (14), empty-netters (9), even-strength (45), third-period goals (29), season hat tricks (4) and career hat tricks (6). Bure also smashed or tied Panther records for points in a period (3), points in a game (4), points per game (1.3), even-strength points (72), season points (94), most shots in a game (11) and in a season (360), along with the best plus-minus (plus-25). As well, he set another four club records in scoring streaks, including for goals (five games), game-winning goals (three games), assists (seven games) and, finally, points (13 games).

10.37 C. The Chicago Blackhawks

"Muldoon's Curse" dates back to Chicago's inaugural season, when Pete Muldoon, the Hawks' first head coach, cursed the team—vowing it would never finish first—after he was sent packing in 1927. And though the story (and the curse) was a fabrication of hockey writer Jim Coleman, Chicago didn't finish in first place until 1966–67, 40 years later. Hawk forward Stan Mikita mocked: "Is the champagne cold? It ought to be—it's been on ice for 40 years."

10.38 B. Montreal (McGill University)

Historians still debate the "real" birthplace of hockey. But most agree it was McGill University students who formed the first organized team, making them instrumental in the evolution of modern-day hockey. The students were responsible for the introduction of codified rules, a flat, circular puck, and the use of goaltenders, goal areas, hockey officials and team uniforms. McGill also played a part in staging the world's first indoor hockey game, played on March 3, 1875, at the Victoria Skating Rink in Montreal. Nine of the 18 players were also McGill students. And two years later, on February 1, 1877, McGill students began hockey's first club, playing an informal squad of players—from lacrosse and football—called the Victorians, in a three-game contest. McGill won the series 2–1. On February 27, 1877, after the McGill games, the first rules of hockey were published in the *Montreal Gazette.*

Game 10

Defunct Teams

THE NHL HAS HAD ITS SHARE of failed franchises. Long before Minnesota, Quebec, Hartford and Winnipeg lost their big-league teams during the 1990s, many other host cities have seen their clubs tank. In this game, match these one-time or current NHL cities with the defunct team's name.

Solutions are on page 563

PART 1

1. _B_ Colorado

2. _C_ Philadelphia

3. _G_ Montreal

4. _E_ Kansas City

5. _A_ Cleveland

6. _F_ Hamilton

7. _D_ Atlanta

A. Barons

B. Rockies

C. Quakers

D. Flames

E. Scouts

F. Tigers

G. Maroons

PART 2

1. _G_ Brooklyn

2. _F_ California

3. _D_ Ottawa

4. _A_ St. Louis

5. _C_ Pittsburgh

6. _B_ Minnesota

7. _E_ Quebec

A. Eagles

B. North Stars

C. Pirates

D. Senators

E. Nordiques

F. Golden Seals

G. Americans

11

This Time It's Personal

AFTER BEANING A HECKLING FAN with a water bottle on November 12, 1998, Chicago's Reid Simpson was handed a two-game suspension by NHL disciplinarian Colin Campbell. TV cameras caught the Chicago defenseman tossing the plastic bottle at a spectator sitting near the penalty box in the United Center. "He was mocking Probie (Bob Probert) a bit," Simpson said. "I think everyone is a bit frustrated right now. I just kind of lost my composure." In this chapter, we also make it personal—all the way to the penalty box.

Answers are on page 285

11.1 **What is the unofficial NHL record for ice time in a game by a player who registered a Gordie Howe hat trick: a goal, an assist and a fight?**
   A. Under five minutes
   B. Between five and 10 minutes
   C. One period
   D. Two periods

11.2 What piece of NHL legislation was dubbed the "Rob Ray Rule"?

    A. Any player who head-butts an opponent receives a game misconduct

    B. Any player engaging in a fight away from the playing surface receives a game misconduct

    C. Any player who removes his jersey before or during a fight receives a game misconduct

    D. Any player who deliberately knees an opponent receives a match penalty

11.3 In a December 2003 game, which NHL team hosted a Santa Claus promotion that, between periods, sparked a wild on-ice mêlée between periods?

    A. The Los Angeles Kings

    B. The New York Islanders

    C. The Boston Bruins

    D. The Philadelphia Flyers

11.4 Who is the only NHLer to lead the league in goals and amass more than 200 penalty minutes in the same season?

    A. Kevin Stevens, with the Pittsburgh Penguins

    B. Peter Forsberg, with the Colorado Avalanche

    C. Keith Tkachuk, with the Phoenix Coyotes

    D. Jarome Iginla, with the Calgary Flames

11.5 In a notorious incident during the 1989 playoffs, Ron Hextall attacked Chris Chelios with his blocker. Which Flyer was Hextall defending?

    A. Tim Kerr

    B. Pelle Eklund

C. Brian Propp

D. Mark Howe

11.6 Which tough guy did the Edmonton Oilers first ice to protect Wayne Gretzky?

A. Marty McSorley

B. Dave Semenko

C. Lee Fogolin

D. Kevin McClelland

11.7 In 1999–2000, which tough guy was instrumental in bringing forth rules that prohibit any NHL player from making a throat-slashing motion towards an opponent?

A. Donald Brashear, with the Vancouver Canucks

B. Gino Odjick, with the Philadelphia Flyers

C. Matthew Barnaby, with the Pittsburgh Penguins

D. Peter Worrell, with the Florida Panthers

11.8 At a practice in 2003–04, which NHL captain got into a highly publicized fight with a teammate?

A. Saku Koivu, with the Montreal Canadiens

B. Chris Pronger, with the St. Louis Blues

C. Markus Naslund, with the Vancouver Canucks

D. Keith Primeau, with the Philadelphia Flyers

11.9 What is the greatest number of penalty minutes recorded by two teams in one NHL game?

A. 319 penalty minutes

B. 359 penalty minutes

C. 419 penalty minutes

D. 459 penalty minutes

11.10 In 2005, what event made fighter Dean Mayrand newsworthy?

- A. The trial over a failed murder plot to kill a hockey agent
- B. The players lockout of 2004–05
- C. The Battle of the Hockey Enforcers slugfest
- D. An impaired driving charge after the death of a prominent athlete

11.11 Why was Ottawa's Peter Schaefer fined US$2,500 in December 2006?

- A. He waved a towel at officials
- B. He sat down during the national anthem
- C. He hit a player with his helmet
- D. He threw a water bottle at a fan

11.12 Since NHL expansion in 1967, how many first-year teams have iced an NHL penalty leader?

- A. Only one club, the Atlanta Thrashers (Denny Lambert)
- B. Three clubs
- C. Six clubs
- D. It has never happened

11.13 Why was netminder Dominik Hasek suspended and fined during the 1997 playoffs while playing with the Buffalo Sabres?

- A. He refused to attend practice
- B. He broke curfew
- C. He assaulted his coach
- D. He assaulted a sportswriter

11.14 What caused the backroom brawl at the beginning of the 1938 finals between the Toronto Maple Leafs and Chicago Blackhawks?

    A. An ongoing feud between opposing goalies

    B. The selection of a substitute goalie for the Hawks

    C. A dispute over the playoff suspension of a goalie

    D. The use of a referee whose brother was the Leafs' goalie

11.15 Who was accused of assaulting the San Jose Sharks' mascot, Sharkie, in 2001–02?

    A. Chris Chelios, with the Detroit Red Wings

    B. Theo Fleury, with the New York Rangers

    C. Ed Belfour, with the Dallas Stars

    D. Darcy Tucker, with the Toronto Maple Leafs

11.16 In league history, how many NHLers have recorded 30-goal, 300-penalty-minute seasons? Name them.

    A. One player

    B. Three players

    C. Five players

    D. Seven players

11.17 What is the greatest number of penalty minutes amassed by all teams in one season?

    A. Between 39,000 and 41,000 penalty minutes

    B. Between 41,000 and 43,000 penalty minutes

    C. Between 43,000 and 45,000 penalty minutes

    D. More than 45,000 penalty minutes

11.18 Which Hart Trophy winner holds the record for amassing the most penalty minutes during the season he was elected MVP?

A. Gordie Howe, in 1952
B. Jean Béliveau, in 1956
C. Mark Messier, in 1990
D. Chris Pronger, in 2000

11.19 What is the NHL record for the worst goals-to-penalty-minutes ratio amongst players with more than 1,000 career penalty minutes?

A. One goal for every 160 PIM
B. One goal for every 260 PIM
C. One goal for every 360 PIM
D. One goal for every 460 PIM

11.20 Who broke his team's all-time penalty-minutes record in 2001–02?

A. Rob Ray, with the Buffalo Sabres
B. Tie Domi, with the Toronto Maple Leafs
C. Scott Stevens, with the New Jersey Devils
D. Derian Hatcher, with the Dallas Stars

11.21 Which NHLer delivered the most hits in 1998–99, the year the league first recorded hits as a statistic?

A. Gary Roberts, with the Carolina Hurricanes
B. Darren McCarty, with the Detroit Red Wings
C. Bobby Holik, with the New Jersey Devils
D. Chris Pronger, with the St. Louis Blues

11.22 In what year did the Philadelphia Flyers play their first game without a penalty? (The Flyers entered the NHL in 1967.)

A. 1969

B. 1979

C. 1989

D. 1999

11.23 How often has an NHL scoring leader recorded more than 100 penalty minutes in the same year he won the Art Ross Trophy?

A. It has never happened

B. Only once

C. Five times

D. 10 times

11.24 According to a study released in 2006, fighting in the NHL does what?

A. Fighting helps a team *win* games

B. Fighting helps a team *lose* games

C. Fighting leads to overtime games

D. Fighting has no impact on the outcome of a game

11.25 After former NHL goon Stu Grimson hung up the gloves, he graduated from university in what discipline?

A. Business

B. Psychiatry

C. Law

D. Medicine

11.26 What is the closest in penalty minutes an NHL scoring leader has come to leading the league in box time in the same season?

A. Within five minutes

B. Between 10 and 20 minutes

C. Between 20 and 40 minutes

D. A scoring leader has led the league in penalty minutes on one occasion

11.27 Before he scored a personal-best 29 goals in 1999–2000, what was bruiser Chris Simon's goal count over seven NHL seasons?

A. 43 goals

B. 63 goals

C. 83 goals

D. 103 goals

11.28 Since the introduction of the 70-game schedule in 1949–50, what is the lowest penalty-minute total for a penalty leader in one season?

A. Fewer than 130 minutes

B. Between 130 and 160 minutes

C. Between 160 and 190 minutes

D. More than 190 minutes

11.29 What is the professional hockey record for most box time in a season?

A. 448 penalty minutes

B. 548 penalty minutes

C. 648 penalty minutes

D. 748 penalty minutes

11.30 After duking it out a few times with Marty McSorley in 1996–97, which NHL brawler took a few more cracks at McSorley in the press, accusing him of being a cheap-shot artist?

A. Gino Odjick, with Vancouver

B. Sandy McCarthy, with Calgary

C. Chris Simon, with Washington

D. Jim Cummins, with Chicago

11.31 Which former NHL brawler died after a struggle with police in 1992?

A. Randy Holt

B. John Kordic

C. Stan Jonathan

D. Steve Durbano

11.32 What is the record for most box time in a season by a goaltender?

A. 53 penalty minutes

B. 83 penalty minutes

C. 113 penalty minutes

D. 143 penalty minutes

11.33 Why was Randy Pierce, with the Colorado Rockies, given a delay-of-game penalty in a November 1979 match?

A. He kissed the puck and threw it into the crowd

B. He pretended to have an equipment malfunction

C. He was caught yapping at an opponent

D. He signed an autograph in the penalty box

11.34 Which Pittsburgh Penguin player did Ray Bourque hit in 1997–98, when he received the first game misconduct of his career?

A. Stu Barnes
B. Jaromir Jagr
C. Kevin Hatcher
D. Ron Francis

11.35 What is the highest penalty count collected by Mario Lemieux in one game?

A. Nine penalty minutes
B. 19 penalty minutes
C. 29 penalty minutes
D. 39 penalty minutes

11.36 Which Toronto Maple Leaf player is remembered for a cheap shot that blew out the knee of New York Islander Michael Peca during the 2002 playoffs—though this player wasn't penalized or suspended for the play.

A. Shayne Corson
B. Darcy Tucker
C. Tie Domi
D. Bryan McCabe

11.37 In 2001–02, which team established an NHL record for most penalty minutes in one period during a fight-filled game?

A. The Calgary Flames
B. The Buffalo Sabres
C. The Chicago Blackhawks
D. The New Jersey Devils

Answers

11.1   **A. Under five minutes**
Gordie Howe was every sniper, passer and battler who ever laced up skates. He was Mr. Hockey *and* Mr. Elbows. On an almost nightly basis, he picked his enemies apart, settling scores in the net and the penalty box with every weapon at his disposal, which meant using his stick to score a goal or an assist and his elbows or fists to fight. And though there is no proof that it has been done in less ice time, former Phoenix tough guy Georges Laraque deserves credit for his Gordie Howe hat trick on November 4, 2006, when he scored on Los Angeles goalie Mathieu Garon in the first frame, assisted on Ed Jovanovski's second-period goal and beat up Raitis Ivanans near the game's start to earn a five-minute fighting major— all in just 4:46 minutes of ice time. Laraque, who was miked for the match, cordially said to Ivanans at the faceoff: "Ya wanna do it? Good luck, then."

11.2   **C. Any player who removes his jersey before or during a fight receives a game misconduct**
The Sabres' Rob Ray was the player chiefly responsible for the NHL rule that penalizes a player for shucking his jersey before or during a scrap. Ray liked to wear a loose jersey, with his protective equipment sewn into it, so he could easily pull it off and fire punches without restraint. (Also, Ray never wore a T-shirt; that way, his opponent had nothing to grab onto.) But even if the technique helped him get the upper hand in

fights, the repeated appearances of Ray's naked torso on the highlight reels was not an image the NHL wanted to project, so it amended its rule.

11.3 B. The New York Islanders

It wasn't the kind of publicity the Islanders envisioned for a promotion that offered a free ticket to anyone fully dressed as Santa Claus, but the footage was good enough to lead ESPN's SportsCenter broadcast. There they were, some 500 fans dressed as Santa Claus in a Santa Claus parade on the ice between periods of an Islanders–Philadelphia game at Nassau Coliseum. In a particularly festive mood, some of the Santas also started sliding across the ice. But then a few ripped off their red costumes to reveal the blue shirts of the Islanders' rivals, the Rangers, and Islander Santas began swarming Ranger Santas, with one Father Christmas yanking at a rival's Pavel Bure jersey. Another Santa carried an anti-Mike Milbury sign that read: "All I want for Christmas is a new GM." Bad publicity aside, no one was hurt and things quieted down in time for the second period to begin.

11.4 C. Keith Tkachuk, with the Phoenix Coyotes

Although a few players share the distinction of putting together a season of 30-goal, 300-minute stats or even a 50–250 record, no one but Tkachuk can claim winning the goal-scoring race with more than 200 minutes in the box. In fact, only five other goal leaders have amassed 100 minutes or more—the next-highest being boy scout Jean Béliveau, a distant 85 minutes behind Tkachuk. But how did the power left-winger find the time to score 52 goals while spending 228 minutes in the box? In his early years, Tkachuk liked to bang; and he owned the corners. But his mean streak was balanced off by an excellent wrist shot and the desire to hit the net hard. Said Tkachuk:

"The bottom line is, I get paid well to play this game. I'm supposed to be the captain of this team and I can't play average."

The Highest PIM Totals by NHL Goal-Scoring Leaders*

PLAYER	TEAM	YEAR	GAMES	GOALS	PIM
Keith Tkachuk	Pho	1996–97	81	52	228
Jean Béliveau	Mtl	1955–56	70	47	143
Maurice Richard	Mtl	1954–55	67	38	125
Nels Stewart	MtlM	1925–26	36	34	119
Maurice Richard	Mtl	1949–50	70	43	114
Maurice Richard	Mtl	1953–54	70	37	112
Gordie Howe	Det	1962–63	70	38	100
Mario Lemieux	Pit	1988–89	76	85	100

Current to 2008–09

11.5   C. Brian Propp

During the 1989 playoffs, Hextall lost it, mugging Chelios with his blocker after the Montreal rearguard elbowed Brian Propp into unconsciousness. Later, Propp called Chelios "a lousy person." Chelios responded with, "He's [Propp] a gutless jerk." Hextall earned a 12-game suspension for the assault; Chelios took home his first Norris Trophy as the league's most outstanding defenseman.

11.6   B. Dave Semenko

Because of the way Wayne Gretzky saw the ice and the play developing, he was always hard to hit. But a few checks connected, particularly in the 1981 playoffs. In fact, the New York Islanders' Dave Langevin and Bryan Trottier slowed him down so much so that he wasn't the same speedy player in the later games of the series. Enter linemate Dave Semenko, the policeman the Oilers needed to protect their greatest asset—for a matchup that benefited both men, for different reasons.

It's "pretty easy when 99 shoots it off your stick," Semenko once said of his newfound scoring touch. But Gretzky, all 170 pounds of him, also fought back in a different way. "If a guy ran him, Wayne would embarrass that guy," said former Oiler Lee Fogolin, as quoted in *Sports Illustrated.* "He'd score six or seven points on him. I saw him do it night after night."

11.7   D. Peter Worrell, with the Florida Panthers

After the Florida Panthers' Peter Worrell made a throat-slashing motion three times towards the New Jersey Devils bench in a game on March 19, 2000, the NHL sent a memo to all teams stating that the league had joined the NFL in banning the gesture. The Devils' Scott Niedermayer had provoked the incident by chopping Worrell in the head with his stick. Niedermayer received a 10-game suspension and had to forfeit US$152,343.74 in salary.

11.8   A. Saku Koivu, with the Montreal Canadiens

Fights amongst teammates at practice aren't uncommon, but they are rare for team captains—the on-ice leaders and player representatives to management. But even more unusual is that this particular captain, who had two stick altercations during a March practice, would be Koivu, the elite Finnish sharpshooter better known for his heroic fight against cancer than any on-ice battle. Koivu's challenger was Mike Ribeiro, the 23-year-old Montreal native and team leader in scoring. And unlike other NHL cities where the press seldom attends practice, in Montreal, the media not only had footage but they turned the skirmish into a full-blown Quebec language issue that dominated the front pages of all four Montreal dailies. French media criticized Koivu while their English counterparts rallied behind him. Worse, at the next home game, boos rained down from the Bell Centre rafters when Koivu stepped on the ice. At the heart of the issue was something facing every Montreal captain: can he lead the Canadiens back to glory?

11.9   C. 419 penalty minutes

It must have brought tears to Dave Schultz's eyes, the way the Philadelphia Flyers pounded it out with the Ottawa Senators on March 5, 2004. Imagine how the Hammer beamed with pride at his former team's 5–3 win in a game that featured five consecutive brawls in the final two minutes and 16 player ejections—all while setting a new NHL record of 419 penalty minutes (breaking the mark of 406 minutes set in a Boston–Minnesota game on February 26, 1981). At the final bell, Schultz couldn't have been more giddy after learning that his born-again Broad Street Bullies established the highest box time total ever for a team in one game, 213 minutes (surpassing Minnesota's 211); and that the Flyers smashed the league's penalty-minute count in one period, 209 minutes (while their adversaries gave as good as they got, 206 minutes all told for Ottawa). Even Schultz's old teammate, Flyer GM Bobby Clarke, couldn't resist a little revenge, having to be restrained by arena personnel in his search for Senators coach Jacques Martin, who Clarke called "that gutless puke" because of a recent February 26 match that included some high-stick work by Ottawa forward Martin Havlat on Mark Recchi. In all, 20 players got fighting penalties and only five players were left on the bench at the final buzzer. Officials needed 90 minutes after the game to figure everything out. Yes, Schultzie would be proud.

11.10   C. The Battle of the Hockey Enforcers slugfest

The idea didn't look good on paper, but promoters of a night of fights on ice weren't deterred. Despite much opposition by hockey purists and anti-violence supporters, two years of searching for a city to host the event and being booted out of Minneapolis, banned in Winnipeg and cancelled in Prince George, the threat of a lawsuit finally brought the Battle of the Hockey Enforcers to the spectators and pay-per-view airwaves. Yet only some 2,000 fans finally watched the slugfest live at the Prince George Multiplex in August 2005, when Dean Mayrand of the Mission Sorel-Tracy of Quebec's North American Professional Hockey League picked up $62,000 for beating up AHL Syracuse Crunch forward Mike Sgroi in the final round. The most familiar name on the card: former NHLer Link Gaetz, who withdrew after his first fight.

11.11   A. He waved a towel at officials

Knowing a little hockey history can save a lot of dough. Peter Schaefer was just five years old when late coach Roger Neilson made hockey headlines by waving a towel in mock surrender at referees during the 1982 playoffs. Had Schaefer known of Neilson's faux pas, he might not have made the same mistake with his own stick-and-towel wave after a string of penalty calls in a Washington–Ottawa tilt on December 6, 2006. "I didn't think about it at all until I got off the ice and I had about five text messages from some buddies," said Schaefer. Within a day, the Ottawa forward also had a Post-it Note on his locker to call NHL executive Colin Campbell, who fined him $2,500—considerably less than the $11,000 that Neilson and the Vancouver Canucks were penalized in 1982. During the 2006 game, referees Kevin Pollack and Justin St. Pierre assessed 11 penalties to each team. The Capitals won 6–2.

11.12   B. Three clubs

The Atlanta Thrashers were not the first expansion club to sport a penalty leader. Before Denny Lambert recorded an

NHL-high 219 penalty minutes with the Thrashers in 1999–2000, two other new teams had penalty kings. Fresh off an outstanding minor-league career, Barklay Plager joined the first-year St. Louis Blues in 1967 and amassed a league-best 153 minutes in the box. Then, in 1979–80, Jimmy Mann collected 287 minutes with the expansion Winnipeg Jets.

11.13 D. He assaulted a sportswriter

The NHL slapped Hasek with a three-game suspension and $10,000 fine for grabbing *Buffalo News* sportswriter Jim Kelley and ripping his shirt after Game 5 of the Sabres–Senators playoff series. Hasek was upset by a column that Kelley had written, in which he questioned the severity of the Buffalo goalie's knee injury. Kelley suggested that Hasek's absence from the Sabres' lineup might have more to do with an inability to cope with the pressure of carrying the club's playoff hopes on his shoulders.

11.14 B. The selection of a substitute goalie for the Hawks

When the Blackhawks arrived in Toronto for the 1938 finals, their first job was to find a backup for injured netminder Mike Karakas. Coach Bill Stewart asked to use Ranger great Davey Kerr, but the Leafs refused and suggested Alfie Moore, an ex-New York American backstopper who was in Toronto. Thinking he was being helpful, Toronto's Frank Selke called up Moore and suggested that he come over to the Gardens. But even as fans arrived for the first game, the issue wasn't settled. When Stewart found out that Selke had called up Moore, he accused Selke of trying to pawn off a half-sober goaltender on his team. Leaf GM Conn Smythe, also at the scene, yelled, "Nobody calls Selke a liar in my presence," and attacked Stewart. But after the fracas was settled, Moore stepped between the pipes for the

Hawks and did an excellent job in a 3–1 Chicago victory. Moore later admitted, "Sure, I had a few beers. But I had no idea I was going to play that night."

11.15 B. Theo Fleury, with the New York Rangers

During a six-game midseason road trip in 2001–02, Fleury exhibited some bizarre behaviour, both on and off the ice. In a January 5 game against Pittsburgh, the Rangers hothead picked up three slashing minors. After the last one, he left the ice and went to the dressing room with 7:37 remaining and his team trailing 3–1. He didn't return. By the time the game ended, Fleury was already on the team bus. Earlier in the same road trip, he was ejected from a game in San Jose after he received a kneeing major for a deliberate attempt to injure. En route to the dressing room, Fleury reportedly punched San Jose's costumed mascot, Sharkie, who suffered a rib injury. Fleury denied the attack, but seemed unrepentant about his emotional outbursts, telling reporters: "So I've had a few cases of snap-itis. That's nothing new. I had plenty of snap-itis attacks in Calgary, didn't I?"

11.16 B. Three players

The 30-goal, 300-penalty-minute club is an exlusive fraternity. Many have tried to join, including Bob Probert, who just missed qualifying by one goal in 1987–88 with a 29–398 record. Obviously, it's a tough act to pull off, that of consistent goal scorer and resident policeman. So membership is limited and, so far, restricted to Tiger Williams, Al Secord and Rick Tocchet. In fact, no old-timer managed it until Williams, who founded the club in 1980–81, when he scored 35 goals and spent 343 minutes in the box. The following year, Secord came aboard with a 44–303 record. Then in 1987–88, Tocchet's 31 goals and 301 penalty minutes edged him nicely into the select group.

11.17 D. More than 45,000 penalty minutes

It's hard to fathom that, with its slate of rule changes, including the first enforcement of calling all fouls, the 2005–06 season did not generate the NHL's highest penalty-minute count. In fact, the season's 39,439 minutes is way off the record established in the early 1990s, when the league introduced a whack of new rules, such as checking from behind, crease infringement and goalie interference, diving, instigating a fight and high sticking (redefined as wielding a stick above waist height). Indeed, three of the top five most-penalized teams—Buffalo, with 2,713 minutes; Chicago, with 2,663 minutes, and Calgary, with 2,643 minutes—collected their penalty highs during 1991–92, the first year of the new rules. But expansion (from 22 to 24 to 26 teams) and two 84-game schedules were the reasons behind the two seasons with the most number of penalties, 1992–93 and 1993–94. So the 1987–88 season must be a blip year: the NHL had a record 15 teams with more than 2,000 penalty minutes.

Most Penalty Minutes in One Season*

SEASONS	PENALTY MINUTES
1992–93	45,650
1993–94	45,559
1987–88	44,380
1991–92	43,781

*Current to 2008–09

11.18 B. Jean Béliveau, in 1956

You could win a few bucks in a bar bet with this one. All of the likely candidates—Gordie Howe, Eddie Shore, Mark Messier, Chris Pronger—rank far behind Jean Béliveau for box time during the years they won their Harts. The Montreal Canadien

MVP led the league with 47 goals and 88 points in 1955–56, despite compiling 143 penalty minutes in 70 games—a heavy total for a guy associated with clean play. Béliveau's closest challenger: Bobby Clarke, who, though never associated with clean play, holds two spots among top penalty-earning MVPs. However, the all-time leader for penalty minutes per game is Nels Stewart. In 1925–26, the Montreal Maroons rookie logged 119 PIM in just 36 games, an average of 3.31 per game.

Most PIM in a Season by NHL MVPs*

PLAYER	YEAR	TEAM	GP	PIM
Jean Béliveau	1956	Montreal	70	143
Bobby Clarke	1976	Philadelphia	76	136
Bobby Orr	1970	Boston	76	125
Bobby Clarke	1975	Philadelphia	80	125
Nels Stewart	1926	Montreal Maroons	36	119

*Current to 2008–09

11.19 C. One goal for every 360 PIM

Randy Holt played 10 NHL seasons and 395 regular-season games despite scoring just four goals. Clearly, he wasn't kept around because of his offensive skills. Holt, who shuttled between defense and the wing, earned a big-league pay-cheque because he wasn't shy about dropping his gloves. And in his career total of 1,438 penalty minutes, he established a record-setting 67 minutes in one game—against the Philadelphia Flyers on March 11, 1979—when, as a member of the Los Angeles Kings, he picked up one minor, three majors, two 10-minute misconducts and three game misconducts. Quite a night's work. Holt's league-leading ratio of one goal for every 360 penalty minutes means that the thug sat through six complete games in the penalty box for every goal scored.

11.20 B. Tie Domi, with the Toronto Maple Leafs

Domi surpassed Tiger Williams as Toronto's penalty king in trademark style: by dispensing vigilante justice. In this case, the Maple Leafs enforcer tossed Montreal's Reid Simpson to the ice after Simpson roughed up mild-mannered Leaf Anders Eriksson. George Thorogood's "Bad to the Bone" then boomed out of the Air Canada Centre speakers as Domi took his seat in the penalty box. The minor gave Domi 1,672 penalty minutes in a Toronto uniform, two more than Williams—a record-setting feat that did not go unrecognized by Domi's team-mates, several of whom glided over to tap him with a stick after he emerged from the sin bin. Coach Pat Quinn also con-gratulated Domi when he returned to the bench. As Quinn said after his club posted a 6–4 victory, "This is a physical, brutal game sometimes and people who can play and who also have that [policeman] ability make the game a little more sane." The only thing that bothered Domi about setting the record was that no mention of it was made to the capacity crowd. "It just goes to show you that certain people don't like that part of the game," said Domi.

11.21 A. Gary Roberts, with the Carolina Hurricanes

The NHL finally entered the computer age in the late 1990s, a move not made soon enough for North America's statistic-mad sports fans. Hockey fans could now feast on a variety of crunched numbers online, from ice time to legal hits. And it's in this last category that Carolina's Gary Roberts led the NHL in 1998–99, with 260 hits on opposing players.

The NHL's Top Hit Men in 1998–99

PLAYER	TEAM	GP	HITS
Gary Roberts	Carolina	77	260
Ken Klee	Washington	78	248
Mattias Norstrom	Los Angeles	78	236
Bob Boughner	Nashville	79	233
Radek Bonk	Ottawa	81	225
Daniel McGillis	Philadelphia	78	220

11.22   B. 1979

It's no surprise that the Flyers led the NHL in team penalty minutes from 1971 to 1982. Built on the Fred Shero model of success through intimidation, Philadelphia bullied its way through the league to capture its first Stanley Cup in 1974 on the strength of a league-high 1,750 minutes in box time. (The next most-penalized team, the St. Louis Blues, had 34 per cent fewer penalties, with just 1,147 minutes.) That early Cup success would define the Flyers franchise of the future, with the club's first penalty-free game coming along 12 years after it entered the NHL, in a 5–3 win over the same Blues on March 18, 1979. Apparently, the boys were on their best behaviour after setting the league record for most penalty minutes (by a team in one period) a week earlier. In that March 11 game against Los Angeles, Philadelphia earned 188 minutes on four minors, eight majors, six 10-minute misconducts and eight game misconducts in the first period.

11.23   D. 10 times

Only seven scoring leaders have recorded 100 minutes in box time. Chicago's Stan Mikita leads the pack with a 1–2 ranking, his highest totals peaking in 1964–65, when he sat out 154 minutes. In a five-year period, Mikita then won the Art Ross Trophy four times. And though his first two scoring championships were marred by 100-plus penalty-minute seasons, his final pair, in 1966–67 and 1967–68, featured uncharacteristic totals of just 12 and 14 minutes each, among the lowest ever by a scoring leader. "I thought I'd try to beat the other guy with my skills instead of knocking his head off," Mikita said.

Most Penalty Minutes by an NHL Scoring Leader*

PLAYER	TEAM	YEAR	POINTS	PIM
Stan Mikita	Chicago	1964–65	87	154
Stan Mikita	Chicago	1963–64	89	146
Jean Béliveau	Montreal	1955–56	88	143
Ted Lindsay	Detroit	1949–50	78	141
Bobby Orr	Boston	1969–70	120	125
Nels Stewart	Maroons	1925–26	42	119
Gordie Howe	Detroit	1953–54	81	109
Bobby Orr	Boston	1974–75	135	101
Gordie Howe	Detroit	1962–63	86	100
Mario Lemieux	Pittsburgh	1988–89	199	100

*Current to 2008–09

11.24 A. Fighting helps a team *win* games

The NHL fight club received some unexpected support from an unlikely source in 2006, when a bunch of university professors dropped the gloves and cold-cocked the scrap-shy NHL with a study that showed fighting is actually a good strategy for team success. Admittedly, the report never concluded that "fighting is a good thing." Its statistical analysis merely showed that major penalties—most often called for fights—increased the total points held by a penalized player's team and lowered the number of goals scored by their opposition. (Only major penalties helped win games; minor penalties decreased a team's success.) "It's clearly a rallying effect, and that's what gets momentum to change in a game," said study author Aju Fenn. The research, conducted by the Department of Economics and Business at Colorado College in Colorado Springs and the School of Business at the University of Sioux Falls, crunched data for all NHL teams during five seasons, 1999–2000 through 2003–04. However, critics of the report said that the post-lockout NHL had changed dramatically, with fights between 2003–04 and 2005–06 dropping from 41 to 29 per cent. Meanwhile, tough guy Georges Laraque, lamenting the fact that only 11 teams regularly dressed enforcers in 2006–07, called the NHL "a ballet league. They want to make this into a European league," he fumed.

11.25 C. Law

Tough guys aren't all mindless ice goons. Stu Grimson, the Grim Reaper of blood, mayhem and 2,113 penalty minutes during his 12-year NHL career, surprised players and fans when he announced his graduation from law school in 2005. Fellow students at the University of Memphis were equally taken aback. "Some of my students say: 'Golly, we've seen video of him beating the heck out of someone.' That's difficult to believe," said Donna Harkness, University of Memphis professor of clinical law. "That was a shock. He just does not have that kind of aura now at all." Grimson's Jekyll and Hyde act is a permanent transformation. He joined the NHL players union in 2006.

11.26 A. Within five minutes

No scoring leader has ever led the league in penalties during the same season, but in 1925–26 the Montreal Maroons' rookie sensation Nels Stewart came within one two-minute penalty of tying tough guy Bert Corbeau's league-high 121-minute mark. Stewart, who ruled the NHL with his 42-point rookie season, finished runner-up in box-time with 119 penalty minutes. A few other scoring leaders also came close in cooler time. Detroit's Ted Lindsay won the scoring crown and finished second in penalties with 141 minutes, just three minutes behind league leader Bill Ezinicki (144). In 1962–63, Stan Mikita won the Art Ross and accumulated 146 minutes—five behind the NHL leader, Vic Hadfield, who had 151.

11.27 A. 43 goals

Chris Simon's extraordinary transition from brawler to first-line forward was the talk of 1999–2000. Washington's comeback kid had a career year, notching 29 goals—just 14 fewer than his entire output of seven previous seasons, 43 goals. What changed? Simon improved his skating and the release of his shot, which earned him more ice time. He also stayed healthy to play 75 games and record 201 shots, almost double the number of shots in his previous best season, 1995–96's 105-shot year. His reputation for toughness was another factor that helped his goal surge; it preceded him into every corner in every NHL arena. But unfortunately, the numbers weren't on the board for Simon in 2000–01. In a story straight out of the Bible's "Samson and Delilah," Simon cut off his long, legendary mane and, like Samson, lost his power. He never again had a 20-goal NHL season and, in 2008, signed with the Vityaz Chekhov of Russia's Continental Hockey League.

11.28 A. Fewer than 130 minutes

In 1952–53, Maurice Richard topped the league with 112 penalty minutes, the lowest total for a penalty leader since the late 1940s. Despite his offensive skills, Richard was one of the NHL's most frequently penalized players. With no team policeman to protect him, he had to defend himself against the league's roughest players and, during his career as hockey's best player, racked up a hefty 1,285 penalty minutes. In 1953–54, when he led the league with 37 goals, Richard finished with 112 penalty minutes, just 20 minutes fewer than Gus Mortson's league-high 132-minute total.

11.29 C. 648 penalty minutes

At five foot ten and 182 pounds, Kevin Evans was no heavyweight, but the rookie winger put up some heavy-duty penalty numbers in 1986–87, racking up 648 minutes in box time in 73 games with the Kalanazoo Wings of the IHL. The bruising total still stands as a record in professional hockey. In 2008, Evans's career mark of 4,419 minutes was surpassed by career leader Dennis Bonvie, with 4,601 minutes. Evans's NHL career path also includes four games with Minnesota (in 1990–91) and five games with San Jose (in 1991–92), where he recorded no goals, one assist and 44 penalty minutes.

11.30 B. Sandy McCarthy, with Calgary

McCarthy made it clear on more than one occasion that he was not a member of the Marty McSorley fan club. "Let's just say I have a grudge against him and a score to settle," said McCarthy. "He's a big man, a strong man and a respected fighter. But he's also a jerk who hands out a lot of cheap shots. He's always cutting guys from behind or giving them cheap shots. There's a code involved here and sometimes McSorley forgets that. He's one of the worst. I respect the guy as a fighter, but I wouldn't trust him."

11.31 B. John Kordic

Kordic's last fight was fatal. On August 8, 1992, police were called to a Quebec City motel where the former enforcer was living, after motel staff complained of abusive behaviour and a loud disturbance in his room. The police officers who responded to the call found Kordic extremely agitated and intoxicated. When they tried to take him to the hospital for treatment, he resisted, throwing punches and screaming. It took nine officers to subdue him, and shortly after the ambulance left the motel, Kordic passed out. He could not be revived. An autopsy showed that he died from heart failure, the result of mixing alcohol, cocaine and steroids. He was only 27.

11.32   C. 113 penalty minutes

Rookie Ron Hextall made a striking impression with the Philadelphia Flyers in 1986–87, combining acrobatic puckstopping with a tomahawk stick hand. When he wasn't using his wood to let fly breakout passes, he was hacking and chopping at opponents who wandered into his crease. It's no wonder that the hotheaded Hextall won the Vezina Trophy as top netminder and logged an unprecedented 104 minutes. The following season, 1987–88, he then duplicated his own mark, with another 104, before besting himself in 1988–89 with a savage 113-minute campaign that ranked him 107th in penalty totals amongst all players in the 21-team NHL.

11.33   A. He kissed the puck and threw it into the crowd

The Colorado Rockies had never beaten the New York Islanders until the two teams met on November 28, 1979, so Randy Pierce was understandably excited when he scored to give the Rockies a 6–4 lead at 19:27 of the third period. Pierce was so thrilled that he impulsively grabbed the puck, kissed it and tossed it into the crowd. He was promptly penalized for delaying the game. Fortunately for Pierce, teammate Wilf Paiement scored a shorthanded goal into the empty net on the ensuing Islanders power play to clinch the win for Colorado.

11.34 B. Jaromir Jagr

Ray Bourque had never been assessed more than 96 penalty minutes in a season and had only two 10-minute misconducts in his illustrious career—until January 29, 1998. In his 1,341st game, the defensive stalwart then received a game misconduct—the first ejection of his 19-year NHL career—after hitting Jagr from behind and sending him headfirst into the boards behind the net. Jagr remained on the ice for five minutes, but returned in the second period. One footnote: A little more than a minute into Bourque's checking-from-behind penalty, Stu Barnes connected on a pass from Ron Francis, who earned his 1,400th career point. Francis became the 11th NHLer to reach the milestone on a winning note, as the Pens beat Boston 4–2.

11.35 C. 29 penalty minutes

On February 6, 2003, Mario Lemieux broke his personal career high of 24 penalty minutes when he received minor penalties for slashing and instigating, a major penalty for fighting, a 10-minute misconduct and a game misconduct—for a total of 29 penalty minutes in a 6–0 loss to Florida. Lemieux's penalties came with 5:12 remaining in the Pittsburgh defeat. Furious over a second-period cross-check from Florida defenseman Brad Ference, Lemieux slashed Ference's wrists, then dropped his gloves and began pummelling the Panther enforcer. It wasn't as pretty as a Lemieux power-play goal, but the point was made. It was Super Mario's first fighting major in regular-season play since a tangle with Washington's Bobby Gould on March 20, 1987.

11.36 B. Darcy Tucker

In its November 2002 issue, *Sports Illustrated* called the Toronto Maple Leafs the most hated club in hockey. A number of players were quoted in the article, which described the city as home to "the NHL's most notorious whiners, divers and cheap-shot artists." The feature article by *SI* senior writer Michael Farber targeted such Leafs as Tie Domi, Shayne Corson and Darcy Tucker for yapping too much, hitting too low and diving too often. As well, opposing players believe the Leafs are favoured by the league, claimed Farber, citing the example of Tucker's unpenalized "low bridge" cheap shot on Peca. The writer also noted that, in what seemed the height of hypocrisy, the league later included Tucker's cheap shot on a tape of unacceptable hits circulated to every club in the 2002–03 season. "That was crap," Ottawa tough guy Rob Ray said in *SI*, "not fining or suspending him and sending the tape saying this can't happen. Why didn't they do anything *when* this happened?"

11.37 A. The Calgary Flames

The mayhem began when Calgary's Craig Berube drew charging and roughing penalties for slamming into Anaheim Mighty Ducks netminder Jean-Sébastien Giguère at 15:44 of the third period in a game on December 8, 2001. A few minutes later, Ducks enforcer Kevin Sawyer steamed into the Calgary crease and cross-checked goalie Mike Vernon in the head, sending him crashing into the net. Several fights broke out, including one in which Anaheim's Denny Lambert traded blows with Calgary scoring star Jarome Iginla. A total of 279 penalty minutes were assessed in the last 85 seconds of the game, while Calgary racked up 190 penalty minues in the period, breaking the 23-year NHL record of 188 minutes set by the Philadelphia Flyers in March 1979. But the Flyers regained their crown in March 2004, when they battled Ottawa and received 209 minutes in the third period.

Game 11

Lowering the Boom

THE NHL'S LONGEST SUSPENSIONS for an on-ice infraction belong to Jesse Boulerice and Chris Simon, each of whom hit with "intent to injure" and received 25 games for their nasty stick work to the faces of their victims. Boulerice cross-checked high and hard, and Simon swung his lumber to deliver a two-handed blow. In this game, match the banished players and their time served on the left with their targets on the right. The dates of the incidents may help your rulings.   *Solutions are on page 563*

PART 1

1. Chris Simon (25 games)
2. Jesse Boulerice (25 games)

3. Marty McSorley (23 games)
4. Gordie Dwyer (23 games)
5. Dale Hunter (21 games)
6. Todd Bertuzzi (20 games)
7. Tom Lysiak (20 games)

A. Donald Brashear (February 2000)
B. Tripping an official (October 1983)
C. Pierre Turgeon (May 1993)
D. Steve Moore (March 2004)
E. Ryan Hollweg (March 2007)
F. Ryan Kesler (October 2007)
G. Abusing officials and exiting the penalty box to fight (September 2000)

PART 2

1. Brad May (20 games)
2. Eddie Shore (16 games)
3. Maurice Richard (15 games)

4. Wilf Paiement (15 games)
5. Dave Brown (15 games)
6. Tony Granato (15 games)

A. Striking an official (March 1955)
B. Dennis Polonich (October 1978)
C. Tomas Sandstrom (November 1987)
D. Steve Heinze (November 2000)
E. Neil Wilkinson (February 1994)
F. Ace Bailey (December 1933)

12

The Deep End

IT'S A DYING BREED: the nutty and neurotic netminder. True, today's elite goalies still follow pre-game rituals and even refuse to meet media on game day, but the strangeness factor has disappeared. No one pukes before games as Glenn Hall did; or showers between periods, a Gary Smith custom; or even believes in reincarnation like Gilles Gratton, who remains convinced he was a soldier during the Spanish Inquisition. And Patrick Roy, the quirkiest of all the bobbing-and-twitching head cases? He hasn't conversed with his goalposts since his retirement in 2003. With the exceptions of nutbar Ed Belfour and the cockroach-eating Ray Emery (both of whom took off to play in Europe), the wackiness is over—gone with the centre red line and $12 tickets. It's a shame, but the crazies have been replaced with more mentally balanced goalies who have benefited from all that specialized coaching. The deep end has never been so shallow.

Answers are on page 314

12.1 In 2006–07, who had his prestigious record for most wins in a season broken by Martin Brodeur?

A. Terry Sawchuk, with the Detroit Red Wings
B. Bernie Parent, with the Philadelphia Flyers
C. Ken Dryden, with the Montreal Canadiens
D. Patrick Roy, with the Colorado Avalanche

12.2 How many NHL games did backup Scott Clemmensen start in four seasons with New Jersey—prior to replacing Martin Brodeur after his elbow injury in November 2008?

A. 17 games

B. 37 games

C. 57 games

D. 77 games

12.3 Bill Durnan, a star netminder with the Montreal Canadiens in the 1940s, was famous for what?

A. His terrible temper

B. His superstitions

C. His incredibly sharp eyesight

D. His ability to catch the puck with either hand

12.4 In 2002–03, which of the following milestones did Patrick Roy reach?

A. First goalie to play 60,000 minutes

B. First goalie to reach 1,000 games played

C. First goalie to record 13 30-win seasons

D. All of the above

12.5 When goalies Ken and Dave Dryden were growing up, which little-known netminder did they idolize?

A. Joe Schaeffer, with the New York Rangers

B. Julian Klymkiw, with the Detroit Red Wings

C. Hal Murphy, with the Montreal Canadiens

D. Moe Roberts, with the Chicago Blackhawks

12.6 Which goalie in 2003–04 recorded the lowest goals-against average in modern-day hockey?

A. Marty Turco, with the Dallas Stars

B. Dwayne Roloson, with the Minnesota Wild

C. Miikka Kiprusoff, with the Calgary Flames

D. Robert Esche, with the Philadelphia Flyers

12.7 **Which famous old-time goalie was known as the "Chicoutimi Cucumber"?**

A. Chuck Gardiner

B. George Hainsworth

C. Alex Connell

D. Georges Vezina

12.8 **What is the fewest number of regular-season games played by a goalie who then led his team to a championship in the Stanley Cup finals?**

A. Zero games

B. Six games

C. 12 games

D. 24 games

12.9 **Hall of Famer Cam Neely scored most of his goals against which netminder?**

A. Mike Richter

B. Dominik Hasek

C. Ed Belfour

D. Patrick Roy

12.10 **In 2006–07, who tried to become the first goalie in NHL history to take a faceoff?**

A. Rick DiPietro, with the New York Islanders

B. Marty Turco, with the Dallas Stars

C. Ray Emery, with the Ottawa Senators

D. Manny Legace, with the St. Louis Blues

12.11 Who is the youngest goalie to play in the NHL?

    A. Frank Brimsek

    B. Terry Sawchuk

    C. Harry Lumley

    D. John Vanbiesbrouck

12.12 In 2001–02, who became the second-youngest goalie in NHL history to see action?

    A. Alex Auld, with the Vancouver Canucks

    B. Jussi Markkanen, with the Edmonton Oilers

    C. Dan Blackburn, with the New York Rangers

    D. Olivier Michaud, with the Montreal Canadiens

12.13 Which goalie piled up the most losses during the 1990s?

    A. Bill Ranford

    B. Jeff Hackett

    C. Sean Burke

    D. Curtis Joseph

12.14 St. Patrick may have been the media's most popular nickname for Patrick Roy, but what was the players' most common moniker for him throughout his career?

    A. Frenchy

    B. Le gros téte (big head)

    C. Superstar

    D. Casseau (a small cardboard box for French fries)

12.15 Why was Hall of Fame defenseman Lionel Conacher called the Travelling Netminder?

    A. He was a goalie coach for several clubs

    B. After hockey, he was a travelling salesman

    C. Because of his unique shot-blocking style

    D. He subbed for many teams before the two-goalie system

12.16 In what year did a goalie first jump directly from college to the NHL?

A. 1949–50

B. 1969–70

C. 1989–90

D. It has never happened

12.17 Only two goalies have put together unbeaten streaks of 30 games or more. Both played for which team?

A. The Montreal Canadiens

B. The New York Rangers

C. The Edmonton Oilers

D. The Boston Bruins

12.18 Ever since he came into a game just for the shootout, who has been considered hockey's first goalie "closer"?

A. Jean-Sébastian Giguère, with the Anaheim Ducks

B. Kari Lehtonen, with the Atlanta Thrashers

C. Mike Morrison, with the Edmonton Oilers

D. Eugeni Nabokov, with the San Jose Sharks

12.19 What is the longest stretch of consecutive shutouts at home recorded by one goalie?

A. Three home shutouts

B. Four home shutouts

C. Five home shutouts

D. Six home shutouts

12.20 What is the briefest career an NHL goalie has had?

A. Three seconds

B. Three minutes

C. Three periods

D. Three games

12.21 What is the greatest number of games played by an NHL goalie who registered only one career shutout?

A. 50 to 100 games

B. 100 to 150 games

C. 150 to 200 games

D. More than 200 games

12.22 Which goalie did Mark Messier victimize the most?

A. Ron Hextall

B. Tom Barrasso

C. Brian Hayward

D. Richard Brodeur

12.23 Both Martin Brodeur and Patrick Roy have recorded 400 wins. But how much younger was Brodeur than Roy when the latter notched his 400th?

A. 66 days

B. 166 days

C. One year and 166 days

D. Two years and 166 days

12.24 Which goalie allowed Bobby Orr's classic Stanley Cup-winning goal of 1970? (In the well-known photo of the goal, Orr is caught airborne, celebrating the Cup-winner.)

A. Jacques Plante

B. Glenn Hall

C. Tony Esposito

D. Ed Giacomin

12.25 With which NHL team did the legendary Jacques Plante play his last game?

A. The New York Rangers

B. The St. Louis Blues

C. The Toronto Maple Leafs

D. The Boston Bruins

12.26 **As of 2008–09, who is the most recent goalie to collect all of his team's wins in one season?**

A. Ron Low, with the Washington Capitals, in 1974–75

B. Kirk McLean, with the Vancouver Canucks, in 1994–95

C. Roberto Luongo, with the Florida Panthers, in 2005–06

D. Martin Brodeur, with the New Jersey Devils, in 2006–07

12.27 **Who led the NHL in shutouts a record seven seasons?**

A. Clint Benedict

B. Glenn Hall

C. Ken Dryden

D. Martin Brodeur

12.28 **What is the most number of goalies one team has iced in one season?**

A. Four goalies

B. Five goalies

C. Six goalies

D. Seven goalies

12.29 **Goalie Lorne Anderson played only three NHL games during the 1950s, but his name is still in the record books for what feat?**

A. Most goals-against in one game

B. Most penalty minutes by a goalie in one game

C. Allowing the fastest hat trick in NHL history

D. All of the above

12.30 Before Tom Barrasso became the U.S.-born goalie with the most wins in NHL history, which old-time netminder held the title?

A. Sam LoPresti

B. Frank Brimsek

C. Mike Karakas

D. Jack McCartan

12.31 What goaltending rarity is shared by Alex Auld and Miikka Kiprusoff?

A. They each recorded a shutout without a win

B. They each registered an assist in the same game

C. They each played in home jerseys during the same game

D. They each received game misconducts for fighting

12.32 What is the NHL record for most consecutive shutouts by a goalie?

A. Four shutouts

B. Five shutouts

C. Six shutouts

D. Seven shutouts

12.33 As of 2008–09, what is the highest number of games played by an NHL goalie who failed to record one shutout during his career?

A. Between 100 and 120 games

B. Between 120 and 140 games

C. Between 140 and 160 games

D. More than 160 games

12.34 In 2006-07, who broke Martin Brodeur's record of most minutes played in a season?

A. Andrew Raycroft, with the Toronto Maple Leafs

B. Miikka Kiprusoff, with the Calgary Flames

C. Roberto Luongo, with the Vancouver Canucks

D. Martin Brodeur, with the New Jersey Devils

12.35 Which former goalie is best known for vigorously whacking his stick on both posts in a swinging motion, alternately hitting one post with the stick's blade, the other with the butt end?

A. Garth Snow

B. Curtis Joseph

C. Ron Hextall

D. Bill Ranford

12.36 Which goalie is known for talking to his goalposts?

A. Ed Belfour

B. Mike Richter

C. Patrick Roy

D. Ron Hextall

12.37 How small is the shortest goalie to see NHL action?

A. Five foot one

B. Five foot three

C. Five foot five

D. Five foot seven

12.38 After goalie Patrick Roy retired in 2003, which sniper did he say he had feared the most during his career when that player was on a breakaway?

A. Jaromir Jagr

B. Pavel Bure

C. Wayne Gretzky

D. No one

Answers

12.1   **B. Bernie Parent, with the Philadelphia Flyers**

When the NHL abolished ties with shootout victories (and over-time, to a lesser degree), a slew of team and individual records were bound to fall, including one of hockey's most famous: Bernie Parent's celebrated 47 wins of 1973–74. But even before Martin Brodeur topped Parent's mark with his 48th victory in 2006–07 (beating Parent's beloved Flyers, no less), the ugly "a"-word was being mentioned. Would an asterisk in the record books really clear the air over who had more wins in a season? Parent himself wouldn't hear of it: "You still have the five minutes of overtime and then the shootout, so you still have to win." Still, Parent's 33-year record was hammered not once but twice in 2006–07. Vancouver's Roberto Luongo equalled Parent with his own 47-win season, notching 11 overtime and five shootout victories, and 13 of Brodeur's 48 wins came either in overtime (3) or the shootout (10). Yet Parent was limited by 12 ties and the 78-game season of 1973–74. "I wish that anyone who ever looks at the record would mention Bernie Parent—and his effort with a shorter season and no shootouts—still having 47 wins," said Brodeur.

12.2   **A. 17 games**

It has been said that the Zamboni driver at the Devils' games gets more ice time than Martin Brodeur's relief goalie. And no one knows that better than career spare Scott Clemmensen, who mostly sat and watched as Brodeur played his typical plus-70-game seasons between 2001–02 and 2006–07, while he worked only 25 games and started just 17 with New Jersey.

Then, in early 2008–09, an injury to the biceps tendon in Brodeur's left elbow thrust the 31-year-old bench warmer into the spotlight: after a couple of losses, Clemmensen took over the number one spot from Kevin Weekes with eight wins in a nine-game stretch that almost had Devils fans asking, "Marty who?" But the real question may have been, Was New Jersey playing better because Brodeur's absence left the team with little margin for error between the pipes? Or did Clemmensen find his game after getting the opportunity to prove himself? When Brodeur returned on February 26, Clemmensen had worked 40 games and earned a 25–1 record for a respectable .917 save percentage on 94 goals in 1,138 shots. Not unexpectedly, after that historic bit of backup work, Clemmensen found himself back toiling with the AHL Lowell Ducks.

12.3 **D. His ability to catch the puck with either hand**
When Bill Durnan was a youngster playing for a church team in Montreal, his coach, Steve Faulkner, taught him to hold his goalie stick in either hand to make up for the fact that he didn't have good lateral movement. By the time he reached the NHL in 1943–44, Durnan was completely ambidextrous. Wearing a catching glove on both hands, he would simply switch his goal stick from one hand to the other during a game, depending on which side of the net he was playing—so no matter which side the shooter approached from he faced Durnan's glove hand. The unorthodox technique helped Dr. Strangeglove win six Vezina Trophies with the Canadiens in his seven-year NHL career. And in 1948–49, he blanked opposition shooters for an amazing 309 minutes and 21 seconds, a modern-day record.

12.4 **D. All of the above**
Roy has established so many important records that we would not be understating the case to say that his dominance in the

goaltending section of the NHL record book is Gretzky-like. Or it was, at least until Roy retired in 2003, after which Martin Brodeur began chipping away at his glory. But as of 2002–03, Roy broke Terry Sawchuk's 971-game total, when he reached the 1,000-game mark on January 20, 2003. Two months later, in a 3–1 win against San Jose on March 31, the Colorado goaltender then eclipsed 60,000 minutes played. That same year, he earned his 30th win for a record 13th time. Along with his mark for most regular-season wins, Roy also owns some prime real estate in the playoff record book as the leader in victories, games played and shutouts. Amen, St. Patrick.

12.5 B. Julian Klymkiw, with the Detroit Red Wings

Julian who? Klymkiw was Detroit's assistant trainer and practice goalie when the Drydens were growing up in the late 1950s, and though he played in only one NHL game, he starred in *Shootout in the* NHL, a CBS between-periods feature. Klymkiw, who zeroed all the top guns of the day, unknowingly became a fan favourite of Ken and Dave, who used to fight over who would pretend to be him. Klymkiw's one real game? It came in 1958, when he played not for his Red Wings but the New York Rangers. With only one goalie per team, all clubs in that era had a substitute netminder available at home games in case of injury to either team's regular goalie. So when New York's Gump Worsley pulled a tendon during the Red Wings' home opener, Klymkiw stepped between the pipes—for the opposition. And though it might have been the pressure of playing against his own team, Klymkiw didn't perform nearly as well as on *Shootout in the* NHL, giving up two goals during his 19 minutes of fame. Detroit won 3–0 and Klymkiw never played in the NHL again. Still, he faced more NHL stars on breakaways than any other one-game goalie.

12.6 C. Miikka Kiprusoff, with the Calgary Flames

If the game needed proof of the decline in goal scoring, it came from a couple of numbers in 2002–03 and 2003–04, when Marty Turco and Miikka Kiprusoff recorded back-to-back years with the lowest goals-against average in modern hockey. In his first year as the Stars' number one goaltender, Turco produced a 1.72 goals-against, the stingiest average in the modern era, topping the NHL record of 1.77 set by Tony Esposito with Chicago in 1971–72 and Al Rollins with Toronto in 1950–51. Then, the following season, Kiprusoff stood on his head in Calgary and busted Turco's measly total with a hot-handed 1.69 in 38 games. Were the duo hockey's proverbial canary in a coal mine? Was Kiprusoff that good? Well, after the lockout year of 2004–05, Kiprusoff stormed back into the new NHL and, despite the increase in goal production league-wide, delivered a league-leading average of 2.07—a higher number than in defense-oriented 2003–04 but still a Vezina Trophy-winning performance as top netminder. Kiprusoff was also nominated for the Hart Trophy as MVP.

12.7 D. Georges Vezina

Georges Vezina, after which the Vezina Trophy is named, became known as the Chicoutimi Cucumber for his ability to remain cool under pressure. Born in Chicoutimi, Quebec, Vezina, joined the Montreal Canadiens in 1910–11 and never missed a regular-season or playoff game over the next 15 years. But his 367-game streak ended in November 1925, when chest pains forced him to the bench. Four months later he died of tuberculosis. The Canadiens donated the Vezina Trophy to honour his memory and the best NHL goalie in future seasons. Vezina was one of two goalies first elected to the Hockey Hall of Fame, in 1945 (Chuck Gardiner was the other).

12.8 A. Zero games

Many mistakenly believe this record belongs to Ken Dryden, who played just six regular-season games with the Montreal Canadiens before leading them to the Stanley Cup in 1971. However, rookie goaltender Earl Robertson didn't play a single regular-season game in 1936–37 before backstopping the Detroit Red Wings to the Cup. Robertson was called up from the minors when starter Normie Smith's injured arm prevented him from playing in the finals against the New York Rangers. In the last two games of a best-of-five series, Detroit then rallied behind Robertson, who played like a bandit and blanked the Rangers 1–0 and 3–0 to win the Stanley Cup. Oddly, Robertson never played a regular-season game for the Red Wings. Two weeks after winning the Cup he was traded to the New York Americans.

12.9 D. Patrick Roy

Of Cam Neely's 452 career goals, 34—his greatest output against any NHL goaltender—were scored on Patrick Roy. "In regards to Patrick, I really understood the way he played. There were only a couple of places to put the puck on him without taking the time to look, the top corner (as Roy did the butterfly) or between his legs (as he was going down)," Neely said in a *Montreal Gazette* interview. Neely's mastery of hockey's winningest goalie included 16 regular-season goals and 18 playoff markers, two of them during a five-game victory in an Adams Division final on April 26, 1988, which handed the Bruins its first series win against Montreal since 1943 and ended its 17-series losing streak against the Canadiens. Neely was inducted into the Hall of Fame in November 2005.

12.10 B. Marty Turco, with the Dallas Stars

Marty Turco's stickhandling abilities have earned him a career 18 assists (to 2008–09), but his offensive talents with the paddle almost won him an unusual NHL first in a Dallas–Los Angeles game on October 14, 2006. It happened during the third period, with both teams playing four-on-four and the faceoff opposite Turco. Dallas's Jeff Halpern got thrown out of the circle, and when no player skated into the dot to replace him, Turco seized the moment: with the linesman about to drop the puck, the netminder lined up opposite Los Angeles winger Derek Armstrong for the draw. But the official motioned Turco out (under rule 76.1, a goalie cannot take faceoffs), thwarting history's first faceoff by a netminder. Still, the tactic earned some time for Dallas, and Eric Lindros took the puck drop.

12.11 C. Harry Lumley

Unless the NHL changes its rules regarding the age of draft picks, this record is set in stone. On December 19, 1943, Lumley donned the pads with the Detroit Red Wings at the age of 17 years, 38 days, and lost 6–2 to the New York Rangers. He would play just one more game before being sent down to the Indianapolis Capitols of the Central Hockey League, then win the starting job the following year. Oddly, during his brief tryout in 1943, Lumley, on loan from Detroit, also played for the New York Rangers, subbing in the third period for an injured Ken McAuley in a game against his own team. The move earned Lumley another distinction: the youngest goalie to play for two NHL teams.

12.12 D. Olivier Michaud, with the Montreal Canadiens

Although no one has seriously threatened Harry Lumley's record as the youngest netminder to play in the NHL, Olivier Michaud has come the closest, debuting with the Canadiens at the age of 18 years and 46 days on October 30, 2001. Michaud, who was on loan from the Shawinigan Cataractes of the QMJHL, replaced Mathieu Garon for the third period of a 3–1 loss to the Edmonton Oilers and stopped all 14 shots he faced. Until

Michaud's appearance, John Vanbiesbrouck, who was 18 years and 93 days old when he saw action with the New York Rangers on December 15, 1981, was the second youngest. Vanbiesbrouck, who beat the Colorado Rockies 2–1 in his debut, remains the youngest goalie to post a win in his first NHL game.

12.13 A. Bill Ranford

It's a good thing Bill Ranford won a couple of Stanley Cups (and a Conn Smythe as playoff NVP) with Edmonton during its glory years in the 1980s, because he saw precious little hardware after that. Instead, in the 1990s he got a lot of rubber and the most losses of any goalie. In fact, Ranford's five-team odyssey through that decade earned him 250 losses (compared to 179 wins) and the fifth-highest shots-against total: 14,686 shots. His next-closest rival, Curtis Joseph, is way back with 211 losses. But Joseph, unlike Ranford, scored no awards or trophies at all. And though he made his three teams—St. Louis, Edmonton and Toronto—better than they were, they rewarded him with a grinding schedule of 60-game seasons, on average. Mike Richter lost 200 games, Sean Burke, 198, Patrick Roy, 197, Jeff Hackett, 195 and Guy Hebert, 192.

12.14 D. Casseau (a small cardboard box for French fries)

Long before Patrick Roy became known as the Canadiens' saviour and viewed as a saint by Montreal's media, he earned the nickname Casseau—French for the small container that French fries are served in. Athletic therapist Gaetan Lefebvre is credited for initially noting that Roy's gangly body inside his oversized suit resembled a box of fries or potato chips spilling out of a bag—an observation made during Roy's first training camp in September 1984. "One day I arrived at the rink with a bag of chips and Gaetan Lefebvre called me a *casseau* in front of the guys," said Roy. The fact that he happens to like junk food just salted the deal. The nickname would follow Roy for the rest of career.

12.15   C. Because of his unique shot-blocking style
Lionel Conacher will forever be known as Big Train and Canada's athlete of the half-century, but he also earned the nickname the Travelling Netminder for his distinctive shot-blocking technique. In a calculated attempt to dissuade opponents from shooting, Conacher would slide across the ice on one knee with his gloves open-palmed to block the puck. The move allowed Conacher to stay upright without being vulnerable to a fake shot or deke, while at the same time cutting down the angle on the net. The move also forced shooters to make quick decisions, such as turning over the puck with a flawed offensive move.

12.16   A. 1949–50
Few NHLers came from the college ranks prior to the 1970s, and even fewer made the leap without some minor pro experience. But Jack Gelineau joined the Bruins late in 1948–49 after graduating from McGill University in Montreal, and the following year, won the Calder Trophy as rookie of the year. Gelineau would play for just a few more seasons before quitting hockey to take a job in insurance.

12.17   D. The Boston Bruins
Only two goalies have managed 30 straight games without a defeat. Gerry Cheevers notched a 32-game unbeaten streak in 1971–72, with 24 wins and eight ties, to earn Boston the league title and the Stanley Cup. Almost a decade later, fellow Bruin netminder Pete Peeters then went on a tear, with 26 wins and five ties in 1982–83, making him the last goalie to go undefeated for 30 games.

12.18 C. Mike Morrison, with the Edmonton Oilers

Edmonton coach Craig MacTavish turned Mike Morrison into hockey's first bullpen closer when he brought the rookie netminder into the game cold to replace starter Ty Conklin for a shootout against Dallas on March 7, 2006. Conklin kicked out 23 of 26 shots through regulation and overtime for the Oilers, but MacTavish figured Morrison's 5–0 shootout record gave him the edge over Conklin in the game-deciding session. However, the Stars jumped all over Morrison, scoring two goals on two shots, while the Oilers were blanked on both their attempts against Marty Turco in the 4–3 loss. On October 26, 2006, Atlanta coach Bob Hartley also tried the switch, relieving Johan Hedberg with Karl Lehtonen. "Just like a baseball manager, you have Mariano Rivera sitting on the bench; he's your closer, and Karl's our number one," said Hartley. In an earlier instance, Buffalo's Martin Biron replaced Mike Noronen *during* the shootout on November 22, 2005. But coach Lindy Ruff only made the move because Noronen had hurt his groin in the third period and was favouring it in the shootout. It was the first goalie swap during a shootout. Interestingly, in all three games, having a goalie come in cold for the shootout allowed a goal in each of the first two shots faced, and the opposition won the game.

12.19 B. Four home shutouts

After a string of three straight shutouts at Nassau Coliseum in December 2006, the Islanders' Rick DiPietro was poised to become only the second netminder in modern-era NHL hockey to record a fourth-consecutive zero on home ice. All that stood in DiPietro's way were the New Jersey Devils and Martin Brodeur, the goalie who had just passed Glenn Hall's record of 84 shutouts with his 85th, for third-best all-time. DiPietro's

play was terrific, but Brodeur blanked the Isles with his 86th
zero, a 2–0 win that halted DiPietro's home shutout streak at
191:04 in the December 30 game. After the final horn, the two
goalies waved and DiPietro passed the puck down to Brodeur,
who had just broken the 50,000-minute mark of his playing
career. "That was a great gesture," said Brodeur. Six-team-era
goalie Terry Sawchuk is the only backstopper to notch four
straight shutouts at home. He did it in January 1955.

12.20 B. Three minutes

In all likelihood some skaters have had shorter NHL stays,
but among netminders no one can challenge the three-
minute career mark held by both Robbie Irons and Christian
Soucy. And while Soucy is known for playing in every North
American pro league possible for someone of his era (NHL, IHL,
CHL, ECHL, AHL, WPHL, WCHL and UHL), his moment of glory—
replacing Chicago starter Jeff Hackett against Washington
on March 31, 1994—isn't nearly as interesting as Irons's brief
tenure between NHL pipes. A career IHLer, Irons's quick-as-
an-eye-blink shift occurred on November 13, 1968, in a game
between New York and St. Louis. Glenn Hall and Jacques
Plante were the Blues' tandem, but on that night Plante sat in
the stands nursing a slight groin pull while Irons backed up
Hall. Then, early in the game, Hall received a game misconduct, forcing St. Louis coach Scotty Bowman to go with Irons.
So Scotty instructed the third stringer to take his warm-up,
then feign an equipment problem to delay the game until
Plante was dressed. But Bowman's stalling tactics earned a
penalty warning from referee Vern Buffey. So out skated Irons,
who played three minutes without facing a single shot on
net. By 5:01 of the first period, Plante was ready, and Irons was
yanked—never to play another second in the big leagues.

12.21   D. More than 200 games

No other NHL goalie has recorded so few shutouts in as
many games as John Garrett. Although a few—Bob Mason
(145 games), Kari Takko (142 games) and Frank Pietrangelo
(141 games)—are up there, Garrett holds the ignoble honour
of recording only one blank in 207 games. It came on March 2,
1983, in a Vancouver win over Winnipeg. "We won 3–0 and
Tiger Williams went out after the game (with the trainer's
scissors) and cut out a piece of the net for me. The Winnipeg
arena crew wasn't too happy about that," recalled Garrett.

12.22   D. Richard Brodeur

Vancouver fans nicknamed Brodeur "King Richard," due to
his sometimes dazzling play. The goalie ruled as number
one backstopper for eight seasons and carried the underdog
Canucks all the way to the stunning Stanley Cup finals of
1982. Brodeur's reign also overlapped Mark Messier's most
prolific scoring period, and though Messier continued to play
for 16 years *after* Brodeur retired, King Richard still holds the
title as Messier's court jester. Brodeur gave up an all-time-high
20 goals to the Moose, followed by Ron Hextall's 16.

12.23   C. One year and 166 days

Based on these numbers, Martin Brodeur could blow by
Patrick Roy and a few other legends to dominate hockey's
most important goaltending records. Roy was 33 years and
123 days old when he registered his 400th win on February 5,
1999; Brodeur was 31 years and 322 days old for win number
400, a 4–3 overtime victory against the Florida Panthers on
March 23, 2004. New Jersey's Scott Niedermayer scored with
1:05 left in the extra period. Brodeur achieved the milestone
in fewer games than any other goalie and was 400–215–105
in 12 seasons. "The scary thing about Martin is that there is

a lot more left," said Devils coach Pat Burns at the time. "He loves the game and he works hard at it, and he's only 31 years old." Brodeur is the eighth and youngest goalie to reach the landmark. He also became the first to win 400 playing every game for the same team. "Not to take anything away from the other guys, but it's tough for an organization to have success for so long," Brodeur said. "It definitely makes it special. It says a lot about the success of the organization."

12.24 B. Glenn Hall

It may be the most famous photo in the history of the NHL: Bobby Orr, frozen by the camera lens of Ray Lussier, sailing mid-air, hands outstretched in celebration after scoring Boston's Stanley Cup winner just 40 seconds into overtime against St. Louis's Glenn Hall on May 10, 1970. Orr had just finished off a give-and-go with teammate Derek Sanderson and, as he fired point blank on Hall, had his skates taken out from beneath him by Blues defenseman Noel Picard. "I told Bobby a couple of times that I had already showered before he landed. I also asked him if that was the only goal he ever scored. I mean, he and I must have autographed a zillion of those pictures people brought to him," said Hall on the 30th anniversary of Orr's goal in May 2000.

12.25 D. The Boston Bruins

For most players, winning six Stanley Cups would be their career legacy, but not for Jacques Plante. In fact, Plante is better remembered for how he changed the game—as the first goalie to consistently wander from his net to play the puck and the first to wear a mask regularly—than he is for his six championships with Montreal in the 1950s. Nor do many remember him tending goal for his last team, the Boston Bruins. Yet Plante played brilliantly in eight games with

Bobby Orr's Bruins in 1972–73, winning seven, losing just one and recording two shutouts as a backup to Eddie Johnston. Unfortunately, the 44-year-old goalie faltered during the 1973 playoffs, giving up 10 goals in two losses. Plante, the masked warrior of 837 NHL games, never played in the league again.

12.26 B. Kirk McLean, with the Vancouver Canucks, in 1994–95

Teams no longer rely on just one goalie as they did back in the 1950s and 1960s, making it difficult for a netminder today to get credit for all of his club's wins in a season. Still, each generation of goalies has a few "win" hogs who have come close: Tony Esposito recorded 25 of Chicago's 26 wins in 1976–77; Martin Brodeur and Roberto Luongo posted near-perfect records in 2006–07, when Brodeur had 48 of 49 wins back-stoppng New Jersey, and Luongo had 47 of 49 in Vancouver. As for Kirk McLean, he is the most recent goalie to collect all of his team's wins in a season, managing the feat in the lockout-shortened season of 1994–95 (when the NHL played just 48 games) by playing in 40 matches and winning all 18 of the Canucks' victories in its second-place finish in the Pacific Division. Backup Kay Whitmore recorded no wins. Prior to McLean, who was the last NHL goalie to do it in a full season? The honour belongs to Ron Low, with the woeful Washington Capitals of 1974–75. The Caps set a modern-era record for fewest wins in a season and, though there wasn't much to salvage from the on-ice disaster, Low recorded all the victories with a record of 8–36–2. It's not much of a silver lining, but Low is the only stopper since the 1960s to account for all of his team's victories in a full season.

12.27 A. Clint Benedict

Benedict paced the NHL in shutouts for seven straight seasons with the Ottawa Senators from 1917–18 to 1923–24. The most zeroes he recorded in one season during that span were five, in 1919–20. And though Benedict logged far more shutouts in his last six seasons than in his first seven—41 as opposed to 17—he did not lead the NHL again, as offense declined in the late 1920s and double-digit shutout totals became common.

12.28 D. Seven goalies

Only three teams in NHL history were forced to dress seven netminders in one season. Quebec set the standard in 1989–90, when the Nordiques tried to stop the ugliness with Ron Tugnutt, Greg Millen, Sergei Mylnikov, Scott Gordon, Stephane Fiset, Mario Brunetta and John Tanner. Yet despite the parade of netminders, Quebec ended its season in last-place overall with a franchise-low of just 12 wins. The Nord's record has since been equalled twice, first in 2002–03 by the slumping St. Louis Blues, when the club iced Brent Johnson, Fred Brathwaite, Tom Barrasso, Cory Rudkovski, Reinhard Divis, Curtis Sandford and Chris Osgood. Then, in 2008–09, Los Angeles became the third team to use seven backstop-pers, with Daniel Taylor, Erik Ersberg, Jason LaBarbera, Jean-Sebastien Aubin, Dan Coultier, Jonathan Bernier and Jonathan Quick filling the Kings' net. Injuries and ineffective rotations were the culprits behind the high turnovers for all three teams, but at least the Blues saved some face by making the playoffs.

12.29 C. Allowing the fastest hat trick in NHL history

On March 23, 1952, fate—in the form of Chicago's Bill Mosienko—met Lorne Anderson and cast a humiliating blow. In only his third NHL contest, Anderson was scored upon three times by Mosienko in a record 21 seconds—the quickest hat trick in league annals. Anderson never recovered, and his NHL career ended with a win and two losses. Anderson's shot at the big time did bring him notoriety in the record books, however—just not for an accomplishment he might have wished for.

12.30 B. Frank Brimsek
Brimsek's route to the NHL began in his hometown of Eveleth, Minnesota, where he played high school hockey before turning amateur in Pittsburgh and pro in New Haven and Providence. Brimsek then went on to become Boston's Mr. Zero by twice recording streaks of three consecutive shutouts during his first month of NHL action in 1938. With the exception of Patrick Roy, few goalies have produced such stellar rookie seasons. Brimsek led the league in shutouts (10) and goals-against (1.56), won the Calder as top rookie and the Vezina as best goalie, and was a selection to the First All-Star Team and captured the Stanley Cup in 1938–39. By the time he retired in 1950, Brimsek had collected 252 victories, the most by an American-born goalie. Remarkably, it took another 44 years before Tom Barrasso surpassed Brimsek's U.S. mark, scoring his 253rd victory on February 15, 1994.

12.31 A. They each recorded a shutout without a win
There was a time in hockey when a shutout meant a win, or at least a tie, and Alex Auld and Miikka Kiprusoff know that better than any other goalies. On November 28, 2006, Auld stopped all Montreal Canadiens shooters during three periods and overtime, but surrendered two goals to Cristobal Huet's one in the shootout. "It's kind of crazy," said Auld after his Panthers fell 1–0. "I never thought I'd get a shutout without a win." Kiprusoff was also left scratching his head after his shutout in Calgary's 1–0 loss to Philadelphia on December 6, 2005. It was the first scoreless tie decided by a shootout since the format was adopted.

12.32 C. Six shutouts

For six straight games in 1927–28, Ottawa Senators netminder Alex Connell was unbeatable. With Connell holding the fort, the Senators beat the Toronto Maple Leafs 4–0 and the Montreal Maroons 1–0, then posted three scoreless ties—two against the New York Rangers and one against the Pittsburgh Pirates—before edging the Montreal Canadiens 1–0. Finally, at 15:50 during the second period of the seventh game of the streak, Chicago Blackhawks forward Duke Keats put a puck past Connell. The final tally: 461 minutes, 29 seconds of shut-out hockey. No goalie has since equalled this mark, which came during the defense-first era, before forward passing was permitted.

12.33 B. Between 120 and 140 games

Pokey Reddick has the longest shutout-less career in NHL annals. He played 132 games with Winnipeg, Edmonton and Florida between 1986–87 and 1993–94 without registering a single zero. In fact, Reddick's best season was his rookie campaign, when he and the Jets' Daniel Berthiaume were nicknamed Pokey and the Bandit as Winnipeg won 40 games and Reddick tallied a 21–21–4 record. Unfortunately, Reddick's career took a dive after his debut, with the exception of one brief shinning moment in 1990, when he played backup to Grant Fuhr and helped win the Stanley Cup.

12.34 D. Martin Brodeur, with the New Jersey Devils

Besides being an all-round nice guy and consummate team player, Martin Brodeur still relishes the spotlight, chasing individual NHL records—even if it's one of his own. Brodeur's NHL-record 4,697 minutes in 2006–07 topped his previous league mark of 4,555 in 2003–04. But the machine with the goalie pads has been known to take a night off, even if it means passing up another record. In New Jersey's last game of 2006–07 (a meaningless match for the playoff-bound Devils), for example, Scott Clemmensen started, preventing Brodeur from tying Grant Fuhr's all-time mark of 79 in one season. Brodeur fell short with 78 games.

12.35 C. Ron Hextall

Much like Ken Dryden's "the thinker" stance during stoppages in play, Hextall had his own unique mannerisms, including one that obviously suited his "take-no-prisoners" temperament. In preparation for a faceoff Hextall would clang his stick on both posts in a distinctive back-and-forth action, hitting the blade off one post and the butt end off the other.

12.36 C. Patrick Roy

During the 1986 playoffs, in Roy's rookie year, Montreal faced the New York Rangers in the Conference finals. After winning Game 3 in "miraculous" fashion in overtime (13 saves in nine minutes before Claude Lemieux scored the game-winner), Roy was asked by New York reporters, "Why did you turn around and stare at your net after the national anthem?" Roy, who spoke very little English at the time, responded, "I was talking to my goalposts." The New York scribes loved the comment and made a big deal out of it, especially after such a spectacular win. (Of course, when his English improved, Roy explained that he really doesn't talk to his posts. He just looks at the net and creates a vision of the net getting smaller. This gives him more confidence and makes him feel bigger.) As for Roy's 1986 season, his inspirational play led the Canadiens, a seventh-place overall team, to a surprise Stanley Cup, while Roy was named playoff MVP and became an overnight goaltending sensation.

12.37 B. Five foot three

Roy "Shrimp" Worters, a 12-year NHL veteran with the New York Americans and the Pittsburgh Pirates, stood only five foot three and weighed just 135 pounds. Yet despite his modest size, Worters played much bigger, winning the Vezina Trophy as top goalie in 1931 and playing five complete seasons without missing a game. His diminutive appearance also contradicted his fiery temperament, which made him a fierce competitor both on-ice and off. When his contract demands with the Pirates in 1928 forced his trade to the New York Americans, for example, Worters refused to report, and NHL President Frank Calder suspended the star netminder. He was only reinstated at a special Board of Governors meeting in December 1928. Throughout that season, his outstanding play in goal kept the Americans on top and earned Worters the first Hart Trophy awarded to a goalie. Only five other netminders since Worters have received such a tribute. And though Worters never won the Stanley Cup, he was named to the Hall of Fame in 1969. (Another small goalie was John Roach, who weighed only 130 pounds and was five foot five.)

12.38 D. No one

Roy never lacked attitude, which proved as important to his success as any skill or piece of equipment in his arsenal. And he left no doubt when he retired that he feared no player. "I've always had confidence in my abilities—so to be honest, no one." Roy, love him or hate him, then snickered at his cockiness, adding: "I guess things haven't changed, eh?"

Lefties and Righties

I N NHL HISTORY, only eight goalies manning the pipes with a right-hand catching glove have won the Vezina Trophy. Why do so many goalies catch with their left hand? Netminders feel they have better control of their stick with the more dominant hand, so they catch left. In this game, match the team and year with the Vezina righties and lefties.

Solutions are on page 564

LEFTIES

1. __F__ Martin Brodeur
2. __E__ Glenn Hall
3. __A__ Miika Kiprusoff
4. __G__ Ron Hextall
5. __C__ Terry Sawchuk
6. __D__ Dominik Hasek
7. __H__ Billy Smith
8. __B__ Patrick Roy

A. Calgary Flames 2006
B. Montreal Canadiens 1992
C. Detroit Red Wings 1955
D. Buffalo Sabres 1999
E. Chicago Blackhawks 1963
F. New Jersey Devils 2003
G. Philadelphia Flyers 1987
H. New York Islanders 1982

RIGHTIES

1. __H__ José Théodore
2. __A__ Chuck Gardiner
3. __G__ Grant Fuhr
4. __C__ Bill Durnan
5. __F__ Tom Barrasso
6. __E__ Gilles Villemure
7. __B__ Dave Kerr
8. __D__ Tony Esposito

A. Chicago Blackhawks 1932
B. New York Rangers 1940
C. Montreal Canadiens 1944
D. Chicago Blackhawks 1970
E. New York Rangers 1971
F. Buffalo Sabres 1984
G. Edmonton Oilers 1988
H. Montreal Canadiens 2002

13

Hockey's Who's Who and the Finnish Flash

THE WINNIPEG JETS WAITED four long years to sign Teemu Selanne after drafting him 10th overall in 1988. Winnipeg showed the virtue of patience and the power of money and finally secured the free-agent rookie by matching Calgary's $1.5-million signing-bonus offer. The investment paid off handsomely. In 1992–93, the "Gretzky of the Fjords" demolished Mike Bossy's record for rookie-season goals, turned Peter Stastny's freshman point totals inside out and stole top rookie honours from presumptive winner Eric Lindros. An astonishing 76 goals and 132 points later, Selanne had become the Finnish Flash. In this chapter: the Who's Who of the hockey world.

Answers are on page 341

13.1 **Which NHL gunner was known as the "Riverton Rifle"?**
- A. Steve Shutt, with the Montreal Canadiens
- B. Danny Grant, with the Minnesota North Stars
- C. Reggie Leach, with the Philadelphia Flyers
- D. Mickey Redmond, with the Detroit Red Wings

13.2 Who was the Holy Goalie?

A. Joe Daley, the WHA's all-time career leader in wins

B. John Garrett, the WHA's all-time career leader in losses

C. Ernie Wakely, the WHA's all-time career leader in minutes played

D. Ron Grahame, the WHA's all-time career leader in goals allowed

13.3 Which coach was known as "Captain Video?"

A. Roger Neilson

B. Scotty Bowman

C. Glen Sather

D. Al Arbour

13.4 Who was "Johnny O" (with the Detroit Red Wings in the 1980s)?

A. Joey Kocur

B. Joe Murphy

C. Eddie Johnstone

D. John Ogrodnick

13.5 Who are considered to be the first twins to play in the NHL?

A. Peter and Chris Ferraro

B. Ron and Rich Sutter

C. Patrik and Peter Sundstrom

D. Daniel and Henrik Sedin

13.6 Who, or what, were "the pirates" in the nickname "Terry and the Pirates"?

A. Terry Sawchuk's fan club

B. Terry Sawchuk's defense corps

C. Terry Sawchuk's equipment bag

D. Terry Sawchuk's drinking buddies

13.7 **Who is Tim Hurlbut?**

A. A Calgary streaker

B. The Zamboni driver at Toronto's Air Canada Centre

C. A controversial Vancouver radio host

D. The new owner of the Buffalo Sabres

13.8 **Who is Rip Simonick?**

A. An alias for NHL free agents

B. The Buffalo Sabres' equipment manager

C. A statistician with the CBC's *Hockey Night in Canada*

D. An IIHF official who criticized the NHL for raiding European leagues

13.9 **Who was the first NHL player to serve as a caddie at the U.S. Open?**

A. Dan Quinn

B. Wayne Gretzky

C. Grant Fuhr

D. Wayne Cashman

13.10 **Which Chicago Blackhawk scored the last goal in Maple Leaf Gardens history?**

A. Doug Gilmour

B. Bob Probert

C. Reid Simpson

D. Tony Amonte

13.11 **Who scored the first goal in New York Ranger franchise history?**

A. The club's first captain, Bill Cook

B. The club's youngest player, Paul Thompson, at 18 years old

C. The club's first multiple-trophy winner, Frank Boucher

D. The club's best defenseman, Ivan "Ching" Johnson

13.12 Who was the Albanian Assassin?

    A. Stu Grimson

    B. Donald Brashear

    C. Tie Domi

    D. Rob Ray

13.13 Who is the only player to be voted to an NHL All-Star team after his death?

    A. Howie Morenz, with the Montreal Canadiens

    B. Bill Barilko, with the Toronto Maple Leafs

    C. Tim Horton, with the Buffalo Sabres

    D. Pelle Lindbergh, with the Philadelphia Flyers

13.14 Who is Arthur Farrell?

    A. A well-known shot-blocking coach for defensemen

    B. The designer of Reebok's player uniforms

    C. The author of the first book written about hockey

    D. The first non-NHLer inducted into the Hockey Hall of Fame

13.15 Who scored the last WHA goal?

    A. Mark Messier, with the Cincinnati Stingers

    B. Mark Howe, with the New England Whalers

    C. Dave Semenko, with the Edmonton Oilers

    D. Bobby Hull, with the Winnipeg Jets

13.16 Who was the first goalie to be nicknamed the "Dominator"?

    A. Johnny Bower, with the Toronto Maple Leafs

    B. Jacques Plante, with the Montreal Canadiens

    C. Tony Esposito, with the Chicago Blackhawks

    D. Dominik Hasek, with the Buffalo Sabres

13.17 In 1994, who was the last Blackhawk to leave the ice after Chicago Stadium's final NHL game?

A. Chris Chelios

B. Tony Amonte

C. Jeremy Roenick

D. Ed Belfour

13.18 Who is Debbie Wright?

A. The NHL's first female TV analyst

B. The NHL's first female goal judge

C. The NHL's first female scout

D. The NHL's first female goalie

13.19 Which NHLer played a record 185 penalty-free games without ever winning the Lady Byng Trophy as the league's most gentlemanly player?

A. Val Fonteyne

B. Dave Keon

C. Mike Bossy

D. Nicklas Lidstrom

13.20 Who was "Leapin' Lou"?

A. Lou Angotti

B. Louie Fontinato

C. Lou Lamoriello

D. Lou Nanne

13.21 Which Hall of Fame defenseman was runner-up for the Norris Trophy as the NHL's most outstanding defenseman six times *and* never won a Stanley Cup despite making the playoffs for 17 consecutive seasons?

A. Borje Salming

B. Brad Park

C. Bill Gadsby

D. Mark Howe

13.22 Who is Mikko Leinonen?

A. The best man at Wayne Gretzky's wedding

B. An NHLer who shares a playoff record with Wayne Gretzky

C. Finland's version of Wayne Gretzky—a cousin of Jari Kurri

D. The peewee goalie who gave up Wayne Gretzky's first goal

13.23 Which NHLer negotiated a contract that allowed him to play in the NHL while playing with his team in the American Hockey League?

A. Jean Béliveau, with the Montreal Canadiens

B. Red Kelly, with the Toronto Maple Leafs

C. Eddie Shore, with the Boston Bruins

D. Ted Lindsay, with the Detroit Red Wings

13.24 Who is John Paris, Jr.?

A. The mascot for the Boston Bruins

B. The inventor of the FoxTrax puck

C. The first African-American pro hockey coach

D. The NHL's official statistician

13.25 Who is the only woman to play for an NHL team?

A. Hayley Wickenheiser

B. Cammi Granato

C. Angela James

D. Manon Rheaume

13.26 Who was "Old Lamplighter"?

A. Roy Conacher

B. Ted Kennedy

C. Max Bentley

D. Toe Blake

13.27 Who was nicknamed "Clark Kent" when he played for the Maple Leafs?

A. Kent Douglas

B. Andy Bathgate

C. Tim Horton

D. Eddie Shack

13.28 Who is Heavy Eric?

A. The Dallas Stars' equipment manager

B. The mascot of the Ottawa Senators

C. A musician who writes songs about the Vancouver Canucks

D. The Zamboni driver at Chicago's United Center

13.29 What distinguished goalie Jacques Plante from his playoff teammates between 1956 and 1960, when the Montreal Canadiens won five consecutive Stanley Cup championships?

A. He was the only player who didn't receive a Stanley Cup ring

B. He was the only player to play every minute of every game

C. He was the only player to travel exclusively by train

D. He was the only player to wear head or face protection in every game

13.30 Who is the first player to be officially credited with raising his stick to signal the scoring of a goal after the NHL initiated a mandatory policy instituting this practice in 1947?

A. Billy Reay, with the Chicago Blackhawks

B. Ted Lindsay, with the Detroit Red Wings

C. Ted Kennedy, with the Toronto Maple Leafs

D. Buddy O'Connor, with the New York Rangers

13.31 Who is goalie Martin Brodeur's father?

A. The first goaltending coach of the Ottawa Senators

B. A one-time conditioning coach for the New Jersey Devils

C. The former photographer for the Montreal Canadiens

D. The NHL's long-time director of Central Scouting

13.32 Who is the only NHLer to sweep hockey's "Triple Crown," winning the Art Ross (top scorer), Hart (MVP) and Lady Byng (good sportsmanship) trophies in one season?

A. Bobby Orr, with the Boston Bruins

B. Stan Mikita, with the Chicago Blackhawks

C. Wayne Gretzky, with the Edmonton Oilers

D. Alexander Ovechkin, with the Washington Capitals

13.33 Who were the "Baby Bulls" of the WHA?

A. A rookie scoring line with the Toronto Toros

B. Underage juniors signed by the Birmingham franchise

C. A defensive duo paired by Glen Sather in Edmonton

D. A trio of 300-plus penalty-minute goons with Minnesota's club

13.34 Who are the Wednesday Nighters?

A. An Edmonton beer league featuring ex-NHL tough guys

B. A barnstorming team of former NHL stars

C. A checking line with the Boston Bruins

D. A pick-up league famous for challenging the NHL's control of the Stanley Cup

13.35 Which high-scoring forward was nicknamed "Killer"?

A. Mike Modano

B. Doug Gilmour

C. Daniel Alfredsson

D. Keith Tkachuk

13.36 Who was the last NHLer to score 50 goals in one season without wearing a helmet?

A. Al Secord, with the Chicago Blackhawks

B. Craig MacTavish, with the St. Louis Blues

C. Rick Vaive, with the Toronto Maple Leafs

D. Dale Hawerchuk, with the Winnipeg Jets

13.37 Which old-time sniper was known as the "Big Bomber"?

A. Nels Stewart

B. Babe Dye

C. Bill Cook

D. Charlie Conacher

Hockey's Who's Who and the Finnish Flash

Answers

13.1 **C. Reggie Leach, with the Philadelphia Flyers**
A natural scorer, who had the power to connect from the blue line and the finesse to take a pass and wrist a shot in one motion, Leach had a brief reign in the mid-1970s as one of the NHL's most dangerous snipers (in 1975–76, he topped

the league with 61 goals for Philadelphia). In fact, born in Riverton, Manitoba, he always took great pride in his shooting ability, and would take hundreds of shots every day at practice, moving the puck around and focussing on specific targets. Unfortunately, he put less effort into other aspects of his game, which, along with a weakness for alcohol, contributed to his rather modest career total of 381 goals. With his talent, Leach could have easily scored 500.

13.2 A. Joe Daley, the WHA's all-time career leader in wins

Joe Daley played 105 NHL games, but is best remembered for the second stage of his career as an original member of the Winnipeg Jets. Daley joined the club in 1972, during the formation of the World Hockey Association, and stayed until the league folded in 1979—one of only five players to have played every season of the WHA's existence with the same team. Some say Daley was a religious man; in fact, to Winnipeggers he was widely known as the Holy Goalie. Certainly the Jets were saviours in a city starved for professional play, with Daley answering their prayers by backstopping the Jets to three Avco Cup championships. And when the WHA merged with the NHL in 1979, Daley retired as the netminder with the most wins in league history.

13.3 A. Roger Neilson

Neilson first hired college kids to shoot game film while coaching the Peterborough Petes of the OHA in the late 1960s. He then continued the practice in the NHL, where he became one of the first coaches to use videotape to analyze team performance, earning him the nickname "Captain Video." Soon more NHL teams hired cameramen and adopted video to study playmaking, and in the 1980s, the league made it obligatory for all clubs to provide game tapes.

13.4   D. John Ogrodnick

During the pre-Jacques Demers days of the 1980s, the cellar-dwelling Red Wings struggled along without much offensive punch, except for the play of Steve Yzerman and the man they called "Johnny O." John Ogrodnick mounted two 40-plus-goal seasons in 1982–83 (41) and 1983–84 (42) before his 105-point year, 1984–85. That was Johnny O's career year, when he popped 55 goals—good enough for seventh place in the NHL scoring race and a berth on the First All-Star Team of 1985. The Wings still finished third in the Norris Division, however, and bowed out 3–0 to Chicago in the first round, wasting Ogrodnick's stellar year.

13.5   B. Ron and Rich Sutter

The Sutters, of Viking, Alberta, are hockey's most productive family, with six siblings of NHL calibre in one generation. Twins Ron and Rich were rookies in 1982–83, sneaking in just ahead of Patrik and Peter Sundstrom by one year. Patrik began in 1982–83 and Peter in 1983–84. The Sutter twins are also the first twins to play on the same team: Philadelphia, in 1983–84.

13.6   B. Terry Sawchuk's defense corps

Sawchuk and his five Red Wings defensemen earned the comic strip nickname in the early 1950s, when Detroit was in the midst of winning seven straight league titles and four Stanley Cups. "The Pirates," who so effectively shut down opposing attackers, were Red Kelly, Marcel Pronovost, Leo Reise, Bob Goldham and Benny Woit. And without fail, every season the press took a photo of the group and called it "Terry and the Pirates." The original comic strip by the same name was created in the 1930s by Milton Caniss of the *New York Daily News*.

13.7   A. A Calgary streaker

Few who saw the news footage have forgotten the story of
Tim Hurlbut, the Calgary streaker who scaled the glass at the
Saddledome during a Boston game on October 17, 2002, fell
on the ice and was knocked out cold for six minutes while
wearing only a pair of red socks. Hurlbut—a name befitting
the man's actions—was intoxicated, and an Alberta judge subsequently ordered him to pay CDN$2,500 to two charities and
do community service, then chastised him for the "pathetic
spectacle of yourself splayed naked on the ice for six minutes
until you were covered." A few weeks later, the Calgary night-
club Cowboys Dance Hall held a fundraiser for Hurlbut, the
man "who brought so much joy into our lives with a simple
pair of red socks."

13.8   B. The Buffalo Sabres' equipment manager

In 2006–07, Rip Simonick was the longest-serving equipment
manager in the NHL. In fact, he has been with Buffalo since the
club entered the league in 1969. Simonick developed a passion
for team sports as a 10-year-old, doing odd jobs around Buffalo
Memorial Stadium. But after playing Junior B and college, he
gave up his dream of playing in the big leagues and settled
into repairing gear and sharpening skates with the Sabres
organization. "Today, we're labourers, psychologists and baby-
sitters. They call me a father figure, because I can do it all,"
Simonick once told the *Montreal Gazette*. At age 57, Simonick
has worked with six Buffalo GMs, 15 coaches and 18 captains,
but the biggest changes he says he has noticed after almost
40 years in the game are bottled water and glove-dryers.

13.9   A. Dan Quinn

After retiring from hockey in 1996, Quinn devoted himself to
golf and became a major player on the Celebrity Tour. Later, at

the 2000 U.S. Open at Pebble Beach, when John Daly's regular caddie had to withdraw with a bad ankle, Quinn was enlisted as his replacement. The honour earned him a close-up look at one of Daly's infamous meltdowns, on the 17th hole, as the golfer smacked one shot into a backyard and deposited three others into the Pacific Ocean. After carding a 14 on the par-5, Daly stormed off the course in disgust.

13.10 B. Bob Probert

Probert made history by scoring the last goal in the last of the Original Six arenas—the 68-year-old Maple Leaf Gardens. The Chicago tough guy notched the Gardens' final marker at 11:02 of the third period in Chicago's 6–2 thumping of Toronto, February 13, 1999. "I've got the puck and it's going to be put on a plaque," said a jubilant Probert. "I'll never forget this moment." Yet the best observation that night may have come from sportswriter Cam Cole, who said, "Bob Probert has closed a lot of buildings in his career—many of them, alas, saloons." For the record, a Chicago player, Harold "Mush" March, also scored the Gardens' first goal—in its 1931 opening game. Oddly, March was also the first to score a goal at the old Chicago Stadium.

13.11 A. The club's first captain, Bill Cook

More than 13,000 fans jammed Madison Square Garden on November 16, 1926, to witness the New York Rangers' first game in the NHL. The Rangers' opponents on that historic night were the Montreal Maroons—the defending Stanley Cup champs. The Rangers defeated the Maroons 1–0 on a goal by captain Bill Cook at 10:37 of the second period. Cook went on to lead the NHL in scoring in 1926–27, while the Rangers finished atop the NHL's American Division.

13.12 C. Tie Domi

Domi never had any illusions about why he was in the NHL: he was a fighter, paid to protect the finesse players. Unlike his fellow goons, however, Domi's swagger matched his pugilistic skills, a combination that earned him steady employment, a top-end us$1.35-million salary with Toronto in his twilight years and recognition as one of the league's most popular players. And through it all, Domi, of Albanian ancestry, did as much as anyone to champion a good fight. While the Assassin was around in the NHL, there was always a place in hockey for the big-time duke-out.

13.13 D. Pelle Lindbergh, with the Philadelphia Flyers

Early on a Sunday morning in November 1985, Philadelphia Flyers goalie Pelle Lindbergh lost control of his customized Porsche 930 Turbo on a sharp curve on Somerdale Road in New Jersey. The car skidded across the street, hit a curb and slammed into a wall. Lindbergh, who had been drinking, did not survive. A day later, he was pronounced brain dead and disconnected from life support in a New Jersey hospital— a tragic end to the 26-year-old's life and promising hockey career. The previous year, the Swedish-born Lindbergh had won the Vezina Trophy as the NHL's top netminder and was named to the First All-Star Team. In an emotional show of support, fans posthumously elected Lindbergh as the starting goalie for the Wales Conference team at the 1986 All-Star game in Hartford.

13.14 C. The author of the first book written about hockey

Hockey: Canada's Royal Winter Game is the oldest surviving book about hockey. And it was written not by a seasoned author or member of the press but by Arthur Farrell, a hockey player who penned the 122-page book in 1899—the year he won one of two Stanley Cups with the Montreal Shamrocks of the Amateur Hockey Association of Canada. Farrell's passion for "our glorious sport" offers a rare glimpse into the game in its infancy: "Hockey thrills the player and fascinates the spectator. The swift race up and down the ice, the dodging, the quick passing and fast skating make it an infatuating game." Only a few hard-copy editions of Farrell's book are known to exist, but digital versions can be found online.

13.15 C. Dave Semenko, with the Edmonton Oilers

On May 20, 1979, Dave Semenko closed a chapter in hockey history, scoring the last WHA goal in a 7–3 loss to the Jets during the final Avco Cup playoff game between Edmonton and Winnipeg.

13.16 D. Dominik Hasek, with the Buffalo Sabres

Most famous goalies earn their nicknames from how they perform between the pipes and not because of their personalities. Johnny Bower became the China Wall because his goaltending was virtually impenetrable. Jacques Plante took the *nom de guerre* of Jake the Snake while revolutionizing the position—by playing the puck outside the crease. Rookie Tony Esposito was christened Tony O after his modern-era record of 15 shutouts in 1969–70. And there could only be one Dominator. After capturing the hockey world's attention with his Cirque de Soliel-like performances on the blue paint during 1993–94 and 1994–95, Dominik Hasek's 1.95 and 2.11 earned him the NHL's best goal-against averages in 20 seasons, back-to-back Vezina trophies and a moniker that cemented his on-ice exploits: the Dominator.

13.17 C. Jeremy Roenick

On April 28, 1994, just moments after the ceremonial hand-shakes to end the Conference quarterfinals and the Hawks' playoff hopes, Jeremy Roenick circled the ice, waved to

Chicago fans and tossed his stick into the stands, saying good-bye forever to the 65-year-old home of the Blackhawks. He was the last Hawk to skate in Chicago Stadium before the club moved into the United Center in 1994–95.

13.18 C. The NHL's first female scout

Debbie Wright, 26, became the first woman to scout for an NHL team when the San Jose Sharks hired her for the 1992–93 season. And in her beat-up Ford Tempo, Wright certainly clocked the miles, scouting—on average—a game every night during the season in the talent-rich territories of Quebec, eastern Ontario and the northeastern U.S.

13.19 A. Val Fonteyne

A steady journeyman who spent most of his NHL career in Detroit and Pittsburgh, Val Fonteyne took only 13 minor penalties and not a single major penalty in 820 regular-season NHL games, just two minors in 149 WHA games and, during one stretch, played 185 straight games without committing a foul. The latter streak began when Fonteyne was with Detroit. He took a minor in a game against Montreal on February 28, 1965, and did not visit the penalty box again until December 1, 1968, when he was with Pittsburgh. Fonteyne's next-cleanest streak, 157 games, is the second-longest in NHL history.

13.20 B. Louie Fontinato

Though not a Hall of Famer by any standard, Fontinato was the kind of character player every team wanted for strength and ruggedness across the blue line—and needed when the gloves came off. And when he joined the league in 1954, he was immediately dubbed "Leapin' Lou" by the New York press for his running and jumping skating style. The media was also quick to discover his prime asset, which he made much use of to amass 1,247 penalty minutes in 535 games, while scoring just 104 points. Fontinato's most memorable heavyweight bout, however, came in 1959 when he challenged Gordie Howe, who in turn broke Fontinato's nose and smashed his face with several lefts and rights. By the time the Ranger brawler delivered three of his own best shots, without inflicting any damage, he knew the fight was lost. Howe's last powerful uppercut knocked Leapin' Lou senseless. Fontinato then went on to play his fearless game for nine more years, with New York and Montreal, before his career ended abruptly in 1963 after he broke his neck crashing headlong into the boards after a check by the Rangers' Vic Hadfield. Leapin' Lou recovered, as he always did, but never played hockey again.

13.21 B. Brad Park

Timing was not on Brad Park's side. He entered the NHL in 1968–69, just as Bobby Orr seemed to be making the Norris Trophy part of his permanent trophy collection, with Park placing second to Orr in the Norris balloting four times. But even after Orr's gimpy knees forced him to retire in 1978–79, Park found himself twice more the bridesmaid in Norris voting, this time to two future Hall of Famers, Denis Potvin and Larry Robinson, who split the award for the next five years. Yet despite surgery-scarred knees of his own, Park lasted 17 seasons in the NHL, qualifying for the playoffs each year but never skating on a Cup-winner.

13.22 B. An NHLer who shares a playoff record with Wayne Gretzky

Among the players Wayne Gretzky shares NHL records with, no one is less famous than Mikko Leinonen, who set a playoff record with six assists in a 7–3 New York Rangers victory over Philadelphia on April 8, 1982. No. 99 then equalled the record five years later, against Los Angeles, in a 13–3 bombing on April 9, 1987.

13.23 C. Eddie Shore, with the Boston Bruins

In 1939, as he neared the end of his NHL career, Eddie Shore purchased the AHL's Springfield Indians for $40,000 and, aware that his presence in Springfield's lineup would be a great drawing card, laced up for the Indians. Soon, Boston manager Art Ross came calling and struck a deal with Shore that would allow the veteran blueliner to play home games for both the Bruins and the Indians during the 1939–40 season. But Shore was soon itching to play in Springfield's road games as well, which prompted an exasperated Ross to trade his troublesome star to the New York Americans. As a result, Shore played eight games in eight nights in one stretch that spring, flying between various cities to maintain his commitments to both the Amerks and the Indians. He was 38 at the time.

13.24 C. The first African-American pro hockey coach

Although far from a household name, John Paris, Jr. has impressive credentials to go with the distinction of being the first African-American coach in pro hockey. In his 24 years behind the bench, Paris was named top coach in five different hockey leagues. After transforming the Atlanta Knights of the International Hockey League into a contender and winning the Turner Cup in 1994, Paris later assumed the coaching reins of the Macon Whoopee of the Central Hockey League in 1996–97. And as a credit to his coaching style, Paris guided the Whoopee roster of 12 first-year players to a second-place finish in the CHL's Eastern Division.

13.25 D. Manon Rheaume

Goalie Manon Rheaume became the first woman to play for an NHL team when she appeared between the pipes for the Tampa Bay Lightning in an exhibition game against the St. Louis Blues on September 23, 1992. Rheaume played one period and allowed two goals on nine shots.

13.26 D. Toe Blake

Blake acquired his nickname, "Old Lamplighter," from the red goal lights (or lamps) he ignited so routinely in his early playing days with the Maroons and the Canadiens. Even before the Punch Line with Maurice Richard and ElmerLach, Blake was a Stanley Cup winner, a league scoring champ and an MVP winner of the Hart Trophy. As senior linemate and Montreal captain, he also directed the Canadiens to two Cups (1944 and 1946). Later, he continued his winning ways behind the bench, coaching Montreal to an unprecedented eight championships—including a record five-in-a-row in his first five seasons (1956 to 1960). Beyond the accolades and silverware, though, Blake was also a teacher whose captaincy was beyond reproach; his on-ice presence and resolve reflected both his skills and leadership. Yes, as a coach, Toe was tough and demanding. Former Canadiens have often said, "Blake didn't know what the word 'lose' meant, because it wasn't in his vocabulary." But with his never-say-die mindset, Blake won 11 Stanley Cups, made the best players better and, ultimately, showed the next generation of coaches, including Scotty Bowman and Mike Keenan, how to win.

13.27 C. Tim Horton

With his horn-rimmed glasses and tremendous athletic strength, Horton was the Superman of the Leafs during the 1960s. Some teammates considered him fearless, and without a doubt, he was Toronto's backbone—an inspirational leader with a clean, hard-hitting defensive style who could turn a game around with one of his patented end-to-end rushes. One of his generation's greatest competitors, he intimidated opponents with his skills and strength, not dirty games, and brought honour to the game each night he played. He was a natural.

13.28 **C. A musician who writes songs about the Vancouver Canucks**

Known in Vancouver music circles as Heavy Eric (with or without his band, the Light Weights), Eric Holmquist has written and recorded more than two dozen songs about the Vancouver Canucks. The former lumberjack, part-time Elvis impersonator and full-time mailman, who has had his music featured on Vancouver radio and TV shows and at the city's GM Place, penned his first hockey hymn, "Gino, Gino," in 1991 as a tribute to enforcer Gino Odjick. A few more Heavy Eric songs were also inspired by the Canucks' one-time controversial No. 44: "They've Freed Todd Bertuzzi" and "It's Called the Todd Bertuzzi." However, Heavy Eric is still waiting to write the song that will crown his music career—the one about his favourite team winning the Stanley Cup.

13.29 **B. He is the only player to play every minute of every game**

Obviously, the only player to play every minute of every play-off game is goaltender Jacques Plante, one of just 12 Canadiens to have won five straight Stanley Cups.

13.30 **A. Billy Reay, with the Chicago Blackhawks**

It was an idea proposed by Frank Patrick (who was the guiding force behind many of hockey's early innovations, including the penalty shot, the blue line and the first playoff system in any sport)—and first tried on November 13, 1947, when Chicago's Billy Reay raised his stick after scoring a goal against the Canadiens. No doubt players before him had celebrated scoring a goal in a similar manner, but Reay was the first scorer to do so under a mandatory policy initiated in 1947, a policy approved by then-league-president Clarence Campbell.

13.31   C. The former photographer for the Montreal Canadiens
Martin Brodeur's hockey bloodline is impeccable. His
father, Denis, the one-time official club photographer of the
Canadiens, tended goal for the Victoriaville Tigers when Jean
Béliveau was the team's star centre in 1949 and, later, won
a bronze medal for Canada in international hockey at the 1956
Olympics. And though his father never played in the six-team
NHL (in an era without substitute goalies, when only extraordinarily talented netminders made it), his 30-year career
in sports photography kept him close to the game and his
son, Martin.

13.32   B. Stan Mikita, with the Chicago Blackhawks
Playing among superstars such as Bobby Hull, Gordie Howe
and Jean Béliveau, Mikita achieved something in 1966–67
never done before or matched since: he won the NHL's scoring
title, most valuable player award and good sportsmanship trophy in one season. But even more impressive is the fact that
Mikita repeated this feat, winning the "Triple Crown" again
the following year.

13.33   B. Underage juniors signed by the Birmingham franchise
When Birmingham Bulls owner John Bassett broke the
league's "gentleman's agreement" against signing underage
juniors by inking 18-year-old Ken Linseman to a contract,
he opened the door to other junior signings, including Indianapolis Racers owner Nelson Skalbania's deal
with 17-year-old scoring ace Wayne Gretzky. In response,
Bassett then signed teenagers Rick Vaive, Craig Hartsburg,
Gaston Gingras and Rob Ramage, who became known as
Birmingham's "Baby Bulls."

13.34 **D. A pick-up league famous for challenging the NHL's control of the Stanley Cup**

The tradition of the Stanley Cup as a challenge trophy was given new life in February 2006, when the NHL reached an out-of-court settlement with Gard Shelley and David Burt, two Toronto-area recreational players who filed a court case to undermine the league's claim that it controlled the Cup. It's unlikely the two beer leaguers' hopes of hoisting hockey's most famous trophy will be realized, but the resulting agreement does stipulate that Cup trustees can award it to a team outside the NHL in a season when the league doesn't operate. Still, though that ruling opened the door, the trustees are under no obligation to award the Cup to just any challengers. Obviously, "our guys weren't going… to court to say the Wednesday Nighters group of geriatric hockey players deserve to have their name on the Cup," said Tim Gilbert, lead counsel for Shelley and Burt, in a *National Post* story. "It was that the Cup is bigger than the NHL." The pact also includes a provision for the NHL to contribute $100,000 a year for five years to leagues for women and underprivileged children.

13.35 **B. Doug Gilmour**

Doug Gilmour was given the nickname early in his career by former Blues teammate Brian Sutter, who began calling Gilmour "Killer" because of the fierce look in his eyes. Few NHLers ever played with more desire or intensity than the 20-year veteran. He always did whatever it took to win a game, both on offense and defense, and still holds single-season records in assists (95) and points (127) with the Toronto Maple Leafs. Gilmour was also a defensive specialist—fearless, intimidating and confident in battle, even against much bigger players, traits that earned him a Selke Trophy as 1992–93's best defensive forward. Still, his greatest individual achievement might be finishing runner-up to Mario Lemieux in voting for the 1993 Hart Trophy as league MVP.

13.36 A. Al Secord, with the Chicago Blackhawks
Even after the NHL passed legislation that made wearing helmets mandatory for any player entering the league after June 1, 1979, it took another 17 seasons before the last helmetless holdout retired, and in 1995–96, Craig MacTavish was the lone NHLer still playing without a helmet. Though an exemption to the rule was passed in 1992–93 (and a few dozen players signed the waivers), only one player, Calgary's Greg Smyth, has exercised the right to play sans helmet, which he did for just one game. The last 50-goal scorer without protective headgear was Al Secord, who scored 54 times in 1982–83.

13.37 D. Charlie Conacher
Two inches taller and 20 pounds heavier than the average player of his era, Conacher dominated the game in the 1930s—not only with his size and strength but with his hustle and heavy shot. His shooting, which terrorized goalies, made him the league's goal-scoring champ five times, the winner of two NHL scoring crowns and a five-time All-Star. Still, though the "Big Bomber" scored more than most of his contemporaries, his scoring prowess was due in part to linemates Busher Jackson and Joe Primeau. The trio were Toronto's number one scoring unit in the 1930s, best remembered as The Kid Line. Conacher played 12 NHL seasons—nine of them in Toronto.

Game 13

MVP Maverick

WHO WAS THE FIRST NON-CANADIAN to win the Conn Smythe Trophy as playoff MVP? To find that exceptional player, unscramble the names of past winners and place each letter in the correct order in the boxes. (To help, each name starts with a bolded letter.) Next, unscramble the letters in the circled boxes to spell the first name of our secret MVP; then unscramble the letters in the diamond-shaped boxes for his last name, the square-shaped boxes for his team.

Solutions are on page 565

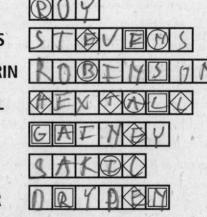

YOR

VESNETS

SNOOBRIN

THAXELL

YANGEI

SIACK

NYDDER

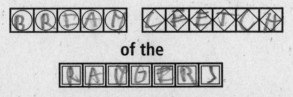

of the

14

The Great One

WAYNE GRETZKY'S CAREER was not only defined by the number of records he smashed but by the incredible margins with which he smashed them. Since his retirement in 1999, for example, only two of Gretzky's 61 records have been broken (both by Mark Messier): most overtime assists and most All-Star game assists. But perhaps even more startling is that, in retirement, the Great One continues to pad his record lead. His 59-record tally was boosted by one when Mario Lemieux came back from retirement to play and lowered his 2.005 career points-per-game average to 1.883, handing Gretzky, with 1.921, the NHL record. In this chapter, we crunch the numbers on the Great One.

Answers are on page 366

14.1 When did Wayne Gretzky register his NHL-record 92-goal season?
   A. 1981–82
   B. 1982–83
   C. 1983–84
   D. 1984–85

14.2 Who was Wayne Gretzky's boyhood idol?
   A. Maurice Richard
   B. Gordie Howe
   C. Bobby Hull
   D. Bobby Orr

14.3 **Against which NHL franchise did Wayne Gretzky score the most goals?**
A. The Calgary Flames
B. The Carolina Hurricanes-Hartford Whalers
C. The Phoenix Coyotes-Winnipeg Jets
D. The Vancouver Canucks

14.4 **Where was Wayne Gretzky's office?**
A. In the goalie crease
B. Behind the opponent's net
C. In the slot in front of the opponent's net
D. At centre ice

14.5 **When Wayne Gretzky scored seven assists on February 15, 1980, he tied an NHL record first set in what decade?**
A. The 1940s
B. The 1950s
C. The 1960s
D. The 1970s

14.6 **Against which former teammate did Wayne Gretzky score his record-breaking career point?**
A. Andy Moog
B. Bill Ranford
C. Kelly Hrudey
D. Grant Fuhr

14.7 **What historic goal did Wayne Gretzky score on December 21, 1991?**
A. The goal that surpassed Maurice Richard's career total
B. The goal that surpassed Bobby Hull's career total
C. The goal that surpassed Phil Esposito's career total
D. The goal that surpassed Marcel Dionne's career total

14.8 Which brand of helmet did Wayne Gretzky wear?

A. CCM

B. Jofa

C. Winn Well

D. Cooper

14.9 In 1981–82, against which team did Wayne Gretzky score his famous 50th goal in 39 games?

A. The Montreal Canadiens

B. The Boston Bruins

C. The Vancouver Canucks

D. The Philadelphia Flyers

14.10 According to Wayne Gretzky, what percentage of his assists came from setting up behind the net?

A. 20 per cent

B. 40 per cent

C. 60 per cent

D. 80 per cent

14.11 Besides No. 99, what was the only other jersey number worn by Wayne Gretzky in his professional career?

A. No. 9

B. No. 10

C. No. 20

D. No. 79

14.12 On average, by how many fans did attendance jump at the Great Western Forum in Los Angeles when Wayne Gretzky was traded to the Kings?

A. By 2,000 fans

B. By 3,000 fans

C. By 4,000 fans

D. By more than 5,000 fans

14.13 In which season did Wayne Gretzky, who began his NHL career in 1979–80, record his 5,000th career shot on goal?

A. 1992–93
B. 1994–95
C. 1996–97
D. 1998–99

14.14 Against which team did Wayne Gretzky score his first professional goal?

A. The Vancouver Canucks
B. The Edmonton Oilers
C. The Quebec Nordiques
D. The Indianapolis Racers

14.15 What is the only league-organized team Wayne Gretzky played for but never scored a goal with?

A. The Brantford Charcon Chargers of the OMHA, a minor league
B. The Seneca Nationals of the OHA, a Junior B league
C. The Peterborough Petes of the OHA, a Junior A league
D. The Indianapolis Racers of the WHA

14.16 What is the greatest number of games Wayne Gretzky went in his NHL career without scoring a goal?

A. 12 games
B. 15 games
C. 18 games
D. 21 games

14.17 Against which NHL goalie did Wayne Gretzky score the most goals?

A. Richard Brodeur, with the Vancouver Canucks
B. Kirk McLean, with the Vancouver Canucks

C. Don Beaupre, with the Minnesota North Stars

D. Mike Liut, with the Hartford Whalers

14.18 How many of the top positions does Wayne Gretzky hold in the NHL record book for most assists in one season?

A. The top two positions

B. The top five positions

C. The top eight positions

D. The top 11 positions

14.19 Wayne Gretzky scored so many assists each season that, on a few occasions, he could have won the NHL scoring race on assist totals alone. How many times did he accomplish this feat?

A. Never

B. Only once

C. Two times

D. Four times

14.20 In which league did Wayne Gretzky produce the greatest margin of points between himself and the next-best player?

A. In minor hockey

B. In junior hockey

C. In the WHA

D. In the NHL

14.21 Which player tied Wayne Gretzky for the scoring lead and prevented him from winning the scoring championship in his first NHL season?

A. Marcel Dionne

B. Gilbert Perreault

C. Bryan Trottier

D. Guy Lafleur

14.22 Wayne Gretzky registered an NHL-record 92 goals in an 80-game schedule in 1981–82. In how many games did Gretzky fail to score a goal that season?

    A. 10 games

    B. 15 games

    C. 20 games

    D. 25 games

14.23 How many shots on net did Wayne Gretzky take during his NHL-record, 92-goal season in 1981–82?

    A. 319 shots

    B. 369 shots

    C. 419 shots

    D. 469 shots

14.24 Which goalie was involved in two of Wayne Gretzky's five-goal games?

    A. Pete Peeters

    B. Don Beaupre

    C. Rick Wamsley

    D. Mike Liut

14.25 After winning an automobile for copping the MVP award at the 1989 All-Star game, Wayne Gretzky announced he was giving his prize to someone else. Who?

    A. His father, Walter Gretzky

    B. His wife, Janet

    C. His agent and personal friend, Mike Barnett

    D. His former teammate, Dave Semenko

14.26 What is the greatest number of goals scored by Wayne Gretzky during a season, *including* the playoffs?

    A. 92 goals

    B. 96 goals

C. 100 goals

D. 104 goals

14.27 In what percentage of games did Wayne Gretzky score at least one point? (We're not looking for the points-per-game average.)

A. 62 per cent

B. 72 per cent

C. 82 per cent

D. 92 per cent

14.28 Which two players assisted on the goal that made Wayne Gretzky the greatest point scorer in NHL history?

A. Jari Kurri and Esa Tikkanen, with Edmonton

B. Larry Robinson and Bernie Nicholls, with Los Angeles

C. Steve Duchesne and Dave Taylor, with Los Angeles

D. Brian Leetch and Adam Graves, with New York

14.29 Among the numerous times that Wayne Gretzky won the Art Ross Trophy as NHL points leader, what was the greatest difference in points between him and the runner up in an NHL scoring race?

A. 69 points

B. 79 points

C. 89 points

D. 99 points

14.30 In his record-setting 215-point season, for how many games did Wayne Gretzky go without a point in the 80-game schedule?

A. None

B. Three games

C. Six games

D. Nine games

14.31 **What was the last Canadian city Wayne Gretzky played in?**
   A. Ottawa
   B. Vancouver
   C. Toronto
   D. Edmonton

14.32 **How many hockey sticks did Wayne Gretzky use in his final NHL game?**
   A. 10 sticks
   B. 20 sticks
   C. 30 sticks
   D. 40 sticks

14.33 **In which road arena did Wayne Gretzky score the most goals?**
   A. Winnipeg Arena
   B. Edmonton's Northlands Coliseum
   C. Toronto's Maple Leaf Gardens
   D. Detroit's Joe Louis Arena

14.34 **Among the 49 arenas in which Wayne Gretzky played, how many venues did he fail to score a point in?**
   A. None—Gretzky scored a point in every rink in which he played
   B. Only one arena
   C. Three arenas
   D. Five arenas

14.35 **Against which NHL team did Wayne Gretzky score the highest percentage of goals?**
   A. The Toronto Maple Leafs
   B. The Vancouver Canucks

C. The Detroit Red Wings

D. The Colorado Avalanche-Quebec Nordiques

14.36 **What is the most number of points Wayne Gretzky scored against one NHL team?**

A. Between 100 and 150 points

B. Between 150 and 200 points

C. Between 200 and 250 points

D. More than 250 points

14.37 **What was Wayne Gretzky's career plus-minus rating?**

A. Between plus-200 and plus-300

B. Between plus-300 and plus-400

C. Between plus-400 and plus-500

D. More than plus-500

14.38 **Including playoff goals, how many more goals than Gordie Howe did Wayne Gretzky compile as a professional?**

A. Only one goal

B. Nine goals, the same number as Howe's sweater number

C. 72 goals, the same year number—1972—of Howe and Gretzky's first meeting

D. 99 goals, the same number as Gretzky's sweater number

14.39 **Five months after his retirement in 1999, Wayne Gretzky said he would have put off retiring for a chance to play with which player?**

A. Jaromir Jagr

B. Mark Messier

C. Pavel Bure

D. Steve Yzerman

Answers

14.1 **A. 1981–82**
Wayne Gretzky smashed a number of hockey's most important scoring records in 1981–82, the season, as Gretzky once
said, that "all heaven broke loose. Pucks started going into
the net on their own. I'd tip 'em in, bounce 'em in, wobble
'em in, elbow 'em in, wish 'em in. No matter what I tried, they
kept finding their way past goaltenders." In one four-game
stretch, Gretzky scored 10 goals. He also nailed the prestigious 50-goal mark in just 39 games, broke Phil Esposito's
76-goal record and became the first player to score 200 points
in a season. Teamed with Finnish sniper Jari Kurri, Gretzky
was the proverbial Energizer Bunny: he just kept going and
going and going. His favourite victims: Los Angeles's Mario
Lessard, whom he netted seven goals against, and Hartford's
Greg Millen, Philadelphia's Pete Peeters and Calgary's Reggie
Lemelin, all of whom he beat five times. No player in hockey
has ever dominated a season the way Gretzky did in 1981–82.

14.2 **B. Gordie Howe**
Gordie Howe was the reason Wayne Gretzky originally wore
No. 9, and when the famed digit wasn't available in the junior
ranks, he switched to No. 99, a tribute to his boyhood hero
and hockey's long-time greatest player. During the 1978–79
WHA All-Star game, Howe and Gretzky, the oldest and youngest players on the ice, then teamed up. Gretzky tucked in
his jersey, as usual. And from nowhere, a hand appeared and
pulled the top back out. Before the game, Howe had somehow
found a needle and thread, sewed up the sides of the jersey to

make it fit properly, then handed it back to the rookie wonder. Gretzky never said a word about any of this. Who argues
with his boyhood idol?

14.3   C. The Phoenix Coyotes-Winnipeg Jets

During his 20-year NHL career, Wayne Gretzky scored at last
one goal against all 27 teams he played against, but his easiest
target was Edmonton's divisional rival, Phoenix-Winnipeg.
The Coyotes-Jets gave up 79 goals, Gretzky's highest goal
count against any NHL franchise, as No. 99 recorded one four-
goal game, three three-goal games, 16 two-goal games and
34 single-goal matches against the club.

14.4   B. Behind the opponent's net

Wayne Gretzky's on-ice "office" was behind the net. The
strategy started in Junior B hockey after Gretzky kept getting knocked over by big defenesmen. At the suggestion of
his coach, No. 99 began setting up behind the net, much as
Bobby Clarke was doing with the Philadelphia Flyers. The net
offered the smaller Gretzky protection but also made defenders turn their backs to his teammates, causing breakdowns
that led to Gretzky-assisted goals. Besides using the net to set
up his slot man, Gretzky could also deke out either way—to
make a pass or score on a wraparound.

14.5   A. The 1940s

Although the Great One did it three times during his stellar
career, the first and only other seven-assist game in the NHL
came courtesy of Billy "The Kid" Taylor. On March 16, 1947,
Taylor caught fire, notching seven helpers in Detroit's 10–6
win over Chicago. Thanks to his playmaking skills, he also
led the league in assists (with 46) and finished third in the
scoring race, with his most-assists-in-a-game record lasting

for a remarkable 33 years until equalled by Gretzky. Taylor's other claims to NHL fame: his 1942 Stanley Cup with Toronto and, later, his life-long suspension from hockey for betting on his own team's games in 1948. (He and Boston linemate Don Gallinger were reinstated in 1970.)

14.6 B. Bill Ranford

In a story only Hollywood could script, when Wayne Gretzky finally scored point number 1,851 to break Gordie Howe's career mark, he did it against the team that brought him his greatest success, the Edmonton Oilers. The historic goal came on October 15, 1989, a little more than a year after Gretzky's trade from Edmonton to the Los Angeles Kings. The Great One flipped the puck over the shoulder of Bill Ranford, No. 99's one-time Oiler teammate, who played just six games with Gretzky after his trade to Edmonton in March 1988—before Gretzky's move to the Kings in August 1988.

14.7 D. The goal that surpassed Marcel Dionne's career total

As the NHL's all-time leader in goals, assists and points, Wayne Gretzky surpassed all of the game's greatest scorers. And on December 21, 1991, he notched his 732nd goal to pass Dionne, the last sniper in his path before his assault on Gordie Howe's 801-goal record.

Wayne Gretzky's Milestone Goals

CAREER GOAL NUMBER	DATE	ACHIEVEMENT
1	10/14/79	First NHL goal
50	04/02/80	First of eight straight 50-goal years
156	12/30/81	50 goals in 39 games
183	02/24/82	Scored 77th goal to break Phil Esposito's single-season record
198	03/26/82	Scored 92nd goal to set highest single-season total
325	01/18/24	Passed Nels Stewart's career-goal total on sixth achievement
500	11/22/86	Passed Mike Bossy's record for fastest 500 goals
545	10/14/87	Passed Maurice Richard's career goal total
611	12/23/88	Passed Bobby Hull's career-goal total
641	10/15/89	Set all-time points total: 1,851
718	03/28/91	Passed Phil Esposito's career-goal total
732	12/21/91	Passed Marcel Dionne's career goal total
802	03/23/94	Passed Gordie Howe's career-goal total
894	03/29/99	Last NHL goal

14.8   B. Jofa

No NHLer was more photographed than Wayne Gretzky, and on the ice, his Jofa 235 was as familiar to fans as his sweater tuck. The custom began in the WHA: "I wore a CCM helmet in Indianopolis. A player in Edmonton told me to try [the Jofa] because it was so much lighter. I never wore anything else [after that]." Then, in the early 1990s, the Great One discovered that his trademark helmet was considered unsafe by the NHL. He fired back: "I've worn my helmet 17 years and now they're afraid I'm going to get hurt. It's a big issue to them, but I'm going to wear the helmet I always have. Let's see if they kick me off the ice."

14.9 D. The Philadelphia Flyers

No player in NHL history had scored 50 goals in fewer than 50 games before Wayne Gretzky accomplished the feat in 1981–82. Maurice Richard and Mike Bossy had 50-in-50 marks in their respective eras, but it was Gretzky who finally broke through with a five-goal spree on December 30, 1981, against the Flyers' Pete Peeters. And even though Gretzky's fifth goal, his 50th of the season, was an empty-netter, Peeters still revels in the memory of that night. "Wayne got, what, five that night?" Peeters said, as quoted in *Sports Illustrated*. "Believe me, it could have been nine or 10. I have vivid memories of coming out, challenging him, stopping him. And he hit at least three pipes. I can still hear them ringing."

14.10 B. 40 per cent

Wayne Gretzky will probably be remembered first for his playmaking. When he was set up in his "office," someone usually scored a goal. In fact, "40 per cent [of my assists] have come from behind the net," Gretzky once said. "The next-biggest number would be hitting the late guy. Between those two plays, I'd say that probably accounts for three-quarters of my assists." Gretzky amassed 2,223 assists, including playoff helpers, during his career.

14.11 C. No. 20

Wayne Gretzky wore only one other sweater number besides No. 99 during his pro career. It happened on November 3, 1978, in his first WHA game with the Edmonton Oilers. The Alberta team didn't have an available jersey bearing the celebrated No. 99, so Gretzky was handed No. 20. The number switch had little adverse effect, however: Gretzky scored his first Oilers goal in the club's 4–3 win over Winnipeg. In the next game, Grezky donned his traditional double nines.

14.12 D. By more than 5,000 fans

Before Wayne Gretzky arrived in Los Angeles in 1988, the Kings averaged about 10,000 fans per game and were the NHL's worst-drawing team on the road. But in Gretzky's seven full seasons in LA, attendance rocketed to 15,700, or 98 per cent capacity of the Forum, while LA became the number one road attraction—playing to near-capacity every night. And in another measure of the Great One's influence, the Kings were the only pro sports team in southern California to sell out every home game in 1991–92.

14.13 D. 1998–99

After being stuck at 4,999 career shots for three games in November 1998, Wayne Gretzky chalked up his 5,000th shot on November 27 against Pittsburgh's Tom Barrasso. He then scored goals in three straight games, including his 890th NHL career marker and his first against New York Islanders goalie Tommy Salo, on December 2. (At the time, Salo was the only goalie with a minimum 10 appearances against Gretzky to blank No. 99.) Gretzky fired a lifetime 5,089 shots in the NHL.

14.14 B. The Edmonton Oilers

Ironically, the club that earned Wayne Gretzky his greatest fame, the Edmonton Oilers, is the same team he scored his first goal against. Before his NHL career began in 1979, Gretzky played the 1978–79 regular season split between the Indianapolis Racers (eight games) and the Edmonton Oilers (72 games) of the WHA—with his first-ever professional goal coming in his fourth pro start. Still, it was anything but spectacular. On October 20, 1978, before 6,386 fans at Indianapolis's Market Place Arena, Gretzky half-fanned a weak backhand against Edmonton, the team he would later turn into an NHL dynasty. He then scored another goal in the 4–3 loss, which history recorded as his first multiple-goal game. Less than a year later, the Great One potted his first NHL goal against the Vancouver Canucks, on October 14, 1979.

14.15   C. The Peterborough Petes of the OHA, a Junior A league
Among No.99's numerous team and league records, there are many personal firsts, including the only club he went goal-less with in his career—the Peterborough Petes of the Ontario Hockey Association. On three occasions in 1976–77 (November 26, January 3 and March 3), Gretzky was called up from the Seneca Nationals' Junior B team to join the Junior A Petes. Gretzky, a skinny 15-year-old centre, registered three assists in three games but no goals. He claims he never really had a good scoring opportunity. That would be another first in the Great One's career.

14.16   D. 21 games
"The drought of '97," as it became known, turned into a goal-scoring dry spell without precedent in the 20-year history of hockey's greatest goal scorer. For 21 agonizing games (five games longer than his previous goal-less streak), the Great One wasn't so great from December 30, 1996, to February 21, 1997—though he continued piling up assists to remain third in points total. "As time goes by, it wears on you," he said. "You want to contribute more offensively." Tighter checking and Wayne's sore back were contributing factors. Gretzky's own theory? "At the beginning of the year, I concentrated on going to the net, and if it opens up, making the play," he explained. "Right now I'm trying to make the play and then go to the net." The drought ended on a 50-foot shot at 17:54 of the second period in a 7–2 New York Rangers loss against Hartford. It was Gretzky's 17th goal of 1996–97, his 854th NHL career goal and the 900th goal of his professional career.

14.17 A. Richard Brodeur, with the Vancouver Canucks

Wayne Gretzky scored on 155 NHL goalies in his career,
most often against Richard Brodeur, who was victimized
29 times—more often than Mike Liut (25), Greg Millen (21),
Don Beaupre (21) and Kirk McLean (21), the only goalies in the
20-goals-against range. Brodeur and Gretzky were so familiar
with each other as Smythe Division neighbours that they
maintained a certain rapport. "When I made a save against
him, I'd say something like, 'Not this time!' " remembered
Brodeur, as quoted in *Sports Illustrated*. "And he'd yell, 'I'll be
back!' " Even in the WHA, Brodeur couldn't shake the Gretzky
jinx. While tending goal for the WHA Quebec Nordiques,
Brodeur gave up two more Gretzky goals (February 9 and
March 7, 1979), in No. 99's first pro season, 1978–79.

14.18 D. The top 11 positions

No record is more indicative of Wayne Gretzky's playmaking
abilities than the number of assists he amassed in one season.
Gretzky owns the first-, second-, third-, fourth-, fifth-, sixth-,
seventh-, eighth-, 10th-, 11th- and 12th-greatest assist seasons
in league annals—each with 100 points or more, including
his record 163 assists in 1985–86. Only Bobby Orr and Mario
Lemieux have assisted on as many as 100 goals in one season.

14.19 D. Four times

Wayne Gretzky led (or shared) the NHL in assists 16 times (13 of
them consecutively). In fact, on four occasions, his assist numbers were so phenomenal that he tied or outscored his nearest
rival's *point* totals *and* won the league scoring crown on assists
alone. In two of those seasons, Gretzky's rival was also his own
linemate, Jari Kurri—a testament to the league-wide dominance of the Gretzky-Kurri line in Edmonton. Furthermore, in
three of those years, No. 99 led the league in goals.

Wayne Gretzky's Most Dominant Seasons

YEAR	PLAYER	GOALS	ASSISTS	TOTALS
1982–83	Wayne Gretzky	71	125	196
	Peter Stastny	47	77	124
1984–85	Wayne Gretzky	73	135	208
	Jari Kurri	71	64	135
1985–86	Wayne Gretzky	52	163	215
	Mario Lemieux	48	93	141
1986–87	Wayne Gretzky	62	121	183
	Jari Kurri	54	54	108

14.20 A. In minor hockey

As a nine-year-old in 1970–71, with the Brantford Nadrofsky Steelers of the Ontario Minor Hockey Association, Wayne Gretzky scored 196 goals and 120 assists in 76 games. "He'll never do that again," people said. And they were right. The next season, wonderboy racked up an astounding 378 goals and 139 assists for 517 points in 69 games. That season Gretzky also won the novice-league scoring race by 238 goals.

14.21 A. Marcel Dionne

Although Wayne Gretzky tied Marcel Dionne with 137 points in the NHL scoring race in 1979–80, No. 99 lost the title because Dionne scored more goals—53 compared to Gretzky's 51. In his autobiography, *Gretzky*, Wayne asks, "What did that say to all the kids who'd heard a thousand times, 'an assist is as important as a goal'?"

14.22 D. 25 games

Although shell-shocked opposition goalies might dispute it, Wayne Gretzky was not unstoppable in 1981–82—with 25 games in which he failed to light the lamp. Still, Gretzky's race to 92 goals was powered by a series of offensive explosions. The Edmonton Oilers dynamo had six three-goal games, three four-goal games and one five-goal game that year. In other words, he scored nearly 40 per cent of his goals in just 10 games. Gretzky didn't give anyone a break, either, scoring against every team in the league while racking up his best total against Los Angeles—13 goals. And if you subtract the 25 contests in which Gretzky didn't score in 1981–82, you're left with this startling fact: he amassed his 92 goals in 55 games.

14.23 B. 369 shots

To establish his NHL goal-scoring record of 92 goals in 1981–82, the Great One directed 369 shots on net in 80 games, an average of 4.6 shots per game, or, incredibly, a goal on every fourth shot on net.

14.24 D. Mike Liut

No NHLer has recorded more five-goal games than Wayne Gretzky, who potted a league-record four five-goal games. His most consistent target was Mike Liut, a victim of two of Gretzky's greatest goal-scoring sprees—though the second time, on December 15, 1984, Liut was only in for No. 99's fifth goal, with Rick Wamsley bearing the brunt of St. Louis's 8–2 loss. But the first time, February 18, 1981, Liut will never forget. He was still on a high from his MVP performance at the 1981 All-Star game. "Kevin Lowe comes in on a breakaway and dekes me into the back of the net," recalled Liut, as quoted in *Sports Illustrated*. "I make the save but I'm floundering, and Gretzky scored on the rebound. I put my head down, and I'm thinking, 'It's okay, we're still in this thing.' But while my head was down, I missed the draw. I look up, and here comes Gretzky on a breakaway. He puts it right through me. Nine seconds, two Gretzky goals. I got the hook." Liut allowed three goals and Ed Staniowski two in Edmonton's 9–2 shellacking of the Blues.

14.25 D. His former teammate, Dave Semenko

The 1989 All-Star game was held in Edmonton, where Wayne Gretzky, who had been traded to Los Angeles before the start of the season, celebrated his return to Northlands Coliseum by notching a goal and two assists and nabbing MVP honours. Afterward, Gretzky surprised everyone, including the recently retired Semenko, by announcing he was giving the Dodge truck he had won as MVP to his former Oilers teammate and on-ice protector. During his career, Gretzky won three All-Star MVP awards and 18 vehicles.

14.26 C. 100 goals

As expected, the NHL mark for most goals in a regular season and postseason belongs to Wayne Gretzky. But No. 99 didn't tally the league's best combined season totals during 1981–82, his record-breaking 92-goal regular season—when he scored five playoff goals in five games before his Edmonton Oilers were defeated by Los Angeles. No, No. 99's best goal-scoring year, including playoffs, came two years later in 1983–84, when he combined 87 regular-season goals and 13 playoff goals. Gretzky is the only player in NHL history to crack the 100-goal plateau.

14.27 C. 82 per cent

In 1,487 regular-season games played, Wayne Gretzky scored at least one point in every four or five games—or 82 per cent of the time. According to hockey's other great one, coach Scotty Bowman, as quoted in *The Sporting News*, "That's like a batter hitting .400 lifetime. It's like a basketball player averaging 50 points for his entire career and a football player running for 3,000 yards a season." Lifetime, Gretzky's points-per-game average is even more remarkable: better than two points per game in 20 NHL seasons.

14.28 C. Steve Duchesne and Dave Taylor, with Los Angeles

Gordie Howe's career total of 1,850 points was considered unassailable until Wayne Gretzky entered the NHL and began destroying all existing scoring records. And fittingly, on October 15, 1989, Howe's number fell in Edmonton, the city where Gretzky rose to prominence, with historic point number 1,851 coming on a game-tying goal with 53 seconds left in regulation time. The setup men: Gretzky's LA teammates Steve Duchesne and Dave Taylor. Rather than playing in his "office," behind the opponent's net, Gretzky had positioned himself in front of Bill Ranford, when Duchesne's pass hopped over a stick, bounced off Taylor's knee and came right to him, and he backhanded it over a sprawling Ranford. The game was then halted while Howe came out to take part in ceremonies honouring the NHL's new point king. Interestingly, the first time Howe met Gretzky, when the latter was just a boy, Howe gave Gretzky some advice—to practice backhand shots. Gretzky was obviously paying attention. He went on to score many backhanders, including his first WHA goal, his first NHL goal and the goal that broke Howe's record, point number 1,851.

14.29 B. 79 points

Between 1981–82 and 1986–87, Wayne Gretzky scored an average of 73 more points per season than his nearest rival in the scoring race, and in his best year, 1983–84, he topped teammate and runner-up Paul Coffey by a staggering 79 points. Gretzky could have quit playing on January 7 and *still* captured the scoring championship—a full three months before the end of the season.

14.30 B. Three games

During his monumental 215-point season in 1985–86, Gretzky failed to score a point in three games: his 10th game against

Buffalo, his 50th versus Chicago and his 69th, again, against the Sabres. But before he got to 215, Gretzky had three-point nights 40 times and 21 four-pointers. His best night: December 11, when he notched a record-tying seven assists in the highest-scoring game in NHL history, a 12–9 Oilers win over Chicago. Meanwhile, Gretzky's assist total of 163 proved to be better than any other player's point total. (Mario Lemieux had 141 points to finish a distant second to Gretzky's 215.) It was the Great One's fourth and final 200-point season.

14.31 A. Ottawa

Wayne Gretzky's last NHL game on Canadian soil was in Ottawa, his homeland's capital, where the city was abuzz and tickets were impossible to find. Federal cabinet ministers begged for seats, then-prime-minister Jean Chrétien tried to rejig his schedule to be at the game, and Gretzky's parents, Phyllis and Walter Gretzky, were flown in and a postgame press conference was scheduled. Unfortunately the New York Rangers earned only a 2–2 tie with the Ottawa Senators, and No. 99 failed to score. Nor did he confirm his retirement—saving the big splash for his final match in New York three days later. Meanwhile, Senators goalie Ron Tugnutt said before the Ottawa game: "I'm hoping for a bench-clearing brawl during the warm-up so I can go out and grab his stick ... his hands are still there. They haven't gone anywhere. It's strange to say, but he's more dangerous behind the net than anyone else. It's a talent no one else has."

14.32 D. 40 sticks

In his final NHL contest on April 18, 1999, Wayne Gretzky used as many as 40 sticks—many of which he later donated to charitable functions or passed on to friends and teammates. He also wore three sweaters in the game (one he kept, another went to

New York general manager Neil Smith and the third was given
to an undetermined lucky soul). As for his play stats: in his last
game, a 2–1 loss to Pittsburgh, Gretzky played 22 shifts (or 22
minutes, 30 seconds), had just two shots on net and recorded
his final NHL point off the lone Ranger goal. He won 10 faceoffs
and lost four. His best pass was a backhanded seeing-eye pass
to Niklas Sundstrom, who set up John MacLean; Tom Barrasso
stopped the low shot. Gretzky's best scoring chance came on
a two-on-one break, but MacLean waited too long and slipped
the puck behind Gretzky and into the corner.

14.33 A. Winnipeg Arena

Gretzky scored goals in 42 of the 49 arenas in which he
played, with his greatest goal count coming at the Winnipeg
Arena, where he totalled 38 regular-season goals. Where *didn't*
the Great One net a regular-season goal? He never scored at
Ottawa's Corel Centre, Miami's National Car Rental Center,
Nashville's Arena, Sacramento's ARCO Arena, Springfield's
Civic Center (in Massachusetts), Chicago's United Center or
Montreal's Molson Centre.

14.34 B. Only one arena

Wayne Gretzky scored at least one point in 48 of the
49 NHL rinks in which he played. The only arena that failed
to witness a No. 99 point was the Springfield Civic Center,
temporary home of his hockey hero Gordie Howe and the
Hartford Whalers while the Hartford Civic Center was
undergoing repairs, because of a 1978 roof collapse, during
Gretzky's first season.

14.35 A. The Toronto Maple Leafs

Wayne Gretzky's best goal-scoring percentage was against
Toronto. He managed an 87.3 per cent success rate with

55 goals in 63 home and away games against the Maple Leafs—slightly better than the 60 goals in 69 matches for an 87 per cent mark opposite his onetime team, the Los Angeles Kings. And when No. 99 played at Maple Leaf Gardens, his favourite road arena, he totalled 30 career goals and 47 assists in 30 appearances, the most by any visiting player in the 68-year history of the famous rink.

14.36 C. Between 200 and 250 points

Wayne Gretzky averaged more than two points per game each time he played the Vancouver Canucks. The Great One scored 239 points in 117 games against the Canucks—the highest point number he tallied against any NHL team.

14.37 D. More than plus-500

Wayne Gretzky recorded 14 seasons in the plus column and six in the minus. He also led the league in plus-minus numbers four times, including in his best year, 1984–85, with a sizzling plus-98. The Great One's worst plus-minus count came in 1993–94, when he won his last Art Ross Trophy with 130 points. Gretzky accumulated a minus-25 with Los Angeles that year. And at the time of his retirement, No. 99 topped all active NHLers with a plus-518 rating. Ray Bourque was second with a plus-453.

14.38 A. Only one goal

Much like baseball's Pete Rose, Wayne Gretzky kept close tabs on his personal statistics and the scoring records he was in range of breaking. But before he retired at the end of the 1998–99 season, Gretzky made sure he set another prestigious, though unpublicized, milestone. By notching goal number 1,072 on March 29, 1999, against the New York

Islanders, the Great One surpassed Gordie Howe's mark for most goals as a professional, including playoff games. It was Gretzky's last goal as a professional and it left him one up on Mr. Hockey, who racked up 869 NHL goals and another 202 in the WHA. Gretzky amassed 1,016 NHL goals plus an additional 56 during his lone season in the WHA.

14.39 C. Pavel Bure

Wayne Gretzky would probably have extended his playing career another year for a chance to play with Jagr, Yzerman or Messier, but in a TSN interview in November 1991, the Great One said: "If (the Rangers) would have traded for Pavel Bure last year, I probably would still be playing right now." Instead Bure went from Vancouver to the Florida Panthers, where he scored a league-high 58 goals in 1999–2000. Meanwhile the Rangers, minus Gretzky, spent us$61 million and still finished 23rd overall. When Panthers executive Bill Torrey heard Gretzky's remarks about staying another year to play with Bure, he said, "You know, I can arrange that."

Game 14

Close, But No Cigar

WAYNE GRETZKY WON a slew of silverware in his career. Every time he took home an Art Ross Trophy as the league's leading scorer or the Hart Trophy as regular-season MVP, someone else was denied that privilege. There are 15 NHLers who can say they were beaten out of hockey's most prestigious awards by the Great One. Once you've figured out who, find them in the puzzle reading down, across or diagonally. As with our example of Mike B-O-S-S-Y, connect the name using letters no more than once. Start with the letters printed in heavy type.

Solutions are on page 565

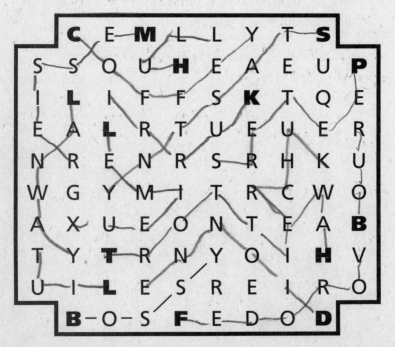

15

All Currency U.S.

WHILE HE WAS PLAYING, few players could give as good lip as Brett Hull. When asked by the *Hockey News* in December 2003 about escalating player salaries, Hull said: "Bob Goodenow [NHLPA president] will kill me, but if we're going to be realistic about things, probably 75 per cent of the league is overpaid." Did the Golden Brett include himself in that group? In this chapter we take stock of the business of hockey.

Answers are on page 393

15.1 The signing of his $85-million* extension in July 2007 meant that Vincent Lecavalier could be with the Tampa Bay Lightning until what age?
   A. Until Lecavalier is 34 years old
   B. Until Lecavalier is 36 years old
   C. Until Lecavalier is 38 years old
   D. Until Lecavalier is past his 40th birthday

15.2 In 2006–07, which NHLer's salary accounted for more of his team's payroll than any other player's?
   A. Brad Richards's, with the Tampa Bay Lightning
   B. Jaromir Jagr's, with the New York Rangers
   C. Nicklas Lidstrom's, with the Detroit Red Wings
   D. Zdeno Chara's, with the Boston Bruins

*All currency in this chapter in U.S. dollars, unless otherwise noted

15.3 Based on the club's $61-million payroll (the highest in hockey history to date), how much did it cost the New York Rangers for each of its wins in 1999–2000?

A. $500,000 per win

B. $1 million per win

C. $1.5 million per win

D. $2 million per win

15.4 In 1995–96, in order to renegotiate his contract with the Ottawa Senators, Alexei Yashin had to maintain a level of point production equal to his previous year's. By how much did he fall short?

A. By one point

B. By five points

C. By 10 points

D. By 20 points

15.5 What was the monetary value of the Stanley Cup when Canada's governor general, Lord Stanley of Preston, donated it as a championship hockey trophy in 1892?

A. Less than $100

B. Between $100 and $1,000

C. Between $1,000 and $5,000

D. More than $5,000

15.6 What were the 1992 Las Vegas odds on the Tampa Bay Lightning or Ottawa Senators winning the Stanley Cup in their first NHL season, 1992–93?

A. 100 to one

B. 500 to one

C. 1,000 to one

D. 2,500 to one

15.7 What was the name of the highly publicized 2006 police investigation into a multi-million-dollar sports betting ring involving prominent NHLers?

A. Investigation Penalty Box
B. Operation Slapshot
C. Investigation Faceoff
D. Operation Betzky

15.8 Conn Smythe built Maple Leaf Gardens at the height of the Depression. Besides attracting investors, how did he raise the capital?

A. He set up a stock-sharing venture with construction workers
B. He oversold seat capacity
C. He mortgaged his Rosedale mansion
D. He organized benefit games at the old Mutual Street Arena

15.9 How much money was involved in Montreal broadcaster Jean Perron's defamation suit against a book publisher in 2004?

A. CDN$600
B. CDN$6,000
C. CDN$60,000
D. CDN$600,000

15.10 How much money did the parents of a 13-year-old girl killed by a puck at an NHL game get in a 2003 court settlement?

A. $600,000
B. $1.2 million
C. $1.8 million
D. $2.4 million

15.11 In 2003–04, who made headlines after losing $5 million on the stock market?

A. Mike Modano

B. Jaromir Jagr

C. Vincent Damphousse

D. Curtis Joseph

15.12 In 2000–01, which player commanded the highest salary package in NHL history?

A. Jaromir Jagr, with the Pittsburgh Penguins

B. Mike Modano, with the Dallas Stars

C. Mario Lemieux, with the Pittsburgh Penguins

D. Paul Kariya, with the Anaheim Mighty Ducks

15.13 How much was Alexander Ovechkin's contract worth when he signed with the Washington Capitals in January 2008?

A. Less than $60 million

B. Between $60 and $90 million

C. Between $90 and $120 million

D. More than $120 million

15.14 How much did Gordie Howe receive as his 1991 NHL pension?

A. $13,000

B. $26,000

C. $52,000

D. $104,000

15.15 How much did ticket prices rise at St. Louis Arena after Brett Hull signed a four-year $7.1-million contract with the St. Louis Blues in 1990?

A. Ticket prices stayed the same

B. $2

C. $5

D. $8

15.16 On a per-game basis, which hockey player earned more money in 1910 than baseball great Ty Cobb?

A. Odie Sprague

B. "Phantom" Joe Malone

C. Fred "Cyclone" Taylor

D. "Newsy" Lalonde

15.17 In 2004–05, how much money did a buyer offer the NHL to sell the league?

A. $2.5 billion

B. $3.5 billion

C. $4.5 billion

D. $5.5 billion

15.18 At a 2002 auction, how much money did the Canadian government spend on Maurice Richard memorabilia?

A. CDN$75,000

B. CDN$150,000

C. CDN$300,000

D. CDN$600,000

15.19 Which hockey card set was the first to sell for $100?

A. 1990–91's Upper Deck

B. 1990–91's O-Pee-Chee Premier

C. 1992–93's Parkhurst

D. 1992–93's Topps Stadium Club

15.20 After he was struck by an errant shot at Los Angeles's Great Western Forum in February 1999, how much money did hockey fan Jonathan Liebert receive as a settlement?

A. $3,000
B. $30,000
C. $300,000
D. $3 million

15.21 According to the *Philadelphia Inquirer*, how much money did Flyers general manager Bobby Clarke blow on bad player deals during the late 1990s?

A. $6 million
B. $16 million
C. $26 million
D. $36 million

15.22 In January 2000, how long did it take the government of Canada to revoke its subsidy package to Canadian-based NHL teams?

A. Four hours
B. Four days
C. Four weeks
D. Four months

15.23 After the Toronto Maple Leafs vacated their former home, Maple Leaf Gardens, in 1999, how much did it cost the general public to rent ice time—when it was still available—at the Gardens?

A. CDN$602.50 per hour
B. CDN$802.50 per hour
C. CDN$1,002.50 per hour
D. CDN$1,202.50 per hour

15.24 How much money did Teemu Selanne once offer former Winnipeg Jet teammate Randy Carlyle for his No. 8 jersey?

A. $100

B. $1,000

C. $10,000

D. $100,000

15.25 How much personal-injury insurance did Eric Lindros have in 2000–01, after he suffered a near-career-ending sixth concussion during the 2000 playoffs?

A. None

B. $5 million

C. $10 million

D. $20 million

15.26 On October 15, 2000, the player's model of Doug Harvey's James Norris Memorial Trophies (five of which he won between 1955 and 1960) was put on the block at a Toronto auction house. What was the selling price of this item?

A. CDN$3,000

B. CDN$5,000

C. CDN$10,000

D. CDN$15,000

15.27 How many millionaires played in the NHL in 1998–99?

A. Less than 100 millionaires

B. Between 100 and 150 millionaires

C. Between 150 and 200 millionaires

D. More than 200 millionaires

15.28 How much money did NHL clubs spend during the first nine days of the 2008 free-agency frenzy?

A. Less than $300 million

B. Between $300 and $500 million

C. Between $500 and $700 million

D. More than $700 million

15.29 Which former NHL tough guy sued Spawn Comics and HBO, originally winning $24.5 million in a lawsuit for misuse of his name?

A. Dave "Tiger" Williams

B. Tony Twist

C. Dale Hunter

D. Dave "The Hammer" Schultz

15.30 At the 1998 NHL All-Star game, a lucky fan had the opportunity to win $5 million if he hit four targets hanging in the corners of a hockey net. How many targets did he hit?

A. One target

B. Two targets

C. Three targets

D. He missed every target

15.31 What is the minimum cost of building a custom backyard rink?

A. CDN$10,000

B. CDN$15,000

C. CDN$20,000

D. CDN$25,000

15.32 In 2001, which Hall of Famer auctioned off most of his personal hockey memorabilia and raised $400,000 in the process?

A. Glenn Hall

B. Mike Bossy

C. Guy Lafleur

D. Frank Mahovlich

15.33 Which former Montreal Hall of Famer wanted to buy the Canadiens when the venerable franchise was up for sale in 2000–01?

A. Bernie Geoffrion

B. Dickie Moore

C. Jean Béliveau

D. Guy Lafleur

15.34 How much money does the Ottawa Senators fine its players for stepping on the Senators logo emblazoned on the carpet of its dressing room at Scotiabank Place?

A. A $1 fine

B. A $10 fine

C. A $100 fine

D. A $1,000 fine

15.35 How long was Paul Kariya's much-publicized contract hold-out during the 1997–98 season?

A. Two games

B. 12 games

C. 32 games

D. 52 games

15.36 Which star forward was almost signed for a record contract of one million dollars during the early 1960s?

- A. Jean Béliveau, by the Montreal Canadiens
- B. Bobby Hull, by the Chicago Blackhawks
- C. Alex Delvecchio, by the Detroit Red Wings
- D. Frank Mahovlich, by the Toronto Maple Leafs

15.37 How much money was involved when the Toronto Maple Leafs offered to sign Maurice Richard in the early 1950s?

- A. $75,000
- B. $135,000
- C. $500,000
- D. $1 million

15.38 It was a precedent-setting amount of money to pay a hockey player—even if he was a top rookie prospect named Bobby Orr. How much was Orr's deal worth in 1966?

- A. Less than $100,000
- B. $100,000 to $200,000
- C. $200,000 to $400,000
- D. More than $400,000

15.39 How much money did collectors spend on Jean Béliveau memorabilia at the Hall of Famer's auction in February 2004?

- A. CDN$500,000
- B. CDN$1 million
- C. CDN$1.5 million
- D. CDN$2 million

Answers

15.1 **D. Until Vincent Lecavalier is past his 40th birthday**
Unless Vincent Lecavalier has a Chris Chelios-like career and
plays past age 40, his 11-year, $85-million contract extension
will likely keep him in a Lightning uniform for the remainder
of his career. The July 2007 deal began in 2008–09 and extends
through the 2019–20 season, when Lecavalier will turn 40.
"I'm proud and honoured to be committing myself... for the
rest of my NHL career," said Tampa's richest millionaire upon
signing. "There's no place else I'd rather be."

15.2 **A. Brad Richards's, with the Tampa Bay Lightning**
Playing in a capped league with a $44-million ceiling on
salaries didn't leave the Lightning with a lot of wiggle room
after they won the Stanley Cup in 2004. The price of success
in the new NHL was a $20-million hit for three forwards:
Brad Richards ($7.8 million), Vincent Lecavalier ($6.9 million)
and Martin St. Louis ($5.2 million), or almost 50 per cent of
Tampa's payroll. Meanwhile, the rest of the team's 2006–07
bench was filled with a supporting cast of mostly minimum-
wage earners who scrimped by on $650,000 or less. Richards,
the highest-paid player, gobbled up the greatest percentage
of his team's $41.7-million salary with a league-leading
18.7 per cent stake. Nicklas Lidstrom commanded $7.6 mil-
lion from Detroit's $42.9-million payroll (17.7 per cent), and
Alexei Yashin, Zdeno Chara and Olaf Kolzig also played in the
17th percentile of their respective clubs' total payrolls. As for
Jaromir Jagr, who took home $8.36 million, just $4.94 million
of his salary went against the Rangers' cap. The remaining

$3.4 million was Washington's headache as part of its 2004 trade with New York. (In 2008–09, Jagr opted to play in Russia's new Continental Hockey League and Richards signed with the Dallas Stars.)

15.3   D. $2 million per win

There is no better proof that money doesn't always buy success than the 1999–2000 New York Rangers. With the NHL's highest payroll in history—$61,194,011—the Rangers finished 23rd overall with a 29–41–15 record. Every victory cost the team $2.11 million, while each of its 218 goals was worth $280,706. The best bargain was the Ottawa Senators, who, with the 23rd-highest payroll, spent $24.89 million and finished 10th overall in the league. The first-place St. Louis Blues had the 12th-biggest payroll: $34,630,019.

15.4   A. By one point

Alexei Yashin's 36-game holdout in 1995–96 with the Senators was sparked by a dispute over a single point, with Ottawa prepared to renegotiate Yashin's contract only if he equalled his scoring rate of the previous year. In 1993–94, Yashin tallied 79 points in 83 games, which works out to .952 points per game. But in the lockout-shortened 1995 campaign, he compiled 44 points in 47 games, an average of .936 points per game—just .016 short of the target of .952. Had Yashin scored just one more point in 1995 (45 points in 47 games), his higher average of .957 would have contractually avoided the pettiness perpetrated by former Ottawa general manager Randy Sexton.

15.5   A. Less than $100

In 1892, Lord Stanley paid a British silversmith 10 guineas, or CDN$48.67, to produce a simple silver bowl called the Dominion Hockey Challenge Cup. It immediately became known as the Stanley Cup, and soon grew in size when a silver barrel was added below its bowl to accommodate the names of each year's champions. Today, the Stanley Cup is the oldest competed-for-trophy in North American sport. It is considered priceless.

15.6 D. 2,500 to one

Las Vegas gave odds of 2,500 to one to anyone who would bet that the Senators or the Lightning would win the 1993 Stanley Cup. That meant a $10 wager would have returned $25,000. The Rangers—who didn't even make the playoffs—had the best odds, at three to one, followed by the defending Cup-champion Penguins, with five to one odds. However, Vegas oddsmakers weren't so generous for either the expansion Panthers or the Mighty Ducks in their first year, 1993–94, giving odds of only 500 to one.

15.7 B. Operation Slapshot

After a three-month police probe (dubbed Operation Slapshot by New Jersey's state police), investigators announced they had uncovered an illegal gambling operation financed by Phoenix Coyote assistant coach Rick Tocchet and supposedly tied to the Bruno-Scarfo organized crime family in Philadelphia and New Jersey. But the big surprise was that Wayne Gretzky's wife, Janet, was mentioned as having placed bets (as much as $500,000 on games) through the underground ring. During a 40-day period between December 29, 2005, and February 5, 2006, police said the betting operation processed more than 1,000 wagers, totalling $17 million, on mostly football and basketball games. And when the case concluded, Tocchet pled guilty to conspiracy and the promotion of gambling—charges that earned him two years' probation and a three-month suspension from the NHL.

15.8 **A. He set up a stock-sharing venture with construction workers**

After raising almost $1.5 million, Conn Smythe was still $200,000 short of capital. The Gardens would not have been built without a scheme he concocted to pay workers with stock certificates in lieu of cash—a gamble that paid off for those who held onto their shares. The stock's value increased tenfold in 10 years.

15.9 **C. CDN$60,000**

In libel action against the book publisher of *Les Perronismes*, Jean Perron claimed the satirical work ridiculed him and damaged his reputation as an on-air analyst. But Justice Daniele Mayrand, the judge in the CDN$60,000 suit, disagreed, stating Perron "could be subject to wisecracks, satire, good-natured ridicule and may be caricatured without his consent." The slim volume of Perron's butchered phrases includes "Don't bite the midget that feeds you" and "The Nordiques should go get some rookies with experience."

15.10 **B. $1.2 million**

No amount of money can ever compensate for the loss of a life, but the Columbus Blue Jackets, the NHL and the Nationwide Arena agreed to pay Brittanie Cecil's family $1.2 million after the 13-year-old died after being struck by a puck at a game in March 2002. Subsequent to the tragedy, every NHL arena installed safety netting around its goal areas to prevent other such incidents.

15.11 **A. Mike Modano**

It was Modano's season to forget. After blowing a reported $5 million on an off-ice stock-market gamble, the Dallas star lost focus and his scoring touch, recording just 44 points in 2003–04. It was his worst regular-season total ever, excluding 1994–95's lockout-shortened year.

15.12 A. Jaromir Jagr, with the Pittsburgh Penguins
While the salary deals of 2000–01 seem almost old-fashioned compared to today's 10- to 12-year hockey packages, it is still interesting to check out what the top players earned just a decade ago. The other three major North American leagues inked $100-million contracts with stars such as Alex Rodriguez, Kevin Garnett and Troy Aikman, but in hockey, the highest figure was a seven-year $48-million pact between Pittsburgh and Jaromir Jagr (1998–2004). The next-best salary packages in hockey at the time were Pavel Bure's $47-million deal over six years with Florida, Mike Modano's six-year $43.5-million agreement with Dallas (1998–2003) and the ill-fated deferred payment deal between Mario Lemieux and Pittsburgh for $42 million between 1992–1997. (None of the contract figures included possible performance bonuses.)

15.13 D. More than $120 million
Hockey has never seen a contract as princely as Alexander Ovechkin's. Though the $124-million deal is not in the ballpark of baseball or basketball's top salaries, such as Alex Rodriguez's annual $27.5-million agreement with the New York Yankees and Kobe Bryant's $19.5-million yearly salary with the Los Angeles Lakers, it is the richest in NHL history and will earn Ovechkin an average of $9.5 million over 13 years. As with Vincent Lecavalier's $85-million package with Tampa Bay, NHL teams are giving their best talent lengthy, big-money contracts to avoid losing their stars through offer sheets from other clubs or unrestricted free agency. As a result, Ovechkin will be

playing with the Capitals until 2020–21. It is the NHL's second-longest contract term after New York Islanders goalie Rick DiPietro's 15-year deal, signed in September 2006.

15.14 A. $13,000

Is there something wrong with this picture? After 26 years in the NHL, hockey's greatest athlete and ambassador receives an annual pension of only $13,000 a year.

15.15 C. $5

Not only was Brett Hull worth the big contract (70 goals, 39 assists and 109 points in 1991–92), but the Blues raised gate revenues by $3.5 million a year thanks to the $5 ticket hike.

15.16 C. Fred "Cyclone" Taylor

Taylor signed with the Renfrew Creamery Kings of the National Hockey Association for the astonishing sum of $5,000. In hockey's early years, with many pro leagues competing for survival, signing the best players not only kept teams afloat but ensured the solvency of entire leagues. What we call "franchise" players today were once "league" players. And "Cyclone" had that kind of impact, pacing the Ottawa Senators to the 1909 Stanley Cup. In a 12-game-season schedule, his $5,000 salary worked out to $416 per game—about 10 times that earned by baseball's premier player at the time, Ty Cobb.

15.17 B. $3.5 billion

In March 2005, Game Plan LLC, a Boston investment company that specializes in sports franchises, pitched the NHL's board of governors with an offer to buy the league—lock, stock and barrel. Under the proposed deal, the NHL would have operated as one big company with the 30 teams acting as franchise outlets (as in the retail industry). Most NHL owners dismissed the idea outright, but the proposed bid would have given the league a new economic structure to overcome its biggest hurdle: market discrepancies related to revenue, which would have been replaced with a money-sharing plan to create better balance league-wide. "When someone is offering over US$3 billion, we felt we had an obligation to the board to have them, at least, hear it from the proposed purchaser," said NHL executive Bill Daly. But in the end, the NHL said Thanks, but no thanks.

15.18   D. CDN$600,000

In a 2002 Internet auction held by the family of the late Maurice Richard, the Canadian government spent CDN$600,000 to buy 47 items of sports memorabilia belonging to the legendary star. On the block were autographed hockey sticks, pucks and trophies, as well as a 1959 Stanley Cup ring and 1953–54 contract (handwritten on a piece of scrap paper) under which Richard was paid a salary of CDN$15,000. But the highest bids were for Richard's game-worn jerseys. The price of his No. 9 sweater from the 1959 Stanley Cup championship climbed to $60,000, while his 1949 All-Star game jersey drew $15,000. The auction received bids from sports fans and collectors around the world. Today, the 47 items are housed at the Canadian Museum of Civilization in Hull, Quebec.

15.19   B. 1990–91's O-Pee-Chee Premier

In the 1960s, a pack of hockey cards with bubble gum cost a nickel. But when the hockey card boom hit in 1990, cards went upscale and the bubble gum disappeared, and with it any vestiges of the hobby's initial innocence. The first set to blast past the $100 mark was the 1990–91 O-Pee-Chee Premier, a relatively tiny 132-card issue, highly prized because of its low production numbers and batch of hot-shot rookies.

15.20 D. $3 million

Fan Jonathan Liebert scored the biggest payoff of his life after
successfully suing the Los Angeles Kings, the San Jose Sharks
and ex-Shark winger Joe Murphy for $3 million, after Murphy
fired a puck out of frustration that hit Liebert in a game at the
Great Western Forum on February 6, 1999. Liebert suffered
post-concussion syndrome and claimed he lost the ability to
work.

15.21 C. $26 million

Philadelphia Inquirer reporter Tim Panaccio calculated that
Bobby Clarke blew $26 million on players who either didn't
play with, or who made little contribution to, the Flyers.
Clarke, in his greatest deal, did steal heavyweights John
LeClair and Eric Desjardins from Montreal, but his record
after that point is abysmal. He paid out $9 million in up-front
money to Chris Gratton, only to send him back later to
Tampa Bay; $1.9 million to underachiever Alexandre Daigle;
$2.6 million for one season (minus the playoffs) to Paul Coffey;
almost a half-million to minor-leaguer Roman Vopat, and
$12.6 million for five years to Luke Richardson, the team's
fifth or sixth defenseman.

15.22 B. Four days

For many years, Canadian-based NHL teams sought government monies and tax breaks to better balance the franchise
economies between themselves and rich American teams.
Finally, on January 18, 2000, Canadian industry minister John
Manley announced a federal government aid package to help
cash-strapped Canadian teams. The plan included $20 million
per year until 2004. But only four days later, Manley stepped
before the cameras and declared the unprecedented deal
"dead" in the wake of negative reaction from politicians, the
media and the public.

15.23 B. CDN$802.50 per hour

Ever since the Maple Leafs skated off to the Air Canada
Centre and abandoned their old home at Carlton and Church,
Maple Leaf Gardens has been mostly a dark and silent place.
For a while it hosted the occasional Junior A and lacrosse game
(including two championships for the Toronto Rock of the
National Lacrosse League). But, for the most part, Canada's most
famous hockey shrine was like a puck without a stick. Still, the
NHL's loss was the public's gain. The rink was rented out periodi-
cally, and, for a cost of CDN$802.50 per hour, non-NHLers could
skate and shoot in the glorious tracks of some of the game's
greatest Leafs, from Charlie Conacher to Mats Sundin. There
were a few annoying rules, however. No pegs were provided for
the nets, no spectators were allowed and only a maximum of
22 skaters could participate each session. In 2004, food retail
giant Loblaw Companies then purchased the Gardens and,
while various redevelopment schemes have been proposed,
few public events have been held at the heritage site since.

15.24 C. $10,000

How much is a number worth? In 2006–07, Selannereflected
on just that while playing alongside present-day Anaheim
coach Randy Carlyle. Carlyle was already wearing Winnipeg's
No. 8, Selanne's jersey number with Jokerit in his native
Finland. So Selanne took his Finnish soccer number, No. 13—
though not before trying to coax the long-time Jet out
of his famous digit. "In Winnipeg, I once offered him [Carlyle]
$10,000 to wear his No. 8 jersey, and he refused," said Selanne.
But Carlyle retired in 1993, and a year later Selanne got No. 8—
free of charge.

15.25 D. $20 million

After six concussions and earnings of about $47.5 million
since 1992, Eric Lindros found himself teamless in 2000–01.

Once hockey's most sought after player who had twice refused early career team offers (Sault St. Marie, Quebec), Lindros was now in limbo, a concussion victim caught in the merciless waiting game imposed by Philadelphia general manager Bob Clarke and a market limited to just a few teams that could afford both his salary and the quality players needed to trade for him. Then there was Lindros's contract caveat: if an injury limited him to fewer than 20 games in 2000–01, he received full payment on a $20-million personal insurance policy. In the end, Lindros never played in 2000–01, but spent the season recovering from his head injuries and dispute with the Flyers.

15.26 D. CDN$15,000

Doug Harvey died a broke and broken man, but his eight-inch silver-plated trophy, awarded to the late Hall of Famer for five of his seven Norris Trophy wins, fetched $15,000 at an auction in October 2000. The dented and tarnished trophy wasn't expected to go for more than $3,000. But the bidding, which was over in 90 seconds, saw the old relic purchased by an unknown tender for $15,000. Harvey had originally given the trophy to a Montreal restaurant owner, who then tried to return it. But the All-Star defenseman yelled, "When I give a gift, I give a gift," hurling the award back at his friend. After hockey, Harvey's life declined into alcoholism and part-time jobs, and his last days were spent in a renovated CN train car at an Ottawa-area racetrack. He died of cirrhosis of the liver on Boxing Day, 1989.

15.27 D. More than 200 millionaires

Amongst the more than 600 NHLers in 1998–99, a total of 244 were millionaires (up from 1997–98, when 215 NHL players earned seven-figure salaries). The 1998–99 average yearly salary also increased, from $1.1 million to $1.2 million between seasons, though there was considerably more disparity between players' income. Sergei Fedorov earned $14 million in a front-end-loaded deal that paid him $2 million in salary and a $12-million bonus, while the lowest-paid players included Ottawa's Steve Leach ($97,000) and Anaheim's Dominic Roussel ($160,000). The average team payroll was $29.6 million, up from $26.6 million a year earlier—a 12 per cent increase.

15.28 D. More than $700 million

It can't be what NHL commissioner Gary Bettman had in mind when his "cost certainty" plan forced a 310-day league lockout and shut down the 2004–05 season. After free agency kicked off on July 1, 2008, clubs spent like drunken sailors to re-sign some of their own players and attract new talent—a staggering $725 million in nine days. The league's salary cap has also increased since the lockout, from between $39 and $44 million to between $50.3 and $56.7 million in 2008–09. And for the first time in league history, teams have been required to spend a salary minimum (of $40.7 million) that is higher than the original cap (of $39 million) after the lockout. The post-lockout deals have pushed team salary totals to $1.48 billion, past the league's $1.34-billion pre-lockout mark.

15.29 B. Tony Twist

It might have been Tony Twist's toughest fight. Unfortunately, after being awarded $24.5 million by a St. Louis jury in a court battle over a comic and animated series featuring a vulgar mobster named Antonio Twistelli (and nicknamed Tony Twist), a judge on appeal tossed out the July 2000 decision, disputing the lower court's ruling that the show hindered Twist's endorsement possibilities. But Twist, who collected only 10 goals and piled up 1,121 penalty minutes in 10 NHL seasons, didn't leave without bloodying his opponent. He settled out of court with HBO for $5 million.

15.30 D. He missed every target

Wayne King, a 37-year-old electronics technician from Dayton, Ohio, had the chance of a lifetime to win a million dollars a target and a bonus of $1 million if he hit all four targets at the 1998 NHL All-Star game. Standing on a rubber mat 31 feet from the net, King had eight seconds to hit the targets. But he blew it, never once raising the puck off the ice. Still, he did take home $10,000 for participating in the event, sponsored by Norelco razors.

15.31 D. CDN$25,000

Creating a backyard rink is no longer a simple matter of hammering a few planks together and then standing around in the freezing cold with a garden hose. The 2008 version of the traditional Canadian experience can cost parents a minimum of CDN$25,000—and even more for those who want to pimp up their garden tractor to turn it into a miniature Zamboni. The brainchild of former NHLer Dave Gagner, these CDN$25,000 "do-it-yourself" kits have everything needed to build a 20-foot-by-30-foot rink, including refrigeration pipes that can be stored each spring. Gagner's top-end Custom Ice Rinks models even include a concrete pad and high-efficiency glycol refrigeration system to defy Mother Nature during warm spells. High boards, glass, goal nets, night lights and electricity are extra.

15.32 C. Guy Lafleur

Stanley Cup rings, trophies, jerseys, pucks, sticks and skates amassed over Guy Lafleur's illustrious 17-year career were all available at the 2001 auction, which lasted two weeks and was conducted via the Internet and telephone. The most expensive of the 122 items was Lafleur's 1977 Conn Smythe Trophy, which sold for $24,423. His 1977 Hart Trophy fetched $21,839, and four of the Hall of Famer's Cup rings went for between $10,000 and $15,000 each. Even Lafleur's frayed first pair of skates, which he wore as a five-year-old, found a buyer, who paid $4,512. Lafleur, who claimed he had no personal attachment to the items, said he would donate $25,000 to charity and keep the rest of the proceeds.

15.33 B. Dickie Moore

Winner of six Stanley Cups with Montreal between 1953 and 1960, Dickie Moore publicly acknowledged after the sale of the Canadiens to Denver businessman George Gillett that he had considered buying the club, but "it was a little out of reach. If I could have raised the money, I would have bought it myself," confirmed Moore, who made a post-hockey fortune in construction equipment rentals and real-estate ventures. The deep-pocketed Gillett purchased the Canadiens and their Molson Centre home for the fire-sale sum of CDN$275 million. Not one Canadian individual, company or consortium made an offer to buy the team. In 2009, eight years after his purchase, Gillett sold the Habs to the Molson family for $CDN550 million.

15.34 C. A $100 fine

It's not a custom of either the division-rival Montreal Canadiens or Toronto Maple Leafs, but the Senators are so serious about penalizing folks who stand on the team's logo (stitched into the red carpet of its dressing room) that fines—$10 for visitors and $100 for players—are handed out to all violators. The no-tread rule was former Senator GM John Muckler's idea; he believed it instilled pride and created a bond between the players. The motif of the scowling centurion with the golden helmet covers about an eighth of the dressing room's total acreage, and is guarded by a club sentry who steers people away from the no-step zone in the middle of the room.

15.35 C. 32 games

Paul Kariya lost almost half of the 1997–98 season due to his contract dispute with the Disney-owned Mighty Ducks. Anaheim wanted its star sniper to sign a multi-year offer, but Kariya was looking for a short-term deal, one that wouldn't restrict future earnings. Disney's hard line held until December 1997, when Kariya was scheduled to join Canada's national team in Europe as part of a training effort to get him ready for the Nagano Olympics. Had he not signed then, the result may have been an Anaheim franchise without Kariya for the season—or forever. In other words, Kariya's power play paid off. He inked a two-year pact worth $5.5 million in 1997–98 and $8.5 million the next season. After the signing, someone in the Ducks organization joked: "He better just show up for practice tomorrow." Kariya did and played 22 games before a Gary Suter cross-check sidelined him for the remainder of the regular season. Kariya played just 22 games in 1997–98. The Ducks were 11–15–6 without Kariya during his contract dispute; a disappointing 6–13–3 with him in the next 22 games, and, after his injury, 9–15–4 to close out the season.

15.36 D. Frank Mahovlich, by the Toronto Maple Leafs

During a party in 1962's All-Star break, Leaf co-owner Harold Ballard accepted a deal worth a record one million dollars from Chicago's James Norris in exchange for the services of Mahovlich. Norris knew that the Leafs were having trouble signing the Big M, and thought he had salted the deal after reportedly handing Ballard a $1,000 bill. But the next day sobering thoughts prevailed—not at the Blackhawks club but at the Maple Leafs'. Toronto's board of directors refused to accept the transaction and the hastily delivered $1-million cheque from Chicago. It was a record amount for a player, but the Maple Leafs said "No" and Mahovlich was quickly signed to Toronto. That season Mahovlich led the Maple Leafs in scoring (36–37–73), and Toronto won both the regular-season title and the Stanley Cup.

15.37 A. $75,000

In the days when players made $5,000 a year, $75,000 was an exorbitant offer, even for the Rocket. Toronto's Conn Smythe, who had publicly criticized Richard's backchecking, proposed the deal to the Canadiens' Senator Donat Raymond, who replied: "I have read that you say Richard won't backcheck . . . Does this mean that, if I get him to play coming and going, you would offer me $150,000?" Two years later Toronto tried to buy the Rocket's playing contract again, this time for $135,000. Still no dice.

15.38 A. Less than $100,000

It sounds almost ludicrous in today's market of million-dollar deals and hefty signing bonuses, but until Orr's landmark contract in 1966, hockey's best rookie was mailed a two-year contract for $10,250, including bonuses. Orr's agent, Alan Eagleson, countered this pittance by hinting that his client might join Canada's Olympic team instead of turning pro. After the noise died down, the Bruins then dealt a $25,000 signing bonus, plus $25,000 in year one and $30,000 in year two. The player agent had arrived. Even more important, so had Bobby Orr.

15.39 B. CDN$1 million

The Jean Béliveau memorabilia auction surpassed all expectations in terms of proceeds—nearly doubling the original dollar figure forecast for the sale of the Hall of Famer's old Stanley Cup rings, miniature replica Cup trophies, sweaters, pucks and skates. In all, 195 souvenirs went on the block during the month-long Internet auction that raised a staggering $799,285—nearly CDN$1 million. The highlight item: Béliveau's 1958–59 championship ring, which a Montreal businessperson known as Bidder 1881 paid $99,077.72 for. Four other mementoes—Béliveau's 1957–58 Stanley Cup Trophy, first-goal NHL puck, 1967 Canadiens sweater and 1950s Quebec Aces jersey—were purchased by one bidder for a combined total of $151,740.54. In comparison, in 2004, the Maurice Richard auction rang up a record $1.6 million, including a $600,000 purchase by the Canadian Museum of Civilization.

Game 15

Drafting Late

WHEN NHL GENERAL MANAGERS and their scouts meet on draft day in search of the next Sidney Crosby or Roberto Luongo, they know the next generation of stars can just as easily come from the late rounds. The selection process after the top five is usually a hit-or-miss venture, one where a highly ranked prospect has every chance of going bust or a deep choice could mature into a Hall of Fame candidate. In this game, match the late draft picks below and their team, draft position and year.

Solutions are on page 565

Pavel Datsyuk   Eric Daze   Michael Ryder

Marty Turco   Daniel Alfredsson   Nikolai Khabibulin

Cristobal Huet   Miikka Kiprusoff   Henrik Zetterberg

Karlis Skrastins   Darcy Tucker   Tomas Kaberle

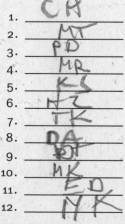

1. _____ CH _____ Los Angeles (214th in 2001)
2. _____ MT _____ Dallas (124th in 1994)
3. _____ PD _____ Detroit (171st in 1998)
4. _____ MR _____ Montreal (216th in 1998)
5. _____ KS _____ Nashville (230th in 1998)
6. _____ HZ _____ Detroit (210th in 1999)
7. _____ TK _____ Toronto (204th in 1996)
8. _____ DA _____ Ottawa (133rd in 1994)
9. _____ DT _____ Montreal (151st in 1993)
10. _____ MKb _____ San Jose (116th in 1994)
11. _____ ED _____ Chicago (90th in 1993)
12. _____ NK _____ Winnipeg (204th in 1992)

409

16

Drafts and Trade Winds

THE PITTSBURGH PENGUINS ICED a record number of first-round draft picks for their improbable run as finalists at the 2008 Stanley Cup. In all, coach Michel Terrien had a long bench, with 13 first-rounders in his battle versus Detroit. The Penguins matured faster as a team than any in NHL history, sporting five players chosen in the top five in five consecutive seasons between 2002 and 2006: Ryan Whitney, Marc-Andre Fleury, Evgeni Malkin, Sidney Crosby and Jordan Staal. Still, while the Red Wings had only three top-round picks in the lineup, they won the Cup, ousting Pittsburgh's roster of top-round picks, including Gary Roberts (1984), Darryl Sidor (1990), Sergei Gonchar (1992), Petr Sykora (1995), Marian Hossa (1997), Kris Beech (1999), Brooks Orpik (2000) and Jeff Taffe (2000).

Answers are on page 419

16.1 Name the only team in NHL history to select two Hall of Famers in the first and second rounds of one draft.
  A. The Edmonton Oilers
  B. The Montreal Canadiens
  C. The New York Islanders
  D. The Boston Bruins

16.2 Which team in 2005–06 dealt away the player who went on to break Bernie Nicholls's record for most points by a player traded midseason?
  A. The Los Angeles Kings
  B. The Boston Bruins

C. The Carolina Hurricanes

D. The New York Rangers

16.3 **When he was traded in March 2004, how many games did Brian Leetch still need as a New York Ranger to surpass Harry Howell's record for most games?**

A. One game

B. 11 games

C. 21 games

D. 31 games

16.4 **Which NHL team drafted Dominik Hasek and, later, traded him to Buffalo?**

A. The Hartford Whalers

B. The Minnesota North Stars

C. The Chicago Blackhawks

D. The Philadelphia Flyers

16.5 **Which player, selected in the first round by the Edmonton Oilers, scored no goals in the season prior to his NHL drafting?**

A. Jeff Beukeboom, in 1983

B. Jason Arnott, in 1993

C. Ryan Smyth, in 1994

D. Ales Hemsky, in 2001

16.6 **What is the shortest time in which one player has scored two goals against his former team after being traded?**

A. One day

B. One week

C. Two weeks

D. One month

16.7 How many of the seven players involved in the Wayne Gretzky trade of August 9, 1988, were still active in the NHL in 2008–09?

    A. None

    B. Only one player, Martin Gelinas

    C. Two players

    D. Three players

16.8 What is the record for most teams by a player in a single NHL season?

    A. Two teams

    B. Three teams

    C. Four teams

    D. Five teams

16.9 What is the most number of expansion teams played by an NHLer during a career?

    A. Two expansion teams

    B. Three expansion teams

    C. Four expansion teams

    D. Five expansion teams

16.10 As of 2008–09, what is the most number of NHL teams a player has been with in his career?

    A. Eight teams

    B. 10 teams

    C. 12 teams

    D. 14 teams

16.11 Two U.S.-born players were first- and second-overall picks in which NHL draft year?

    A. 2001

    B. 2003

C. 2005

D. 2007

16.12 **How many, if any, number one overall picks never went on to play in the NHL?**

A. None, all number one picks have played in at least one NHL contest

B. Only one player, Rick Pagnutti—with Los Angeles in 1969

C. Two players

D. Three players

16.13 **As of 2008, how many draft picks chosen last overall have played in an NHL game?**

A. Three players

B. Six players

C. Nine players

D. 12 players

16.14 **Among active goalies in 2008–09, which goalie has been with the NHL franchise that drafted him longer than any other netminder?**

A. Martin Brodeur, with the New Jersey Devils

B. Marty Turco, with the Dallas Stars

C. Evgeni Nabokov, with the San Jose Sharks

D. Olaf Kolzig, with the Washington Capitals

16.15 **Perhaps inspired by the Mexican fast food chain Taco Bell, which two NHL general managers traded Kari Takko for Rob Bell?**

A. Nick Beverly and Mel Bridgman

B. Mike Milbury and Rejean Houle

C. Harry Sinden and Brian Burke

D. Bobby Clarke and Glen Sather

16.16 When was the first time, if ever, two goalies were selected
in the top 10 overall at the NHL Entry Draft?

A. At the 2000 NHL draft
B. At the 2002 NHL draft
C. At the 2004 NHL draft
D. At the 2006 NHL draft

16.17 What is the most number of goalies drafted in an NHL first
round?

A. Two goalies
B. Three goalies
C. Four goalies
D. Five goalies

16.18 After he became Calgary's all-time leading point producer
in February 1999, how many more games did Theo Fleury
play as a member of the Flames?

A. One game
B. Four games
C. Eight games
D. 16 games

16.19 At the time of his January 1999 trade from the Vancouver
Canucks to the Florida Panthers, Pavel Bure had scored a
goal against every other NHL team except one. Which team
blanked Bure?

A. The Florida Panthers
B. The Philadelphia Flyers
C. The Ottawa Senators
D. The Detroit Red Wings

16.20 From which team did the Florida Panthers claim John Vanbiesbrouck in the 1994 Expansion Draft?

A. The Vancouver Canucks

B. The Washington Capitals

C. The New York Rangers

D. The Calgary Flames

16.21 Which scoring line of the 1940s had all of its members traded away at the same time?

A. The Pony Line of the Chicago Blackhawks

B. The Flying Forts Line of the Toronto Maple Leafs

C. The Punch Line of the Montreal Canadiens

D. The Kid Line of the Toronto Maple Leafs

16.22 How much did the WHA Edmonton Oilers pay to acquire the rights to Wayne Gretzky in 1978?

A. Less than $1 million

B. $1 million

C. $2 million

D. $3 million

16.23 Which GM drafted the first international player in NHL history?

A. Bill Torrey, with the New York Islanders

B. Keith Allen, with the Philadelphia Flyers

C. Jim Gregory, with the Toronto Maple Leafs

D. Scotty Bowman, with the St. Louis Blues

16.24 Who was the first big-name NHL player to sign a WHA contract?

A. Derek Sanderson

B. Wayne Connelly

C. Bernie Parent

D. Bobby Hull

16.25 Which NHLer and his son were both selected in the same draft position in their respective years?

A. Brent Sutter and son Brandon

B. Dave Gagner and son Sam

C. Mike Foligno and son Nick

D. Darryl Sutter and son Brett

16.26 Just before Red Kelly's highly publicized trade from Detroit to Toronto in the 1960s, he was involved in another deal that fizzled on Red Wings manager Jack Adams. Which team did Kelly almost play for instead of the Maple Leafs?

A. The New York Rangers

B. The Montreal Canadiens

C. The Boston Bruins

D. The Chicago Blackhawks

16.27 Which NHLer was recruited by Dallas Stars owner Tom Hicks to court baseball's Alex Rodriguez—before Rodriguez signed the richest contract in sports history with the Texas Rangers in December 2000?

A. Wayne Gretzky

B. Mike Modano

C. Mario Lemieux

D. Brett Hull

16.28 How many Ranger players did Phil Esposito trade in his first season as GM in New York?

A. 11 players

B. 15 players

C. 19 players

D. 23 players

16.29 After the NHL-WHA merger in 1979, how many former WHA players were chosen in the first round (among 21 draft selections) of the 1979 NHL Entry Draft?

A. One WHA player, Mike Gartner

B. Three WHA players

C. Five WHA players

D. No WHA players were selected in the first round

16.30 When Ray Bourque was traded in March 2000, which player then became the longest-serving still-active NHLer in games played with one team?

A. New Jersey's Ken Daneyko

B. Detroit's Steve Yzerman

C. Minnesota's Mike Modano

D. New York's Brian Leetch

16.31 Who is the youngest number one overall pick?

A. Mike Modano

B. Eric Lindros

C. Pierre Turgeon

D. Sidney Crosby

16.32 How many more points did Wayne Gretzky score after his trade to Los Angeles than all five players/picks Edmonton received?

A. Less than 10 points

B. Between 10 and 100 points

C. Between 100 and 200 points

D. Gretzky scored fewer points than the five players' combined totals

16.33 Which Stanley Cup finals series featured two starting goaltenders who were previously traded for each other?

    A. Edmonton's Bill Ranford vs. Boston's Andy Moog, in 1990

    B. Chicago's Ed Belfour vs. Pittsburgh's Tom Barrasso, in 1992

    C. Dallas's Ed Belfour vs. Buffalo's Dominik Hasek, in 1999

    D. Detroit's Dominik Hasek vs. Carolina's Arturs Irbe, in 2002

16.34 In what position was Wayne Gretzky selected at the 1977
Junior A OHA draft?

    A. Number one overall

    B. Number two overall

    C. Number three overall

    D. Number four overall

16.35 How many, if any, NHL rookies of the year have been traded
midseason during their Calder Trophy-winning season?

    A. None, it has never happened

    B. Only one rookie, Carl Voss

    C. Two rookies

    D. Three rookies

16.36 As of 2008, how many sets of twins have been drafted into
the NHL?

    A. Three sets of twins

    B. Five sets of twins

    C. Seven sets of twins

    D. Nine sets of twins

16.37 As of 2008, how many goalies have been selected first overall since the NHL draft became universal in 1969—when all
players of qualifying age became eligible for selection?

    A. Only one, Marc-Andre Fleury

    B. Two goalies

C. Four goalies

D. Six goalies

16.38 What was so unusual about Phil Roberto's last NHL season, 1976–77?

A. His season was split, as he played between two expansion teams

B. He was mistakenly drafted by the Colorado Rockies

C. He was traded for his brother

D. His contract was up for renewal but he never signed

Drafts and Trade Winds

Answers

16.1   C. The New York Islanders

The 1980s Edmonton Oilers might be the most obvious team that comes to mind to settle this draft rarity. In 1979, Glen Sather turned the expansion Oilers into a Stanley Cup dynasty team with his first three choices: Kevin Lowe, Mark Messier and Glenn Anderson. But his one-two-three combination was spread over four rounds, since Sather had no pick in the second. The only team to pick up Hall of Famers in the two first rounds of the draft is the Islanders, in 1974, when they took Clark Gillies first, followed by Bryan Trottier. Gillies earned Hall of Fame status in 2002 and Trottier in 1997.

16.2   B. The Boston Bruins

A lot of raised eyebrows greeted the trade of Boston fan favourite and captain Joe Thornton to the San Jose Sharks in November 2005. Thornton went on to have a career year, winning the NHL scoring race on a record 125 points—split

between the Bruins (33) and the Sharks (92)—and besting
Bernie Nicholls's mark of 112 with Los Angeles and the New
York Rangers of 1989–90.

16.3   D. 31 games

It's impossible to estimate the loss of Brian Leetch to the
Rangers (or to New York City as a sports icon for more than a
decade). But as Mark Messier observed at the time, the team
"bottomed out" after his best friend's trade. As a lifetime
Ranger, the Conn Smythe Trophy-winning Leetch had experienced everything that's wonderful about the game yet also
some of its misery, from the Stanley Cup highs of 1994 to six
desperate seasons missing the playoffs. Leetch, the seventh-
highest-scoring defenseman in NHL history, played 1,129
games as a Blueshirt, just 31 short of old-time rearguard Harry
Howell's team record of 1,160. Leetch's trade signalled the end
of an era at Madison Square Garden. It came on his birthday,
March 3, 2004.

16.4   C. The Chicago Blackhawks

Hasek's career moves off-ice are as unique as his acrobatic
goaltending style. In fact, a number of teams failed to recog-
nize his full potential when he was within their reach. Hasek
was drafted an incredible 199th by Chicago in the 1983 draft—
late in the 11th round. The Hawks obviously weren't gambling
much on the 18-year-old, whose immediate plans lay in playing for his hometown team in Pardubice, Czechoslovakia—yet
when he finally hit the NHL in 1990–91 and 1991–92, he
notched a 2.53 goals-against average in 25 games. But Hawks
general manager Mike Keenan still preferred the red-hot Ed
Belfour; he sent Hasek to Buffalo. A year later, at the 1993 NHL
Expansion Draft, the Sabres, unimpressed after a mediocre

season, then left Hasek unprotected when the newly formed
Anaheim Mighty Ducks and the Florida Panthers were filling their ranks. Fortunately for the Sabres, neither expansion
team picked Hasek, who stayed in Buffalo to become a major
star, winning multiple Vezina Trophies, First All-Star Team
appearances and the coveted MVP award twice (a league first
for goalies). Ironically, Hasek's first NHL victory came against
Buffalo in a 5–3 Chicago win on March 8, 1991.

16.5   A. Jeff Beukeboom, in 1983

Despite scoring no goals in 70 games with the OHL Sault
St. Marie Greyhounds in 1982–83, the Oilers made Jeff
Beukeboom their first pick, 19th overall, in the 1983 NHL
draft. He may be the only non-goalie ever chosen in the
first round who didn't score a goal in the season prior to
his NHL draft.

16.6   A. One day

There is no record holder in this category, but Steve Thomas
is probably the best candidate. Only one day after Thomas
was traded by Chicago to Anaheim, he scored two goals—
including the game-winner—in his first two shots against his
former team. "It was weird. There were times out there when
I thought I was in a red jersey," said the ex-Hawk. Thomas had
scored just four goals in 69 games with the Blackhawks before
his trade on March 11, 2003. So what's the record for quickest
goal from the start of a game against former teammates? No
conclusive results are available on this one, either. But Detroit
winger Kyle Calder may have inflicted the fastest hurt, on
February 27, 2007, the day after being axed by the Blackhawks.
In his Red Wings debut versus Chicago, Calder scored at 1:46
of the first period.

16.7 C. Two players

Tears in Edmonton were mirrored by wide grins in Los Angeles after Wayne Gretzky became a King in 1988. Los Angeles also got Mike Krushelnyski and Marty McSorley, while the Oilers picked up Jimmy Carson, Martin Gelinas, three first-round picks (Martin Rucinsky, Nick Stajduhar and Jason Miller—in a New Jersey trade) and US$15 million. Almost 10 years after Gretzky retired in 1999, only two members from the transaction were still active: Gelinas and Rucinsky, who were both on their seventh NHL teams.

16.8 C. Four teams

Two players—Dennis O'Brien and Dave McLlwain—hold the record for most NHL teams in one season, but neither are as well-travelled as Rick Tabaracci, who ping-ponged between six different pro and international clubs in 1999–2000. It was a fitting end to a career that saw the veteran goalie play for seven different NHL franchises. His 46-game season in 1999–2000 included only three NHL matches, between Atlanta and Colorado, but he was everywhere, making stops for Canada's national team at the 1999 World Championships and three different clubs in the IHL: the Cleveland Lumberjacks, Orlando Solar Bears and Utah Grizzlies.

16.9 B. Three expansion teams

Butch Deadmarsh and Poul Popiel. They're not exactly household names, but these guys produced NHL careers with three expansion teams, all in different seasons. Deadmarsh joined Buffalo in 1970–71, Atlanta in 1972–73 and Kansas City in 1974–75; Popiel played in Los Angeles in 1967–68, Vancouver in 1970–71 and Edmonton in 1979–80. Two other players—Ron Low and Jean-Guy Talbot—also suited up with three expansion clubs, though both played with two of their teams in the same year. Talbot was with St. Louis and Minnesota in 1967–68, and later joined Buffalo in 1970–71. Low played with Washington in 1974–75, then with Quebec and Edmonton in 1979–80.

16.10 C. 12 teams

Well-travelled players have been branded several classic nicknames. Goaltender Gary Smith's seven-team odyssey through the league, for example, earned him the moniker "Suitcase." And, unofficially, airline ticket agents called Sergei Samsonov, who played with Dynamo Moscow, Boston, Edmonton and Montreal between 2005 and 2007, Sergei Samsonite. In the case of Mike Sillinger, though, his journeyman status has yet to inspire a nickname that has stuck. Presumably, he hasn't been around long enough with any club to get labelled after suiting up for almost half of the league's 30 NHL teams—his record 12th with the New York Islanders in 18 seasons (as of 2008–09). Instead, Sillinger owns a slew of NHL "trade" records, including most times traded (10), most midseason trades (8), most consecutive midseason trades (4) and most different teams (9), with 10 goals in a season. Sillinger was drafted by Detroit in 1989 and was signed as a free agent twice (with Columbus and the Islanders). And in 2005–06 he scored a career-high 32 goals between St. Louis and Nashville, yet still got traded to Long Island. What does this guy do to deserve such treatment—take showers with the worst case of foot fungus in league history? Of his 12 teams (not including Dallas, to whom he was traded in 2003, then traded out of later that day), Sillinger had full seasons with only Detroit, Vancouver and Columbus. He has only once been asked to be traded (from Detroit) and has been dealt from non-playoff teams to contenders more times than not. When he joined the Islanders, in 2006–07, he was tied with baseball pitcher Mike Morgan for the most teams played for in any North American professional sport.

16.11 D. 2007

The 2007 NHL draft was the year of the American, with several records set or tied by U.S.-born players. Of the 211 players chosen, a record 63—or 29.9 per cent—came from the U.S., a record 21 were picked up in the first two rounds and a record-tying 10 (as in 2006) were spoken for in the first round. Fourteen states contributed players, including first- and second-overall picks Patrick Kane from Buffalo, New York, and James vanRiemsdyk from Middletown, New Jersey. Kane's selection marked the first time U.S.-born players were drafted number one in consecutive years—Kane in 2007 and Erik Johnson in 2006.

16.12 D. Three players

Prior to 1969 and the first universal NHL draft, few top junior prospects were eligible for selection, most already being under contract to NHL teams through sponsored junior teams. This created some unusual circumstances between 1963—the draft's first year—and 1969. Rick Pagnutti, a defenseman chosen first overall by the Kings in 1967, played 10 years in five pro leagues but never made the NHL. And he was not alone: Claude Gauthier (1964) and Andre Veilleux (1965) were two other first picks whose NHL futures never materialized.

16.13 A. Three players

Given the unwritten rule that higher draft picks get better opportunities to play at the NHL level, it's a wonder that any late-rounder makes it onto NHL radar screens after draft day. But NHL managers and scouts are famous for selecting some gems late, such as Luc Robitaille (171st), and others not at all, such as free-agent Ed Belfour. Of course, no last-overall pick has embarrassed managers and scouts the way Robitaille and Belfour did, though the experiences of Andy Brickley, Hans Jonsson and Kim Johnsson also make a case for sticking with it, despite the ignominy of one's draft position. Brickley, taken last, or 210th, by Philadelphia in 1980, scored 82 goals in 385 NHL games. Jonsson, chosen last as Pittsburgh's 286th in 1993, played six years in Sweden before his four-year NHL stint. And Johnsson, picked last as the New York Rangers' 286th overall in 1994, came to the NHL five years later and recorded his 500th game in 2006–07—the most tallied among last-pick draftees.

16.14 A. Martin Brodeur, with the New Jersey Devils
In 2008–09, only Joe Sakic and Mike Modano have been with the club they were drafted to longer than netminder Martin Brodeur, who was selected by New Jersey 20th overall in 1990. Olaf Kolzig had held the title among netminders until July 2008, when the Washington Capitals' pick of 1989 signed as a free agent with Tampa Bay. For Brodeur, it's hard to imagine the Devils ever trading or releasing him. The three-time Stanley Cup winner has been their franchise player since the early 1990s and is closing in on 1,000 games with the club—more than any one-team goalie in NHL history.

16.15 D. Bobby Clarke and Glen Sather
We have always suspected that Bobby Clarke and Glen Sather have evil minds. Now here's more proof. In November 1990, Clarke, who was then general manager of the Minnesota North Stars, and Sather, then general manager of the

Edmonton Oilers, engineered a player trade that appears to have been made merely to satisfy both men's warped sense of humour. Clarke sent backup goalie Kari Takko to the Oilers in return for defenseman Bruce Bell, thus completing the first and only Takko-Bell deal. Only Bell had an NHL career, and played just one more game—for the Oilers.

16.16 A. At the 2000 NHL draft

A number of goalie firsts shook up the 2000 NHL Entry Draft. The New York Islanders chose Rick DiPietro first overall (the first goalie ever selected number one at an entry draft) while Calgary picked Brent Krahn ninth (marking the first time a second goalie was chosen in the top 10).

16.17 C. Four goalies

Unlike John Davidson, who went directly from the WCJHL Calgary Centennials to backstopping the St. Louis Blues for 39 games in 1973–74, goalies usually require several years of development before they are NHL calibre. As a result, unless managers and scouts spot a surefire netminder such as Davidson, they are hard-pressed to choose a goalie as first-round pick. Of course, there have been exceptions, with varying results. In 1994, 1995, 2004 and 2006, a record four goalies were chosen in each of the first rounds of those draft years. And while some are still maturing, as of 2008–09 it looks like the best of those 16 may have come from 1995, when Patrick Roy wannabes Jean-Sébastien Giguère (13th overall), Martin Biron (16th), Brian Boucher (22nd) and Marc Denis (25th) were picked in the first round.

16.18 B. Four games

After almost 800 games and more than 11 seasons as a Flame, Fleury became Calgary's all-time leading scorer on February 19, 1999, just nine days and four matches before he was traded to Colorado on February 28. The milestone goal, a shorthanded marker between the legs of Anaheim goalie Guy Hebert, was Fleury's 823rd point—one more than Al MacInnis's club record of 822. Fleury's final tally in Calgary was 830 points.

16.19 A. The Florida Panthers
Players are often acquired in trades by teams they have tormented on the ice. But this wasn't the case in the Bure-to-Florida deal. The only team the Russian Rocket had failed to score a goal against was the Panthers. In five career games against Florida, Bure managed only four assists.

16.20 A. The Vancouver Canucks
Many have forgotten that Vancouver acquired John Vanbiesbrouck from the Rangers in exchange for Doug Lidster shortly before the 1994 Expansion Draft, but Pat Quinn undoubtedly remembers. The Canucks' general manager took Vanbiesbrouck for the sole purpose of leaving him unprotected in the Expansion Draft. The reason? Quinn wanted to keep backup netminder Kay Whitmore out of the clutches of the expansion Anaheim Mighty Ducks and Florida Panthers. The Panthers, of course, chose the Beezer with their first pick, while Whitmore remained in Vancouver and played only 11 more games before being traded to the Rangers. In retrospect, Quinn would have been better advised to keep Vanbiesbrouck and expose Kirk McLean to the draft. But McLean, who had just come off a sensational playoffs, was considered untouchable—a description the Panthers would soon apply to Vanbiesbrouck.

16.21 B. The Flying Forts Line of the Toronto Maple Leafs
Despite the fact they helped win him a Stanley Cup in 1947, Toronto GM Conn Smythe dealt five of his Leafs, including the talented Flying Forts Gus Bodnar, Bud Poile and Gaye Stewart,

for defending scoring champion Max Bentley of Chicago. In the process, Smythe pulled off the "deal of the century," which worked like magic. Toronto won three more Cups in four years with Bentley. Meanwhile, Chicago, despite its new personnel, failed to make the playoffs for six seasons. And by the time they did, only Bodnar from the Flying Forts Line remained.

16.22   A. Less than $1 million

In 1978, after just eight games and six points as an Indianapolis Racer, 17-year-old rookie Wayne Gretzky (as well as Peter Driscoll and Eddie Mio) were sold for $850,000 by Racers owner Nelson Skalbania to Peter Pocklington of the Oilers. Skalbania had originally signed Gretzky to a personal-services contract, but after losing $40,000 a game in Indianapolis, he severed his ties with the teenager. The rest is history.

16.23   D. Scotty Bowman, with the St. Louis Blues

The first international player selected in an NHL draft was Finnish-born Tommi Salmalainen, who played hockey for HIFK Helsinki in Finland before being picked 66th overall by St. Louis coach and general manager Scotty Bowman in 1969. Ultimately, Salmalainen never played a game in the NHL, but Bowman's willingness to experiment with European players and their free-flowing style of game proved essential to his success in Montreal, Buffalo, Pittsburgh and Detroit. Interestingly, after the selection of Salmalainen, another five years would pass before other teams started bringing Europeans into the NHL.

16.24   C. Bernie Parent

Two weeks after the WHA's inaugural player draft, the Miami Screaming Eagles announced the signing of Toronto Maple Leafs goalie Bernie Parent to a $750,000 long-term deal. The outlaw league had landed its first "name" player. "At my present salary, it would take me 10 to 15 years to make the kind of money I'm going to make in Miami," said Parent. But the Eagles folded before playing a game and Parent found himself backstopping their successors, the Philadelphia Blazers, and it took only one WHA season before he crossed town to begin his Hall of Fame career with the Flyers. After Parent jumped to the WHA, Wayne Connelly also signed a WHA contract, early in 1972. The Parent and Connelly deals happened months before the Bobby Hull signing, which sparked an explosion of NHL defections, including those of established stars Gerry Cheevers, Ted Green and J.C. Tremblay.

16.25 D. Darryl Sutter and son Brett

Louis Sutter sired an unprecedented six NHL-playing sons, who between them managed a total of 4,994 games—5,603 games, if you include the playoffs. In fact, no other hockey dynasty family, including the Howes, Hulls or Richards, can claim the legacy of the Sutters in NHL action, which features a 1,320 goal count, 2,935 point total and 7,224 minutes in box time. Also, during a five-year span in the 1980s, all six brothers played in the league at the same time, and Louis Sutter, who passed away in February 2005, lived to see all six of his sons working for the NHL after they retired as players. And now his grandsons are showing potential, including Brent's son, Brandon, and Darryl's son, Brett, who was drafted by Calgary 179th overall—the same draft position his father held 27 years earlier with Chicago in 1978.

16.26 A. The New York Rangers

Before the 1960 Toronto deal, Detroit general manager Jack Adams traded Kelly (and Bill McNeill) to New York in exchange for Bill Gadsby and Eddie Shack. But Kelly refused to report to the Rangers. The deal was nixed and the Simcoe, Ontario, native soon found himself homeward bound to Toronto and the Maple Leafs.

16.27 B. Mike Modano

To nab shortstop Alex Rodriguez, Dallas Stars and Texas Rangers owner Tom Hicks asked the Stars' Mike Modano to show A-Rod the sights of Dallas and then join them for dinner at Bob's Steak and Chop House. "I knew for sure he [Hicks] would be as aggressive as he is in his business dealings," said Modano. "Nobody ever thought that Brett Hull would sign with the Stars because of the style of game we played, but Mr. Hicks knew he [Hull] could help us win." The 25-year-old Rodriguez signed a 10-year, us$252-million contract with the Rangers, the richest in sports history to date—topped only by Rodriguez' us$275-million deal with the Yankees in November 2007.

16.28 C. 19 players

Never one to shun any spotlight, not even Broadway's brightest, Phil Esposito quickly earned the nickname "Trader Phil" in New York by completing 19 player trades in his first season as GM. He also fired or replaced two head coaches before going behind the bench himself.

16.29 C. Five WHA players

Ten players from the WHA were chosen in the 1979 NHL Entry Draft, including five in the first round. Of those 10 draftees, seven came from the WHA Birmingham Bulls, a team with huge potential. Overall, NHL scouts had a relatively accurate bead on the talent. Quality players such as Rob Ramage, Mike Gartner and Michel Goulet went in the first round, but young

Mark Messier was selected 48th overall. Wayne Gretzky was never drafted, since he had signed an extended personal-services contract with Edmonton owner Peter Pocklington.

WHA Players Selected in the 1979 NHL Entry Draft

DRAFT ROUND	PREVIOUS WHA TEAM	DRAFTED BY NHL TEAM
FIRST ROUND		
1. Rob Ramage	Birmingham	Colorado
4. Mike Gartner	Cincinnati	Washington
5. Rick Vaive	Birmingham	Vancouver
6. Craig Hartsburg	Birmingham	Minnesota
20. Michel Goulet	Birmingham	Quebec
SECOND ROUND		
27. Gaston Gingras	Birmingham	Montreal
28. Pat Riggin	Birmingham	Atlanta
THIRD ROUND		
48. Mark Messier	Cincinnati	Edmonton
49. Keith Crowder	Birmingham	Boston
FOURTH ROUND		
71. John Gibson	Winnipeg	Los Angeles

16.30 B. Detroit's Steve Yzerman

It was unthinkable—Ray Bourque in a uniform other than the black-and-gold of his beloved Bs. But after almost 21 seasons, 18 All-Star selections, five Norris Trophies as the NHL's best defenseman and a Calder Trophy as top rookie, Bourque was finally traded to a Stanley Cup contender—the Colorado Avalanche—at his request. Four teams, including Philadelphia (his first choice), made a pitch for the future Hall-of-Fame rearguard, but the Avalanche pulled the trigger and bagged Bourque for the playoff drive. (Interestingly, it was Patrick Roy who laid the groundwork for the Avalanche by selling Bourque on the idea of coming to Colorado when they were teammates playing for Canada at the 1998 Olympics.) Of course, the trade wasn't completely unexpected. During the mid-1990s, Bourque settled for less money to stay in Boston, expecting that the Bruins would turn the corner. But as things in Beantown went from bad to worse, it looked like the veteran had made the wrong decision. Bourque could have signed as an unrestricted free agent with Detroit and won two Stanley Cups by the time he was finally dealt to Colorado in 2000. His departure left Ken Daneyko and Steve Yzerman as the longest-serving active players in the league.

16.31 C. Pierre Turgeon

When Buffalo called Turgeon to the podium at the Joe Louis Arena in 1987, the Granby Bison was 17 years, 10 months old, the youngest-ever junior selected first overall in an NHL draft. Modano, Hawerchuk and Lindros were all 18-year-olds.

16.32 B. Between 10 and 100 points

From the start of 1988–89 through to the end of 1998–99, Wayne Gretzky outscored the combined total of the five players he was traded for: Jimmy Carson, Martin Gelinas, Jason Miller, Martin Rucinsky and Nick Stajduhar. No. 99 had 1,118 points in 791 games, compared to the combined sum of 1,040 points in 1,599 games amassed by the five.

16.33 A. Edmonton's Bill Ranford vs. Boston's Andy Moog, in 1990

At the 1988 Entry Draft, Boston and Edmonton exchanged goalies Bill Ranford and Andy Moog, who two years later battled each other in the Oilers–Bruins 1990 Stanley Cup finals. The goaltenders' duel turned into hockey history in the first game as Moog and Ranford protected a 2–2 tie until 55:13 of overtime, a marathon match that represents the longest game in Stanley Cup finals play. Moog faced 31 shots in the 3–2 loss; Ranford, who had been beaten twice in the third period by Ray Bourque to force overtime, kicked out everything else in his 52-shot effort. Backstopped by Ranford's spectacular play, the Oilers whipped the Bruins 4–1 in the best-of-seven series. Ranford won the Conn Smythe Trophy as playoff MVP.

16.34   C. Number three overall

Despite off-the-chart numbers in scoring in minor hockey and Junior B, Wayne Gretzky was selected third in the 1977 Ontario Junior A draft. The Oshawa Generals, who picked first, chose Tom McCarthy; the Kitchener Rangers, with second pick, took Paul Reinhart; the Sault Ste. Marie Greyhounds, who drafted third, chose the 17-year-old Gretzky, who lit up the OHA in his rookie season, scoring 182 points in 64 games. Why wasn't Gretzky drafted first? The Peterborough Petes, who drew fourth pick, wanted Gretzky badly and made deals with Oshawa and Kitchener, but they didn't work anything out with the Greyhounds. So Sault Ste. Marie got Gretzky, and, despite protests by Walter Gretzky concerning the distance from Brantford (500 miles), Wayne played his only full OHA season in the Soo.

16.35   C. Two rookies

Since 1933 there have been only two occasions when NHL teams traded away rookies in midseason who went on to win the Calder Trophy as the league's top freshman. Carl Voss, the very first Calder winner, was traded by New York for cash to Detroit in 1932 just 10 games (and three points) into the 1932–33 season. Voss scored 20 points in the next 38 games to win rookie of the year with the Red Wings. And in 1954–55, Montreal literally gave away promising rookie Ed

Litzenberger to shore up Chicago's faltering franchise. In 29 games with the sniper-rich Canadiens, Litzenberger scored just 11 points. But in Chicago, as his ice time soared so did his point totals, and he collected 40 points in 44 games to claim top rookie honours.

16.36 C. Seven sets of twins

Daniel and Henrik Sedin may be the NHL's most famous twins after being picked second and third by Vancouver in the 1999 Entry Draft, but they are only one of seven sets of twin brothers drafted into the league. Patrik and Peter Sundstrom, the first and only twins drafted in separate years, were selected in 1980 and 1981. Ron and Rich Sutter both went in the first round of 1982. Peter and Chris Ferraro were picked in the 1992 draft. And three sets of twins were drafted in 2000: Matt and Mark McRae (both of whom went to the Atlanta Thrashers), Paul and Peter Flache, and Hedrik and Joel Lundqvuist. As mentioned in an earlier chapter, the latter also became the third set of twins to play against each other and the first in goalie and forward positions. Patrik and Peter Sundstrom played as opponents 18 times, the Sutters on 17 occasions.

16.37 B. Two goalies

New York Islanders general manager Mike Milbury made NHL history in June 2000, when he chose Boston University goalie Rick DiPietro first overall. DiPietro was the first netminder chosen first in an entry draft, though goalie Michel Plasse was the top overall pick in 1968, when few top prospects were eligible to NHL teams in the Amateur Draft. DiPietro, a native of Winthrop, Massachusetts, was named best goalie at the 2000 World Junior Championships and set an NCAA record with 77 saves in one game for Boston University in 1999–2000. The only other puckstopper chosen first was Marc-Andre Fleury, in 2003. Fleury played junior hockey with the QMJHL Cape Breton Screaming Eagles, where he won Second All-Star Team honours in 2002–03, the same year he won one of two silver medals (the other came in 2003–04) with Team Canada at the IIHF World Junior Championships. In 2008, Fleury's No. 29 was retired by the Screaming Eagles.

16.38 A. His season was split, as he played with two expansion teams

Phil Roberto's ying-yang career generated a Stanley Cup during his rookie year with Montreal in 1971 and one oddity in his final season: playing on two new teams that had been transferred from other cities (due to their failure in Kansas City and California, respectively). In 1976, each club moved and set up franchises in Denver and Cleveland, and Robero ended his 385-game NHL career as the only player on two newly relocated clubs, the Rockies and the Barons.

Game 16

Bench Boss Blues

IN NHL HISTORY ONLY one man has won the Jack Adams Award as coach of the year with the same team he set an NHL record with as a player. Unscramble the names of these other Jack Adams winners by placing each letter in the correct order in the correct box. (To help, each name starts with the bolded letter.) Next, unscramble the three letters in the square-shaped boxes to spell out the first name of our secret coach; then unscramble the letters in all the circled boxes for the family name and all the diamond-shaped boxes for his team.

Solutions are on page 566

RETUTS   SUTTER

MEDSER   DEMERS

SRUNB   BURNS

HEARTS   SATHER

LANON   NOLAN

BWAMNO   BOWMAN

REMAILE   LEMAIRE

RED BERENSON

ST LOUIS BLUES

436

17

The Bench Boss

WHICH ORIGINAL COACH of an expansion team has recorded the most games behind the bench? In this era of "win-now-or-else" coaching, few thought any coach would seriously challenge Lester Patrick's reign of 604 games with the New York Rangers from 1926–27 to 1938–39. But Nashville's Barry Trotz changed all that when he topped Terry Crisp's 391-game run in Tampa Bay with his 392nd match (in the Predators' 5–4 win against Chicago) on March 1, 2003, to become the modern-day leader for most games coached by the first coach of an NHL expansion franchise. Then, Trotz took the Predators to four consecutive postseasons and, during 2006–07, beat Patrick's all-time mark with his 605th game as the first coach of an NHL club. The historic match came on December 14, 2006, in a 6–0 win versus Ottawa. Since Trotz became the Predators' first coach in 1998, 28 of the 30 NHL teams have changed bench bosses. As of 2008–09, only Lindy Ruff has had a longer run with his current team. In this chapter, the bench boss rules.

Answers are on page 447

17.1 **In what season did Scotty Bowman become the winningest coach in NHL history?**
   A. In 1978–79, with the Montreal Canadiens
   B. In 1984–85, with the Buffalo Sabres
   C. In 1991–92, with the Pittsburgh Penguins
   D. In 1994–95, with the Detroit Red Wings

17.2 **Which 1980s coach displayed the Stanley Cup in his team's dressing room to motivate the players during the finals?**

A. Glen Sather, with the Edmonton Oilers

B. Al Arbour, with the New York Islanders

C. Terry Crisp, with the Calgary Flames

D. Mike Keenan, with the Philadelphia Flyers

17.3 **Who was the first goalie to coach an NHL team?**

A. Hugh Lehman, with the Chicago Blackhawks

B. Emile Francis, with the New York Rangers

C. Percy LeSueur, with the Hamilton Tigers

D. Gerry Cheevers, with the Boston Bruins

17.4 **Which coach introduced "pyramid power" to the NHL?**

A. Barry Melrose, with the Los Angeles Kings

B. Herb Brooks, with the New York Rangers

C. Bob Hartley, with the Colorado Avalanche

D. Red Kelly, with the Toronto Maple Leafs

17.5 **Which NHL coach was criticizing Wayne Gretzky when he said: "You have to expect your best players to carry the team, and that's not happening."**

A. Glen Sather, with the Edmonton Oilers

B. John Muckler, with the New York Rangers

C. Mike Keenan, with the St. Louis Blues

D. Barry Melrose, with the Los Angeles Kings

17.6 **How many different players wore a St. Louis uniform during Mike Keenan's two-and-a-half-year reign as coach and general manager of the Blues?**

A. 52 players

B. 62 players

C. 72 players
D. 82 players

17.7 **Who was the first coach to remove his goalie during a delayed penalty?**
A. Dick Irvin, with Montreal
B. Hap Day, with Toronto
C. Milt Schmidt, with Boston
D. Tommy Ivan, with Detroit

17.8 **How many Chicago head coaches did Denis Savard serve under as assistant coach before the Blackhawks hired him as head coach in 2006–07?**
A. Only one head coach, Trent Yawney
B. Three head coaches
C. Five head coaches
D. Seven head coaches

17.9 **In 2005, which former NHL tough guy coached the London Knights to the Memorial Cup?**
A. Chris Nilan
B. Marty McSorley
C. Dale Hunter
D. Bob Probert

17.10 **Which old-time coach is famous for punching a referee after a playoff game—and was subsequently nailed with the largest NHL fine at the time?**
A. Toe Blake, with the Montreal Canadiens
B. Billy Reay, with the Chicago Blackhawks
C. Punch Imlach, with the Toronto Maple Leafs
D. John Ferguson, with the New York Rangers

17.11 The Philadelphia Flyers went undefeated a record 35 consecutive games in 1979–80. Who coached the Flyers that season?

A. Fred Shero

B. Pat Quinn

C. Bob McCammon

D. Mike Keenan

17.12 In 2002–03, which NHL coach was fired—losing his chance to tie the Islanders' Al Arbour record of improving his team's points total in six consecutive seasons?

A. Bob Hartley, with the Colorado Avalanche

B. Paul Maurice, with the Caroline Hurricanes

C. Darryl Sutter, with the San Jose Sharks

D. Scotty Bowman, with the Detroit Red Wngs

17.13 Which NHL coach was fired twice from two different teams in the final days of a winning regular season?

A. Larry Robinson

B. Pat Burns

C. Robbie Ftorek

D. Jacques Demers

17.14 In his 2005 biography, what former Stanley Cup-winning coach revealed that he was illiterate?

A. Mike Keenan

B. Jacques Demers

C. John Muckler

D. Harry Sinden

17.15 Which NHL team hired the first European-trained head coach in league history?

A. The Pittsburgh Penguins

B. The Detroit Red Wings

C. The Washington Capitals

D. The Chicago Blackhawks

17.16 What team has captured the most Stanley Cups with rookie head coaches?

A. The Toronto Maple Leafs

B. The Detroit Red Wings

C. The old Ottawa Senators

D. The Montreal Canadiens

17.17 Among the six NHL coaches fired in 1997–98, how many were from the league's Atlantic Division?

A. Two coaches

B. Three coaches

C. Four coaches

D. Five coaches

17.18 Who is the only NHL coach to be fired and then, two days later, re-hired by the same team?

A. Don Cherry, by the Boston Bruins

B. Lou Lamorello, by the New Jersey Devils

C. Roger Neilson, by the Toronto Maple Leafs

D. Al McNeil, by the Montreal Canadiens

17.19 Which bench boss began his NHL coaching career with a record six straight wins?

A. Mario Tremblay, with the Montreal Canadiens

B. Mike Keenan, with the Philadelphia Flyers

C. Craig MacTavish, with the Edmonton Oilers

D. Randy Carlyle, with the Anaheim Mighty Ducks

17.20 What International Hockey League club had its coach suspended for attacking an opposing team's mascot in the stands during a 1995 game? (And name the unfortunate mascot.)

A. The Las Vegas Thunder

B. The Cincinnati Cyclones

C. The Detroit Vipers

D. The Peoria Rivermen

17.21 Which is the only other team, besides the New York Islanders, that Al Arbour has coached?

A. The Detroit Red Wings

B. The Chicago Blackhawks

C. The Toronto Maple Leafs

D. The St. Louis Blues

17.22 Responding to a reporter, Minnesota Wild coach Jacques Lemaire once said: "No? Really? That's why I'm so tired. That's definitely why I'm so tired." Why was Lemaire "tired"?

A. He held the longest practice in team history

B. His Wild set a league record for longest road trip

C. His Wild played back-to-back games in less than 24 hours

D. He had coached his 1,000th career game

17.23 What future NHL bench boss coached the most games in WHA history?
  A. Jacques Demers
  B. Glen Sather
  C. Bill Dineen
  D. Harry Neale

17.24 Who is the only bench boss to win coach of the year honours in both the WHA and the NHL?
  A. Bill Dineen
  B. Jacques Demers
  C. John Brophy
  D. Bobby Kromm

17.25 Which Stanley Cup-winning coach was a great admirer of the Russian hockey system, even travelling to Moscow to take a course taught by Soviet national coach Anatoly Tarasov?
  A. Al Arbour, with the New York Islanders
  B. Fred Shero, with the Philadelphia Flyers
  C. Scotty Bowman, with the Montreal Canadiens
  D. Glen Sather, with the Edmonton Oilers

17.26 What is the highest number of coaches fired during one regular season?
  A. Three coaches
  B. Six coaches
  C. Nine coaches
  D. 12 coaches

17.27 Who was Patrick Roy's coach when he got his first NHL victory?

A. Pat Burns
B. Jacques Demers
C. Jean Perron
D. Jacques Lemaire

17.28 What is the fewest number of regular-season games worked in a year by an NHL head coach who then went on to lead his team to a Stanley Cup?

A. Fewer than 10 games
B. Between 10 and 44 games
C. Between 44 and 70 games
D. More than 70 games

17.29 Who was Detroit coach Scotty Bowman targeting when he said, "The only thing he didn't do was win an Olympic medal. And I was kind of glad he didn't because we wouldn't have heard the end of it."

A. Chris Chelios, with the Chicago Blackhawks
B. Eric Lindros, with the Philadelphia Flyers
C. Patrick Roy, with the Colorado Avalanche
D. Brett Hull, with the Dallas Stars

17.30 "Take the shortest route to the puck—and arrive in ill humour" was which coach's advice on how to play hockey?

A. Philadelphia Flyers coach Fred Shero's
B. New Jersey Devils coach Claude Julien's
C. Toronto Maple Leafs coach Pat Quinn's
D. Vancouver Canucks coach Harry Neale's

17.31 In 2006–07, coach Ted Nolan's first return to Buffalo as coach of the Islanders resulted in what outcome?
A. A shutout win for the New York Islanders
B. A victory for the Buffalo Sabres
C. A double-digit win for the New York Islanders
D. A scoreless tie before a shootout victory for the Buffalo Sabres

17.32 During the 1970s, which head coach bucked the trend during NHL games of dressing in a suit by wearing an athletic tracksuit behind the bench?
A. Barclay Plager, with the St. Louis Blues
B. Bob Pulford, with the Chicago Blackhawks
C. Ron Stewart, with the Los Angeles Kings
D. Jean-Guy Talbot, with the New York Rangers

17.33 What was the age of the oldest NHL rookie coach?
A. 53 years old
B. 56 years old
C. 59 years old
D. 62 years old

17.34 Which future NHL coach was the first American to score more than 100 points in a season in pro hockey?
A. Robbie Ftorek
B. Herb Brooks
C. Ron Wilson
D. Craig Patrick

17.35 Which coach formed Detroit's Production Line?

A. Jimmy Skinner

B. Jack Adams

C. Sid Abel

D. Tommy Ivan

17.36 What NHL tough guy suffered an on-ice, near-career-ending injury in 1969, only to return to action and later become an NHL coach?

A. Scotty Bowman

B. Ted Green

C. Al Arbour

D. Terry Crisp

17.37 Which NHL coach has received the longest suspension to date for a game-related incident?

A. Mike Keenan, with the Calgary Flames

B. Tom Webster, with the Los Angeles Kings

C. Pat Quinn, with the Vancouver Canucks

D. Michel Terrien, with the Pittsburgh Penguins

17.38 When, if ever, was the last time a player-coach won the Stanley Cup?

A. During the 1920s

B. During the 1940s

C. During the 1960s

D. It has never happened

17.39 How old was the youngest head coach in NHL history? (Hint: it happened in 1979.)

A. Under 30 years old

B. 32 years old

C. 34 years old

D. 36 years old

17.40 Who was the first coach in NHL history to win 50 or more games in his first three seasons with a team?

    A. Mike Babcock, with the Detroit Red Wings

    B. Toe Blake, with the Montreal Canadiens

    C. Scotty Bowman, with the Detroit Red Wings

    D. Jacques Lemaire, with the New Jersey Devils

The Bench Boss

Answers

17.1 B. In 1984–85, with the Buffalo Sabres

Bowman's NHL mark of 1,244 wins is about as safe as Glenn Hall's record stretch of 502 games between the pipes. Neither will ever be beaten. Bowman's reign began on December 26, 1984, when the Buffalo Sabres shut out Toronto 6–0 and won their coach his 693rd victory—one more than managed by Dick Irvin, who recorded 692 wins during his distinguished career. The coach who came closest to toppling Bowman was Al Arbour. In 1990–91, while Bowman was in the fourth year of his first retirement, Arbour hit 661 wins. Still, Bowman was untouchable. He had 739 victories and was just starting the second half of his career, in which he added another 504 wins and four Stanley Cups.

17.2 D. Mike Keenan, with the Philadelphia Flyers

Superstition has it that if you touch the Stanley Cup before you compete for it—even while as a child—you will never win the trophy. But there were few believers in this myth during the 1987 finals. With Philadelphia trailing Edmonton three games to one, Keenan brought the Cup into the dressing room before Game 5 to fire up his players. The Flyers won 4–3, so Keenan repeated the ploy before Game 6, which Philadelphia also won, 3–2. But the Oilers finally caught wind of Keenan's shenanigans, and, before Game 7 in Edmonton, Oilers GM Glen Sather instructed team trainer Sparky Kulchisky to stash the Cup in the trunk of his car. Without their pre-game fix, the Flyers were defeated 3–1. Amongst the 22 Philadelphia players who participated in the 1987 finals, five went on to win Cups with other teams. So too did Keenan, who sipped champagne at New York's 1994 Cup celebration. So much for superstitions.

17.3   C. Percy LeSueur, with the Hamilton Tigers

Despite their storied history as the game's most important and brightest players, few goaltenders have made the leap to bench boss. The first was Percy LeSueur, who never played in the NHL but won three Stanley Cups with the Ottawa Senators before the league was formed in 1917. LeSueur's early fame came backstopping the Senators, but he later earned hockey titles as coach, manager, referee, inventor, arena manager and columnist. He was the first manager of the old Detroit Olympia, the inventor of a gauntlet-type glove to protect a goalie's forearm and the creator of the first goal net that could trap rising shots. As a reporter for the *Hamilton Spectator*, LeSueur also introduced the statistic "shots on goal" to box scores. Yet despite his well-documented career of hockey firsts, LeSueur has never been credited as the first goalie to coach an NHL team, according to our research. (Perhaps that's just as well. It proved to be the low point in his Hall of Fame career, given that LeSueur guided the outmatched Hamilton Tigers to last place with a 3–7–0 record in

10 games during 1923–24.) Instead, the first NHL goalie to be credited with coaching in the league was Hugh Lehman, who served Chicago for 21 games in 1927–28.

17.4 D. Red Kelly, with the Toronto Maple Leafs

When Red Kelly coached the Toronto Maple Leafs he was always trying to dream up motivational gimmicks—including pyramid power, which he introduced during the Leafs' playoff run in 1976. As Brian McFarlane notes in his book *The Leafs,* Kelly had heard about the mystical powers associated with pyramids and ordered that a large one be suspended from the ceiling of the Leafs' dressing room, with smaller versions arranged beneath the team bench. If players sat beneath these triangles or even placed their sticks under them, Kelly insisted, they could tap into psychic energy sources. The players were sceptical. But when captain Darryl Sittler tried it and scored five times in an 8–5 romp over the Philadelphia Flyers, many of them jumped on the bandwagon. Kelly scrapped his pyramid scheme after the Flyers bounced Toronto from the quarterfinals in seven games.

17.5 C. Mike Keenan, with the St. Louis Blues

During the 1996 Detroit–St. Louis Western Conference semifinals, Mike Keenan publicly questioned Gretzky's performance, saying, amongst other things, "If he's not injured, then something must be bothering him." Keenan also berated the Great One in front of his teammates, which left Oilers general manager Glen Sather to muse: "I think (Keenan) should have his head examined. As far as I'm concerned, he must be touched by the wind or something to be critical of a guy like Wayne Gretzky." Later, Keenan apologized to Gretzky, saying he may have "overstepped" himself in his comments.

17.6   D. 82 players

They may as well have installed a revolving door in the Blues'
dressing room during Keenan's two-and-a-half-year St. Louis
tenure. Before his compulsive trading habits cost him his job,
a total of 82 players wore the Bluenote—some didn't even stick
long enough to sweat their jerseys. As well, dealing draft picks,
discarding fan favourites such as Brendan Shanahan and Curtis
Joseph and unloading skill players for plodding muckers such
as Adam Creighton, Craig MacTavish, Greg Gilbert, Mike Peluso
and Stephane Matteau didn't turn the Blues around, but it did
drive fans away. Season ticket renewals dropped from 97 per
cent to 85 per cent and attendance declined by 3,000 per game.
The growing alienation of the Blues' fans and Keenan's ongoing feud with star Brett Hull finally prompted management to
hand Iron Mike his pink slip in December 1996.

17.7   C. Milt Schmidt, with Boston

The Bruins didn't have to be losing late in the game for
Schmidt to pull his goalie—he was known to add an extra
attacker in the offenisve zone with five seconds remaining,
no matter the period or the score. So the next logical offensive
move? Pull your goalie for an extra skater during a delayed
penalty because the opposition can't score—since any play on
their part will be immediately whistled dead. And on October
20, 1960, that is exactly what Schmidt did, probably for the
first time ever, introducing what is now standard hockey
strategy by pulling goalie Don Simmons and adding forward
Bronco Horvath after referee John Ashley signalled a delayed
penalty against Detroit. Boston didn't score, but they held the
extra offensive punch for 10 seconds before the whistle.

17.8   D. Seven head coaches

If numbers were kept on this sort of thing, Denis Savard probably set an NHL record when he became Chicago's head coach

in November 2006. In his nine years as assistant coach, he had seen Craig Hartsburg, Dirk Graham, Lorne Molleken, Bob Pulford, Alpo Suhonen, Brian Sutter and Trent Yawney take their turn on Chicago's merry-go-round of bench bosses. Unfortunately, his hot start behind the bench, when he became only the second coach in club history to win his first three games, soon fizzled, and Savard was fired just four games into 2008–09 after posting a 65–66–16 record in 147 matches. Meanwhile, the Hawks missed both playoff seasons under his guidance—lending credence to the old theory that superstar athletes don't make good head coaches.

17.9 C. Dale Hunter

From the start, Dale and Mark Hunter believed that the London Knights could be a powerhouse franchise in the Ontario Hockey League. In fact, the brothers felt so strongly about their vision that they purchased the team for $3.8 million from Doug Tarry in March 2000. They then began drafting character and role players, making smart trades and developing a pro-club atmosphere with conditioning programs and fitness trainers. Further, the city of London chipped in and built a $45-million 9,100-seat downtown arena that rivalled many NHL rinks (except in seating capacity). Dale proved to be an excellent coach, too, shedding the notoriously volatile behaviour he displayed during his 19-year NHL career to remain calm and cool behind the bench. "I've taken bits and pieces from all the coaches I've had," he said in a *Globe and Mail* story. "And one of the things I liked in a coach was a guy who could stay composed. If you get riled up, the team gets riled up and takes too many penalties...As a player, you have to get emotional, play on the edge. But as a coach you need to stay in control." It was a strategy that would pave the way for one of the most memorable years in Canadian Hockey League history. The Knights celebrated their 40th season by setting a

CHL record with a 32-game undefeated streak that lasted until January, in the process shattering several junior records and becoming the first OHL team to record back-to-back 100-point seasons. The year was then capped by a 4–0 victory over Sidney Crosby's Rimouski Oceanic to claim the Memorial Cup. "I played 19 years (in the NHL) and never won a Stanley Cup, and I could never do this—celebrate on the ice," said Hunter.

17.10 **A. Toe Blake, with the Montreal Canadiens**

For most coaches, winning five consecutive Stanley Cups might take the pressure off in terms of going for another championship. But not for Toe Blake. Furious after several game-changing calls in favour of the opposition during the 1961 playoffs, Blake jumped the bench and bareknuckled referee Dalton McArthur. Blake was fined an all-time high of $2,000. In addition, league president Clarence Campbell stipulated that Blake must pay the fine personally, without team assistance.

17.11 **B. Pat Quinn**

After losing to the Atlanta Flames in their second game of the 1979–80 season, the Flyers decided to get serious. Very serious. They went on a rampage, going 35 straight games without a loss—the longest undefeated streak in NHL history. Under the direction of coach Pat Quinn, the "Broad Street Bullies" had changed their style, emphasizing speed and quickness and cutting back on the violence that had been the club's hallmark. The result: Philadelphia finished the season with 116 points for the highest total in the league.

17.12 **C. Darryl Sutter, with the San Jose Sharks**

The 2002–03 season was supposed to be the year of the Shark. In fact, Sutter had many believing his team was ready to dominate the Western Conference and rival such power clubs as

Colorado, Detroit and Dallas. Having already tied Al Arbour's record of five straight seasons of point improvement with a five-year climb from 1997–98 to 2001–02, Sutter led San Jose to a franchise-record five consecutive playoff berths and one near upset against the Avalanche in the second round of the 2002 playoffs. But the bubble burst early in 2002–03. A few key players—Evgeni Nabokov and Brad Stuart—played holdout at training camp, and San Jose never found its groove. And after an 8–12–2–2 start, the Sharks dumped Sutter, who was followed by Owen Nolan, Matt Bradley and Bryan Marchment in a fire sale at the trade deadline. A week later, GM Dean Lombardi was fired. San Jose finished 25th overall with a disappointing 28–37–9–8 record.

17.13   C. Robbie Ftorek

Ftorek has coached three NHL teams, but never lasted past two seasons with any of them. He was fired in LA in 1988–89 after a year and half at the helm, blown out in New Jersey during his second season with only eight games left in 1999–2000 and, three seasons later, given the hook again in his second year just weeks before the playoffs, when Boston unloaded him with nine games remaining in 2002–03. Ftorek's record was 41–20–8–5 in New Jersey and 33–28–8–4 in Boston. But perhaps the best story of how Ftorek alienated himself from his players occurred when he scratched Ken Daneyko from the lineup in St. Louis so that the career-playing Devil couldn't record his 1,000th game a few nights later before New Jersey fans on October 27, 1999. It was a slight never forgiven in the Devils' dressing room.

17.14   B. Jacques Demers

It's not a disability that a coach could hide in today's game, but in Jacques Demers's time he found a way to fool everyone, including players, trainers, general managers and, for a while, even his wife. A Grade 8 dropout, Demers had taken many low-level jobs to care for his three younger siblings after his parents died a few years apart in the 1960s. He later turned to coaching to overcome his lack of education and to channel his anger from having an abusive father, he says in *Jacques Demers: Toutes en Lettres*, a biography written by Mario Leclerc. The charismatic Demers then worked around his illiteracy by bluffing his way through scouting reports, getting trainers to do his lineup sheets and writing big when signing autographs. Yet his literacy handicap never affected his coaching. Demers's 1,000-plus-game NHL career included two Jack Adams Awards as coach of the year with Detroit and a Stanley Cup with Montreal. He quit coaching in 1999 with a 409–467–130 record; his career playoff mark was a respectable 55–43.

17.15 **D. The Chicago Blackhawks**

After signing a three-year contract in February 2000 as assistant coach with Pittsburgh, Ivan Hlinka looked to be the replacement for the Penguins' Herb Brooks and the first born-and-bred European head coach in the NHL. Then Chicago director of hockey operations Mike Smith, no stranger to international hockey, hired Finnish native Alpo Suhonen in April 2000—just prior to Hlinka's appointment in Pittsburgh in June of that year. The hiring of two European-trained coaches after 82 years of NHL play (Russian-born Johnny Gottselig, who coached Chicago in the mid-1940s, was raised in Winnipeg) was long overdue and, like the arrival of European players, "broke new ground" as international coach Dave King said at the time. Why did it take so long to hire Europeans? Good question. Suhonen coached more than 1,500 games in Europe and 300 as an assistant coach in the NHL, and Hlinka, coach of the 1998 Czech Olympic gold-medal team, is credited with building his country's ice hockey program into one of the world's best.

17.16   D. The Montreal Canadiens

The Montreal Canadiens captured an unprecedented four of their record 24 Stanley Cups with rookie coaches, each Cup in successive decades between the 1950s and 1980s. The great Toe Blake coached just 70 games in the NHL before winning the Cup in 1955–56. Claude Ruel won 1968–69's championship after 76 games with the Habs; rookie Al MacNeil replaced Ruel with 55 games remaining in 1970–71 and won the Cup; and Jean Perron became Montreal's fourth Cup-winning rookie head coach after coaching 80 games in 1985–86. As of 2009, only 13 head coaches won the Stanley Cup as rookies, the most recent being Pittsburgh's Dan Bylsma in 2009.

17.17   D. Five coaches

During 1997–98, an epidemic of bench firings swept through the weak Atlantic Division, knocking out five coaches in the seven-team NHL division. Florida replaced Doug MacLean with Bryan Murray; Tampa Bay's Terry Crisp vacated the bench for Jacques Demers; Wayne Cashman was demoted by the Flyers to bring in Roger Neilson; the New York Rangers let go Colin Campbell for John Muckler, and the Islanders' Rick Bowness was replaced by Mike Milbury. The five firings in the Atlantic Division might be a record (if any statistics in this category were kept). Only one other coach was canned during the 1997–98 regular season. In the Pacific Division, the Vancouver Canucks hired Mike Keenan to replace Tom Renney.

17.18   C. Roger Neilson, by the Toronto Maple Leafs

As owner of the Maple Leafs, Harold Ballard can take credit for many fiascoes in his time, but few debacles compare to the outrageousness of the Roger Neilson firing-rehiring episode. After the club fell below .500 in February 1979, Ballard promised a TV audience that he would fire Neilson if the Leafs lost their next game. True to his word and blind in his arrogance, after Toronto bowed to Montreal, he fired Neilson—on TV. Unfortunately for the Leafs, however, Ballard had no replacement in mind, and after scout Gerry McNamara and AHL coach Eddie Johnston turned down the job, Ballard was forced to rehire Neilson. To save face and make it appear as if it was all a well-concocted hoax, Ballard instructed Neilson— through Leaf GM Jim Gregory—to appear behind the bench at the start of the next game wearing a paper bag over his head. At the appropriate dramatic moment, after the national anthem, Neilson was to come out and rip the bag off his head to reveal to the expectant Maple Leaf Gardens crowd the next coach of Toronto. As Toronto captain Darryl Sittler said in a *National Post* story, "I remember we were waiting to go on the ice for the start of the game, and Harold was standing at the dressing room door with the paper bag. As Roger walked by, Harold said, 'C'mon, c'mon, put it on.'" Neilson refused, and strode by Ballard to take his position behind the bench. The Leafs won the game. But at the end of the season, Neilson was once again fired.

17.19 A. Mario Tremblay, with the Montreal Canadiens

Who says you need experience? Despite having never previously coached pro hockey, Mario Tremblay earned a spot in the record books when Montreal defeated Boston 3–1 on October 31, 1995. The victory was Tremblay's sixth in a row, the longest winning streak at the start of an NHL coaching career. The previous mark of five was set by Bep Guidolin of the Bruins in 1973 and equalled by Marc Crawford of the Quebec Nordiques in 1994.

17.20 B. The Cincinnati Cyclones

Fights occur between opposing players, between opposing coaches, between coaches and referees, and even between coaches, players and fans. But no head coach had ever taken down a mascot until February 4, 1995. That's when the usually even-tempered Don Jackson, coach of the Cyclones, completely lost it after the Atlanta Knights' mascot "Sir Slap Shot" banged the glass partition separating the fans from the Cincinnati players. Jackson, leaning against the glass at the time, was knocked into his players, and seconds later, he climbed over the glass divider and began pummelling Sir Slap Shot. The IHL suspended Jackson for 10 games and fined him $1,000, the same fine levied against Atlanta (because of their mascot's conduct). The Knights won 7–2.

17.21 D. The St. Louis Blues

Following a 15-year NHL playing career, including his last four with St. Louis, Arbour moved behind the Blues' bench and notched a 42–40–25 record in 107 games from 1970–71 to 1972–73. He then scouted briefly for the Atlanta Flames before becoming the Islanders' third coach in 1973–74, and, within two years, New York was a playoff contender. Before the decade ended, Arbour was named 1979's NHL coach of the year, and the next season he won the Islanders' first of four-in-a-row Cups, in 1980, 1981, 1982 and 1983.

17.22 D. He had coached his 1,000th career game

Jacques Lemaire is one of the very few NHL coaches with long-term experience who has never been fired. He quit Montreal's bench after 97 games, plagued by the media locust swarm; resigned from New Jersey with 378 games and a Stanley Cup, and, currently, mentors in Minnesota, where he coached his 1,000th career game, a 3–2 win against Los Angeles, on

November 11, 2006. Yet the self-deprecating Lemaire, well known for his attention to detail, appeared oblivious to his milestone match—either that or he was just toying with the press when he said, "That's why I'm so tired." At the 1,000-game mark, his record stood at 423–348–129.

17.23 C. Bill Dineen

Dineen, with a record 554 WHA games (322–204–28), was the only bench boss to coach in every WHA season, guiding Houston from 1972–73 to 1977–78 and New England in 1978–79. Dineen also holds the distinction of being the only WHA coach to win two Avco Cups (for Houston, in 1974 and 1975). Later, in 1991, he became the head coach of the Philadelphia Flyers.

17.24 D. Bobby Kromm

Kromm took coach of the year honours for guiding the WHA Winnipeg Jets to the Avco Trophy in 1975–76 before moving to the Detroit Red Wings, where he copped his second coaching trophy, the NHL's Jack Adams Award, in 1977–78. Kromm's "think defense" team strategy worked well in both leagues. Although the Jets possessed great firepower, built around finesse players such as Bobby Hull, Kromm believed that "teams that give up the fewest goals usually claim first place more often than teams that score the most goals." And based on that strategy, he whittled the Jets' goals-against numbers down from 293 to 254 goals in 1974–75, their championship year. Then, in Detroit, Kromm took the cellar-dwelling Red Wings to second place in the Norris Division, while reducing the team's goals-against total from 309 to 266 in 1977–78, the year he won the Jack Adams Award.

17.25 B. Fred Shero, with the Philadelphia Flyers

Although Shero was the architect who put together the infamous brawling Flyers teams of the mid-1970s, he had long been a student and admirer of the Russian game. Just weeks after he coached Philadelphia to its first Stanley Cup in May 1974, for example, Shero attended a three-week course in Moscow on sport and physical education conducted by Soviet national coach Anatoly Tarasov. However, few, if any, of Tarasov's theories were ever used by Shero, whose approach to hockey he once candidly described as "controlled mayhem."

17.26 C. Nine coaches

Trigger-happy GMs made an all-time high nine in-season coaching changes during 1981–82 and 2000–01. Those who took the bullet in 2000–01: Craig Hartsburg (Anaheim), Pat Burns (Boston), Don Hay (Calgary), Alpo Suhonen (Chicago), Terry Murray (Florida), Alain Vigneault (Montreal), Butch Goring (New York Islanders), Craig Ramsay (Philadelphia) and Steve Ludzik (Tampa Bay). The highest number of new coaches league-wide at the start of a season was recorded in 1997–98, when 10 teams had new bosses behind the bench.

17.27 D. Jacques Lemaire

Jacques Lemaire coached only 97 games in Montreal, the team he won eight Stanley Cups with as a player, but in one of those games he inserted 19-year-old Patrick Roy in his first game. Roy, a prospect drafted 51st overall by Montreal in 1984, was called up from Granby of the Quebec Major Junior Hockey League as a backup against Winnipeg on February 23, 1985. To Roy's surprise, Lemaire then put him in after two periods in the 4–4 game. "Jacques Lemaire came into the dressing room and he said, 'Roy, get in the net,' " Roy recalled. "My English was not very good. I turned around and I looked at Guy Carbonneau. I said: 'Did he mention my name?' Carbo goes, 'Yeah, you're going in.' " Montreal won the game but Roy headed back to the minors before joining the team full-time in 1985–86—and leading the Canadiens to the Stanley Cup.

17.28 A. Fewer than 10 games

A dozen NHL coaches have led their teams to the Stanley Cup in their first season behind the bench, but the leader in this category is not a rookie coach. New Jersey's Larry Robinson worked for four years (328 games) in Los Angeles before returning to the Devils as an assistant coach in 1999–2000. (Robinson had first tenured as a Devils assistant coach under Jacques Lemaire.) With just eight games remaining in the season, New Jersey general manager Lou Lamoriello then fired head coach Robbie Ftorek and moved Robinson into the hot seat, where he gelled the underachieving Devils into Stanley Cup winners. The Devils went just 4–4–0 before the playoffs, but under Robinson they dismissed Florida in four games, Toronto in six, Philadelphia in seven and Dallas in six, including an extraordinary triple-overtime loss in Game 5 and a double-overtime Cup-clincher in Game 6. In the process, New Jersey became the first team in two decades (since the 1980 Islanders) to whip three 100-point teams en route to the Cup, while Robinson became the only NHL head coach to coach so few regular-season games with a team that went on to win the Stanley Cup. Ironically, just a year earlier, after a miserable final season in Los Angeles, Robinson was asked whether he planned to return behind the bench next season. He said: "Oh, yes, I love sleepless nights."

17.29 C. Patrick Roy, with the Colorado Avalanche

Bowman directed his comments at Patrick Roy in April 1998, after another mêlée erupted in the ongoing blood feud between Detroit and the Colorado Avalanche. This time the mayhem began when Colorado tough guys Jeff Odgers and Warren Rychel took on, amongst others, the Wings' Kirk Maltby, Martin Lapointe, Bob Rouse and Aaron Ward. With Lapointe on top of the Avs' Tom Fitzgerald, Roy moved in and briefly tried to intervene, before focussing his attention on centre ice and challenging Chris Osgood, who had left his crease and dropped his gloves. Osgood, two inches shorter and 15 pounds lighter than Roy, seemed reluctant at first, but the dare had been made. After the two duked it out, the fight ended with a pileup in front of the Detroit bench, with Osgood on top of Roy. The next day Bowman admonished Roy, stating that he was "kind of glad he [Roy] didn't win the Olympic medal because we wouldn't have heard the end of it." To which Roy shot back, "Isn't he a Canadian? I wonder what [Brendan] Shanahan and [Steve] Yzerman are thinking right now." Each side, including Osgood's mom, declared its man the victor in the goalie battle. The Detroit goalie left the ice to the chant of "Ozz-ie, Ozz-ie."

17.30 A. Philadelphia Flyers coach Fred Shero's
Bobby Clarke is often cited as the source of this gem, but he likely got it from the same individual who developed the search-and-destroy mindset of the Flyers during the 1970s: coach Fred Shero. Led by thugs Dave "the Hammer" Schultz, Andre "Moose" Dupont and Bob "Hound Dog" Kelly, the Broad Street Bullies perfected the art of strategic intimidation to become the first post-1967 expansion team to win the Stanley Cup. And in response to critics who accused the Flyers of playing too violently, Shero said, "If you keep the opposition on their butts, they don't score goals. If you want to see pretty skating, go to the Ice Capades."

17.31 B. A victory for the Buffalo Sabres
If two previous straight shutout losses were not incentive enough, winning one for their coach should have lit the Islanders' fire. Unfortunately, neither provided much motivation, and Ted Nolan's first visit to Buffalo after a nine-year

absence was spoiled by a 3–1 loss to the surging Sabres that set a new Islanders scoreless streak, 186:31. Still, Nolan had his club playing better than expected in 2006–07. "It's always nice to come back here," said Nolan, who won NHL coach of the year with Buffalo in 1997 and is one of the most beloved bench bosses in the Sabres' history. Fans cheered, and one sign read: "We wish you well Teddy… just not tonight"— far better treatment than they gave former Sabres forward Miroslav Satan, who was booed every time he touched the puck during the game.

17.32 D. Jean-Guy Talbot, with the New York Rangers

Talbot coached the Rangers for just one season. But more memorable than his win and loss record was his game attire—a sweatsuit and turtleneck that drew few raves in fashion-conscious New York. His players weren't impressed either, finishing 1977–78 with a 30–37–13 before losing the preliminary round of the playoffs. "I wore a sweatsuit because it was a job and I sweat," Talbot said in a *Montreal Gazette* story. "Look at baseball and football coaches. They don't wear a shirt and tie."

17.33 C. 59 years old

Scotty Bowman, at 69 years old, was the oldest coach in NHL history. But amongst rookies, Bill Dineen gets the golden cane—for being just a few years away from old-age security payments when, at age 59, he took over the helm of the Philadelphia Flyers in 1991–92. Dineen, who was born on September 18, 1932, played five NHL seasons, including two with the Stanley Cup-winning Detroit Red Wings during the 1950s; Toronto great George Armstrong was 58 when he was handed the reins of the Maple Leafs for one season, 1988–89. Several rookie coaches joined the NHL ranks in their early 50s, including Toronto's John Brophy in 1986–87 and the Rangers' Steve Stirling in 2003–04, both when they were 53 years old, and, most recently, Bruce Boudreau, at age 52, of the Washington Capitals in 2007–08.

17.34 A. Robbie Ftorek

Before graduating to the NHL, Robbie Ftorek of Needham, Massachusetts, was a bona fide star in the WHA. In 1976–77, he finished fourth in league scoring with a 46–71–117 record and earned MVP status, one of the first Americans in pro hockey to do so. And though the WHA standard of hockey was a level below the NHL calibre of play, he also made it in the NHL, though he never achieved similar offensive numbers once the two leagues merged. During his five WHA seasons, Ftorek chalked up an impressive four consecutive 100-point seasons in Phoenix and Cincinnati. His first century mark in 1975–76 was the first 100-point season for a U.S.-born player in pro hockey.

17.35 D. Tommy Ivan

Although Jack Adams is often credited with forming the Production Line (he put Sid Abel and Gordie Howe together), it wasn't until Tommy Ivan took over in 1947, in his coaching debut, that Ted Lindsay was tried as a left-wing linemate. It was a match made in hockey heaven. The line gelled into the league's most dominant offensive unit, with at least one member finishing first in the NHL scoring race for five successive years and, in 1949–50, the trio going 1–2–3 amongst all point-getters. The original Production Line played together until 1952, when Abel became player-coach with Chicago.

17.36 B. Ted Green

Oilers coach Ted Green was once one of the game's roughest players, but when he battled with St. Louis's Wayne Maki in

1969, the ex-Bruins defenseman met his greatest challenge. In Green's book *High Stick*, Phil Esposito describes what happened: "They were sparring over in the corner near the Bruins' goal, when Maki went down on one knee. He got right up and hit Greenie over the head with the hardest part of his stick—at the bend where the shaft joins the blade. Greenie was down when I reached him and he looked awful." Maki's stick had smashed Green's skull, driving bone chips into the area of the brain that controls speech and movement of the left arm and leg—in light of which, Green's subsequent comeback was extraordinary. Three delicate brain operations and 14 months of therapy later, Green was back skating on Boston ice. He ended his NHL playing career after the Bruins' 1972 Stanley Cup; Maki played until 1973.

17.37 B. Tom Webster, with the Los Angeles Kings
Webster was nailed for 12 games, the longest game-related suspension in league history for a coach, after showing his "displeasure" at a penalty call in November 1991 by hurling a player's stick at referee Kerry Fraser. The stick grazed Fraser's skates. But it wasn't the first tantrum for Webster, who was ejected three times the previous season, once for another bit of "sticky" business against Calgary, once for cursing at a referee and once for punching Doug Gilmour, a move that landed him a four-game suspension and $5,000 fine. Webster later called the Fraser incident "regrettable" and praised the referee for his "professionalism." During his 12-game absence, the Kings slipped from second to fifth in the Smythe Division.

17.38 B. During the 1940s
Only a few individuals have ever been a player-coach in NHL hockey. Boston defenseman Dit Clapper managed the dual role while he was captain of the Bruins during 1945–46 and

1946–47. And a few years earlier, Ebbie Goodfellow played his final two campaigns as Detroit coach Jack Adams's unofficial assistant, making fewer and shorter appearances on the ice, particularly after Adams was suspended indefinitely for accosting an official during the 1942 playoffs. Goodfellow first took over the helm with the Red Wings up 3–0 in the final series. But Toronto stormed back to stage playoff hockey's greatest comeback and claim the Stanley Cup. The following season, 1942–43, Goodfellow then played even more sparingly and scratched himself from the playoffs entirely, realizing, despite the previous spring's debacle against the Maple Leafs, that he could be more help behind the bench than on the ice. It proved the right decision. Detroit swept Boston 4–0 in the finals, and though Adams is often credited as the Cup-winning coach, etched in silver on the Cup's patina is "Ebbie Goodfellow Coach."

17.39 A. Under 30 years old

When the Washington Capitals hired Gary Green in November 1979, he was 26 years old, the youngest NHL bench boss ever. Already a Memorial Cup-winning coach with the Peterborough Petes, Green had only been coaching the Caps' farm team in Hershey for a month when he got the call from the big club. Green would coach for two and a half seasons in Washington, finishing just out of playoff contention in 1980 and 1981.

17.40 A. Mike Babcock, with the Detroit Red Wings

Is Mike Babcock the new Scotty Bowman? He had a decent record as Anaheim's head coach, but when Babcock moved to Hockeytown he registered an unprecedented three plus-50-win seasons with 58, 50 and 54 victories between 2005–06 and 2007–08. Not even Bowman, hockey's winningest bench boss, had that kind of early success.

Game 17

Hockey Crossword 3

Solutions are on page 566

ACROSS

1. Detroit's Steve _____
5. Detroit's Brendan _____
10. Calgary/St. Louis's Cory _____
11. Eric _____
12. Pittsburgh/Colorado's Darius _____
16. Ottawa's Radek _____
19. Toronto's Garry _____
20. Old-timer, retired in 1973, Montreal's Dave _____
21. 17-year veteran Murray _____
24. "_____ and grab" hockey
26. Edmonton _____
27. Colorado's Patrick _____
29. Old-time NYR goalie Chuck _____
30. Eight-year veteran Todd _____
31. Paper or electronic _____
35. One-time Florida goalie John _____
37. Abbreviation for overtime
39. Buffalo tough guy Rob _____

40. Retired Buffalo Sabre Mark _____
41. One-time Senator Wade _____

DOWN

1. Toronto's Dmitry _____
2. New Jersey's Patrik _____
3. Florida/St.Louis's Scott _____
4. _____ Broten
6. Brett _____
7. Gordie Howe's uniform, No. _____
8. From pucks to donuts, Tim _____
9. St. Louis's Tyson _____
13. Anaheim's Antti _____
14. NYI's John _____
15. _____ Apps Jr. and Sr.
17. Anaheim's Paul _____
18. NYR's Theo _____
22. 500-goal man Pat _____
23. 13-year veteran Uwe _____
25. Detroit D-man Chris _____
28. Don Cherry once called Pavel Bure this kind of animal

32. Buffalo's Miroslav _____
33. Old-timer, Toronto's _____ Bathgate

34. Bland colour
36. _____ Krupp
38. Old-timer _____ Van Impe

18

Lugging the Jug

I**T'S NOT OFTEN THAT** a son follows in the footsteps of his *mother* to become a Stanley Cup winner, but that's exactly what John Grahame did after winning the Cup as Nikolai Khabibulin's backup on the Tampa Bay Lightning in 2004. Grahame's mother, Charlotte, one of only a dozen women to have her name engraved on the Cup, was Colorado's director of hockey administration when the Avalanche won the Cup in 2001. This mother-son combination on the Cup is an NHL first.

Answers are on page 479

18.1   As of 2008, who has appeared in the most postseasons?
   A. Gordie Howe
   B. Larry Robinson
   C. Raymond Bourque
   D. Chris Chelios

18.2   Which New York Islander scored the overtime-series-winning goal against Washington during the 1987 playoff game known as the "Easter Epic"?
   A. Bryan Trottier
   B. Mike Bossy
   C. Brent Sutter
   D. Pat LaFontaine

18.3 As of 2008, what is the NHL record for most shutouts by a goalie in one playoff year?

A. Five shutouts

B. Six shutouts

C. Seven shutouts

D. Eight shutouts

18.4 Which NHLer has played in the most Stanley Cup finals games without winning the Cup?

A. Brad Park

B. Bruce MacGregor

C. Brian Propp

D. Dale Hunter

18.5 What is the longest span between Stanley Cup championships by a coach?

A. Nine years

B. 11 years

C. 13 years

D. 15 years

18.6 Prior to Wayne Gretzky, how many players earned the distinction of winning postseason scoring titles with two different teams?

A. None, Wayne Gretzky was the first

B. Only one player

C. Three players

D. Five players

18.7 Who was the first goalie to record 50 playoff wins in an NHL career?

A. Turk Broda

B. Glenn Hall

C. Jacques Plante

D. Terry Sawchuk

18.8 Who was the first goalie to record 50 playoff losses in an NHL career?

A. Terry Sawchuk

B. Glenn Hall

C. Gump Worsley

D. Johnny Bower

18.9 What is the NHL record for most goals scored by a player in one playoff season?

A. 15 goals

B. 17 goals

C. 19 goals

D. 21 goals

18.10 How many games did Roberto Luongo play before experiencing his first playoff match?

A. Less than 200 regular-season games

B. Between 200 and 300 regular-season games

C. Between 300 and 400 regular-season games

D. More than 400 regular-season games

18.11 Which third-line winger was the goal-scoring hero for the Montreal Canadiens when the club won the Stanley Cup in 1959?

A. Marcel Bonin

B. Claude Provost

C. Don Marshall

D. Phil Goyette

18.12 **How long did Toronto forward Jack McLean have to wait for his Stanley Cup ring after helping the Maple Leafs win the Stanley Cup in 1945?**

A. 57 hours

B. 57 days

C. 57 months

D. 57 years

18.13 **When Dallas's Jonathan Sim and Kirk Muller scored two goals 12 seconds apart in the 2000 finals, it tied an NHL record set in what year?**

A. 1935

B. 1955

C. 1975

D. 1995

18.14 **Which NHL superstar single-handedly tied the 12-second record for the two fastest goals in a playoff series?**

A. Bernie Geoffrion, with the Montreal Canadiens

B. Gordie Howe, with the Detroit Red Wings

C. Jean Béliveau, with the Montreal Canadiens

D. Ted Lindsay, with the Detroit Red Wings

18.15 **What NHL first did Chris Pronger produce during the 2006 Stanley Cup finals?**

A. The first shorthanded breakaway goal in finals history

B. The first penalty-shot goal in finals history

C. The first hat trick by a defenseman in finals history

D. The first game misconduct in finals history

18.16 Which coach is credited with first using regular line changes, a strategy he employed to help win the Stanley Cup in 1925?

A. Lester Patrick, with the Victoria Cougars
B. Eddie Powers, with the Toronto St. Patricks
C. Leo Dandurand, with the Montreal Canadiens
D. Percy Thompson, with the Hamilton Tigers

18.17 Which NHLer set a new playoff record for game-winning goals after Joe Nieuwendyk tied Joe Sakic's record of six in 1999?

A. Brett Hull, with the Dallas Stars, in 2000
B. Peter Forsberg, with the Colorado Avalanche, in 2002
C. Jamie Langebrunner, with the New Jersey Devils, in 2003
D. Brad Richards, with the Tampa Bay Lightning, in 2004

18.18 What is the longest span between the first and last Stanley Cup wins by a player?

A. 13 years
B. 16 years
C. 19 years
D. 22 years

18.19 Since 1967, which Stanley Cup-winning goalie has had the biggest difference in his goals-against averages between the regular season and the playoffs in which he won the Cup?

A. Patrick Roy, with the Colorado Avalanche
B. Chris Osgood, with the Detroit Red Wings
C. Rogatien Vachon, with the Montreal Canadiens
D. Cam Ward, with the Carolina Hurricanes

18.20 What is the greatest number of different teams a goalie has won a Stanley Cup with?
A. Two different teams
B. Three different teams
C. Four different teams
D. Five different teams

18.21 What is the fastest time in which a netminder gave up a goal in overtime in the playoffs? Name the goalie.
A. Nine seconds
B. 19 seconds
C. 29 seconds
D. 39 seconds

18.22 Who owns the longest shutout streak by a rookie in the playoffs?
A. Normie Smith in 1936, with Detroit
B. Brent Johnson in 2002, with St. Louis
C. Jean-Sébastien Giguère in 2003, with Anaheim
D. Ilya Bryzgalov in 2006, with Anaheim

18.23 How many times in history has an NHLer got his name on the Stanley Cup *without* playing for his team during the championship season?
A. It has never happened
B. Only once: Vladimir Konstantinov, with Detroit in 1998
C. On four occasions
D. More than five times

18.24 During the 2006 Stanley Cup playoffs, who scored the first overtime shorthanded goal in finals history?

A. Fernando Pisani, with Edmonton

B. Rob Brind'Amour, with Carolina

C. Eric Staal, with Carolina

D. Chris Pronger, with Edmonton

18.25 Which long-time NHL playoff record held by Maurice Richard did Joe Sakic break in 2006?

A. Most overtime goals in a career

B. Most overtime goals in one playoff year

C. Most overtime goals in one playoff series

D. All of the above

18.26 In 2001, Patrick Roy came within one minute and 41 seconds of breaking the mark for the longest span of shutout goaltending in the Cup finals. Which New Jersey player broke Roy's streak?

A. Bob Corkum

B. John Madden

C. Patrik Elias

D. Sergei Brylin

18.27 As of 2008, how old is the oldest player to win the Stanley Cup?

A. 38 years old

B. 42 years old

C. 46 years old

D. 52 years old

18.28 "Mighty Mouse" was the nickname of which 1954 Detroit Red Wings playoff hero?

A. Alex Delvecchio

B. Tony Leswick

C. Johnny Wilson

D. Marty Pavelich

18.29 During the 1976 playoffs, Reggie Leach equalled an NHL record by scoring five goals for the Philadelphia Flyers. What made Leach's effort doubly impressive?

A. He had an injured wrist

B. He had not slept the night before

C. He was wearing someone else's skates

D. He was drunk

18.30 During the 1999–2000 playoffs, New Jersey coach Larry Robinson blew up at his players in a tirade that is credited for inspiring the Devils to win the Stanley Cup. In which playoff series did Robinson explode in anger?

A. In the first playoff round against Florida

B. In the second playoff round against Toronto

C. In the third playoff round against Philadelphia

D. In the final playoff round against Dallas

18.31 Who is the only rookie to record double-digit goal totals in his first playoffs after playing fewer than 20 regular-season games?

A. Jeremy Roenick, with the Chicago Blackhawks

B. Pat Flatley, with the New York Islanders

C. Claude Lemieux, with the Montreal Canadiens

D. Dino Ciccarelli, with the Minnesota North Stars

18.32 What is the age of the oldest individual whose name is engraved on the Stanley Cup?

A. 67 years old

B. 77 years old

C. 87 years old

D. 97 years old

18.33 Which player in the 2006 playoffs joined the ranks of hockey legends Newsy Lalonde and Maurice Richard—the only NHLers to score all four or more of their team's goals in a playoff game?

A. Joffrey Lupul, with the Anaheim Mighty Ducks

B. Fernando Pisani, with the Edmonton Oilers

C. Patrick Marleau, with the San Jose Sharks

D. Rod Brind'Amour, with the Carolina Hurricanes

18.34 Which NHL goaltending record did Miikka Kiprusoff set during the 2004 playoffs?

A. Most minutes played in one postseason

B. Most shots faced in one postseason

C. Most shutouts in one postseason

D. Most losses in one postseason

18.35 Why was Sergei Fedorov's overtime goal in Game 6 of the 1992 Norris Division semifinals an historic NHL event?

A. It was the fastest overtime goal ever scored

B. It was the first shorthanded goal in overtime

C. It was the first time a video replay was used to decide a playoff game

D. It was the first overtime playoff goal scored on a penalty shot

18.36 What is the longest time one goalie has blanked the opposition in one playoff series?

    A. For less than 120 minutes of play

    B. For between 120 and 180 minutes of play

    C. For between 180 and 240 minutes of play

    D. For more than 240 minutes of play

18.37 Given that he retired in 1928, why is Boston goalie Hal Winkler's name on the Stanley Cup with the names of the Bruins' victorious 1929 team?

    A. He was the Bruins' manager in 1929

    B. Boston wanted to honour him

    C. The Cup engraver added Winkler's name by mistake

    D. He came out of retirement to play one game in the 1929 finals

18.38 What is the record for most points by a defenseman in a Stanley Cup finals game?

    A. Three points

    B. Four points

    C. Five points

    D. Six points

18.39 What is the greatest number of Stanley Cup losses by a team captain?

    A. Three Cup losses

    B. Four Cup losses

    C. Five Cup losses

    D. Six Cup losses

18.40 During the 2003 playoffs, who became the first player in 70 years to score an overtime goal on a five-on-three power play?

    A. Vincent Lecavalier, with the Tampa Bay Lightning

    B. Joe Sakic, with the Colorado Avalanche

    C. Todd Bertuzzi, with the Vancouver Canucks

    D. Marian Hossa, with the Ottawa Senators

18.41 Who was the first goalie to register two 60-save games in one postseason?

    A. Ed Belfour, with the Dallas Stars

    B. Olaf Kolzig, with the Washington Capitals

    C. Jean-Sébastien Giguère, with the Anaheim Mighty Ducks

    D. Martin Brodeur, with the New Jersey Devils

18.42 Who is the youngest player ever to lead the Stanley Cup playoffs in scoring?

    A. Howie Morenz, with Montreal, in 1924

    B. Andy Blair, with Toronto, in 1929

    C. Gordie Howe, with Detroit, in 1949

    D. Eric Staal, with Carolina, in 2006

18.43 Before his dramatic double overtime Stanley Cup win against the Dallas Stars in 1999–2000, what kind of overtime playoff streak did New Jersey's Martin Brodeur take into the game?

    A. Four straight wins

    B. Seven straight wins

    C. Four straight losses

    D. Seven straight losses

18.44 Who holds the NHL record for scoring the most points in a playoff year without reaching the Stanley Cup finals?

    A. Doug Gilmour, with the Toronto Maple Leafs

    B. Rick Middleton, with the Boston Bruins

    C. Denis Savard, with the Chicago Blackhawks

    D. Mario Lemieux, with the Pittsburgh Penguins

18.45 What is the NHL record for the most series-deciding overtime goals in a career?

    A. Two overtime goals

    B. Three overtime goals

    C. Four overtime goals

    D. Five overtime goals

18.46 What is the longest span between the first and last time the same individual had his name engraved on the Stanley Cup?

    A. 23 years

    B. 33 years

    C. 43 years

    D. 53 years

Lugging the Jug

Answers

18.1   **D. Chris Chelios**

In 24 regular seasons, Chris Chelios has participated in the playoffs a near-perfect 23 times—eclipsing Raymond Bourque's previous record of 21. The only postseason without Chelios between 1984 and 2008 was in 1998, when his Chicago Blackhawks finished ninth in the Western Conference. Still, while Chelios leads all greybeards in years, Gordie Howe remains the oldest player to compete in the playoffs. To match Howe, Chelios would have to play until he was 52—Howe's age in his last playoff game in 1980. But Chelios leads another playoff category as games-played leader. In 2008 he topped Patrick Roy's 247 with 260. Chelios won Cups with Montreal in 1986 and Detroit in 2002 and 2008.

18.2   **D. Pat LaFontaine**

New York Islander fans still recall where they were during the Easter Epic, and Pat LaFontaine knows this well, because fans never fail to remind him of his famous goal. It was the one he scored during a gruelling match that went into the fourth overtime of the seventh and deciding game against the Washington Capitals in April 1987. The game started on Saturday, April 18, and concluded just before 2 AM on the 19th, Easter Sunday. As for the Goal, it was New York's 57th shot. Near the Capitals' blue line, LaFontaine picked up a deflected puck that was on its edge, then spun around and drilled it through a maze of players. The shot streaked by a shot-blocking Rod Langway—and several other players—without changing direction and into the net past Bob Mason, who never saw it until it was too late. "It was the most memorable moment in my hockey life," LaFontaine later said.

18.3   **C. Seven shutouts**

The New Jersey Devils earned each of their three Stanley Cups with a winning combination of timely offense, killer defense and the stellar netminding of Martin Brodeur. During the 2003 playoff run, however, the hockey wasn't particularly entertaining or compelling, with the Devils' "D" choking the life out of its opponents with traps, dump-ins and dump-outs. But it won the day as Brodeur netted an unheard of seven shutouts in a 16-victory march to the Cup. Still, despite Brodeur's magnificent play, the Conn Smythe Trophy was awarded to playoff MVP and final series loser Jean-Sébastien Giguère, who recorded five shutouts with Anaheim. Brodeur had shutouts in each series: two against Boston, one versus Tampa Bay and Ottawa and three blankings of the Ducks in the final round.

18.4 B. Bruce MacGregor

Brad Park and Brian Propp are the first NHLers who come to mind when tallying the most frustrated NHLers without a Cup. Park's Hall of Fame career included numerous All-Star appearances and 161 postseason matches, but no silver chalice. Propp, at 160, managed one less playoff game than Park, but he has more goals (64) than any other postseason performer without a Cup. Although Dale Hunter has more to complain about than anyone, with 186 fruitless playoff games, he is a less likely choice considering he had one chance in a final— with Washington in 1998—during his lengthy 19-year career. The surprise is the Cup-less Bruce MacGregor, way back of the pack with 107 playoff contests but a league-high 30 appearances in the finals. MacGregor's string of frustrations began with his first career goal, a playoff game-winner that tied Detroit and Chicago 2–2 in the 1961 finals. The Blackhawks won the next two matches and the Cup, ushering in the MacGregor curse on playoff-bound teams. Each of his five finals series ended in failure, but earned MacGregor this dubious distinction after 24 final games with Detroit and six with New York. Propp is second with 29 and Norm Ullman has 28.

18.5 C. 13 years

After winning multiple Stanley Cups with Montreal, his last in 1979, Scotty Bowman was squeezed out of the organization in a front-office power play that left him bitter and determined to find another NHL job. It came in Buffalo. After seven seasons with the Sabres, Bowman then quit coaching and only returned in 1991–92 to lead Pittsburgh to its second straight championship. It had been 13 years since Bowman's last Cup victory in 1979. Dick Irvin knew drought better than most coaches, winning only four of 16 Cup finals. His longest stretch was 12 years between Cups: Toronto in 1932 and Montreal in 1944.

18.6   B. Only one player

Hockey statisticians went into overdrive researching the last time someone duplicated Gretzky's playoff feat of scoring titles with two different teams. Only one name came up. Hall of Famer Marty Barry shared the scoring derby lead with Boston in 1930 and led all playoff performers with Detroit in 1937. A polished stickhandler and policeman with Boston, Barry then caught the eye of Detroit GM Jack Adams, who acquired the tough centre in 1935. The Red Wings won successive Stanley Cups with Barry in 1936 and 1937. The Great One claimed five postseason scoring titles with Edmonton and his sixth and last in 1993 as a member of the Los Angeles Kings.

18.7   A. Turk Broda

Broda was early hockey's best money goalie. He appeared in 21 playoff series and won 15 of them, with Toronto racking up five Stanley Cups during his distinguished career, from 1937 to 1952. His overtime record was outstanding as well: 15 wins and eight losses. His 50th playoff victory, a league first, came in a 3–1 win against Detroit on April 10, 1949.

18.8   B. Glenn Hall

Only a handful of netminders have had the staying power
to withstand 50 playoff defeats, including Glenn Hall, who
became the NHL's first netminder with a 50-loss record when
his St. Louis Blues were defeated 2–1 in double overtime by
Philadelphia on April 16, 1968. Hall's Blues were swept by the
Montreal Canadiens during the finals, but Hall won the Conn
Smythe Trophy as playoff MVP. Mr. Goalie earned a playoff
record of 49 wins and 65 losses between 1956 and 1971. He
won one Stanley Cup, with Chicago, in 1961.

18.9   C. 19 goals

Reggie Leach won two successive Stanley Cups with
Philadelphia. But his finest playoffs came the following
year, in 1976, when the Flyers crashed and burned against
Montreal in the finals. Despite the Canadiens' sweep, Leach
was the best player on the ice and was honoured with the
Conn Smythe Trophy. His 19 goals in 16 games broke Newsy
Lalonde's legendary mark of 17 goals, set with Montreal in
1919, and he topped Maurice Richard's goal-scoring streak by
denting the twine in 10 consecutive games. Unlike Leach,
however, Jari Kurri's sizzling performance with Edmonton in
1985 was rewarded with the Stanley Cup. The Finnish winger
loaded up his 19-goal count against Chicago in the Conference
finals, where he scored 12 times and established a new mark
of three hat tricks, including one four-goal game. No player
has ever notched as many goals in one series, and Kurri did it
in six games—just one more match than Newsy Lalonde's
11 goals in five contests. But Kurri went cold in the finals, scoring only once in five games against Philadelphia. Remarkably,
both Leach and Kurri reached their records with virtually no
help from the power play. Leach had two goals and Kurri only
one, with the man-advantage.

18.10 D. More than 400 regular-season games

It took Roberto Luongo a league-record 417 games to get a taste of postseason, but he made up for lost time in his first start on April 11, 2007. It might also have been a case of "be careful what you wish for," except for the results. Luongo's Vancouver Canucks and Marty Turco's Dallas Stars battled through seven periods and 138-plus minutes of hockey before Henrik Sedin scored at 18:06 of the fourth overtime, the sixth-longest match in league history. The game dragged on for exactly five hours and 21 minutes, ending at 12:32 AM Pacific Daylight Time, with Bobby Lu facing a modern-day record of 76 shots and stopping 72 in the 5–4 Canucks win. "I got all the experience I needed in one game," Luongo said afterwards of the career-defining experience he categorized as the "most exhausted I've ever been." Amongst modern-era netminders, Luongo's herculean effort falls only one short of Kelly Hrudey's 73 saves on April 18, 1987, but leads all debuts by rookies (including Jean Sébastien Giguère's 63-save performance in April 2003) since the NHL began compiling shots on goal in 1956. The all-time leader is Detroit's Normie Smith, who stopped all 90 shots in his first playoff game, on March 24, 1936—the longest overtime in NHL history.

18.11 A. Marcel Bonin

With the awesome firepower of Jean Béliveau, Dickie Moore, Bernie Geoffion and brothers Maurice and Henri Richard on its scoring lines, it's hard to imagine any other Canadien getting sufficient ice time to compete for the playoff scoring race. But Marcel Bonin, a solid third-line winger without a goal in his 25-game playoff career, became just that hero when he subbed for an injured Maurice Richard during the 1959 playoffs. Vaulted onto Montreal's first line with Jean Béliveau and Dickie Moore (until Béliveau himself got injured), the left-shooting winger racked up 10 goals in 11 playoff games and led the Canadiens to their fourth straight Cup. The next-highest goal count that season was six goals. Montreal originally picked up Bonin for a song from Boston at the Inter-League Draft in 1957.

18.12 D. 57 years

Let's hope Maple Leaf fans don't have to wait as long to see their team win another Stanley Cup as McLean waited to receive his Cup ring. McLean played three seasons for Toronto during the 1940s, his last on 1944–45's Cup-winning team. But he only received his ring in August 2002, when the Toronto franchise decided to pay tribute to surviving players from championship seasons prior to 1948 (which was when the Maple Leafs first issued team rings to commemorate Cup wins). McLean was one of only nine players honoured. "I haven't been sleeping nights because I've been so excited about this," McLean, 79, said after slipping the ring on his finger for the first time. McLean's name had long been engraved on the Cup for the 1945 Cup win.

18.13 A. 1935

The fastest two goals scored by one team in final series action was first set on April 9, 1935 (and later tied by Montreal on April 7, 1955). In the 1935 game between Toronto and the Montreal Maroons, Baldy Northcott and Cy Wentworth scored 12 seconds apart—at 16:18 and 16:30 in period two—to give the Maroons a 3–1 lead that left "very little starch in Toronto," as one newspaper reported. Montreal won the game 4–1 and the Stanley Cup in three straight games to salt the best-of-five finals series. In the 2000 playoffs, Dallas's Jonathan Sim and Kirk Muller tied the 12-second record in their final series round against New Jersey, notching goals at 7:43 and 7:55 of the third period in the May 30 opening game, a shocker that saw the Stars trail 7–1 before the Sim and Muller goals. Dallas failed to generate any more offense, losing 7–3.

18.14 A. Bernie Geoffrion, with the Montreal Canadiens

The quickest time teammates have scored in finals history is 12 seconds (see above question), but one player has matched that mark. Bernie Geoffrion fired two goals 12 seconds apart in Game 3 of the Montreal–Detroit finals in 1955. Geoffrion's markers came at 8:30 and 8:42 of the first period on April 7, 1955, with the Canadiens beating the Wings 4–2, though they lost the Stanley Cup. Wayne Gretzky is runner-up (a rarity for the Great One), with two goals in 15 seconds against Philadelphia in May 1985.

18.15 B. The first penalty-shot goal in finals history

Chris Pronger's historic goal on a penalty shot during Game 1 of the 2006 finals received little attention after the match. But at the time it was seismic—giving Edmonton a 2–0 lead against Carolina at 10:36 of the second period. Pronger was awarded the penalty shot after referee Mick McGeough called Hurricanes defenseman Niclas Wallin for covering the puck in the crease. Edmonton coach Craig MacTavish then chose Pronger, who lumbered in on Cam Ward and snapped a 14-foot riser past the Carolina goalie. It was the ninth penalty shot awarded in finals history. All previous shots were unsuccessful.

18.16 A. Lester Patrick, with the Victoria Cougars

Lester Patrick is one of those hockey immortals whose contributions triggered major advancements in game play, organization and expansion of the sport. Throughout his career as a player, coach, manager and owner, Patrick also established numerous firsts, including a new strategy of line changes to beat the defending champion Montreal Canadiens during the 1925 finals. Obviously, Patrick knew that his aging team, though they had plenty of Cup experience, would be no match for the 60-minute men of Montreal, a team that had set endurance records the previous postseason by playing its regulars without substitution. So while most teams carried spares who rarely saw ice time, Patrick devised a novel strategy for his subs: line changes every two to three minutes with the regulars. "Who could stop Morenz, Joliat and Boucher?" Patrick later said. "Who could score on the great Vezina? But I knew we'd win because our second line would just tire them out, and it did." While games alternated between eastern and western rules, fatigue and frustration set in on the Montreal bench by Game 2, and the Canadiens managed just one win in the best-of-five series—with Victoria soundly defeating its eastern foe 3–1. Patrick's on-ice tactics had won the day, and the Cougars captured the Cup. The proud era of the 60-minute man was history. (Prior to the 1927–28 season, the NHL passed a rule that allowed players to change on the fly.)

18.17   D. Brad Richards, with the Tampa Bay Lightning, in 2004
The pride of Murray Harbour, Prince Edward Island, Brad Richards earned his Conn Smythe Trophy in 2004 with an MVP-worthy performance, scoring a postseason-leading 26 points that included 12 goals and a record-setting seven game-winners. Richards's uncanny talent for scoring the goals that matter most began in Game 3 of the first round against the New York Islanders. He then scored the deciding goals in Games 3 and 4 of the second-round sweep of Montreal and Games 1 and 5 against Philadelphia in the Tampa Bay's first Conference finals. In the Cup's final series, he tied Joe Sakic's record of six game-winners in the Lightning's 4–1 win in Game 2 and netted his record seventh in Game 4, when Tampa

Bay evened the series at two in its 1–0 win against Calgary. Richards also led all players in the playoffs in average ice time per game, with 23:28.

18.18   D. 22 years

In Stanley Cup history, two players have won championships 22 years apart: early era forward Lester Patrick and modern-day marathon man Chris Chelios. But there's a great big asterisk next to Patrick's name, considering the heroics he displayed as coach of the New York Rangers during the 1928 Cup finals by strapping on the blood- and sweat-stained pads of injured Ranger goalie Lorne Chabot. After losing Chabot to an eye injury midway through Game 2, the 44-year-old Patrick took over between the pipes and stopped all but one shot through two periods and sudden-death overtime. The Rangers won 2–1 and eventually defeated the Montreal Maroons for their first Cup in franchise history. Of course, while Patrick's stint in net marked the last time he played and won a Cup, it is unofficial, considering he was a head coach filling in for his injured netminder. But it did happen 22 years after his first championship as a star forward with the Montreal Wanderers in 1906. Chelios, on the other hand, decided to have a Gordie Howe-like career with the champion Detroit Red Wings. After winning the 2008 Cup, he equalled Patrick's long-standing mark with his own 22-year spread, bookended by Cups in 1986 and 2008.

18.19   D. Cam Ward, with the Carolina Hurricanes

A few goalies in NHL history have cut their regular-season goals-against averages by as much as one goal during the playoffs, but Rogatien Vachon and Cam Ward have dropped the greatest amount since 1967. Splitting Montreal's goaltending duties with Gump Worsley in 1968–69, Vachon lowered his 2.87 average in 36 regular-season matches to 1.42 in eight playoff games, a drop of almost one and a half goals per game, though Ward did slightly better than Vachon in 2005–06. After playing backup to the Hurricanes' Martin Gerber for 28 games and registering an average of 3.68 during the regular season, Ward turned in a Conn Smythe-MVP-winning performance during postseason, winning Carolina its first Cup and slicing his goals-against average to 2.14.

18.20 B. Three different teams

Although a few modern goalies, such as Patrick Roy, have succeeded in leading two different teams to the Stanley Cup, no one can match Harry "Hap" Holmes's four championships with three NHL clubs. During his 17-year career, the journeyman goalie played in four pro leagues, winning four Cups with the 1914 Toronto Blueshirts, the 1917 Seattle Metropolitans, the 1918 Toronto Arenas and the 1925 Victoria Cougars. Holmes's versatility and "nerveless" cage work earned him Hall of Fame status and his name on the American Hockey League's top goalie award, the Hap Holmes Memorial Trophy.

18.21 A. Nine seconds

On May 18, 1986, Calgary's Mike Vernon was beaten just nine seconds into overtime on a goal by Brian Skrudland, resulting in a 3–2 Canadiens victory. The goal, scored in Game 2 of the Stanley Cup finals, set a new record for the fastest overtime goal (and shortest overtime period) in playoff history, passing the old mark of 11 seconds established by Jean-Paul Parise of the New York Islanders in 1975.

18.22 D. Ilya Bryzgalov in 2006, with Anaheim

George Hainsworth's legendary playoff shutout streak has
had real estate in the NHL record books since he set down
stakes with 270 minutes and eight seconds in 1930. Contenders
such as old-time puckstoppers Dave Kerr (248:35) and Normie
Smith (248:32) have taken their legitimate run, but, until
Ilya Bryzgalov, no one in 75 years of playoff action has come
as close to claiming hockey's greatest postseason shutout
record. For that, Hainsworth can thank Colorado's Dan
Hinote. Bryzgalov's streak began after Stephane Yelle scored
Calgary's lone goal at 10:18 of the first period on May 1 and
ended on Hinote's late first-period goal at 19:33 on May 9, a
shutout sequence of 249 minutes and 15 seconds. Bryzgalov
fell agonizingly short of Hainsworth by 20:53, or roughly, a
period of hockey. But the Russian rookie actually came much
closer. After Hinote's goal, Bryzgalov held Colorado until
Jim Dowd scored at 4:47 of the third period. Had Bryzgalov
denied Hinote, he would have passed Hainsworth's record by
more than four minutes, breaking the long-standing mark.
As it is, Bryzgalov's 249:15 established a new rookie mark.
Unfortunately, though the league recognizes goal- and point-
scoring feats by rookies, it still does not acknowledge the
accomplishments of freshmen goalies such as Bryzgalov.

Longest Shutout Sequence in One Playoff Year*

LENGTH	GOALIE	TEAM	DATES
270:08	George Hainsworth	Montreal	March 28 to April 3, 1930
249:15	Ilya Bryzgalov	Anaheim	May 1 to May 9, 2006
248:35	Dave Kerr	New York Rangers	March 25 to April 6, 1937
248:32	Normie Smith	Detroit	March 24 to 28, 1936
218:42	Gerry McNeil	Montreal	March 27 to 31, 1951
217:54	J.S. Giguère	Anaheim	May 5 to 16, 2003

*Current to 2008

18.23 D. More than five times

Vladimir Konstantinov is the most recent player to have his name etched in silver, despite being inactive during a championship season. The Russian defenseman was considered Detroit's spiritual leader in 1997–98, and the team's Cup win was a tribute to him—after his career was abruptly terminated by a car accident the previous spring. In an emotional ceremony at centre ice, captain Steve Yzerman passed the Cup to the wheelchair-bound Konstantinov, then the entire team wheeled him around the rink in celebration. A few other teams have honoured inactive players with Cup inscriptions, including the Montreal Canadiens, who recognized goalies Richard Sevigny (1979) and Ernie Wakely (1965 and 1968), even though they hadn't played a shift all year. (In Wakely's case, he did suit up in two career games for Montreal, one in 1962–63 and the other in 1968–69. His two championships for two games' worth of work must be the best Cups-per-game average by a player on one team.) And in 1929, the Boston Bruins favoured retired goalie Hal Winkler with Cup status despite the fact that he was replaced in nets by Tiny Thompson the preceding season. The Bruins also added the names Ted Green and John Adams to the Cup's gleaming patina in 1970. Green had been sidelined the entire season with a fractured skull, and Adams was the Bruins' third goalie, a minor-leaguer in Oklahoma City who didn't see NHL action until 1972–73.

18.24 A. Fernando Pisani, with Edmonton

Hometown hero Fernando Pisani scored a playoff-high five game-winners during Edmonton's improbable 24-game Cup run in 2006, but his most important game-winner came in Game 5 against Carolina with his team down 3–1 in the series. At 3:03 of overtime, Edmonton looked in deep trouble. Moments earlier, the Hurricanes' Michael Peca had rung a shot off the post and Oilers defenseman Steve Staios has been called for tripping, giving Carolina the man-advantage and a huge opportunity to win the game and claim the Cup. But Cory Stillman's cross-ice breakout pass failed to reach Eric Staal, when, moving in to disrupt the play, Pisani performed a little miracle. "The puck was kind of going slow and I decided to go for it. [Staal] has a long reach, and I got my stick on it as well. It hit me in the chest, and all of a sudden I looked up and I've got a breakaway on the goalie." Carolina goalie Cam Ward cheated on his blocker side, so Pisani shot it in at the top half of the net, glove side. The breakaway goal was the first over-time shorthanded goal in finals history and the first of its kind to prevent a team from being eliminated. Final score: 4–3.

18.25 A. Most overtime goals in a career

When Maurice Richard retired in 1960, he held an amazing eight of the 14 playoff records available to scorers. Almost 50 years later, however, his legendary collection has shrunk to include just a few shared marks, and his achievements as hockey's most dominant clutch performer have all but disappeared from the books. The last record Richard owned outright was finally broken on April 24, 2006, by Joe Sakic, when the Colorado sniper scored his seventh career overtime goal against Dallas's Marty Turco. The goal ended the Rocket's 46-year reign as the all-time leader of six extra-period tallies. Sakic scored on a tip-in off a John-Michael Liles slap shot from the point at 4:36 of overtime in the 5–4 Colorado win. It was Sakic's 79th goal in 12 playoff seasons. Richard's career-high 82-playoff-goals record has long since been broken several times.

18.26 A. Bob Corkum

Patrick Roy entered Game 2 of the 2001 Stanley Cup finals against New Jersey riding a streak of 213 minutes and 12 seconds of shutout hockey in the finals. He hadn't been scored on since Game 3 of the 1996 finals. Roy needed to blank the Devils for 16 minutes and 11 seconds to snap the all-time mark of 229:22 set by Clint Benedict between 1923 and 1926. But Roy's run at the record came up 1:41 short, when he was beaten through the five-hole by Bob Corkum, who had just helped kill off a Devils penalty. Corkum was a surprise starter, having been added to the lineup to replace injured winger Randy McKay.

18.27 C. 46 years old

The 2008 Stanley Cup proved to be a watershed year for playoff records by elder statesmen on skates. Detroit's championship broke both of Johnny Bower's marks—as the oldest goalie and player on a Cup-winner—with Dominik Hasek and Chris Chelios setting new standards in each category. And while there is an argument that would support New York coach Lester Patrick (who at age 44 replaced his injured netminder for two periods in the Rangers' 1928 Cup win) as the oldest Cup-winning player, his case is iffy, considering he did it as a former forward replacing an injured goalie on a team he coached. Nevertheless, the Red Wings settled all that in 2008. Bower, age 42 years nine months when the Toronto Maple Leafs won their last championship in 1967, gave up his 41-year NHL reign in 2008 to Hasek, 43 years five months old at the time, and to Chelios, then 46 years five months old. Chelios is the oldest U.S.-born player in NHL history.

18.28 B. Tony Leswick

Tony Leswick, who died of cancer at age 79 in July 2001, is best remembered as the scoring hero of the 1954 Stanley Cup finals. Although he usually played a checking role with the Red Wings, on April 16, 1954, Leswick scored the winning goal against Montreal in the seventh game in overtime. Leswick's Cup-clincher was no work of art, though. Near the end of his first shift in the extra period, he flipped the puck into the Canadiens' zone, then watched in amazement as it deflected off defenseman Doug Harvey's arm and past goalie Gerry McNeil. The diminutive but feisty winger, who was nicknamed "Mighty Mouse," stood five foot six and weighed 160 pounds.

18.29 **D. He was drunk**

On May 6, 1976, Philadelphia Flyers winger Reggie Leach scored five goals in a 6–3 win over the Boston Bruins in Game 5 of the semifinals. The stunning performance was even more remarkable considering that Leach was, by his own admission, "stone drunk." As described in the book *When the Final Buzzer Sounds,* Leach had gotten hammered the night before and only made the rink that afternoon thanks to two teammates, who went to his house and revived him from a drunken stupor with a cold shower and a quart of coffee. After this treatment, Leach decided that his best chance of making it through the Sunday matinee was to have a few more drinks. With a few fresh beers in his system, he then arrived at the Spectrum feeling "really loose." Leach told line-mate Bobby Clarke, "Just get me the puck. I'll put it in." Two hours later, the Flyers had posted a 6–3 victory, Leach had matched the record for most goals in a playoff game and the Bruins were gone from the playoffs.

18.30 **C. In the third playoff round against Philadelphia**

After a 3–1 Game 4 loss to the Flyers during the Conference finals—a game that put New Jersey down 3–1 in the series—Larry Robinson blew a fuse and exploded in an uncharacteristic fit, yelling at players and kicking over garbage cans in the Devils' dressing room. But Robinson's outburst, known as "The Tirade" in the media, became the catalyst that regrouped the slumping Devils, who went on to beat Philadephia and ultimately defeat Dallas to win the Stanley Cup. Robinson refused to take credit for the championship, however, stating over and over: "It isn't about me. It's about the players." But the Devil players, to a man, didn't believe they would have won the Cup if not for Robinson. "He's honest. It's hard to find a man in hockey like that, but that's why we love to play hard for him," said Bobby Holik.

18.31 C. Claude Lemieux, with the Montreal Canadiens

Lemieux's fame as a playoff standout was well-established long before 1994–95, when he doubled his regular-season goal count of six goals to score 13 playoff markers during New Jersey's Stanley Cup run. In fact, his reputation was established in his rookie year, 1985–86, when Lemieux, after just one goal in 10 regular-season games, surprised everyone with 10 goals in 20 postseason games. The result: Montreal won its 23rd Stanley Cup and Lemieux was the playoff sensation. Ciccarelli leads all rookies with 14 goals (1981) and Roenick is second with 11 goals (1991), but neither played as few regular-season games in his rookie year as Lemieux. Roenick had 78 games of experience and Ciccarelli had 32 games against Lemieux's 10-game total.

18.32 C. 87 years old

Chris Chelios, with Detroit, may be the oldest player to win the Stanley Cup (at age 46). But the oldest person to get his name etched on it is Wally Crossman, who worked in the Detroit dressing room for half a century—dating back to the early years of the Olympia. Crossman was a rink rat and hung around the old arena so much that the Red Wings offered him a job as stick boy. His name is on the Cup four times between 1951 and 1998—the last time as dressing room assistant, when he was 87 years old.

18.33 A. Joffrey Lupul, with the Anaheim Mighty Ducks

Let's face it, Joffrey Lupul isn't likely to ever garner the kind of greatness bestowed on Hall of Famers Newsy Lalonde or Maurice Richard. Maybe it's the name. Pronounced forwards or backwards, "Lupul" just doesn't have a regal ring to it. Yet after the night of May 9, 2006, when he potted all four of Anaheim's goals in a 4–3 overtime win against Colorado, Lupul can lay claim to some fame because he duplicated what only Lalonde and Richard had managed previously: scoring all four, or more, of his team's goals in a single playoff contest. (Lalonde recorded four goals in a 4–2 victory against Seattle on March 22, 1919; 25 years later, on March 23, 1944, Richard notched five tallies in a 5–1 match over Toronto.) Lupul can also tuck in another little accolade for immortality's sake. He is the first player in playoff history to cap a four-goal night with an overtime score. After the match, Lupul said he hadn't scored four times in a game since junior hockey.

18.34 A. Most minutes played in one postseason

The trade that sent Miikka Kiprusoff from San Jose to Calgary on November 16, 2003, was the spark that the struggling Flames needed to make the playoffs for the first time in seven years. Thanks to the Finnish-born netminder's heroics, Calgary upset Vancouver and Detroit and advanced to the 2004 Stanley Cup finals before losing to Tampa Bay in seven games. Along the way, Kiprusoff set a new NHL record by playing 1,655 minutes in 26 postseason games, breaking the former mark of 1,544 minutes jointly held by Ed Belfour and Kirk McLean. Kiprusoff finished the 2004 playffs with 15 wins, 11 losses, a 1.86 GAA and five shutouts.

18.35 **C. It was the first time a video replay was used to decide a playoff game**

In overtime of Game 6 of the Detroit–Minnesota divisional semfinal, the Wings' Sergei Fedorov wired a shot past Stars netminder Jon Casey that appeared to ricochet off the crossbar. After a stoppage in play, referee Rob Shick consulted with video replay supervisor Wally Harris, who determined that the puck *had* entered the net, giving the Wings a 1–0 victory. It was also an historic goal for another reason—it was the first time a Russian-trained player had scored an overtime goal in the playoffs.

18.36 **D. For more than 240 minutes of play**

Norm Smith may not be remembered today, but in 1936 no one could stop talking about his 248:32 shutout sequence during the Red Wings—Maroons semifinal series. Smith's record began on March 24 in Game 1 as Detroit battled Montreal through three regulation periods until 16:30 of the *sixth* overtime period, when the Red Wings' Mud Bruneteau scored on Maroon goalie Lorne Chabot. The 176:30 minutes not only marked the longest game in playoff history, but the longest overtime shutout at 116:30. Smith then continued his streak through three more periods of Game 2, zeroing Montreal 3–0. Finally, at 12:02 of Game 3, Gus Marker scored on Smith, stopping the clock on his record: 248 minutes and 32 seconds of shutout hockey, a playoff record that may never be broken. It's also worth noting that, though Smith's record does not beat George Hainsworth's famous shutout sequence of 270:08 in 1930, unlike Hainsworth, Smith did it against one opponent in one series (Hainsworth managed it in two rounds) and, most remarkably, he was a playoff rookie.

18.37 B. Boston wanted to honour him

Hal Winkler is probably the oldest individual to begin a pro hockey career, given that he didn't play pro hockey until age 30, when he backstopped the WCHL Edmonton Eskimos in 1922. After the western-based league folded in 1926, he then landed in New York and Boston, playing almost two years for the Bruins before retiring at age 36. Interestingly, however, Winkler's last season was his best. He led the NHL in minutes played (2,780) and tied the great Alex Connell for most shutouts (15), leaving the game on top with a sparkling 1.59 GAA—or so he thought. In his retirement year, the Bruins, with rookie goalie Tiny Thompson, led the American Division and then beat the Rangers for the coveted Stanley Cup. Yet despite no games played that season, Boston felt Winkler deserved some credit, so they included him in the team's championship picture and added his name on the Cup: "Hal Winkler, sub-goaltender."

18.38 C. Five points

For his brief NHL tenure of just 26 regular-season games and 11 more in playoff action, little-known Eddie Bush garnered some fame—most notably for his 43 years as the league's leader amongst defenseman, with five points in a playoff game. Paul Coffey's six-pointer changed all that in May 1985, but Bush still shares the lead in final series play. Remarkably, amongst those half-dozen players are forwards Sid Abel, Toe Blake and Jari Kurri; Bush is the only rearguard. His date with destiny came on April 9, 1942, when he scored one goal and four assists to figure in every Detroit goal of a 5–2 win against Toronto. It would be the last time the Red Wings won in the round. They took a commanding 3–0 series lead—only to tank in the next four contests, handing the Maple Leafs the most incredible comeback in Stanley Cup history.

18.39 B. Four Cup losses

Butch Bouchard holds the distinction of captaining more losing teams in the Stanley Cup finals than any other captain
in league history. Bouchard wore the "C" with the Montreal
Canadiens for eight seasons from 1948–49 to 1955–56, winning
two championships in 1953 and 1956, but losing to Toronto in
1951 and Detroit in 1952, 1954 and 1955.

18.40 A. Vincent Lecavalier, with the Tampa Bay Lightning

In a playoff series filled with bizarre penalties, including a
too-many-men-on-the-ice call during triple overtime and a
four-minute high-sticking penalty on goalie Olaf Kolzig, one
might expect a penalty-goal combination that only comes
along every 70 years. With Washington's Jaromir Jagr (roughing) and Ken Klee (elbowing) in the penalty box, Vincent
Lecavalier fired in a rebound at 2:29 of overtime to give the
Lightning a 4–3 win against Washington. Lecavalier's winner came in Game 3 of the Conference quarterfinals on April
15, 2003. It was the first five-on-three playoff overtime goal
since April 13, 1933, when New York's Bill Cook scored in the
extra period with a two-man advantage against Toronto. (Alex
Levinsky and Bill Thoms were the penalized Maple Leafs.)
Cook's goal won the Rangers their second Stanley Cup.

18.41 C. Jean-Sébastien Giguère, with the Anaheim Mighty Ducks

During the 2003 playoffs Giguère put on a clinic for backstop-
pers. His Mighty Ducks swept the defending Stanley Cup
champion Detroit Red Wings in the first round and then
took a commanding 2–0 lead over the Dallas Stars in the next
series. In those 18 days Giguère was undefeated, winning all
six by one-goal margins. Four games had been decided in
overtime. And in two contests, the Ducks' playoff rookie kept
the fairy tale alive with two 60-save performances: 63 saves

in a 2–1 triple-overtime win against Detroit on April 10 and
60 saves in a 4–3 marathon game that took five overtime
periods to decide on April 24. The six-foot-one Giguère lost
"10 to 15 pounds" in the Dallas game, which turned into the
fourth-longest overtime game in playoff history. Anaheim's
Petr Sykora, who scored the winner at 80:48 of overtime, ate
seven Power Bars during the epic battle, and most players
from both teams changed gloves, skates, sweaters, socks and
T-shirts between periods. Dallas defenseman Sergei Zubov
logged 64 minutes of ice time, the most amongst skaters, and
Adam Oates, the oldest player in the game at age 40, played 39
minutes. At least 10,000 fans were still in the stands when the
game ended at 12:36 AM Dallas time.

18.42 C. Gordie Howe, with Detroit, in 1949

One of the best stories from the 2006 playoffs was the stellar play of sophomore Eric Staal, who averaged better than
a point per game to lead Carolina to the Stanley Cup. Staal
scored 28 points in 25 playoff games to became one of only
four 21-year-olds to lead all postseason scorers in NHL annals—
the youngest since Gordie Howe topped all point-earners in
1949 and the third-youngest of all time. Howe was 21 years
and 16 days old, followed closely by Toronto's Andy Blair at
21 years and 32 days of age in 1929. Neither Howe nor Blair,
however, won the Cup during their postseasons. Staal was
21 years and 233 days old, Howie Morenz 21 years and 277 days
old in 1924. Remarkably, Howe is also the oldest playoff scoring leader, topping all shooters with 19 points in 1964. He was
36 years old.

18.43 D. Seven straight losses

When the Devils won the Stanley Cup in 2000, goalie Martin
Brodeur clinched the Cup by outduelling Dallas netminder

Ed Belfour in a double-overtime heart-stopper that ended on Jason Arnott's goal at 28:20 of overtime. That win ended Brodeur's personal streak of seven consecutive playoff over-time losses dating back to May 26, 1995. In fact, prior to winning the Devils' second Stanley Cup in 2000, Brodeur had won only three overtime games in 14 postseason matches since his rookie year, 1993–94.

18.44 A. Doug Gilmour, with the Toronto Maple Leafs

Gilmour's valiant efforts in the 1993 playoffs failed to pro-pel the Maple Leafs to the Cup finals, but he did establish a milestone for most points by a player who failed to reach the final series. The Leafs waged three seven-game series in 1993 and Gilmour collected 35 points in 21 games to break Rick Middleton's record of 33 points, set in 17 games with the Boston Bruins in 1983.

Most Playoff Points Without Reaching the Cup Finals

PLAYER	YEAR	TEAM	GP	G	A	POINTS
Doug Gilmour	1993	Toronto	21	10	25	35
Rick Middleton	1983	Boston	17	11	22	33
Barry Pederson	1983	Boston	17	14	18	32
Denis Savard	1985	Chicago	15	9	20	29
Doug Gilmour	1994	Toronto	18	6	22	28

Current to 2008

18.45 B. Three overtime goals

Had Martin Gelinas lived 100 years ago he might have been a hired gun in the Old West. Before signing with Florida in 2005, he played on Stanley Cup finalists with every team that sought his services except Quebec. Based on his postseason record with Edmonton, Vancouver, Carolina and Calgary, one could argue Gelinas is the ultimate playoff triggerman, a reliable third-liner who provides momentum-changing shifts with his energy and work ethic and a role player able to grind it out or fill in on better lines in case of injuries. Gelinas notched final appearances with the Stanley Cup-winning Oilers in 1990, the Canucks in 1994, the Hurricanes in 2002 and the Flames in 2004. But his one Cup aside, it is what he did in 2002 and 2004 that shines on his resumé. Gelinas took Carolina to the finals after knocking off Toronto with his Conference-finals winner in overtime. Then, in 2004, Calgary eliminated Vancouver in the first round and Detroit in the second thanks to overtime winners by Gelinas. He is the first and only NHLer to end three playoff series with overtime goals.

18.46 D. 53 years

Marcel Pronovost has had a long and rewarding association with the game. He won five Stanley Cups as a hard-hitting defenseman with Detroit and Toronto—beginning in 1950, when he was called up during the playoffs to replace Red Kelly on the Red Wings' blue line. And when Detroit won the Stanley Cup, Pronovost's name was etched in silver without him playing a single regular-season game. During his career, Pronovost would never take home any individual awards, but he was named to All-Star teams on four occasions. After retiring in 1970, he coached junior hockey and scouted for the NHL's Central Scouting Bureau. He then landed a scouting job with New Jersey and saw his name on the Cup three more times, after the Devils won championships in 1995, 2000 and 2003, more than a half-century after Pronovost's first Cup celebration.

Game 18

Chris Who?

FOR EVERY VINCENT LECAVALIER of Tampa Bay or Martin Brodeur of New Jersey, there are dozens of champions like Chris Dingman, who win the Stanley Cup but rarely get the ink or air time of their high-profile teammates. In this game, all of the Cup-winners in the left column played with their respective championship clubs for the majority of the regular and postseason, including Dingman with his two-Cup performances in 2001 and 2004. Try to match them with their Cup-winning teams on the right.

Solutions are on page 567

PART 1

1. _C_ Chris Dingman
2. _E_ Jiri Fischer
3. _F_ Kevin Haller
4. _D_ Hector Marini
5. _B_ Troy Loney
6. _A_ Craig Muni

A. Edmonton Oilers, 1988
B. Pittsburgh Penguins, 1992
C. Tampa Bay Lightning, 2004
D. New York Islanders, 1982
E. Detroit Red Wings, 2002
F. Montreal Canadiens, 1993

PART 2

1. _D_ Colin Patterson
2. _B_ Ace Bailey
3. _E_ Dave Reid
4. _F_ Jay Pandolfo
5. _A_ Dan Hinote
6. _C_ Brian Noonan

A. Colorado Avalanche, 2001
B. Boston Bruins, 1972
C. New York Rangers, 1994
D. Calgary Flames, 1989
E. Dallas Stars, 1999
F. New Jersey Devils, 2003

19

True or False Stanley Cup

WHEN RAY BOURQUE BLASTED a shot past New Jersey Devils goalie Martin Brodeur in the third period of Game 3 of the 2001 Stanley Cup finals, the 40-year-old defenseman became the oldest player to score in the finals. *True or False?* Yes, it's true, but is Bourque still the oldest NHLer to score in finals action? Nope. On June 8, 2002, Detroit's Igor Larionov scored twice against Carolina, including a triple-overtime marathon goal in Game 3. Larionov scored the game-winner on a beautiful rush, with a deke past Bates Battaglia and then a slick backhand upstairs behind Arturs Irbe. It came at 54:47 into overtime. Not bad for the oldest guy on the ice. Two nights later, on June 10, the "professor" broke his own NHL finals record with another goal against the Hurricanes. He was 41 years and six months old.

Answers are on page 509

19.1 The last goalie to win the Stanley Cup without wearing a mask played for the same NHL club that iced the first goalie to win the Cup wearing a mask. *True or False?*

19.2 When Brennan Evans joined Calgary during the 2004 playoffs, he became just the second player to appear in postseason without ever playing in the regular season. The only other player to do this is TV hockey personality Don Cherry. *True or False?*

19.3 Stanley Cup finalists have never both failed to make the playoffs the following year. *True or False?*

19.4 Curtis Joseph has appeared in more playoff games than any goalie in NHL history who has not won a Stanley Cup. *True or False?*

19.5 The first European-trained player to win the Stanley Cup came from the former Soviet Union. *True or False?*

19.6 Stanley appears more often on the Stanley Cup than any other family name. *True or False?*

19.7 Besides Mike Bossy, only one other player in NHL history has scored back-to-back Stanley Cup-winning goals. *True or False?*

19.8 As of 2009, Patrick Roy holds the NHL record for most career shutouts in the playoffs. *True or False?*

19.9 No brothers have ever captained Stanley Cup champions. *True or False?*

19.10 No individual has his name on both the Stanley Cup and the Canadian Football League's Grey Cup as a player. *True or False?*

19.11 Since Toronto and Montreal met in the Stanley Cup finals in 1967, only one all-Canadian Cup finals has occurred. *True or False?*

19.12 Former U.S. president Bill Clinton and former Canadian prime minister Jean Chretien made a bet on the outcome of the 1998 Eastern Conference semifinal between the Washington Capitals and the Ottawa Senators. *True or False?*

19.13 Adam Oates is the most prolific point-earner never to win the Stanley Cup. *True or False?*

19.14 No NHLer has won the Conn Smythe Trophy as playoff MVP before winning the Calder Trophy as rookie of the year. *True or False?*

19.15 Wayne Gretzky owns the NHL record for points in the most consecutive playoff games. *True or False?*

19.16 Vancouver was the first city west of Winnipeg to host the Stanley Cup finals. *True or False?*

19.17 During the 1997 Detroit–Philadelphia Stanley Cup finals, Flyers coach Terry Murray used the "c" word, as in choking, to describe the poor play of his players. *True or False?*

19.18 In the 40-year history of the Jack Adams Award, the only bench boss to win coach-of-the-year honours and the Stanley Cup in the same season is John Tortorella—with Tampa Bay in 2003–04. *True or False?*

19.19 Sweden produced the first players to win the World Championships, the Olympics and the Stanley Cup. *True or False?*

19.20 The New York Islanders iced the first Czech-trained player to win the Stanley Cup. *True or False?*

19.21 Vancouver's Kirk McLean not only leads all netminders in shots faced and saves in one playoff season, he also holds the mark for minutes played in one postseason. *True or False?*

19.22 Montreal Canadiens coach Toe Blake was the first coach to win five Stanley Cups. *True or False?*

19.23 According to Henri Richard, winner of 11 Stanley Cups, he has only one Cup ring still in his possession. *True or False?*

19.24 The first Russian-trained player to score a goal in a Stanley Cup final was Pavel Bure of the Vancouver Canucks. *True or False?*

19.25 Mario Lemieux experienced his first playoff game in his rookie season. *True or False?*

19.26 The first time two former WHA teams met in the Stanley Cup finals was when Carolina battled Edmonton in 2006. *True or False?*

19.27 Mark Messier was the first former WHA player to score a Stanley Cup-winning goal after the NHL and WHA merged in 1979–80. *True or False?*

19.28 The 1974 Philadelphia Flyers was the last team composed entirely of Canadian-born players to win the Stanley Cup. *True or False?*

19.29 The first U.S. team to win the Stanley Cup was from San Francisco. *True or False?*

19.30 New Jersey's Larry Robinson was not the first coach to win the Stanley Cup after taking over a team during the regular season. *True or False?*

19.31 During the 1990s, no player won the Stanley Cup with more teams than Claude Lemieux. *True or False?*

19.32 Wayne Gretzky holds the NHL mark for the most points in a single playoff series. *True or False?*

19.33 Super pest Claude Lemieux is second after Wayne Gretzky and Brett Hull for most game-winning playoff goals. *True or False?*

19.34 The great Guy Lafleur once kidnapped the Stanley Cup. *True or False?*

19.35 Mario Lemieux, not Wayne Gretzky, owns the NHL record for most points in one playoff year. *True or False?*

19.36 When goal totals are counted, the four-time Stanley Cup-winning New York Islanders of the early 1980s outscored the four-time Cup-winning Edmonton Oilers of the mid- and late-1980s. *True or False?*

19.37 Wayne Gretzky holds the record for most career points in the Stanley Cup finals. *True or False?*

19.38 Montreal's Jacques Plante is the only goalie to captain a Stanley Cup champion. *True or False?*

19.39 Opposing goalie greats Turk Broda and Bill Durnan, each of whom won multiple Stanley Cups and Vezina Trophies during the 1940s, died within weeks of each other. *True or False?*

19.40 Maurice Richard was once named first, second and third star in a playoff game. *True or False?*

19.41 The 2005 Stanley Cup playoff finals between Carolina and Edmonton marked the first time in NHL history that rookies started in nets for an entire finals round. *True or False?*

19.42 The first player from a losing team to win the Conn Smythe Trophy as playoff MVP was a goalie. *True or False?*

19.43 Kevin Lowe was the last active member of the Edmonton Oilers' Stanley Cup dynasty teams of the 1980s. *True or False?*

True or False Stanley Cup

Answers

19.1 **True**

Gump Worsley, the last maskless goalie to win the Cup, played on the same team—wearing sweater No. 1—as the first masked netminder to win the Cup, Jacques Plante. Nine years after Plante's historic first with the Montreal Canadiens (April 14, 1960), Worsley played the last Cup-winning match by a barefaced puckstopper. It happened on May 4, 1969, as the Canadiens swept St. Louis. From that point on, all Cup-winning goalies wore face protection, beginning with Boston's Gerry Cheevers in 1970.

19.2 **False**

At least 25 players have made their only NHL appearance during the playoffs, the most famous being Don Cherry, who suited up for one NHL game during the 1951 Boston–Montreal semifinals. Brennan Evans joined this exclusive group after being called up by the Flames on an emergency basis when injuries claimed several Calgary defensemen during the 2004 playoffs. Evans appeared in two games against Detroit and has not been seen in an NHL uniform since. To date, only three players have won Stanley Cups without a regular-season appearance: Gord Haidy (1950), Doug McKay (1952) and Chris Hayes (1972). New Jersey's Steve Brule played just one playoff match when the Devils won the Cup in 2000, but he later played for Colorado in two regular-season games.

19.3 **False**

A few champions, such as the 1969 Montreal Canadiens and 1995 New Jersey Devils, had Cup hangovers the following season, but it wasn't until 2006–07 that both the previous season's Cup-winner and finalist failed to make the next playoffs. Carolina followed up their third-overall, 112-point finish and Stanley Cup victory in 2005–06 with a disappointing 20th-place showing, enough to keep the Hurricanes out of the 2006–07 postseason. Edmonton also fell from grace after its electrifying Cup run, sliding from 95 points for 13th place overall in 2005–06 to 71 points and a 26th place finish in 2006–07.

19.4 **True**

Although Curtis Joseph has enjoyed a stellar NHL career, he has not claimed any of the big goalie prizes. Cujo has never been named to an All-Star team, for example, or captured a Vezina Trophy or won the Stanley Cup. Yet, as of 2009, Joseph has appeared in 133 playoff games with the Red Wings, Oilers, Maple Leafs, Blues and Flames—the most postseason action seen by any goaltender who hasn't raised Lord Stanley's mug.

19.5 False

Because of their free-flowing finesse game, it's hard to imagine the Europeans not playing a part in a Stanley Cup-winning team in today's NHL. But it wasn't until the New York Islanders won the Cup in 1980 that a Euro-trained player had his name engraved on hockey's most cherished award. In fact, that year two Europeans—defenseman Stefan Persson and forward Anders Kallur—became the NHL's first European-taught Cup-winners and multiple Cup-winners as members of the Islanders' four consecutive championship teams between 1980 and 1983.

19.6 False

As of 2008, Smith is the most popular name on the Stanley Cup, with 19 different Smiths (both players and hockey personnel) winning the Cup 33 times. Hooley Smith is the only Smith to win the Cup with two different teams (Ottawa in 1927 and the Montreal Maroons in 1935). Billy Smith has won the most Cups (four betwen 1980 and 1983). The only two Smiths to backstop Cup-winners (Normie Smith and Billy Smith) have both done so on multiple occasions (Normie with Detroit in 1936 and 1937 and Billy four times, as mentioned). Smiths have been on Boston's last three Stanley Cups (Des Smith in 1941 and Dallas and Rick Smith in 1970 and 1972). On four occasions two Smiths have been on Stanley Cup-winning teams: Alex and Hooley in Ottawa (1927), Clint and Stan in New York (1940), Dallas and Rick in Boston (1970) and Steve and Geoff in Edmonton (1990). With the exception of Chicago, five of the Original Six teams have won the Cup with a Smith.

19.7   **True**

A few NHLers have scored more than one Stanley Cup winner during their careers. Boston's Bobby Orr (1970 and 1972) and Toe Blake (1944 and 1946) of the Montreal Canadiens each did it, though not in consecutive years. The first to notch two Stanley Cup winners, Jack Darragh, also did it consecutively, in 1920 and 1921, when the old Ottawa Senators recorded two championships. Darragh scored three times in the 1920 Cup-winning game and only became available for the 1921 finals after Ottawa mayor Frank Plant persuaded Darragh's employer, the Ottawa Dairy Company, to grant him a leave of absence to play in the series. It was another 62 years before Mike Bossy became the NHL's second player to notch back-to-back Cup-winners. His came in 1982 and 1983 to lead the New York Islanders to their third and fourth championships. In those four postseason drives between 1980 and 1983, Bossy scored 61 goals, posting three straight postseasons of 17 goals apiece. Wayne Gretzky didn't even do that during his Cup years with Edmonton.

19.8   **True**

As with a few of Patrick Roy's most impressive career records, this one will fall to Martin Brodeur, too. In 2009, Brodeur finally tied Roy's NHL-high of 23. Roy took over the league lead in 2001 with his 16th shutout, surpassing Clint Benedict's amazing 73-year reign of 15 zeroes. But Roy's massive 247-playoff-games mark dwarfs Benedict's career total of just 48, a sublime postseason performance that includes four Stanley Cups in nine playoff years with the old Ottawa Senators and Montreal Maroons. Benedict is the only netminder in NHL history to notch two postseasons of four shutouts. Compared to Roy, Brodeur amassed his 23 goose eggs in just 176 games.

19.9   False

Montreal's Maurice and Henri Richard are the only siblings in
NHL history to captain their teams to the Cup. Maurice managed it four times—during the 1950s—and Henri twice—in
the early 1970s.

19.10   False

At least four sports figures have their names on the Grey
Cup and Stanley Cup, but in our research we came across
only one individual who has sipped champagne from both
trophies as a player: Lionel Conacher. The old-time great
could be found on several fields of play during his era. He was
Canada's athlete of the half-century, a multi-sport player who
excelled at the highest levels in lacrosse, baseball, football
and hockey. (Though he was regarded as a better football
and lacrosse player, he made more money playing hockey.)
And amongst the great Canadian sports stories is Conacher's
Grey Cup victory with the Toronto Argonauts in 1921, when,
after starring in the game, he left the football field early
to play semi-pro hockey for Aura Lee. Conacher would win
Stanley Cups with Chicago in 1934 and the Montreal Maroons
in 1935. The other three individuals with Cups in football
and hockey are Harold Ballard, who won championships as
owner of the NHL Toronto Maple Leafs and the CFL Hamilton
Tiger-Cats; Normie Kwong, who earned four Grey Cups with
the Edmonton Eskimos and was part-owner of the Stanley
Cup-winning Calgary Flames in 1989; and Wayne Gretzky,
as part-owner of the 1991 Toronto Argonauts and four-time
Stanley Cup winner. Interestingly, Gretzky's name was only
added to the Grey Cup in 2007, 16 years after the Argos won
the championship.

19.11   False

Since Toronto downed Montreal to win the Stanley Cup in 1967, only two other finals series in more than 40 years were entirely Canadian affairs: both the 1986 and 1989 Cup finals pitted Calgary against Montreal, with each team winning one championship.

19.12   True

After Washington beat Ottawa 4–1 in 1998's semifinals, Clinton clinched the bet between the two nations' leaders and provided Chretien with the Capitals' blue-black-and-white sweater to wear in public. The Canadian prime minister donned the Caps sweater in front of cameras in England, where world leaders of the G8 were meeting. Clinton and Chretien also exchanged hockey sticks.

19.13   False

It's too bad that Marcel Dionne didn't find a Stanley Cup contender like the Colorado Avalanche. Such a career move brought Ray Bourque his only championship after 21 years of futility and more than 1,500 points as a Boston Bruin. For Dionne, with a Hall-of-Fame career 1,771 points, moving to a playoff hopeful would have meant all those goals and assists counted for something more than individual effort. Unfortunately, it didn't work out that way, and Dionne remains the lone NHLer in the all-time top 10 list of scorers without a Cup. Dionne's teams never got closer than the quarterfinals in 18 seasons with Detroit, Los Angeles and the New York Rangers, and on nine occasions failed to make postseason play entirely. As for Adam Oates, he came up Cupless after 19 NHL seasons with seven teams and 1,420 points. Upon retirement in 2004, Oates ranked 13th amongst all-time point leaders.

19.14 False

New Jersey's Scott Gomez accomplished what only four previous NHL players had done—he won the Stanley Cup before claiming Calder Trophy honours. But Gomez's Cup and Calder wins both happened in 2000, while Gaye Stewart, Tony Esposito, Danny Grant and Ken Dryden won the Stanley Cup the season *before* they claimed top rookie status. Still, amongst this select group, Ken Dryden stands alone. With just six regular-season games behind him, Dryden led the underdog Montreal Canadiens to a surprise Stanley Cup in 1971, winning the Conn Smythe as postseason MVP. The following season he scored his Calder as the top rookie of 1972.

19.15 False

The New York Islanders' championship squads of the early 1980s boasted a host of talented performers, but none contributed more to the club's success than Bryan Trottier. The hard-driving centre counted a point in 27 consecutive playoff games between 1980 and 1982, setting a record that no other player has approached. Even Wayne Gretzky's point-scoring streak of 19 straight games in 1988 and 1989 is a distant second. Trottier logged 42 points (16 G, 26 A) in those 27 games, but he was especially impressive during the 1981 playoffs, when he scored a point in all 18 games the Islanders played to set a record for the longest consecutive point-scoring streak in one playoff year.

19.16 True

In 1915, Vancouver became the first city west of Winnipeg to host the Stanley Cup finals, when the National Hockey Association champion Ottawa Senators journeyed west to meet the Pacific Coast Hockey Association champion Vancouver Millionaires. The best-of-five series was played at

Vancouver's Denman Street Arena, a cavernous 10,500-seat space that was the second-largest indoor sports stadium in the world, after New York's Madison Square Garden. Built in 1912, at a cost of $300,000, it was a wildly ambitious structure for a city with a population of only 150,000. And here, spurred on by a sellout hometown crowd, the Millionaires trounced the eastern invaders 6–2, 8–3 and 12–3. The Denman Street Arena would play host to one more Stanley Cup final, in 1921, before being destroyed by fire in 1936.

19.17 True

With the Flyers trailing the Red Wings three games to none in the 1997 Cup finals, Murray resorted to a risky and unusual psychological ploy, suggesting his team was in the process of choking. While discussing the Flyers' waning confidence level with reporters, Murray said, "I don't know where it has gone. Many teams have been through this problem before and it is basically a choking situation." Philadelphia played better in Game 4, but still lost, going down in four straight. It was the first time the Flyers had lost four games in a row since March 1993.

19.18 False

By definition, the Jack Adams Award is presented to the coach who contributes the most to his team's success. But the superstition surrounding the award suggests that the Adams contributes nothing to the recipient's success, and, instead that the winner is just one step away from being fired. Three-time Adams-winner Pat Burns knows this better than anyone, after receiving pink slips upon winning the Adams with Montreal, Toronto and Boston. And if the Adams offers no guarantee of future employment, it also has little to do with success beyond the regular season. Besides Tortorella, only Cup-winning coaches Fred Shero (in 1974) and Scotty Bowman (in 1977) have received the top coach trophy since its inception in 1974.

19.19 True

The first players to win World, Olympic and Stanley Cup championships were Swedes Tomas Jonsson, Mats Naslund and Hakan Loob. Each captured the World title with Sweden in 1991, an Olympic gold medal in 1994 and, on different occasions with different teams, the Stanley Cup (Jonsson in 1982 and 1983 with the Islanders, Naslund in 1986 with Montreal and Loob with Calgary in 1989).

19.20 False

The first Czech-trained NHLer to win the Stanley Cup is Jaroslav Pouzar. Selected in the fourth round (83rd overall) by the Oilers in the 1982 draft, Pouzar, age 30, was already a Czech veteran of six World Championship tournaments and two Olympics when he joined Edmonton for the 1982–83 season. His NHL entrance was a classic case of joining the right team at the right time. He won his first Stanley Cup the following year, 1983–84, and two more Oiler Cups before heading back to Europe in 1987. Pouzar won three Stanley Cups and played only 186 NHL regular-season games. (Another Czech player who hit the NHL jackpot was Jiri Hrdina. Hrdina played just four complete seasons, but during that time he won the Stanley Cup with the 1989 Calgary Flames in his first year and two more Cups in his third and fourth years with the Pittsburgh Penguins. Hrdina won three Cups on two different teams and played in just 250 NHL games.)

19.21 False

Team shot totals reveal a number of interesting facts about netminders. For example, since 1982–83, the six highest shots-against counts are owned by goalies who succeeded in reaching the finals but lost the Cup. Vancouver's Kirk McLean ranks first in the rubber parade, facing a record 820 shots on net in 24 playoff games during 1994. McLean stared down an average of 34 shots per game and made 761 saves, another playoff mark. But amongst minutes-played leaders, he ranks tied for second with Ed Belfour, with both players tallying 1,544 minutes during their respective years. Calgary's Miikka Kiprusoff, one of the six most-shot-upon playoff losers (with 710 shots), leads this category, having played 1,655 minutes in 26 games during the Flames' Cup run in 2004.

19.22 False

While Toe Blake won an unprecedented five consecutive Stanley Cups, Toronto's Hap Day was the first to claim five championships. Day began his NHL employment as a player, and was Toronto's first team captain, anchoring the blue line with Red Horner and King Clancy. Later, as the coach of the Maple Leafs, he had a highlight-reel career with five Cups in a 10-year span (1940–41 to 1949–50). In the process, he coached the Leafs to the greatest comeback in league annals (the team rebounded from a 0–3 deficit to win 1942's championship), led Toronto to another Cup in 1945 and then three in a row, in 1947, 1948 and 1949, a first for an NHL coach. Day was elected to the Hall of Fame in 1961.

19.23 True

Henri Richard won more Stanley Cups than any other NHLer, but amongst those 11 Cups he owns only one ring. Unfortunately, thieves stole the others from his Montreal-area home after he retired in 1975. The Canadiens great began his Hall of Fame career winning an unprecedented five consecutive Cups with Montreal between 1956 and 1960, though only one ring was issued for that dynasty. "The team paid half (the cost) of the ring and we paid half," Richard recalled in a *Montreal Gazette* story. The stolen rings were from the 1960, 1965, 1966, 1968, 1969 and 1971 seasons. His last Cup ring, 1973's, is the only one Richard still owns. The king of the rings keeps that treasure in a safe place and wears his 1979-issued Hall of Fame ring.

19.24 False

The NHL record book notes that Alexei Kovalev was the first Russian to score a Stanley Cup finals goal, but there's no mention of how close Pavel Bure came to beating him for the record. Kovalev scored at 8:29 of the third period of Game 1 of the 1994 Rangers–Canucks finals, while Bure, the second Russian to notch a Cup-final goal, potted his just a little more than a game later, at 1:03 of the first period in Game 3. Although Igor Kravchuk was the first former Soviet player to appear in a Cup-final game, with Chicago in 1992, he did not score. Alexei Zhitnik, with the Kings, was the first ex-Soviet to post a point in the finals, an assist on a Luc Robitaille goal in the 1993 Cup showdown.

19.25 False

Mario Lemieux's first career playoff game was a 3–1 win over the New York Rangers on April 5, 1989. He had played five NHL seasons, or 368 games, without a whiff of postseason action. By the time the Penguins seriously challenged for the Stanley Cup in 1991, Lemieux had just 11 playoff games under his belt in seven NHL seasons.

19.26 True

Since the four WHA franchises from Hartford, Edmonton, Quebec and Winnipeg merged with the 17-team NHL in 1979–80, no two WHA teams had faced off in a Stanley Cup finals until 2006, when the Edmonton Oilers challenged the Carolina Hurricanes (formerly the old Hartford Whalers). The 2006 matchup was a classic seven-game duel, with Carolina winning one of the most intense and frenzied series in playoff history. The first WHA team to win the Cup was the Oilers, in 1984.

19.27 False

Three former WHA players have scored Stanley Cup winners: Mark Messier (1994), Wayne Gretzky (1988) and Ken Linseman, who bagged the Oilers' first Cup-winning goal on May 19, 1984. Linseman, who was drafted by Birmingham as an underage junior, recorded a 38–38–76 rookie season with the Bulls in 1977–78. He spent the next four years playing for the Philadelphia Flyers before joining Edmonton in 1982.

19.28 True

The infamous Broad Street Bullies club was the last all-Canadian-born contingent of players to win the Stanley Cup. While a few other teams may have been up for consideration, none qualify in this category. For example, the 1977 Montreal Canadiens iced American-born Bill Nyrop and Mike Polich and Venezuelan-born Rick Chartraw; the 1980 Islanders sported Stefan Persson, Bob Nystrom and Anders Kallur of Sweden; and the 1989 Flames had Americans Joe Mullen and Gary Suter and Swede Hakan Loob.

19.29 False

Curiously, the last team to win the Stanley Cup before 1917–18, the year the NHL was formed, was a U.S.-based Cup-winner:

the Pacific Coast Hockey Association's Seattle Metropolitans. Seattle was also the first U.S. team to host a Stanley Cup series. The Metropolitans defeated the defending Cup champs, the Montreal Canadiens, 3–1 in the best-of-five finals.

19.30 True

Prior to the New Jersey Devils' stunning coaching change in 1999–2000, when Larry Robinson took over from Robbie Ftorek with just eight regular-season games remaining and captured the Stanley Cup, only two other Cup-winning coaches were midseason replacements. Dick Irvin Sr. took over from Art Duncan to win Toronto's Stanley Cup in 1931–32, and Claude Ruel was bounced in favour of Al McNeil during 1970–71, when Montreal won the championship.

19.31 False

The Stanley Cup has a way of following some players around. Hard-nosed Mike Keane, the ultimate depth player, is one of those lucky few. Keane is the only player during the 1990s to win Stanley Cups on three different teams: Montreal in 1993, Colorado in 1996 and Dallas in 1999. Claude Lemieux won four Cups in his career: with Montreal in 1986, New Jersey in 1995, Colorado in 1996 and the Devils in 2000.

19.32 False

An overtime goal by Brad Park lifted the Boston Bruins past the Buffalo Sabres in Game 7 of the 1983 Adams Division finals, but the real hero of the series was Rick Middleton. The shifty Bruin forward repeatedly bamboozled Buffalo's defense, collecting a single-series-record 19 points on five goals and 14 assists. Wayne Gretzky missed this record by one point, scoring four goals and 14 assists for 18 points in 1985's Conference finals blitz against Chicago.

19.33 True

No matter how much criticism Lemieux attracted for his
subpar offensive numbers during the regular season, all
was forgiven come playoff time. In the postseason he was
the model of consistency. As of 2008, Lemieux's 19 postseason game-winners tally is second only to Gretzky and Hull's
record 24 and tied with one of the more conspicuous playoff
heroes, Joe Sakic.

19.34 True

Lafleur caused some tense moments for club officials after
the 1979 finals, when he "borrowed" the Cup during an afternoon downtown tour. Unnoticed, Lafleur slipped away with
the trophy and drove to his parents' home in Thurso, Quebec,
where he placed the Cup on the front lawn and watched as
hundreds of people from miles around paraded past it. After
an afternoon of picture-taking, Lafleur then returned it to
Montreal, much to the relief of officials. Lafleur was repri-
manded for his prank, but only for appearances' sake. What
could the club do to hockey's greatest scorer of the late 1970s?

19.35 False

If Wayne Gretzky set the standard by which Mario Lemieux
is measured, then perhaps Lemieux's greatest scoring act is
his 44-point playoff year of 1991—just three points behind
Gretzky's all-time record of 47. During the 23 games, Lemieux
fired a playoff-high 93 shots, scored 16 times and assisted on
28 others. His most important goal, however, may have come
with Pittsburgh leading Minnesota 2–1 in Game 2 of the
Cup finals, when Lemieux wheeled through centre ice, split
Minnesota defensemen Shawn Chambers and Neil Wilkinson
with a deft move, then deked goalie Jon Casey and flipped a
backhander between the posts as he fell to the ice. From that

moment on, the Stars knew a healthy Lemieux was almost impossible to contain. For many, it was the play that turned the series.

19.36 True

Because of the sheer volume of team and individual records established by Wayne Gretzky and the Edmonton Oilers during their dynasty years of the 1980s, we tend to overlook the scoring prowess of the New York Islanders in their glory years. Between 1980 and 1983, the Isles, led by Mike Bossy, Bryan Trottier and Denis Potvin, scored an unreal 87 goals in just 19 final-series games to capture four Stanley Cups. By comparison, Edmonton's powerhouse needed more games (22) and scored fewer goals (85) to win its four championships.

19.37 False

Unlike Wayne Gretzky, who failed to make the playoffs in his last two seasons, Jean Béliveau went out on top, captaining the Montreal Canadiens to the Stanley Cup in 1970–71, the 10th of his illustrious career. Béliveau finished the playoffs with six goals and a then-record 16 assists, leaving the sport as the all-time leader in playoff points. He has since been eclipsed in that category, but still holds the mark for most points in the finals. Béliveau has 62 points, compared to Gretzky's 53. But while the great Canadiens centre played in 64 finals matches, No. 99 was in only 31 games.

19.38 False

Only a handful of goalies have served as team captains, and just one, the great Chuck Gardiner, captained his team to a Stanley Cup title. Gardiner was handed the captaincy in 1933–34 after six seasons with the Blackhawks—a perennial cellar dweller that once set the record for fewest goals scored.

Yet despite the lack of support, Gardiner maintained consistently solid averages, won two Vezina Trophies (top goalie) and was named to four All-Star teams. During 1933–34, for example, Gardiner was instrumental in the Hawks' second-place finish, even though the club had the league's worst offensive record—and it was no secret that throughout that regular-season campaign, Gardiner suffered from headaches so severe that at times he clutched the goalposts to keep from collapsing. Even so, Gardiner limited the first-place Red Wings to two goals in his club's three victories. In the Stanley Cup clincher, Gardiner made 40 saves, shutting out the Wings 1–0 in a rare double-overtime victory. It was the Blackhawks' first Stanley Cup. Two months later, Gardiner, only 29 years old, died of a brain hemorrhage. The Hawks honoured their fallen chief by not appointing a player to the captaincy the following season, one of the few occasions in Chicago's 80-year-plus history that the club played without a captain.

19.39 True

One of hockey's greatest old-time rivalries was the Toronto–Montreal ice feuds of the 1940s. The intensity was due, in no small measure, to Broda and Durnan, arguably the two best goalies of the era. While Broda won the Stanley Cup five times, Durnan dominated individual awards in his seven NHL seasons, winning the Vezina Trophy as top goalie six times and getting named to six First All-Star Teams. As brothers-in-arms in the goaltending trade, the two men definitely dominated the game, managing consecutive seasons of silverware streaks that were broken only by the other. Broda and Durnan won *everything*. Curiously, both goalies died within weeks of each other in October 1972.

19.40 True

The only time in NHL history that one player has been named all three game stars in playoff action occurred on March 23, 1944, after Richard's one-man scoring show during Game 2 of the 1944 Toronto–Montreal semifinals. Richard predicted a big night, boldly telling Maple Leaf goalie Paul Bibeault: "You were too hot for us in Game 1, Paul. But I'll give you a lot to think about in Game 2, my friend." True to his word, Richard, in only his second career-playoff game, came out storming in an offensive display that blew five goals past his Leaf pal. When Richard was named the third star, the crowd was aghast. Who could have topped the Rocket's five-goal night? Then Richard was selected the second star as well. The Forum crowd immediately caught on, cheering in anticipation of the next announcement. The night turned into pure theatre as another loud roar ungulfed the Forum in approval of Richard's first-star selection. After the 5–1 win, the Canadiens never looked back, pummelling Toronto and then Chicago and racking up seven consecutive victories to win the Stanley Cup.

19.41 False

The 2005 Cup finals featured two rookie goalies, with Carolina's Cam Ward challenging Jussi Markkanen of Edmonton—though Markkanen didn't play the entire series (he replaced injured starter Dwayne Roloson after Game 1 against the Hurricanes.) But on two other occasions in post-season history, rookies *did* meet in the finals and each time something special happened. The first freshmen to face each other were Toronto's Frank McCool and Detroit's Harry Lumley, in 1945. Far from the expected shooter's free-for-all, McCool posted shutouts in the first three games to set a Stanley Cup record. Lumley then responded with two of his own—in Games 5 and 6—to tie the series. McCool won the Cup with a 2–1 victory in Game 7, but never played in another final series. In his 16-year career, Lumley went to the finals three more times, eventually winning a Cup in 1949–50 in another seven-game series with Detroit. The next rookie-versus-rookie matchup occurred 41 years later, when Mike Vernon and Patrick Roy manned opposing nets in the 1986 Montreal–Calgary Stanley Cup playoffs. The Canadiens easily handled the Flames, while 22-year-old Roy became the youngest playoff MVP ever. Only one other freshman duel took place in finals action, but it involved Maple Leaf veteran netminder Turk Broda, who played the first two games of the classic 1951 Toronto–Montreal showdown between rookies Al Rollins of Toronto and Gerry McNeil of Montreal. After Broda, the veteran, split overtimes with McNeil in Games 1 and 2, Rollins, the rookie, returned from a knee injury to win the next three from the Canadiens, all in extra periods. It marked the first and only time in Stanley Cup history that every game of a final series ended in overtime—proving to be another oddity in playoff rookie matchups.

19.42 True

As of 2008, only five players have taken home the Conn Smythe for their extraordinary play—despite losing the championship. The first was MPV-winning goalie Roger Crozier of the Detroit Red Wings in 1966. Outpowered by heavily favoured Montreal, Crozier kept the long-shot Red Wings alive to survive six games, including early back-to-back wins at the Montreal Forum. But during Game 4, he went down with a wrenched leg and the Red Wings lost confidence. He returned with a taped knee only to lose Game 5 (5–1) and Game 6 (3–2), an overtime heartbreaker. The other Cup-losing MVPs are Glenn Hall, in 1968, Reggie Leach, in 1976, Brian Hextall, in 1987, and Jean-Sébastien Giguère, in 2003.

19.43 False

At the start of 1997–98, Kelly Buchberger and Kevin Lowe were the only remaining members from the Oilers' championship era. Lowe, a five-time Cup-winner with Edmonton, played just five games in 1997–98 before ending his 19-year career to become an assistant coach. Buchberger, who won two Oilers Cups in 1987 and 1990, remained with the team until 1998–99 before being traded to four teams in five seasons and then retiring during the lockout season of 2004–05.

Game 19

Magnetic Attractions

SOME PLAYERS ARE LIKE magnets when it comes to attracting the game's silverware. Throughout their careers, the Stanley Cup follows them from one team to another, drawn by mysterious forces that have turned players such as Mike Keane and Claude Lemieux into multiple Cup-winners. Other NHLers can't get a sniff of playoff action past the second round. In this game, match the two-time Cup-winners on the left and their championship teams on the right.

Solutions are on page 567

PART 1

1. __D__ Joe Nieuwendyk	A.	NY Rangers 1994, Detroit 1998
2. __E__ Terry Sawchuk	B.	Edmonton 1984, Pittsburgh 1991
3. __F__ Mark Messier	C.	NY Islanders 1980, Pittsburgh 1991
4. __G__ Ted Harris	D.	Dallas 1999, New Jersey 2003
5. __A__ Joe Kocur	E.	Edmonton 1984, NY Rangers 1994
6. __C__ Bryan Trottier	F.	Detroit 1952, Toronto 1967
7. __B__ Paul Coffey	G.	Montreal 1965, Philadelphia 1975

PART 2

1. __B__ Patrick Roy	A.	Toronto 1967, Montreal 1971
2. __E__ Brett Hull	B.	Montreal 1986, Colorado 1996
3. __F__ Dick Duff	C.	Montreal 1986, Detroit 2002
4. __G__ Larry Murphy	D.	Calgary 1989, Pittsburgh 1991
5. __D__ Joe Mullen	E.	Dallas 1999, Detroit 2002
6. __A__ Frank Mahovlich	F.	Toronto 1962, Montreal 1965
7. __C__ Chris Chelios	G.	Pittsburgh 1992, Detroit 1997

20

The Hardest Act

WELCOME TO THE TOUGHEST tournament in sports. After doing battle in the 2006 Stanley Cup finals, the Carolina Hurricanes and Edmonton Oilers became inextricably linked by a much less honourable distinction after each failed to qualify for the 2007 playoffs. In NHL history, Carolina and Edmonton are the only finalists to both miss postseason play the following year. Worse, the 'Canes joined only six other defending Cup champions, including the 1969–70 Montreal Canadiens and the 1995–96 New Jersey Devils, that stalled the next season. Sometimes the hardest act to follow is your own.

Answers are on page 538

20.1 **In which city was the first Stanley Cup parade held?**
- A. Winnipeg
- B. Toronto
- C. Montreal
- D. Ottawa

20.2 **When researchers measured noise levels at Edmonton's Rexall Place during the 2006 Stanley Cup finals, they compared the fan noise after an Oilers goal to what sound?**
- A. A shotgun blast
- B. A small bomb detonating
- C. Screeching tires
- D. A jet taking flight

20.3 Which NHL bench boss coached the same team the longest without winning the Stanley Cup?

A. Billy Reay, with the Chicago Blackhawks

B. Milt Schmidt, with the Boston Bruins

C. Sid Abel, with the Detroit Red Wings

D. Brian Murray, with the Washington Capitals

20.4 What is the most number of NHL teams for which a head coach has worked before winning a Stanley Cup?

A. Three teams

B. Four teams

C. Five teams

D. Six teams

20.5 Since 1987, when each of the four playoff series required best-of-seven formats, what championship team won the Stanley Cup in the fewest number of postseason games? And how many games were played (if the minimum is 16 matches and the maximum is 28)?

A. The Edmonton Oilers in 1988

B. The Pittsburgh Penguins in 1991

C. The Montreal Canadiens in 1993

D. The New Jersey Devils in 1995

20.6 What is the greatest margin in shot totals between two teams in one playoff series?

A. Less than 60 shots

B. Between 60 and 90 shots

C. Between 90 and 120 shots

D. More than 120 shots

20.7 Which NHL team was first to have a 40-year-old player and a teenager score in the same playoff game? (It happened during the 2007 postseason.)

A. The Buffalo Sabres
B. The San Jose Sharks
C. The Pittsburgh Penguins
D. The Chicago Blackhawks

20.8 Which Stanley Cup finals featured a bizarre game in which the play was delayed several times by heavy fog?

A. The 1948 Toronto–Detroit finals
B. The 1965 Montreal–Chicago finals
C. The 1970 Boston–St. Louis finals
D. The 1975 Philadelphia–Buffalo finals

20.9 Which of the following playoff records set by the 1985 Edmonton Oilers has since been surpassed?

A. Most games in one playoff game
B. Most goals in one playoff series
C. Most shorthanded goals in one playoff year
D. Most three-or-more goals in one playoff year

20.10 Montreal and Boston have one of hockey's greatest rivalries. But for much of the 20th century, it was a one-sided affair. How many consecutive playoff series did Montreal take from Boston between 1946 and 1988?

A. Nine consecutive series
B. 12 consecutive series
C. 15 consecutive series
D. 18 consecutive series

20.11 What is the fewest number of total goals scored by a winning team in a playoff round?

A. One goal

B. Four goals

C. Six goals

D. Eight goals

20.12 What is the fewest number of goals allowed in a best-of-seven playoff series? The NHL record was set during the 2003 playoffs.

A. No goals

B. One goal

C. Two goals

D. Three goals

20.13 Before Anaheim's surprising four-game sweep of the Detroit Red Wings during the preliminary round of the 2003 playoffs, when was the last time the defending Stanley Cup champions lost four straight in the first round?

A. In 1932: Montreal vs. the New York Rangers

B. In 1952: Toronto vs. Detroit

C. In 1972: Montreal vs. the New York Rangers

D. In 1992: Pittsburgh vs. Washington

20.14 Which team was the first to win the Stanley Cup without a captain?

A. The Detroit Red Wings, in 1943

B. The Toronto Maple Leafs, in 1962

C. The Boston Bruins, in 1970

D. The Montreal Canadiens, in 1986

20.15 What is the most number of goals scored in a seventh game in playoff action?

A. Seven goals

B. Nine goals

C. 11 goals

D. 13 goals

20.16 What was Detroit's regular-season point difference between 1995–96, the year it recorded a league-high 62 regular-season wins, and 1996–97, the year it won the Stanley Cup?

A. Less than 15 points

B. 15 to 25 points

C. 25 to 35 points

D. More than 35 points

20.17 After losing the 1999 Stanley Cup to Dallas on Brett Hull's disputed goal, how long did it take the Buffalo Sabres to get their first victory in 1999–2000?

A. The Sabres won the first game of 1999–2000

B. Three games

C. Five games

D. Seven games

20.18 Prior to the Tampa Bay Lightning in 2004, when was the last time a team beat the Montreal Canadiens in the rounds before the finals and went on to win the Stanley Cup?

A. In the 1964 playoffs

B. In the 1974 playoffs

C. In the 1984 playoffs

D. In the 1994 playoffs

20.19 Which NHL club first rewarded the team's hardest-working player of a game with a hard hat?

A. The Boston Bruins

B. The Calgary Flames

C. The New Jersey Devils

D. The Edmonton Oilers

20.20 How much time does each player on the Stanley Cup-winning team get to spend with the Cup during the summer?

A. Six hours

B. One day

C. Three days

D. Six days

20.21 During the 2000 postseason, what team established an NHL record for the fewest power-play goals allowed?

A. The Stanley Cup-winning New Jersey Devils

B. The Philadelphia Flyers

C. The Stanley Cup-finalist Dallas Stars

D. The Colorado Avalanche

20.22 What is the highest number of seventh games that have occurred in one playoff year?

A. Three seventh games

B. Five seventh games

C. Seven seventh games

D. Nine seventh games

20.23 In August 2004, in which NHL city did airport agents "lose" the Stanley Cup?

A. Calgary

B. Tampa Bay

C. Vancouver

D. Chicago

20.24 What is the longest layoff between playoff series by a modern-day team?

A. Seven days

B. Nine days

C. 11 days

D. 13 days

20.25 The greatest single-game comeback in postseason history belongs to Los Angeles, which erased a record five-goal deficit against Edmonton in April 1982. What is the largest comeback—in goals scored—in Stanley Cup finals play?

A. Two goals

B. Three goals

C. Four goals

D. Five goals

20.26 How many Devils won Stanley Cups with New Jersey's championship teams of 1995 and 2000?

A. Six players

B. Nine players

C. 12 players

D. 15 players

20.27 Although NHL teams didn't use tandem goalies until the 1950s, in which year were the names of two goalies first engraved on the Stanley Cup?

A. 1928–29

B. 1938–39

C. 1948–49

D. 1958–59

20.28 What is the greatest number of different NHL franchises a general manager has led to the Stanley Cup?

A. Two franchises

B. Three franchises

C. Four franchises

D. Five franchises

20.29 In what decade did the first on-ice awarding of the Stanley Cup take place?

A. In the 1920s

B. In the 1930s

C. In the 1940s

D. In the 1950s

20.30 Which NHL owner was taken hostage during the 1982 play-offs by an armed man who demanded $1 million in ransom money?

A. Bill Wirtz of the Chicago Blackhawks

B. Harold Ballard of the Toronto Maple Leafs

C. Jerry Buss of the Los Angeles Kings

D. Peter Pocklington of the Edmonton Oilers

20.31 The year 1925 marks the last time a non-NHL team captured the Stanley Cup. Which team holds that honour?

A. The Regina Capitals

B. The Calgary Tigers

C. The Victoria Cougars

D. The Edmonton Eskimos

20.32 How many hours was the longest Stanley Cup parade?

A. Less than four hours

B. Between four and six hours

C. Between six and eight hours

D. More than eight hours

20.33 The smallest town to win the Stanley Cup celebrated the 100th anniversary of its championship in January 2007. Which town and team were the improbable Cup-winners of 1907?

A. Ontario's Kenora Thistles

B. Manitoba's Winnipeg Victorias

C. Ontario's Renfrew Creamery Kings (Millionaires)

D. The Yukon's Dawson City Nuggets

20.34 Which team's surprising collapse during the 1930 Stanley Cup playoffs is credited with bringing about the best-of-five format in the finals?

A. The Montreal Canadiens'

B. The Boston Bruins'

C. The Chicago Blackhawks'

D. The New York Rangers'

20.35 As of 2008, which Stanley Cup finalist was the last to avenge its Cup loss by winning the championship the following year?

A. The Edmonton Oilers

B. The Calgary Flames

C. The Colorado Avalanche

D. The New Jersey Devils

20.36 What is the most number of current or former captains on a Stanley Cup-winning team?

A. Six captains

B. Seven captains

C. Eight captains

D. Nine captains

20.37 Which club set an unwanted record in the 2000 playoffs, when it recorded an all-time NHL low of six shots in a game?

A. The Edmonton Oilers

B. The Toronto Maple Leafs

C. The Florida Panthers

D. The Ottawa Senators

20.38 In which NHL city is the Red Mile?

A. Detroit

B. Calgary

C. Nashville

D. San Jose

20.39 Which Stanley Cup champion has travelled the greatest distance on his summer trip with the Stanley Cup?

A. Jere Lehtinen, with the Dallas Stars

B. Peter Forsberg, with the Colorado Avalanche

C. Pavel Datsyuk, with the Detroit Red Wings

D. Alexander Mogilny, with the New Jersey Devils

The Hardest Act

Answers

20.1   A. Winnipeg

Stanley Cup champions had previously been honoured with just gifts, banquets and celebrations at their home rink, until the first Cup parade took place in Winnipeg in February 1896 for the hometown Victorias. After stunning the Montreal Victorias with a 2–0 winner-take-all victory at Montreal's Victoria Rink (yes, apparently everything was named after the great dame in the Victorian age), Winnipeg held many celebrations, including a parade on Main Street with the Stanley Cup travelling in a cab. It was the first time a western club had won the Cup, and, upon its return by train from Montreal, the team had the locomotive's cow catcher festooned with hockey sticks and brooms to symbolize the Vic's clean sweep in Montreal. (Cup parades as we know them today began in 1907, when the Montreal Wanderers were celebrated with a long parade through Montreal streets that concluded at the famous Savoy Hotel.)

20.2   D. A jet taking flight

Researchers admitted they weren't looking to take the fun out of hockey, only to alert spectators to the potential for hearing loss at big games. Their findings were deafening. The roar of Oilers fans when Edmonton scored against Carolina during Games 3, 4 and 6 of the 2006 Cup finals in Rexall Place reached 120 decibels, or roughly the equivalent of a jet taking off. As for the average noise level—104 decibels—during each match, researchers likened it to sitting next to a chainsaw revved at full throttle for three straight hours. Bottom line: hockey spectators were subjecting themselves to 3,100 per cent of their "daily allowable noise dose" during each contest. The study suggested that fans, like players, should wear earplugs.

20.3   A. Billy Reay, with the Chicago Blackhawks

Billy Reay coached some of the 1960s' and early 1970s' highest-scoring teams but never a Stanley Cup winner. Chicago's coach for 14 seasons, Reay was an institution in the Blackhawk organization, leading the club to numerous West Division titles, a first-place finish overall in regular-season standings for the first time in franchise history (1966–67) and, unfortunately, to the Cup finals an agonizing three times without sipping champagne. During the regular season Reay coached

1,102 games in Chicago—more matches with one team than any other Cup-less coach in league history. But he also won more (542 games) than any other bench boss of his era except Dick Irvin. No other coach challenges Reay's games-coached numbers on one team in this category, though a few are in the rearview mirror, including Buffalo's Lindy Ruff and Barry Trotz.

Most Games Coaching One Team by a Cup-Less Coach

COACH	TEAM	YEARS	GC
Billy Reay	Chicago	1963–1977	1,102
Lindy Ruff	Buffalo	1997–2009	902
Barry Trotz	Nashville	1998–2009	820
Sid Abel	Detroit	1957–1970	811
Paul Maurice	Hartford/Carolina	1995–2009	731
Milt Schmidt	Boston	1954–1966	726
Jacques Martin	Ottawa	1995–2004	692

*Current to 2008–09

20.4 B. Four teams

No coaches have been behind the bench with as many teams before winning the Stanley Cup as Jacques Demers and Pat Burns. Demers was working on his fourth NHL team, the Montreal Canadiens, when he led them to the championship in 1993. His career began in the NHL-rival WHA, where he had already coached another four clubs during the 1970s, bringing his total to eight pro teams before his Cup in 1993. When the WHA merged with the NHL in 1979–80, Demers coached the Quebec Nordiques before moving on to St. Louis and Detroit, where the master motivator won back-to-back Jack Adams Awards as the league's top coach, an NHL first. Pat Burns, a coach of the year with each of his first three clubs, in Montreal, Toronto and Boston, finally won his Stanley Cup in New Jersey in 2003.

20.5 A. The Edmonton Oilers in 1988

The Edmonton Oilers won the 1988 Stanley Cup in 18 games, losing just twice during their best-of-seven, four-round playoff series—once to Winnipeg in the division semifinals and another in the Conference finals to the Detroit Red Wings. Edmonton won the other two series, the Division finals against Calgary and the Cup finals versus Boston, both in four games straight.

20.6 D. More than 120 shots

Since shot counts were first tabulated in 1967, no two teams have amassed a greater shot difference in one playoff round than Calgary and Detroit during the 2007 Western Conference quarterfinals. It was the West's first overall team versus its worst postseason qualifier, and the results were not pretty. Although Calgary made a series out of it, extending Detroit to six games, there wasn't much that Flames goalie Miikka Kiprusoff could do against the battering from Red Wings shooters. In those six games, however, Kiprusoff faced a wicked 255 shots (or more than half the aggregate Jean-Sébastien Giguère faced in the four rounds Anaheim needed to win the Stanley Cup that season). At the other end, Calgary's skaters directed just 129 shots at Dominik Hasek for a record disparity of 126 shots between the two clubs. Despite games of 55, 51, 46, 38, 35 and 30 shots against, however, Kiprusoff made 237 saves, giving up just 18 goals and winning two contests. His best match may have been Game 6, an overtime loss that ended Calgary's playoff hopes. The Red Wings won 2–1, but it took 55 shots through five periods of hockey to subdue the stubborn Flames. Hasek faced just 21 shots that night.

20.7 C. The Pittsburgh Penguins

On April 14, 2007, the Penguins became the first playoff club in NHL history to have goals scored by a 40-year-old player and a teenager in the same game. Gary Roberts (age 40) tied the contest against Ottawa at 2–2, Jordan Staal (age 18) scored the equalizer after a go-ahead goal by the Senators' Chris Kelly, Sidney Crosby (age 19) potted the game-winner—and all scored in the same period, the third. The final score was Pittsburgh 4—Ottawa 3.

20.8 D. The 1975 Philadelphia–Buffalo finals

Stifling heat and oppressive humidity in Buffalo's Memorial Auditorium created an eerie, low-lying fog in Game 3 of the 1975 finals. Surveying the thick soup, Philadelphia Flyers goalie Bernie Parent cracked, "I wouldn't take my boat out in these conditions." Play had to be halted 12 times during the game because visibility was so poor, and officials finally resorted to having rink attendants skate around waving blankets to disperse the mist. In the end, the fog worked to the Sabres' advantage. Rene Robert scored the winner in overtime, beating Parent on a shot from a nearly impossible angle. "It went in between his pads and the post," said Robert. "It was pure luck. Any other time I wouldn't have shot the puck, but because of the fog you could score from anywhere."

20.9 A. Most goals in one playoff game

It's difficult to decide which Edmonton Oilers team of the 1980s was the most explosive; they all had supersonic weaponry. During the 1985 playoffs, Wayne Gretzky (47 points) and Paul Coffey (37 points) each set new scoring records in one postseason in their positions. The Oilers also bagged team records for most goals in a series (44 against Chicago in the Conference finals), most shorthanded goals in one playoff year (10 in 16 games) and most players scoring hat tricks in one playoff year (six). The 11 goals that the Oilers scored against Chicago in Game 1 of the Conference finals (equalling Montreal's 1944 record) is one of the few records set that did not survive. It was broken in 1987 by another Oilers club that pumped in a baker's dozen in a 13–3 massacre of Los Angeles in the Division semifinals. In 1990, the Kings challenged the record with 12 goals against Calgary in a 12–4 on April 10, 1990.

20.10 D. 18 consecutive series

Montreal has defeated many teams in the playoffs, but no club has suffered so much at the hands of the Canadiens as the Bruins. Montreal's mysterious postseason mastery of Boston spanned 41 years and a record-setting 18 straight series. The streak began in 1946, when Rocket Richard and his mates defeated the Beantowners in the Cup finals, and continued until 1988, when the Terry O'Reilly-coached Bruins finally subdued the Habs in five games in the Adams Division finals.

20.11 A. One goal

It's impossible for a team today to win a playoff series by scoring just one goal, but prior to 1936, when early rounds were decided by total-goals format, it was doable. (Under that format, teams with the highest goal count after two games won the series and scoreless games ended in regulation.) So what is the lowest goal total accumulated by a winning team? On two occasions, NHL clubs staved off playoff elimination by scoring just one goal. First, in 1929's quarterfinal subway series between New York's Americans and Rangers, neither team scored until the second overtime period in Game 2. The Rangers' Melville Keeling notched the series-winner on Roy Worters, and, despite surrendering just one goal, the Americans were eliminated—with the Rangers winning the total-goals series 1–0. More dramatically, in 1935, the same one-goal total lifted the Montreal Maroons over the Chicago Blackhawks in quarterfinals action and took the team to the semis, where the Maroons' slim, 5–4 total-goals win against the Rangers earned them a Cup finals berth. The Maroons faced Toronto, the first-place team that had beaten them in five of six games during the regular season. But the Maroons were in the zone after two squeaker series and swept the Maple Leafs in three games in the best-of-five round. It was a Cup victory that began on Baldy Northcott's lone goal against Chicago in one of the last total-goals series in NHL history.

20.12 B. One goal

Before the start of the 2003 Cup finals against New Jersey, Anaheim goalie Jean-Sébastien Giguère's work between the pipes was being measured in Conn Smythe Trophy proportions. After disposing of Detroit and Dallas, Giguère shut out the Minnesota Wild in the first three games of the Conference finals—only the second time in history a goalie had opened a series with three straight zeroes. And in Game 4 he allowed just one goal, when Andrew Brunette connected at 4:47 of the first period to end Giguère's shutout run of 217:44, the fifth-longest streak in NHL history. The 2–1 win earned the Mighty Ducks a ticket to their first Cup finals and the record for the fewest goals given up in a best-of-seven series.

20.13 B. In 1952: Toronto vs. Detroit

In more than a half-century of playoff hockey, only two Cup champions have been swept in the first round. Fifty-one years after Detroit swept the defending Cup-champion Maple Leafs in the first round of the 1952 playoffs, the Red Wings went down four straight to Anaheim during the preliminary round of 2003. (In both series, hot rookie netminders stoned the defending Cup champions.) In 1952, a kid named Terry Sawchuk broom-handled Toronto. Then in 2003, Jean-Sébastien Giguère did the honours for the Mighty Ducks by stopping 165 of 171 shots while posting a stingy 1.24 goals-against average against the high-powered Wings. After being humbled in the series, forward Brendan Shanahan put Guguère's play in perspective: "I saw Dominik Hasek in the Olympics in 1998 in a zone. And I haven't seen that before or since until this week with that kid," said Shanahan. According to Las Vegas odds-makers, the Ducks were 10–1 underdogs to win the series and would have been 150–1 underdogs to sweep.

20.14 C. The Boston Bruins, in 1970
Boston is the first, last and only NHL franchise to ice a Stanley Cup winner without a full captain. Between 1967–68 and 1972–73, the Bruins named no captain to their squad, including during the Cup-winning years of 1970 and 1972. There were four co-captains—Johnny Bucyk, Ed Westfall, Phil Esposito and the injured Ted Green—during the 1970 championship, with Bucyk accepting the Cup from NHL president Clarence Campbell. When Boston repeated as champions in 1972, no Bruin wore the "C" above his heart. It was the last time a Cup-winner was declared without a captain.

20.15 D. 13 goals
In 124 seventh games between 1938 and 2008, 56 games, or 45 per cent, have ended in 1–0, 2–0, 2–1, 3–1 or 3–2 scores. The seventh game of the 1968 Western quarterfinals between Los Angeles and Minnesota looked to be another squeaker, after six games of home team wins by close scores. But contrary to what was expected, the Kings fell apart at home in a 9–4 defeat to the North Stars, the greatest goal count in

a seventh and deciding game in NHL history. The biggest blowout in a Game 7 belongs to Patrick Roy's Colorado Avalanche, who were whipped 7–0 by Detroit in the 2002 Conference finals.

20.16 D. More than 35 points

A big regular season guarantees nothing but home-ice advantage in the playoffs. Detroit found that out in 1995–96 after establishing the best wins and points in NHL history, with a 62–13–7 record. They finished the season 27 points ahead of second-place Colorado, but lost their playoff bid in the third round to the Avalanche. The following season, 1996–97, Detroit wised up and saved something for the playoffs, finishing with twice as many regular-season losses over the previous year and 13 points back of first-place. The strategy worked. With just 94 points in 1996–97, Detroit finished 37 points behind 1995–96's mark of 131, and the Red Wings went on to win their first Stanley Cup since 1955.

20.17 D. Seven games

After losing the 1999 Stanley Cup on Brett Hull's controversial toe-in-the-crease goal, the Sabres went winless in their first seven games (0–5–2) in 1999–2000. The season-opening slump equalled the team's worst start in franchise history (0–4–3 in 1990–91). "Our attitudes aren't great right now. There's too many guys just showing up," said Sabres captain Mike Peca. Buffalo winger Dixon Ward joked: "Until we get an apology we're not going to win a game. We vow not to win until we get an apology from [NHL commissioner Gary] Bettman." But the Sabres didn't get one, and had to walk away from a regular season where the NHL reviewed 289 goals on video and disallowed 137, most for a toe in the crease. Hull's Cup-winner was a bitter pill for Buffalo, who were down 3–2 against Dallas in the series. Their first win of the following season, 1999–2000, came in a 7–3 victory over Carolina on October 22. It was Buffalo's eighth game of the season.

20.18   A. In the 1964 playoffs

They're a sensitive and superstitious bunch those Boston fans, but there may be something to their "Canadiens Hex," a bit of postseason hocus-pocus concocted by the hockey gods to curse any club that beats Montreal in the early round. After seeing his beloved Bruins lose for the fourth time in five years after eliminating the Canadiens, tortured fan Dave Bontempo discovered statististical evidence that he believed was more than coincidental: on 19 consecutive occasions, winners over Montreal were later defeated in the playoffs. "Do teams suffer a letdown after defeating the Canadiens in a playoff series?" Bontempo asked in a *Montreal Gazette* story. "Or is defeating the Canadiens like winning the Stanley Cup in a figurative sense?" Good questions, considering the last Cup-winner to knock out Montreal before the finals was the Toronto Maple Leafs in 1964. The Lightning finally broke the hex with their Cup victory in 2004. Oddly, the following postseason, Carolina repeated Tampa's feat when they captured the Cup after defeating the Habs in the 2006 Conference quarterfinals.

20.19   B. The Calgary Flames

Born out of the improbable season that led to Calgary's stunning run at the Stanley Cup finals in 2004, the hard hat honours the Flames' hardest-working player each game—awarded by the players to one of their peers. The hard hat is one of several franchise traditions amongst hockey fans, including the throwing of octopi in Detroit, the waving of white towels in Vancouver and the now-banned practice of tossing plastic rats in Florida.

20.20 B. One day

The custom that sees each player on a championship team spending 24 hours with the Stanley Cup is a recent innovation. It started in 1995, when the New Jersey Devils won the Cup for the first time and Hockey Hall of Fame curator Phil Pritchard and three of his colleagues first took turns accompanying the trophy on its travels. Since then, players have taken the Cup up mountains, to strip clubs and even to gravesites. But one of the stranger trips occurred in 1999, when Jere Lehtinen of the Dallas Stars had the Finnish army ferry the Cup on a hovercraft to an island in the Baltic Sea, where he had a sauna party with all of his childhood buddies.

20.21 A. The Stanley Cup-winning New Jersey Devils

When the New Jersey Devils won the Stanley Cup in 1999–2000, their penalty killing unit set a modern-day league record for fewest power-play goals—allowing just five goals, including only two (by Sylvain Cote and Joe Nieuwendyk) in 16 opportunities by Dallas in the Cup finals. The playoff mark highlights the importance of disciplined play in any championship. In 23 games, the Devils were assessed 192 penalty minutes or 8.3 minutes per game, the lowest penalty-minute average per game in the 2000 postseason.

20.22 C. Seven seventh games

An NHL record seven series, or almost half of the 15 series played over four rounds during the 1994 Stanley Cup playoffs, were decided by seventh games. The two Stanley Cup contenders, Vancouver and New York, were each stretched to the seventh-game limit in earlier rounds before reaching the finals, where they played a dramatic seventh game for the championship. In the first round there were a record four Game 7s. Vancouver rallied from a 3–1 series deficit to nip Calgary, San Jose upset Detroit, New Jersey finished off pesky Buffalo and Boston scraped by Montreal, the defending Cup champions. In the second round, San Jose succumbed to Toronto's bid in seven games. In round three the Rangers were stretched by New Jersey, a series decided in double overtime in Game 7. In the finals, New York jumped out to a 3–1 series lead, only to see the Canucks rally to tie the series and force a deciding game at Madison Square Garden. The Rangers ended a 54-year Stanley Cup drought before a record television audience worldwide, defeating the Canucks 3–2 in Game 7. It was only the 10th time the Cup was captured in a seventh game.

20.23 C. Vancouver

So how does hockey's most revered trophy go missing? If you ask Air Canada officials in Vancouver, they would say the Stanley Cup was never actually lost or misplaced on their jet bound for Fort St. John, B.C., in August 2004. Apparently, the 35-pound (16-kg) Cup was booted from a full plane in Vancouver because of weight restrictions. But no one told Cup handler Walter Neubrand, who went into a tailspin after arriving in Fort St. John without it. Each summer, Lord Stanley's prize travels with members of the Stanley Cup winners, and it was Tampa Bay head scout Jake Goertzen's turn. After many anxious hours and a few cancelled showings of the Cup, a red-faced spokesperson confirmed that "the Cup was held in a secure facility overnight. We always knew where it was." Truly lame.

20.24 C. 11 days

During Anaheim's remarkable trip to the 2003 Stanley Cup finals, the Mighty Ducks set a record of 11 days downtime after polishing off the Minnesota Wild in the semifinals

on May 16 and before their finals matchup against the New
Jersey Devils on May 27. Unfortunately history wasn't on
Anaheim's side. Their finals-loss represented only the second
time a modern-day team failed to win the championship
after a rest of seven days or more. Of the last six longest lay-
offs, the club that was well-rested won five of the six final
series. Montreal had nine days off before their Cup-winning
series in 1966; the 1984 Edmonton Oilers, the 1952 Detroit Red
Wings and the 1949 Toronto Maple Leafs had eight days rest,
and the 1999 Buffalo Sabres and 1993 Montreal Canadiens had
seven days off.

20.25 B. Three goals

The 2006 finals featured a series of stunning comebacks. The
most dramatic belongs to Edmonton, which clawed its way
back from a 3–1 deficit in games against Carolina to force
a do-or-die seventh match for the Cup. But the Hurricanes
established the battleground with their comeback in the first
game. Down by three Oilers goals, captain Rod Brind'Amour
sparked the charge with a late second-period marker. In the
third frame, Ray Whitney scored twice and Justin Williams
added another on a shorthanded breakaway, giving Carolina
its first lead of the game. Three minutes after Williams's goal,
Alex Hemsky tied it 4–4. The earth then crumbled beneath
the Oilers: playoff star and MVP contender Dwayne Roloson
suffered a devastating series-ending injury, little-used Ty
Conklin took over and made a game-deciding blunder in the
final minute after mixing up a routine play to teammate
Jason Smith, and Brind'Amour tucked the puck into an open
net, handing Carolina a 1–0 series lead and the biggest comeback in finals history. (Five other teams have come from three
goals down to win, including Pittsburgh in 1992 in a 5–4 victory against Chicago.)

20.26 B. Nine players

New Jersey general manager Lou Lamoriello's sixth sense for team building is the main reason the Devils captured a couple of Stanley Cups between 1995 and 2000. Give credit to the intimidating play of Scott Stevens, the return to form of Martin Brodeur and the inspired coaching of Larry Robinson, but it was Lamoriello who built the Devils around a core of character and role players designed to win over the long haul. He also kept them together, even in an age where player mobility is a given amongst managers. (How many teams have more than a half-dozen players still in the fold six years later?) Robinson, assistant coach Bobby Carpenter and nine players—Scott Stevens, Martin Brodeur, Sergei Brylin, Ken Daneyko, Bobby Holik, Claude Lemieux, Randy McKay, Scott Niedermayer and Chris Terreri—won two Cups with the Devils. Only Lemieux left during the years between championships.

20.27 A. 1928–29

The first time two goalies from the same team were co-credited on the Stanley Cup was in 1928–29, when Boston won the championship backstopped by famed goalkeeper Tiny Thompson. Thompson played the entire 44-game schedule and every game of the playoffs, but he shared the championship with goalie Hal Winkler, who is listed as Boston's "sub-goaltender" on the Cup. So what happened? Although Winkler didn't start a single game in 1928–29, his name was etched on the Cup (and his picture included in the official team photo) for sentimental reasons after he performed admirably in the 1927 finals against Ottawa and, again, during the 1927–28 regular season, leading the Bruins to third-place overall. Boston did not win the Cup in 1928, and, when Winkler was replaced by Thompson the following year, many on the team felt that he deserved to be part of hockey's greatest award.

20.28 C. Four franchises

One of early hockey's most extraordinary and successful individuals, Tommy Gorman hasn't received his due among the pantheon of builders in NHL history. Icons such as Conn Smythe and Jack Adams never won as consistently with as many teams as Gorman. After turning Ottawa into the league's first dynasty (1920, 1921, 1923), he took over the New York Americans, then the Chicago Blackhawks (1934), the Montreal Maroons (1935) and the Montreal Canadiens (1944, 1946)—for seven Stanley Cups on four different franchises.

20.29 B. In the 1930s

Until the 1930s, it was likely that it had never been done before: not on a baseball diamond, a basketball court, a football gridiron or a hockey-ice surface. Championship trophy presentations were typically reserved for the locker room or black-tie banquets, until the NHL moved the ceremony on-ice during the 1930s. But by no means did the practice become a league-wide tradition—that wouldn't happen until the 1950s. It was sporadic at best, with newspaper reports of jubilant speeches by Conn Smythe and others at Maple Leafs Gardens in 1932. Then, two years later, immediately following Chicago's stunning victory over Detroit, NHL president Frank Calder presented the Cup to club owner Fred McLaughlin and his triumphant Blackhawks before a euphoric crowd at Chicago Stadium. The *Detroit News* reported that, during the 1934 on-ice celebrations, Hawks winger Louis Trudel "grabbed the Stanley Cup as soon as it was brought on the ice for the presentation and skated wildly around the rink" (which takes the shine away from Ted Lindsay, who is recognized as the first player to pick up the Cup and carry it around the rink—after the Red Wings won in 1950). It wasn't until the 1980s that the other three major team sports adopted hockey's rink ritual and made the fans part of their year-end celebration.

20.30 D. Peter Pocklington of the Edmonton Oilers

The Oilers' owner emerged from a bizarre and harrowing hostage-taking drama with a bullet in his arm but his life intact. The incident began on April 20, 1982, when a masked gunman burst into Pocklington's Edmonton mansion. Pocklington was bound and gagged by the intruder, but his wife, Eva, escaped and alerted police. After a 12-hour standoff, in which the kidnapper demanded $1 million in ransom money and an airplane to take him to an undisclosed location, police stormed the house and fired a shot that passed through the gunman's chest, winging Pocklington in the shouder. The kidnapper, who had a pistol pointed at Pocklington's head when he was shot, was taken into custody.

20.31 C. The Victoria Cougars

It was a sweet playoff victory for Lester Patrick's Victoria Cougars in 1925. Patrick's team won the final series against the Montreal Canadiens as much on strategy as on talent, with the east-west game rules in effect. At the time, the eastern rules were not much different from those of the West, with a few exceptions. Eastern rules, for example, allowed player changes only after the ref's whistle had blown, which suited the Canadiens' All-Star lineup of 60-minute men such as Howie Morenz, Aurel Joliat and Sprague Cleghorn, who were renowned for their endurance. Patrick, on the other hand, had perfected smooth, quick, on-the-move line changes that, under western rules, were allowed as play continued. So when western rules were played in alternate games, the Canadiens were confused. And when eastern rules applied, Patrick smartly had his team stop play frequently to make line changes, frustrating the Canadiens, who were used to wearing down their opponents. The Cougars won the Stanley Cup in four games, and Patrick's on-the-fly line changes became an integral part of game strategy.

20.32 D. More than eight hours

Montreal mayor Jean Drapeau had a knack for the spectacular. His world's fair to celebrate Canada's centennial, Expo 67, was a marvel that drew international praise and 50 million visitors to man-made islands in the St. Lawrence River. At the same time, he built an underground city that was connected by a sleek and innovative subway system. Drapeau also had a hand in landing a Major League Baseball franchise and brought the 1976 Olympics Games to town. These accomplishments might have all been predicted, however, considering his grand plans to organize a Stanley Cup parade for the Canadiens in 1956. Drapeau's parade route took the team along 30 miles of Montreal streets, from the Montreal Forum through all 11 city districts and finishing up at City Hall—a gruelling eight-hour-30-minute parade that was nearly twice as long as expected. Legendary coach Toe Blake was furious, and threatened to never win another Cup if the mayor subjected his team to such celebrations again.

20.33 A. Ontario's Kenora Thistles

When Kenora challenged the Montreal Wanderers for the Stanley Cup in January 1907, the playoff matchup was billed as "a battle between a small town and a big city, rough and raw Western Canada against the rich and refined East" by John Danakas and Rick Brignall in *Small Town Glory*. At the time, Montreal was Canada's most modern city, while Kenora was just a speck in the wilderness of northwestern Ontario. Still, the rugged mining and lumber outpost boasted a Hudson's Bay fort, a Mounties police house and the Canadian Pacific Railway running through its heart, with sports as big as the outdoors—lacrosse, baseball, rowing and sailing in the warm months and hockey the rest of the year. The local winter game was played mostly on frozen creeks and rivers, but Kenora did have Victoria Rink, where the Thistles refined their fast-skating brand of play. The team iced five locals from town and two ringers, goalie Eddie Geroux and the famous Art Ross. (Two other players made the trip but did not play: Joe Hall and Russell Phillips.) And after two previous Cup losses (in 1903 and 1905), the club was skilled, road-tested and ready to take on the Wanderers—even in front of Montreal crowds at Westmount Arena. The result: the Thistles stunned the defending-Cup-champion Wanderers by stealing both games (4–2 and 8–6) in an improbable best-of-two total-goals series victory, and, receiving the news via telegraph, euphoric Thistles fans celebrated on the small-town streets of Kenora. The Thistles' unforgettable championship was then again honoured, in January 2007, with minor hockey games, an exhibition match between Kenora players and NHL old-timers and a long-overdue visit by the Stanley Cup. Kenora remains the smallest town to win the Stanley Cup or any major sports championship, while the upstart Thistles are a lasting reminder of how the West was really won.

20.34 B. The Boston Bruins'
Although their postseason rivalry dates back to the 1929 semi-finals (with a 3–0 series win by Boston), Montreal's playoff hex over the Bruins began in earnest during the 1930 finals. In the regular season, Boston dominated the NHL with a record .875 winning percentage and won all four meetings against the Canadiens. By the time the finals rolled around, the Bruins were already planning a parade route and their roster list for the Cup engravers. But then something happened to the team that had not lost back-to-back games all season. It was swept in consecutive games, 3–0 and 4–3, and lost the Cup to

Montreal in the best-of-three series. Boston's quick demise at the hands of the Canadiens prompted the NHL to extend the finals from a best-of-three to a best-of-five series.

20.35 A. The Edmonton Oilers

For most teams, reaching the Stanley Cup finals is the height of their success, not a stepping stone to greater glory the following spring. In fact, finalists often find themselves further away from a championship come the next playoff year. Chicago, for example, is still waiting for a return to the big dance since the 1992 finals, as are Los Angeles (1993), Vancouver (1994), Florida (1996), Washington (1998) and Buffalo (1999). As of 2008, the last team to break the bridesmaid curse is the Cup-winning Edmonton Oilers, who in 1984 averaged four straight losses to the New York Islanders in the 1983 Cup finals.

20.36 B. Seven captains

The most captain-loaded team in NHL history was the 1998–99 Dallas Stars. Dallas GM Bob Gainey, a captain himself with Montreal from 1981 to 1989, built a club boasting seven players who had worn the "C" on other NHL teams: Joe Nieuwendyk (Flames, 1991–1995), Guy Carbonneau (Canadiens, 1988–1994), Pat Verbeek (Whalers, 1992–1995), Mike Keane (Canadiens, 1994–1996), Brett Hull (St. Louis, 1992–1996) and Brian Skrudland (Panthers, 1993–1997), in addition to Stars captain Derian Hatcher.

20.37 B. The Toronto Maple Leafs

Like a doomed rat in the suffocating grasp of a python, the Leafs quietly expired 3–0 to the New Jersey Devils in Game 6 of their 2000 semifinals series. Facing elimination, Toronto managed only three quality scoring chances in the entire game and missed the net on each one, allowing Martin Brodeur to breeze to the easiest shutout of his career. The Leafs directed a paltry six shots on net: three in the first period, two in the second and one in the third. That's the fewest shots recorded in an NHL game since the stat was first compiled in 1967–68. The previous record-holder was the Washington Capitals, who had seven shots on net in a 4–1 loss to Philadelphia on February 12, 1978.

20.38 B. Calgary

During the Flames' amazing 26-game run at the Stanley Cup in 2004, a four-block area west of the Saddledome was dubbed the Red Mile. Thousands of Calgary fans, thirsting for a Cup and sporting their team's scarlet jersey, flooded into the strip of bars, pubs and cafés to watch the big-screen TVs and celebrate. Cars with horns blaring and festooned with Flames pennants cruised along 17th Avenue amidst throngs of fans and thunderous, fist-pumping cheers of "Go Flames Go." It was Calgary's first playoff series in seven seasons. But it all ended in heartbreak when Tampa Bay doused the Flames and their fans' celebratory mood with a 2–1 win in Game 7 of the finals.

20.39 C. Pavel Datsyuk, with the Detroit Red Wings

The Stanley Cup has gone from the bottom of Mario Lemieux's swimming pool to the top of some of Canada's highest mountains, but no player has taken the Cup further than Pavel Datsyuk. After Detroit won the 2002 championship, Datsyuk lugged the jug to the Urals city of Yekaterinburg, Russia, where he paraded it up and down the Continental Divide between Europe and Asia. The Cup doesn't have an on-board odometer, but we suspect that was the furthest it has travelled from its home base, the Hall of Fame in Toronto.

Solutions to Games

Game 1: Odd Man Out

1. Steve Yzerman
2. Brett Hull
3. Chris Pronger
4. Mario Lemieux
5. Patrick Roy
6. Dave Schultz
7. Gerry Cheevers
8. Marcel Dionne
9. Wayne Gretzky
10. Phil Esposito

Game 2: What's in a Name?

1. Nashville
2. Glenn Hall
3. No Holds Barred
4. Bernie Nicholls
5. Bench-clearing brawl
6. Randy Holt
7. Kevin Haller
8. Punch Line
9. Andy Van Hellemond
10. Final Whistle

Game 3: Hockey Crossword 1

Game 4: The Best Rookie Class Ever?

1. Alexander Ovechkin set an NHL rookie record with 425 shots on goal, topping Teemu Selanne's mark of 387 in 1992–93.

2. Josh Harding is the first goalie to play his first NHL game and record his first win in a shootout. It happened in Minnesota's 5–4 win against the St. Louis Blues on April 4, 2006.

3. On April 7, 2006, Sidney Crosby became the youngest player in NHL history to score 90 points, when he notched four points against the Florida Panthers. He was 18 years and 243 days old, 100 days younger than Dale Hawerchuk, who hit 90 points at the age of 18 years, 343 days, during his remarkable rookie year of 1982–83. Then on April 17, Crosby set up three goals in a 6–1 win against the Islanders to reach his 100th point. He was three months younger than Hawerchuk. Only Wayne Gretzky was this good so young; and Gretzky was in the WHA.

4. Dion Phaneuf is only the third rookie defenseman to reach the 20-goal plateau in one season. He did it on April 13, 2006, versus the Colorado Avalanche.

5. Alexander Ovechkin is the second rookie in NHL history to record 50 goals and 100 points in one season. In 2005–06, he amassed 52 goals and 54 assists for 106 points, compared to Teemu Selanne's 76–56–132 in his first season, 1992–93.

6. Henrik Lundqvist set the New York Rangers' record for most wins by a rookie goalie on March 29, 2006, when he made 18 saves in a 5–1 win over the New York Islanders. It was his 30th win, the most by a Ranger goalie since Mike Richter in 1996–97.

7. Alexander Ovechkin is the first rookie to lead an NHL regular season in shots on goal, with 425 in 2005–06.

8. Marek Svatos tied the NHL rookie record with nine game-winning goals in one season, set by Steve Larmer in 1982–83. His nine game-winners for Colorado led the entire NHL at the time of his season-ending shoulder injury on March 4 in Dallas. At that point, only Alexander Ovechkin had more than Svatos's 32 goals and only Ovechkin and Sidney Crosby had more points amongst first-year players.

9. Sidney Crosby is second in most points by a rookie who entered the league in the same year he was drafted, behind only Dale Hawerchuk's 103 points in 1981–82. Crosby netted 102 points in 2005–06.

10. Jussi Jokinen led all players with 10 shootout goals in 13 attempts during 2005–06, the first shootout year in the NHL.

11. Kari Lehtonen of the Atlanta Thrashers had the best save percentage in shootouts, stopping 17 of 20 shots for .850.

12. Alexander Ovechkin is only the fourth rookie in NHL history to reach the 50-goal mark in one season, after Teemu Selanne, Mike Bossy and Joe Nieuwendyk.

13. Ottawa's Ray Emery posted a 12–2–2 record in March 2006, tying Bernie Parent's mark of 12 wins in a calendar month, March 1974.

14. As 100-point earners, Alexander Ovechkin (106) and Sidney Crosby (102) produced two NHL firsts. It was the first time that two rookies scored 100 points and that two rookies finished top 10 in scoring.

15. Henrik Lundqvist (30), Ryan Miller (30), Antero Niittymaki (23). Ray Emery (23) and Kari Lehtonen (20) equalled the league record set in 1981–82 for most rookie netminders posting 20 or more victories.

Game 5: The Third Jersey

1. E. NYR; *The Statue of Liberty*'s head
2. F. Calgary; Horse head snorting fire
3. K. Columbus; A star, wrapped in the Ohio State flag
4. J. Ottawa; A Roman's head, looking out
5. I. Edmonton; Drop of oil in a gear-like design
6. H. Los Angeles; Coat of arms
7. G. Montreal; Replica of a 1945 jersey
8. B. Nashville; Sabre-tooth tiger protruding out of a triangle
9. A. Boston; Brown bear
10. D. Dallas; Bull's head with a star constellation
11. C. Toronto; Replica of a 1938 jersey

Game 6: The Last Original Six Survivor

Game 7: Lockout Lingo
PART 1

1. Flyers goalie Robert Esche, a vocal opponent to the salary cap, later apologized for calling Gary Bettman a "madman"

2. TV host Jay Leno

3. Wayne Gretzky, on his and Mario Lemieux's attempt to help negotiations between players and management

4. Ottawa enforcer Rob Ray, on why he would be happy to be a replacement player, one of the first to make such a damning comment in October 2004

5. Former NHL great Marcel Dionne

6. Mike Lupica, the *New York Daily News,* on the poor-performing, high-salaried Ranger players

7. LA Kings forward Sean Avery, on the way negotiations were conducted and the results

PART 2

1. Bob Goodenow

2. Jill Armstrong, the *Denver Post*

3. All-time minor-league goal leader Kevin Kerr, on playing as a replacement player if he were asked

4. Flyers GM Bobby Clarke, on NHLPA president Bob Goodenow

5. Greg Cote, the *Miami Herald*

6. New Jersey's general manager Lou Lamoriello, using the death of Pope John Paul II as an analogy

7. Gary Bettman, making it clear replacement players would not be used

Game 8: Hockey Crossword 2

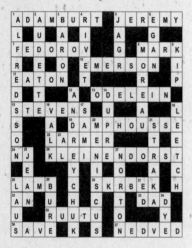

Game 9: The First Five-Team 20-Goal Man

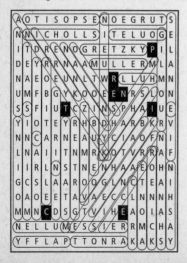

The first NHLer with 20 goals on five teams is Dean PRENTICE, who scored at least 20 goals with each team he played on—the New York Rangers, Boston, Detroit, Pittsburgh and Minnesota—between 1952–53 and 1973–74.

Game 10: Defunct Teams
PART 1

1. B. Colorado Rockies
2. C. Philadelphia Quakers
3. G. Montreal Maroons
4. E. Kansas City Scouts
5. A. Cleveland Barons
6. F. Hamilton Tigers
7. D. Atlanta Flames

PART 2

1. G. Brooklyn Americans
2. F. California Golden Seals
3. D. Ottawa Senators
4. A. St. Louis Eagles
5. C. Pittsburgh Pirates
6. B. Minnesota North Stars
7. E. Quebec Nordiques

Game 11: Lowering the Boom
PART 1

1. E. Chris Simon got 25 games for hitting Ryan Hollweg in the face with his stick, March 2007

2. F Jesse Boulerice got 25 games for cross-checking Ryan Kesler in the face with his stick, October 2007

3. A. Marty McSorley got 23 games for a slash to the head of Donald Brashear, February 2000

4. G. Gordie Dwyer got 23 games for abusing officials and exiting the penalty box to fight, September 2000

5. C. Dale Hunter got 21 games for hitting from behind on Pierre Turgeon, May 1993

6. D. Todd Bertuzzi got 20 games for a punch to the head of Steve Moore, March 2004

7. B. Tom Lysiak got 20 games for tripping an official, October 1983

PART 2

1. D. Brad May got 20 games for a slash to the head of Steve Heinze, November 2000

2. F. Eddie Shore got 16 games for hitting from behind on Ace Bailey, December 1933

3. A. Maurice Richard got 15 games for striking an official, March 1955

4. B. Wilf Paiement got 15 games for a stick swing on Dennis Polonich, October 1978

5. C. Dave Brown got 15 games for cross-checking Tomas Sandstrom, November 1987

6. E. Tony Granato got 15 games for slashing Neil Wilkinson, February 1994

Game 12: Lefties and Righties

LEFTIES

1.	Martin Brodeur	F.	New Jersey Devils 2003
2.	Glenn Hall	E.	Chicago Blackhawks 1963
3.	Mikka Kiprusoff	A.	Calgary Flames 2006
4.	Ron Hextall	G.	Philadelphia Flyers 1987
5.	Terry Sawchuk	C.	Detroit Red Wings 1955
6.	Dominik Hasek	D.	Buffalo Sabres 1999
7.	Billy Smith	D.	New York Islanders 1982
8.	Patrick Roy	B.	Montreal Canadiens 1992

RIGHTIES

1.	José Théodore	H.	Montreal Canadiens 2002
2.	Chuck Gardiner	A.	Chicago Blackhawks 1932
3.	Grant Fuhr	G.	Edmonton Oilers 1988
4.	Bill Durnan	C.	Montreal Canadiens 1944
5.	Tom Barrasso	F.	Buffalo Sabres 1984
6.	Gilles Villemure	E.	New York Rangers 1971
7.	Dave Kerr	B.	New York Rangers 1940
8.	Tony Esposito	D.	Chicago Blackhawks 1970

Game 13: MVP Maverick

```
R O Y
S T E V E N S
R O B I N S O N
H E X T A L L
G A I N E Y
S A K I C
D R Y D E N
```

```
B R I A N   L E E T C H
```
of the
```
R A N G E R S
```

Dominated by Canadian players since 1965, when the first playoff MVP was selected, the Conn Smythe has been won in recent years by Nicklas Lidstrom and Henrik Zetterberg. The first non-Canadian to win MVP status was American-born Brian Leetch, with the New York Rangers, in 1994.

Game 14: Close, But No Cigar

```
C  E-M  L-L  Y  T-S
S-S  O  U-H  E  A  E-U  P
I  L  I-F-F  S  K  T  Q  E
E  A  L  R  T  U  E  U  E  R
N  R  E  N  R  S-R  H  K  U
W-G  Y  M-I  T  R-C  W  O
A  X-U-E  O  N  T  E  A  B
T  Y  T-R  N  Y  O  I  H  V
U-I-L  E  S  R-E  I  R-O
B-O-S  F-E-D-O  D
```

Game 15: Drafting Late

1. Cristobal Huet: Los Angeles (214th in 2001)
2. Marty Turco: Dallas (124th in 1994)
3. Pavel Datsyuk: Detroit (171st in 1998)
4. Michael Ryder: Montreal (216th in 1998)
5. Karlis Skrastins: Nashville (230th in 1998)
6. Henrik Zetterberg: Detroit (210th in 1999)
7. Tomas Kaberle: Toronto (204th in 1996)
8. Daniel Alfredsson: Ottawa (133rd in 1994)

9. Darcy Tucker: Montreal (151st in 1993)
10. Miikka Kiprusoff: San Jose (116th in 1994)
11. Eric Daze: Chicago (90th in 1993)
12. Nikolai Khabibulin: Winnipeg (204th in 1992)

Game 16: Bench Boss Blues

SUTTER
DEMERS
BURNS
SATHER
NOLAN
BOWMAN
LEMAIRE

RED BERENSON
ST LOUIS BLUES

On November 7, 1968, St. Louis' Red Berenson scored an NHL-record six goals in an 8–0 win on the road against the Philadelphia Flyers. In 1981 he was awarded the Jack Adams, as bench boss of those same Blues.

Game 17: Hockey Crossword 3

Y	Z	E	R	M	A	N	S	H	A	N	A	H	A	N
U		L		E		U		I		O			A
S	T	I	L	L	M	A	N	L	I	N	D	R	O	S
H		A		L		L		E		T		H
K	A	S	P	A	R	A	I	T	I	S	B	O	N	K
E		F		N		A	O		Y		N		A
V	A	L	K	B	A	L	O	N	O	L	I	V	E	R
I		E		Y		T		E	K		E		I
C	L	U	T	C	H	O	I	L	E	R	S	R	O	Y
H		R		H		W		L		U		B		A
R	A	Y	N	E	R	E	L	I	K	P	R	E	S	S
O		A		L		A		G		P		E		A
V	A	N	B	I	E	S	B	R	O	U	C	K	O	T
E		D		O		E		A		W		E		A
R	A	Y	A	S	T	L	E	Y	R	E	D	D	E	N

Game 18: Chris Who?
PART 1

1. C. Chris Dingman; Tampa Bay Lightning, 2004
2. E. Jiri Fischer; Detroit Red Wings, 2002
3. F. Kevin Haller; Montreal Canadiens, 1993
4. D. Hector Marini; New York Islanders, 1982
5. B. Troy Loney; Pittsburgh Penguins, 1992
6. A. Craig Muni; Edmonton Oilers, 1988

PART 2

1. D. Colin Patterson; Calgary Flames, 1989
2. B. Ace Bailey; Boston Bruins, 1972
3. E. Dave Reid; Dallas Stars, 1999
4. F. Jay Pandolfo; New Jersey Devils, 2003
5. A. Dan Hinote; Colorado Avalanche, 2001
6. C. Brian Noonan; New York Rangers, 1994

Game 19: Magnetic Attractions
PART 1

1. Joe Nieuwendyk — D. Dallas 1999, New Jersey 2003
2. Terry Sawchuk — F. Detroit 1952, Toronto 1967
3. Mark Messier — E. Edmonton 1984, NY Rangers 1994
4. Ted Harris — G. Montreal 1965, Philadelphia 1975
5. Joe Kocur — A. NY Rangers 1994, Detroit 1998
6. Bryan Trottier — C. NY Islanders 1980, Pittsburgh 1991
7. Paul Coffey — B. Edmonton 1984, Pittsburgh 1991

PART 2

1. Patrick Roy — B. Montreal 1986, Colorado 1996
2. Brett Hull — E. Dallas 1999, Detroit 2002
3. Dick Duff — F. Toronto 1962, Montreal 1965
4. Larry Murphy — G. Pittsburgh 1992, Detroit 1997
5. Joe Mullen — D. Calgary 1989, Pittsburgh 1991
6. Frank Mahovlich — A. Toronto 1967, Montreal 1971
7. Chris Chelios — C. Montreal 1986, Detroit 2002

Acknowledgements

Thanks to the following publishers and organizations for the use of quoted and/or statistical material:

- *The Best of Hockey Night in Canada.* Stephen Cole. 2003. Canadian Broadcasting Corporation (CBC). McArthur & Company.
- *The Game.* Ken Dryden. 1983. Macmillan of Canada.
- *Gordie: A Hockey Legend.* Roy MacSkimming. 1994. Greystone Books.
- *Gretzky, An Autobiography.* Wayne Gretzky. 1990. Harper Collins.
- *High Stick.* Al Hirshberg, Ted Green. 1971. Dodd, Mead & Company.
- *Hockey: Canada's Royal Winter Game.* Arthur Farrell. 1899. R. Corneil Print, made available digitally by Library and Archives Canada.
- The *Hockey News,* various excerpts. Reprinted with permission of the *Hockey News,* a division of Transcontinental Media G.P.
- "The Hockey Song." Stompin' Tom Connors. 1973. EMI Music Canada.
- *Jacques Demers: Toutes en Lettres.* Mario Leclerc. 2005. Stanké.
- *The National Hockey League Official Guide and Record Book.* The National Hockey League. Various years. Dan Diamond and Associates Inc.
- *Pavel Bure: The Riddle of the Russian Rocket.* Kerry Banks. 1999. Greystone Books.
- *The Physics of Hockey.* Dr. Alain Haché. 2002. The John Hopkins University Press. Raincoast Books.
- *Players, The Ultimate A–Z Guide.* Andrew Podnieks. 2003. Doubleday Canada.
- *Total Hockey.* Dan Diamond and Associates Inc. 1998, 2000. Total Sports.
- *Total* NHL. Dan Diamond and Associates Inc. 2003. Total Sports.

When the Final Buzzer Sounds. Colleen Howe, Gordie Howe, Carles Wilkins. 2000. Triumph Books.

As well:

The Associated Press; *Buffalo News; Calgary Sun;* Canadian Press; *Globe and Mail; Montreal Gazette; National Post; Newark Star-Ledger; Philadelphia Inquirer; Sporting News; Tampa Bay Tribune; Toronto Star;* plus *Sports Illustrated,* USA *Today* and numerous other publications and books, including *The Straight Facts About Making It in Pro Hockey;* television programs on CBC and NBC, and Internet sources such as NHL.com, IIHF.com, hockeydb.com, faceoff.com, HHF.com and shrpsports.com—all of which both guided and corroborated our research.

Care has been taken to trace ownership of copyright material contained in this book. The publishers welcome any information that will enable them to rectify any reference or credit in subsequent editions.

The author gratefully acknowledges all the help throughout the years from everyone at the *Hockey News;* Gary Meagher and Benny Ercolani of the NHL; Phil Prichard and Craig Campbell at the Hockey Hall of Fame; the staff at the McLellan-Redpath Library at McGill University; Rob Sanders and Susan Rana at Greystone Books; designers Peter Cocking and Heather Pringle; the many hockey writers, broadcast journalists, media and Internet staff who have made the game better through their own work; as well as statistical resources such as the Elias Sports Bureau, inputter Joy Woodsworth, editors Kerry Banks and Anne Rose and puzzle designer Adrian van Vlaardingen for their dedication, expertise and creativity. Special thanks to Kerry Banks for his additional contributions, from research to writing; and for being my "second pair of eyes" on the facts.